McKeachie's

Teaching Tips

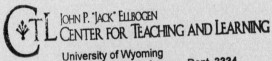

 John P. "Jack" Ellbogen
Center for Teaching and Learning

University of Wyoming
1000 E. University Avenue, Dept. 3334
Coe Library 510
Laramie, WY 82071
Phone: (307) 766-4847 Fax: (307) 766-4822
www.uwyo.edu/ctl

TWELFTH EDITION

McKeachie's
Teaching Tips

Strategies, Research, and Theory for College and University Teachers

Wilbert J. McKeachie
University of Michigan

Marilla Svinicki
University of Texas at Austin

with chapters by

Barbara Hofer, Middlebury College
Richard M. Suinn, Colorado State University
Peter Elbow and Mary Deane Sorcinelli, University of Massachusetts Amherst
Erping Zhu and Matthew Kaplan, University of Michigan
Brian Coppola, University of Michigan
Richard Mann, University of Michigan
Andrew Northedge, The Open University
Claire Ellen Weinstein, University of Texas at Austin
Jane Halonen, University of West Florida

WADSWORTH
CENGAGE Learning

Australia • Brazil • Japan • Korea • Mexico • Singapore • Spain • United Kingdom • United States

We dedicate this edition to all the teachers over the years who have said that they have been introduced to more systematic, reflective ways of teaching by reading this book. We appreciate their interest and applaud their efforts.

WADSWORTH
CENGAGE Learning™

McKeachie's Teaching Tips: Strategies, Research, and Theory for College and University Teachers, Twelfth Edition
Wilbert J. McKeachie, Marilla Svinicki

Publisher: Patricia Coryell
Senior Sponsoring Editor: Sue Pulvermacher-Alt
Senior Development Editor: Lisa Mafrici
Editorial Assistant: Dayna Pell
Associate Project Editor: Teresa Huang
Editorial Assistant: Michelle O'Berg
Senior Art and Design Coordinator: Jill Haber
Senior Composition Buyer: Sarah Ambrose
Manufacturing Coordinator: Chuck Dutton
Marketing Manager: Laura McGinn
Marketing Assistant: Erin Lane

For product information and technology assistance, contact us at **Cengage Learning Customer & Sales Support, 1-800-354-9706**

For permission to use material from this text or product, submit all requests online at **www.cengage.com/permissions**
Further permissions questions can be emailed to **permissionrequest@cengage.com**

Library of Congress Control Number: 2005925784

ISBN-13: 978-0-618-51556-1
ISBN-10: 0-618-51556-9

Wadsworth
10 Davis Drive
Belmont, CA 94002-3098
USA

Cengage Learning is a leading provider of customized learning solutions with office locations around the globe, including Singapore, the United Kingdom, Australia, Mexico, Brazil, and Japan. Locate your local office at: **www.cengage.com/global**

Cengage Learning products are represented in Canada by Nelson Education, Ltd.

To learn more about Wadsworth, visit **www.cengage.com/wadsworth**
Purchase any of our products at your local college store or at our preferred online store **www.ichapters.com**

Printed in the United States of America
11 12 13 14 15 16 17 12 11 10 09

Contents

Part 1 Getting Started   1

CHAPTER **3** Meeting a Class for the First Time 21

Part 2 Basic Skills for Facilitating Student Learning 29

CHAPTER **4** Reading as Active Learning 30

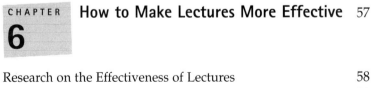

CHAPTER
6
How to Make Lectures More Effective   57

CHAPTER
7

Assessing, Testing, and Evaluating: Grading Is Not the Most Important Function

CHAPTER
8

Testing: The Details

CHAPTER 9 Tests from the Students' Perspective   105

CHAPTER 10 What to Do About Cheating   113

CHAPTER 11 The ABC's of Assigning Grades   123

Part 3 Understanding Students   139

CHAPTER
12
Motivation in the College Classroom   140
By Barbara K. Hofer, Middlebury College

CHAPTER
13
Teaching Culturally Diverse Students   151
By Richard M. Suinn, Colorado State University

CHAPTER 14   Dealing with Student Problems and Problem Students (There's Almost Always at Least One!)   172

Part 4 Adding to Your Repertoire of Skills and Strategies for Facilitating Active Learning   191

CHAPTER 15   How to Enhance Learning by Using High-Stakes and Low-Stakes Writing   192
By Peter Elbow and Mary Deane Sorcinelli, University of Massachusetts Amherst

CHAPTER **16**

Active Learning: Cooperative, Collaborative, and Peer Learning   213

 CHAPTER **17**

Problem–Based Learning: Teaching with Cases, Simulations, and Games   221

CHAPTER
21

The Teacher's Role in Experiential Learning   278
By Richard D. Mann, University of Michigan

CHAPTER
22

Teaching by Distance Education   288
By Andrew Northedge, The Open University

Part 6 Teaching for Higher-Level Goals

CHAPTER 23

Teaching Students How to Become More Strategic and Self-Regulated Learners

By Claire Ellen Weinstein, University of Texas at Austin

CHAPTER 24

Teaching Thinking

By Jane S. Halonen, University of West Florida

Preface

TEACHING TIPS was originally written to answer the questions posed by new college teachers, to place them at ease in their jobs, and to get them started effectively in the classroom. It has proven useful as well to experienced instructors, to teachers in community colleges, to distance educators, adult educators, adjunct faculty, and faculty members in many other countries.

The organization of the book begins with the issues involved in getting started, then moves on to the basic skills needed by all teachers—getting student participation, lecturing, assessing learning, and assigning grades (Parts 1 and 2). Equally important are awareness of, respect for, and ability to adapt to differences among students (Part 3). Parts 4 and 5 deal with additional skills and strategies important for other aspects of teaching. In Part 6 we discuss goals of education going beyond simple memorization of facts, concepts, and theories, and in Part 7 we point toward your continued development as a teacher.

Effective teaching demands more than the acquisition of skills. To adapt to the educational needs of a particular class at a particular time, the teacher needs to understand the underlying theory of learning and teaching so that each teacher can develop his or her own methods. Thus the "teaching tips" are supported by discussion of relevant research and theory. Skill in teaching is not something to be learned and simply repeated; what makes it exciting is that there is always room to grow. As you reflect on your classes, you will get new insights and will continue to develop both your theory of teaching and learning and your repertoire of skills and strategies.

As with any revision, the Twelfth Edition reflects new developments in almost every chapter. Probably the fastest moving field is instructional technology. The thoroughly updated chapter titled "Technology and Teaching," by my colleagues Erping Zhu and Matthew Kaplan, will be helpful both to novices and more experienced teachers who want to use technology where and when it can help students learn. This edition also features completely new chapters on the topics of using high- and low-stakes writing (by Peter Elbow and Mary Deane Sorcinelli), experiential learning (by Richard D. Mann) and teaching culturally diverse students (by Richard M. Suinn).

Teaching Tips has stressed learner-centered teaching since the very first edition, in which I emphasized the importance of active learning. In the second edition I introduced a longer section on learner-centered teaching and the role of the teacher as a facilitator of learning. It is gratifying that in the last several years authors have begun to write about the shift from teacher-centered to learner-centered education and the shift of the teacher's role from that of dispenser of information to facilitator of learning. Whether *Teaching Tips* has contributed to that shift, I do not know, but I hope that "learning-centered" does not become one of the buzz words that come and go—like the fifties' "master teachers" (who were to be televised and teach large numbers of students), or the sixties' "programmed learning" (which would teach more efficiently), or the seventies' "technological revolution." All were believed to be panaceas (and all contained worthwhile elements), but after a period of ascendancy, all faded before the next great enthusiasm. What counts in education is not so much what the teacher does as what goes on in the students' minds, and this will be true even if the term "learner-centered" falls into disuse. This does not mean, however, that "learner-centered" implies a particular method of teaching.

"Learner-centered" may appear to diminish the importance of the teacher. Not so! Your unique qualities as a person, your integrity, your commitment to your students' development—these are even more important than they were when the teacher's role was simply that of a talking textbook. Your role is now expanded to include that of mediator between your content and your students' understanding of it, on multiple, and increasingly higher, levels. *There is no one best way of teaching.* If you are to continue to develop as a teacher, you will need well-practiced skills, but you also need fresh thinking about why some things worked or didn't work in your last class. I do not offer a set of rules to follow. Rather I suggest strategies to consider and modify as needed by the ever-changing dynamics of your classes. What is best for you may be quite different from what is best for me. By introducing research and theory relevant to the strategies suggested, I hope to encourage your reflection and continuing development as a thinking, observing, and caring teacher. Also, while providing current research is always a major goal, in this edition, you will see that "classic" references are now denoted with a diamond icon in the end-of-text references section. This has been added to point out the classic, seminal works that still offer the most reliable scholarship on their topic.

I am pleased that so many copies of previous editions of this guide have been used outside the United States. My increased interaction with colleagues in other countries who are concerned about improving teaching makes me aware of the cultural bias of much of my writing. I trust that *Teaching Tips* will nevertheless have value for everyone concerned with teaching and student learning.

The first edition of this book was prepared in collaboration with Gregory Kimble. His wit and wisdom are still evident at many points in the Twelfth Edition. I have asked Marilla Svinicki to join me as co-author of this edition. Marilla is not only an award-winning teacher but also a nationally recognized expert on helping faculty members improve their teaching. My thanks go to Janet Young, my development editor; Lisa Mafrici at Cengage Learning, who made many helpful suggestions; and to all the reviewers, who will see evidence of the impact of their comments:

T. Binfet, *Loyola Marymount University*
Iris Engstrand, *University of San Diego*
Jacqueline Hansen, *Murray State University*
Mary Heppner, *University of Missouri–Columbia*
June Gary Hopps, *University of Georgia*
Paula S. Krist, *Florida Institute of Technology*
Judy Reinhartz, *The University of Texas at Arlington*
Stewart Wood, *Madonna University*

WILBERT J. McKEACHIE

A Special Preface

For Teaching Assistants and Graduate Student Instructors

TEACHING TIPS was originally written for my own teaching assistants. I am pleased that more experienced teachers have also found it to be helpful, but I still think of my primary audience as being beginning teachers. I began teaching as a teaching assistant (TA) and have worked with teaching assistants ever since. I try to involve my TAs in course planning both before and during the term. We grade tests in a group the evening after a test is given, bringing in sandwiches and brownies to maintain our energy and good spirits during sessions that may last until midnight. In short, I try to develop the spirit of a collaborative team.

However, I recognize that TAs are in the difficult position of being in the middle between the students and me. As TAs you want to be liked and respected by your students as well as by your professor; yet there are times when you don't agree with the professor's point of view or even with some of the course policies. You will be tempted to blame the professor or the system when students complain, but overusing this strategy only leads to students perceiving you as weak and powerless. On the other hand, this doesn't mean that you have to defend everything your professor says. Students, particularly first-year students, need to learn that absolute truth is hard to come by and that it is possible to have well-reasoned differences.

Yet one must be aware of student anxiety when TA and lecturer seem always to be at odds with one another. Support your lecturer when you can, disagree when you must, but recognize that sometimes your students' learning will be best served by your silence. Often your role is that of a coach helping students develop skills in learning and thinking, using the knowledge provided by the lecturer and textbook.

Many of you will find it hard to believe that the students will accept your authority and expertise, and you will be ambivalent about whether to dazzle them with your brilliance or to play the role of being just one of the group. Relax! The power of role expectations always amazes me. If you are the teacher, students will accept your authority and expertise. You don't need to be dictatorial, but you do need to be clear about your expectations of the students. Think of yourself as a more experienced scholar who can be a valuable coach. You may not know everything, but you have enough subject-matter expertise to be helpful. I hope this book will add to your helpfulness. Have fun!

Note: A great book written especially for graduate students is Anne Curzon and Lisa Damour's *First Day to Final Grade* (Ann Arbor: University of Michigan Press, 2000).

W. J. M.

MCKEACHIE'S
Teaching Tips

Part 1

Getting Started

Chapter 1

Introduction

The first few months and years of teaching are all-important. Experiences during this period can blight a promising teaching career or start one on a path of continued growth and development.

Most of us go into our first classes as teachers with a good deal of fear and trembling. We don't want to appear to be fools; so we have prepared well, but we dread the embarrassment of not being able to answer students' questions. We want to be liked and respected by our students; yet we know that we have to achieve liking and respect in a new role which carries expectations, such as evaluation, that make our relationship with students edgy and uneasy. We want to get through the first class with éclat, but we don't know how much material we can cover in a class period.

In most cases anxiety passes as one finds that students do respond positively, that one does have some expertise in the subject, and that class periods can be exciting. But for some teachers the first days are not happy experiences. Classes get off on the wrong foot. Sullen hostility sets in. The teacher asserts authority and the students resist. The teacher knows that things are not going well but doesn't know what to do about it.

One likely response of the teacher is retreat—retreat to reading lectures with as little eye contact with students as possible, retreat to threats of low grades as a motivating device, retreat to research and other aspects of the professional role.

What makes the difference in these first few days?

It's probably not the subject matter. More often than not, the key to a good start is not the choice of interesting content (important as that may be) but rather the ability to manage the activities of the class effectively. Simple teaching techniques get the students involved so that they can get to work and learn.

The new teacher who has techniques for breaking the ice, for encouraging class participation, and for getting the course organized is more likely to get off to a good start. Once you find that teaching can be fun, you will enjoy devoting time to it, you will think about it, and you will develop into a competent teacher.

When you are just starting, discussions of philosophy of education and theories of learning and teaching can be helpful, but they are probably not as important as learning enough techniques and simple skills to get through the first few weeks without great stress and with some satisfaction. Once some comfort has been achieved, you can think more deeply about the larger issues discussed in later chapters.

THE COLLEGE OR UNIVERSITY CULTURE

A course cannot be divorced from the total college or university culture.

First of all, the institution makes certain requirements of instructors. In most you must submit grades for the students' work. You probably must give a final course examination. A classroom is assigned for the class, and the class meets in this assigned place. The class meets at certain regularly scheduled periods.

There are, in addition, areas not covered by the formal rules or routine practices of the college, in which instructors must tread lightly. For example, in most college cultures instructors who become intimately involved with their students are overstepping the bounds of propriety. Certain limits on class discussion of religion, sex, or politics may exist. Instructors must learn not only to operate within the fences of college regulations but also to skirt the pitfalls of the college mores. And it is not just the culture of the institution that matters. Each department or discipline has its own culture with customs related to teaching methods, testing, standards, and styles of communication and instruction.

Each reader will need to adapt my suggestions to the college culture of which he or she is a part. When you begin a new teaching position, talk to other faculty members about their perceptions of the students, about how these instructors teach and perceive others as teaching. Ask for examples of syllabi, tests, and other course materials.

In many institutions, students have had experience in previous classes with instructors who, in a more or less parental way, gave information and rewarded those students who could best give it back. The sort of tests, frequency of tests, and methods of grading also have conformed closely to certain norms. As a result, instructors who attempt to revolutionize teaching with new methods or techniques may find that they are only frustrating the needs and expectations their students have developed in the culture of the college. So, if you are trying something new, be sure that students understand why the new method is likely to be valuable.

Although there are many norms and folkways that characterize an entire campus, you need to recognize that there are many subcultures. Some of them are subcultures of faculty in different disciplines, but it is important to recognize that there are student subcultures that have their own norms and expectations. And within the student cultures there are important individual differences among students. Taking account of the diversity of students is so important in teaching that "Understanding Students" is a separate part (Part 3) of this book.

RESEARCH VERSUS TEACHING?

One aspect of the local culture critical for new teachers is the definition of the proper role of a faculty member. In many universities, for example, formal definitions of the criteria for promotion give research and teaching equal weight, but it is not uncommon to find that research is "more equal."

Studies have demonstrated that research and teaching are not necessarily in conflict. Many faculty members are excellent researchers and excellent teachers as well. Some excellent researchers are poor teachers; some excellent teachers do not publish research. Most faculty members enjoy both teaching and scholarship. Most also provide service to their institutions, and many provide service to their community and nation.

Teaching as Scholarship

In 1990, Ernest Boyer's book *Scholarship Reconsidered* stimulated discussion throughout higher education about the nature of scholarship. In most American universities scholarship has been evaluated in terms of published research. Boyer suggested that teachers who keep up with current developments, who devise and assess better ways to help students learn, or who do research on methods of teaching are also scholars. As a result of the debates about Boyer's proposal, there is increasing acceptance of the idea that good teaching involves much scholarly activity.

Find out what the local norms are, and if you feel a conflict, choose the balance that suits your own talents and interests with an informed awareness of the likelihood of support for that self-definition. Although time is not infinitely elastic, most faculty members find that a 50- to 60-hour work week is satisfying because they enjoy both teaching and research.

Whatever your choice, it is likely that teaching will be a part of your role. *Teaching skillfully may be less time consuming than teaching badly.* Teaching well is more fun than teaching poorly. Moreover, you will be better able to focus on your research if you are not worrying about teaching. Thus some investment of time and attention to developing skill in teaching is likely to have substantial payoff in self-satisfaction and effectiveness in your career.

IN CONCLUSION

Because the suggestions I make are based on my own philosophy of teaching, you should be forewarned of six of my biases or hypotheses.

1. What is important is learning, not teaching. Teaching effectiveness depends not just on what the teacher does, but rather on what the student does. Teaching involves listening as much as talking. It's important that both teacher and students are actively thinking, but most important is what goes on in the students' minds. Those minds are not blank slates. They hold expectations, experiences, and conceptions that will shape their interpretation of the knowledge you present. Your task is to help them develop mental representations of your subject matter that will provide a basis for further learning, thinking, and use.

2. Teachers can occasionally be wrong. If they are wrong too often, they should not be teaching. If they are never wrong, they belong in heaven, not a college classroom.

3. Classes are unpredictable. This can be frustrating, but it also makes teaching continually fascinating. Don't be discouraged if some students don't appreciate your teaching. You can interest all of your students some of the time; you can interest some of your students all of the time; but you can't interest all of your students all of the time.

4. There are many important goals of college and university teaching. Not the least of these is that of increasing the student's motivation and ability to *continue* learning after leaving college.

5. Most student learning occurs outside the classroom. This is both humbling and reassuring for the beginning teacher. It means that the students' education will neither succeed nor fail simply because of what you do or don't do in the classroom. At the same time it reminds one to direct attention to stimulating and guiding student learning outside class even more than to preparing to give a dazzling classroom performance.

6. One key to improvement is reflection—thinking about what you want to accomplish, and what you and the students need to do to achieve these goals. What is contained in this book will not make you a Great Teacher. It may be that Great Teachers are born and not made, but anyone with ability enough to get a job as a college teacher can be a *good* teacher. This book will give you some tips for avoiding common problems and some concepts to think

with, but eventually it comes down to you, your personality, and your values. My hope is that this book will help you feel enough at ease that you can reveal the best that is in you.

Supplementary Reading

When the first edition of *Teaching Tips* was published, it was almost the only book offering guidance to college teachers. Now there are a great many, as well as journals and newsletters published in the United States and other countries. Almost every discipline has a journal concerned with teaching that discipline. Check out the holdings of your institution's library. If your institution has a faculty/instructional developmental center, it will have lots of material and a helpful staff.

I am reluctant to list only a few of the many good books on college teaching because I see them all as meeting a need and complementing one another as well as *Teaching Tips*. I will limit myself to fewer than twenty.

- Robert Boice, *Advice for New Faculty Members: Nihil Nimus* (Boston: Allyn and Bacon, 2000).

- B. G. Davis, *Tools for Teaching* (San Francisco: Jossey-Bass, 1993).

- S. F. Davis and W. Buskist (eds.), *The Teaching of Psychology: Essays in Honor of Wilbert J. McKeachie and Charles L. Brewer* (Mahwah, NJ: Erlbaum, 2002).

- L. Dee Fink, *Creating Significant Learning Experiences* (San Francisco: Jossey-Bass, 2003).

- Deborah DeZure (ed.), *Learning from Change: Landmarks in Teaching and Learning in* Change Magazine, *1969–1999* (Sterling, VA: Stylus Publishing, 2000).

- K. Eble, *The Craft of Teaching*, 2nd ed. (San Francisco: Jossey-Bass, 1988). Don't think that a 1988 book must be out of date by now. This is a good book to read when you've lost your initial anxiety and want to think about teaching as a craft and a calling.

- Linc Fisch, *The Chalk Dust Collection: Thoughts and Reflections on Teaching in Colleges and Universities* (Stillwater, OK: New Forums Press, 1996). A thoughtful, often amusing collection of essays with much good sense.

- A. Grasha, *Teaching with Style* (Pittsburgh: Alliance Publishers, 1996).

- Diane F. Halpern and Milton D. Hakel (eds.), "Applying the Science of Learning to University Teaching and Beyond," *New Directions for Teaching and Learning*, no. 89, March 2002.

■I Ray Perry and John Smart (eds.), *Effective Teaching in Higher Education* (New York: Agathon Press, 1997).

■I R. Prieto and S. A. Meyers, *The Teaching Assistant Handbook* (Stillwater, OK: New Forums Press, 2001).

David E. Johnson has a good chapter, "Teaching, Research, and Scholarship," in S. F. Davis and W. Buskist (eds.), *The Teaching of Psychology: Essays in Honor of Wilbert J. McKeachie and Charles L. Brewer* (Mahwah, NJ: Erlbaum, 2002).

Parker Palmer's book, *The Courage to Teach: Exploring the Inner Landscape of a Teacher's Life* (San Francisco: Jossey-Bass, 1998), will inspire you.

The following five books come from authors writing from the perspective of experience in other countries. Their contents are relevant to university teachers in all countries.

■I J. Biggs, *Teaching for Quality Learning at University* (Buckingham, UK, and Philadelphia: Society for Research into Higher Education and Open University Press, 1999).

■I Nira Hativa, *Teaching for Effective Learning in Higher Education* (Dordrecht: Kluwer, 2000).

■I Linda B. Nilson, *Teaching at Its Best*, 2nd ed. (Bolton, MA: Anker, 2003).

■I Daphne Pan, *Learning to Teach, Learning to Learn* (Singapore: National University of Singapore, 2001).

■I P. Ramsden, *Learning to Teach in Higher Education* (London and New York: Routledge, 1992).

Many university faculty development centers publish newsletters for their own faculties. In addition there are two national publications on college teaching: *The National Teaching and Learning Forum* and *The Teaching Professor*. Both have helpful articles.

Countdown for Course Preparation

For teachers, courses do not start on the first day of classes. Rather, a course begins well before you meet your students. I shall present a series of steps, but planning does not usually follow a perfectly orderly, linear pattern. The components of course planning are all shown in Figure 2.1. Experts typically say that you should start with your objectives, but don't get stuck on this. In all your planning, you'll do at least one thing that will remind you to modify earlier steps. So, you move back and forth as you progress. The main thing is to get started!

This chapter incorporates material from Graham Gibbs's chapter in the tenth edition, "Planning Your Students' Learning Activities."

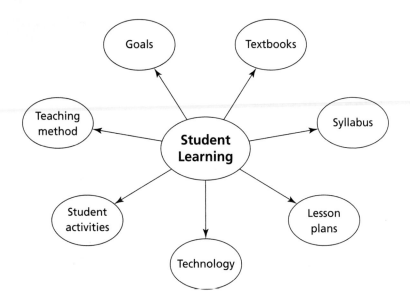

FIGURE 2.1   **Course Preparation Components**

TIME: THREE MONTHS BEFORE THE FIRST CLASS*

Write Objectives, Goals, or Outcomes

The first step in preparing for a course is working out course objectives, because the choice of textbook, the selection of the type and order of assignments, the choice of teaching techniques, and all the decisions involved in course planning should derive from your objectives. What are your students like? What do they expect? What outcomes do you expect them to achieve? At this point your list of goals or objectives should be taken only as a

---

*I borrowed the idea of three months, two months, and so on from P. G. Zimbardo and J. W. Newton, *Instructor's Resource Book to Accompany Psychology and Life* (Glenview, IL: Scott, Foresman, 1975). Don't take the "three months" too seriously. You may not have three months, but get started as soon as you can.

rough reminder to be revised as you develop other aspects of the course plan and to be further revised in interaction with students. Writing out your goals helps clarify your thinking.

Your objectives have the great advantage of pointing clearly to what you can look for as evidence that the objective has been achieved. Your students see your methods of assessing or testing achievement of the objectives as the most important operational definition of your goals; hence goals and testing are inseparable teaching tasks. This does not mean that all of your goals should be assessed and count toward a grade. Some of your goals will involve motivational, attitudinal, and value outcomes, as discussed in the chapters "Motivation in the College Classroom," "Teaching Students How to Become More Strategic and Self-Regulated Learners," and "The Ethics of Teaching and the Teaching of Ethics." Course grades are typically based only on cognitive and skill outcomes.

What Goals?

The answer obviously depends on the course and discipline, but it is important to note that the overall course objectives involve *educating students;* the objective of a course is not just to cover a certain set of topics, but rather *to facilitate student learning and thinking.* Ordinarily we are concerned not simply with the learning of a set of facts, but rather with learning that can be applied and used in situations outside course examinations. In fact, *in most courses we are concerned about helping our students in a lifelong learning process;* that is, *we want to develop interest in further learning and provide a base of concepts and skills that will facilitate further learning, thinking, and appreciation.* Thus in framing your goals, think about what will be meaningful to your students. Will these goals really be relevant to them now and in the future?

Your personal values inevitably enter into your choice of goals. Although many of us were taught to be strictly objective, I have come to believe that this is impossible. Our teaching is always influenced by our values, and students have a fairer chance to evaluate our biases or to accept our model if we are explicit about them. Hiding behind the cloak of objectivity simply prevents honest discussion of vital issues.

In thinking about your goals, remember that each course contributes to other general goals of a university education that transcend specific subject matter, such as critical thinking, being willing to explore ideas contrary to one's own beliefs, knowing when information or data are relevant to an issue and how to find that information, and developing skills for learning and self-regulation (see the chapters "Teaching Students How to Become More Strategic and Self-Regulated Learners" and "Teaching Thinking").

In addition to this general perspective, you need to keep in mind characteristics of the setting in which you teach. What is the role of this course in the curriculum? Are other instructors depending on this course to provide specific kinds of background knowledge or skill? What are your students like? How do they differ? (See the part on "Understanding Students.") What are their current concerns? Self-discovery? Social action? Getting a job? How can their goals be integrated with other goals of the course? Talk to some of your colleagues.

A committee of college and university examiners developed two books, which are now classics, to assist faculty members in thinking about their objectives: *Taxonomy of Educational Objectives, Handbook I: Cognitive Domain* (Bloom, 1956) and *Handbook II: Affective Domain* (Krathwohl et al., 1964). Krathwohl and others have completed a revision (Anderson et al., 2001). Another good framework is the SOLO (Structure of the Observed Learning Outcome) taxonomy (see Biggs, 1999).

Having said all this about the importance of starting with clear goals, I would nonetheless not want to make you feel guilty if you started on your syllabus with only vague notions about goals. Although it seems logical to start with goals, content, teaching methods, and the nature of the students, all of these interact in dynamic ways. So if you find it easier to start by outlining the content of the course, do so. Ideally you would then tie the content to goals, but many effective teachers never state their goals very explicitly, yet their students achieve the kinds of motivational and cognitive outcomes that we all desire. College teachers are individualists. There are lots of different ways to do a good job. Goals emerge as you teach.

Order Textbooks, Lab Supplies, or Other Resources Students May Need

Should You Use a Textbook?* With paperback books, reprint series, photocopiers,** and the World Wide Web, young instructors are immediately beguiled by the thought that they can do a much better job of compiling a set of required readings than any previous author or editor. "Coursepacks"—compilations of relevant articles and book chapters—may be used in place of a textbook or as supplementary reading.

There is much to be said for such a procedure. It provides flexibility, a variety of points of view, and an opportunity to maintain maximum interest. Moreover, since no single text covers every topic equally well, the use of a variety of sources enables the teacher to provide more uniformly excellent materials, ranging from theoretical papers and research reports to applications.

The disadvantages of not using a textbook are apparent. Without a textbook the task of integration may be so overwhelming that great pressure is placed on instructors to provide integration. This may limit your freedom to use the class period for problem solving, applications, or other purposes. With a well-chosen textbook, you may rely on the students to obtain the basic content and structure of the subject matter through reading and thus be freer to vary procedures in the classroom. Moreover, the managerial task of determining appropriate readings and arranging to have them available for students is not to be taken lightly. If students are expected to use certain print sources in the library, consult a librarian to be sure enough copies are available. Access to course resources is particularly important in distance learning.

A final consideration is the extent to which you want to use required versus free reading, as in my use of a journal (see the chapter "How to Enhance Learning by Using High-Stakes and Low-Stakes Writing"). I use a textbook as a base to provide structure and then require students to write journal entries on readings

---

*You can skip this section if your department has already chosen the textbook.

**Check the copyright laws before making multiple copies.

they choose. To assign diverse required readings and additional free reading seems to me to require too much integration even for well-prepared, bright students.

Choose a Textbook or Other Reading Materials*

In choosing reading materials the most important thing is that they fit your objectives. One of the most annoying and confusing practices for students is instructor disagreement with the text-book. It is doubtful that any book will satisfy you completely, but if you use a textbook, choose one that is as much in line with your view as possible.

Students prefer going through a book as it was written. If the author wrote the book in a systematic way, building one concept on another, there may be good pedagogical reasons for following the author's order. I know of no text that completely suits every teacher, however, so I can only recommend that you keep skipping around to a minimum and make sure that students understand why.

There is no substitute for detailed review of the competing texts for the course you are teaching. As textbooks multiply, it becomes increasingly tempting to throw up your hands in frustration over the time required for a conscientious review and to choose the book primarily on the basis of appearance, the personality of the sales representative, or the inclusion of your name as author of one of the studies cited. Yet research on teaching suggests that the major influence on what students learn is not the teaching method but the textbook. What should you do?

1. Winnow the possibilities down to two to five. You may be able to do some winnowing on the basis of the table of contents and preface, by checking with colleagues who have taught the course, or by reading reviews.

2. Read a couple of chapters. It is tempting to simply leaf through each book, reading snatches here and there. But reading a couple of complete chapters will give you a better idea of the difficulty

---

*Some of these ideas were stimulated by Russell Dewey's article, "Finding the right introductory psychology textbook," *APS Observer*, March 1995, 32–35.

and interest level of each book. Try picking one chapter on a topic you know well and one that is not in your area of expertise.

3. Pick three or four key concepts. See how each text explains them. Will the explanations be clear to students? Interesting?

4. Beware of seductive details or pictures that were included to make the book more attractive but may distract from the basic concepts.

TIME: TWO MONTHS BEFORE THE FIRST CLASS

Begin Drafting a Syllabus for the Course

When we think about teaching, we usually think about what goes on in the classroom, but most student learning occurs outside the classroom. Planning assignments and out-of-class activities is even more important than planning for class meetings. A syllabus typically contains such a plan, with assignments correlated with topics to be discussed in class. If you are teaching a distance learning course, a syllabus is indispensable. Like a contract, a syllabus should help students understand both their responsibilities and yours.

Constructing your syllabus will force you to begin thinking about the practicalities of what you must give up in order to achieve the most important objectives within the limitations of time, place, students, and resources. If you have taught the course before, what worked? What didn't?

How Much Student Time Does Your Course Involve?   It is easy to imagine that your course is the only one your students are taking. After all, it is the only one you see. However, your students may be taking three, four, or five other courses in parallel. Given a realistic studying week of about 40 hours, you therefore have between about 6 and 10 hours a week of your students' time available to allocate to learning on your course, including in-class time. If your students spend 3 hours a week in class with you, then you have between 3 and 6 hours a week of out-of-class learning activity to plan. You should expect to use all of this time, and you should be quite explicit with your students about what you expect them to do with it. Exactly how many hours you have and are taking up is rather important. Students experience wide variations in demands among courses because teachers often do not estimate or plan this time carefully. The most common problems are caused by, at one extreme, specifying nothing and leaving students to their own devices. At the other extreme, teachers overload students with inappropriate and unproductive activities that actually limit their learning. For example, science teachers often fill their students' time with writing up lab reports, leaving them no time to read. It can be helpful to calculate the total number of study hours available to your course and to plan what all of those hours would ideally be used for, estimating the time demands of each activity. In reality students will vary. Some will work harder or slower than others, and some will spend more of their time on some learning activities, and on some of their courses, than on others. But being explicit will help you to make realistic demands and will help students to see what is expected of them.

What Should Be in the Syllabus?   There is no one model. Take the following as suggestions, not rules. If you have followed my recommendations up to this point, you now have a list of goals, have chosen a textbook, and have a general schedule of when you will cover each topic. The core of your syllabus will be that schedule. In introducing the schedule, explain the purpose for the organization you have chosen.

Under the topic headings, you can schedule assignments and the dates when they are due. This relieves you of the task of making assignments every few days and of repeating the assignments for students who were absent when each assignment was announced. State your expectations and policies about class attendance.

As you lay out your schedule, consider alternate ways students might achieve the goals of a particular day or week of class. You will seldom have perfect attendance at every class. Why not build in periodic alternatives to your lecture or class discussion? Be sure also to consider the diversity of your students. Alternative assignments can help. Students who have options and a sense of personal control are likely to be more highly motivated for learning.

Be clear about when and how learning will be assessed. What students do is strongly influenced by their anticipation of the ways learning will be evaluated. You may also include other items that will be helpful for student learning, such as sites on the World Wide Web, interesting readings to supplement textbook assignments, strategies for maximizing learning, and what to do when having difficulty.

Finally, you may include any special rules you want to emphasize, such as a statement to the effect that assignments for the course are to be completed by the dates indicated in the course outline.

But isn't a syllabus that is printed or on a web site a cue that the course is really instructor centered and that student needs are not going to be considered? Not necessarily so. Research by Mann and colleagues (1970) suggests that students may see a less organized approach as an indication that the teacher is not interested in their learning. The syllabus helps students discover at the outset what is expected of them and gives them the security of knowing where they are going. At the same time, your wording of assignment topics can convey excitement and stimulate curiosity. Ken Takeuchi of the State University of New York at Buffalo has a nice acronym for guiding syllabus construction:

S—Specific

M—Measurable

A—Agreed (clearly understood)

R—Related, with a clear structure and links between assignments

T—Time frame

TIME: ONE MONTH BEFORE THE FIRST CLASS

Begin Preparing Lesson Plans

If you are planning to lecture, outline the content of the first few lectures and the ways you will get student involvement. If you are planning to teach by discussion, cooperative learning, or other methods, don't assume that they will take less preparation. Work out your plans. (See also the chapters "Meeting a Class for the First

Time" and "Facilitating Discussion.") Think about what students need for the tests you will give. If you spend a little time on your plans each day and let them percolate in your mind, ideas will come to you while driving, jogging, or walking to your office.

Plan for Out-of-Class Learning

It is easy for teachers to imagine that what happens in class is overwhelmingly important to students' learning and that they and their classes are at the center of students' learning universe. It is the component of student learning that teachers see—the rest is often invisible. When they do their planning, most teachers give their attention to covering content in class rather than to what happens out of class (Stark & Lattuca, 1997). However, in studies of what students believe most influenced change during the college years, and of what students believe were their most important experiences at college, ideas presented by instructors in courses, and instructors themselves, rank far behind a range of other influences (Feldman & Newcomb, 1969). In most courses students spend at least as much time studying out of class as they do in class. Thus you need to focus as much on what you expect students to do outside class as on what goes on in class. Look at your objectives. If you want students to become better problem solvers or critical thinkers, they need to practice these skills.

Reading an assignment passively will produce poorer learning than reading with an activity in mind, such as preparing a question for class discussion, drawing a concept map, or writing examples or possible applications.

Choose Appropriate Teaching Methods

A final point at which your preparation for a course is determined by your objectives is in the type of instruction you will use. For some goals and for some materials, an orthodox lecture presentation is as good as or better than any other. For others, discussion may be preferable. For the accomplishment of still other ends, cooperative learning or role-playing techniques described later in the book may be useful. Probably most successful teachers vary their methods to suit their objectives. Thus you may wish one day to present some new material in a lecture. You may then follow this with a class discussion on implications of this material or with a laboratory or field exercise. Since your choice in the matter is determined as much by your own personality as by your course objectives, I shall not dwell on it here. From the description of these techniques in later sections of the book, you may be able to decide which techniques are suited to your philosophy of teaching, your abilities, the class you are teaching, and the particular goals you are emphasizing at a particular time.

Select Appropriate Technology

It is quite possible to teach an effective course without technology. Nonetheless there is much that can be helpful. The chapter "Technology and Teaching" gives you a good overview of some of the possibilities. When used appropriately, technology can provide opportunities for students to interact with the content and with one another. It is an important instructional resource. But just as in considering other resources, ask yourself, "Will this help my students learn more effectively?"

TIME: TWO WEEKS BEFORE THE FIRST CLASS

Check Resources

Preparation and planning are not done when you've firmed up the syllabus. Now look back over the syllabus to see what resources are required. Presumably your check with a colleague (as suggested in the chapter "Introduction") has turned up any gross problems—such as assuming an unlimited budget for films. This is a good time for another check. What are the library policies relevant to putting on reserve any books you may want? What computer resources are available? Can you assume unlimited photocopying of exams and course materials to give to students? What do you do if you want to show a film? Go on a field trip?

Visit the classroom you've been assigned. Will the seating be conducive to discussion? Can you use the technology you need? If the room is unsuitable, ask for another.

Start a Portfolio

A teaching portfolio not only will be useful when you discuss your teaching with your department head or superior, it will also be useful in your thinking about teaching and your development.

TIME: ONE WEEK BEFORE THE FIRST CLASS

If you teach first-year students and have a class list and e-mail addresses, send an e-mail welcoming the students to your class. (It's also not a bad idea to do this with more advanced students.)

At this point you're ready to prepare for the first class. For ideas about what to do and how to handle this meeting, read the next chapter.

Supplementary Reading

Robert Diamond's *Designing and Assessing Courses and Curricula: A Practical Guide* (San Francisco: Jossey-Bass, 1998) has a good chapter, "Developing a Learning-Centered Syllabus."

Barbara Davis's book *Tools for Teaching,* 2nd ed. (San Francisco: Jossey-Bass, 1993), has a fine chapter on the syllabus (pp. 14–28).

Chapter 6, "The Natural History of the Classroom," in *The College Classroom* by Richard Mann, S. M. Arnold, J. Bender, S. Cytrynbaum, B. M. Newman, B. Ringwald, J. Ringwald, and R. Rosenwein (New York: Wiley, 1970), is still the best material on the changing needs of classes over the course of a semester.

Teaching Within the Rhythms of the Semester by Donna K. Duffy and Janet W. Jones (San Francisco: Jossey-Bass, 1995) is also a perceptive and read-able guide to thinking about the flow of the course over the term.

An excellent aid for preparing your syllabus is M. A. Lowther, J. S. Stark, and G. G. Martens, *Preparing Course Syllabi for Improved Communication* (Ann Arbor: NCRIPTAL, University of Michigan, 1989).

If you are teaching first-year students, the book *Teaching College Freshmen* by Bette Erickson and D. W. Strommer (San Francisco: Jossey-Bass, 1991) will be helpful to you.

Meeting a Class for the First Time

The first class meeting, like any other situation in which you are meeting a group of strangers who will affect your well-being, is at the same time exciting and anxiety-producing for both students and teacher. Some teachers handle their anxiety by postponing it, simply handing out the syllabus and leaving. This does not convey the idea that class time is valuable, nor does it capitalize on the fact that first-day excitement can be constructive. If you have prepared as suggested in the previous chapter, you're in good shape; the students will be pleased that the instruction is under control, and focusing on meeting the students' concerns can not only help you quell your own anxiety but also make the first class interesting and challenging.

Other things being equal, anxiety is less disruptive in situations where stimulus events are clear and unambiguous. When the students know what to expect, they can direct their energy more productively. An important function of the first day's meeting in any class is to provide this structure; that is, to present the classroom situation clearly, so that the students will know from the date of this meeting what you are like and what you expect. They come to the first class wanting to know what the course is all about and what kind of person the teacher is. You need to know what the students expect. To these ends, the following concrete suggestions are offered.

SETTING THE STAGE

One point to keep in mind on the first day and throughout the term is that yours is not the students' only class. They come to you from classes in chemistry, music, English, or physical education, or rushing from their dormitory beds or from parking lots. The first few minutes need to help this varied group shift their thoughts and feelings to you and your subject.

You can ease them into the course gradually, or you can grab their attention with something dramatically different, but in either case you need to think consciously about how you set the stage to facilitate achieving the course objectives. Even before the class period begins, you can communicate nonverbally with such actions as arranging the seats in a circle, posting an agenda, putting your name on the board, and chatting with early arrivals about what class they have come from or anything else that would indicate your interest in them. While students are coming in, suggest that they spend the time before class starts by getting acquainted with the students sitting near them.

BREAKING THE ICE

You will probably want to use the first period for getting acquainted and establishing goals. You might begin by informally asking first-year students to raise their hands, then sophomores, juniors, seniors, or out-of-staters. This gives you some idea of the composition of the class and gets students started participating. Make it clear that you value diversity. Varied student backgrounds enrich discussions.

In my relatively large lecture classes I have then asked the students to take a minute or two to write down words and phrases that describe their feelings on the first day of class. I then ask them, "What have you written?" and list their responses on the board.

Next I ask them, "How do you think your teacher feels on the first day of class?" This takes them aback, but they begin writing. We now list these responses in a second column, and they see some parallels. I comment briefly on my own feelings. (I remember with special affection the senior who came up to me after class and said, "I've been at this university almost four years, and this is the first time it ever occurred to me that professors have feelings.")

I admit to them that I'm anxious—that I'm concerned about how the students will relate to me and the material, but I'm not sure that everyone should do this. Students need to feel that you're secure enough to admit your own feelings. If they see you as being uncertain about your ability to fill the roles of authority and expert when needed, students may become more anxious.

In a small class you might then ask all class members (including yourself) to introduce themselves, tell where they're from, mention their field of concentration, and answer any questions the group has. Or you can ask each student to get acquainted with the persons sitting on each side and then go around the class with each student introducing the next or each repeating the names of all those who have been introduced—a good device for developing rapport and for helping you learn the names, too. A more demanding but surprisingly effective device is to have each person introduce everyone who was introduced before, ending with the teacher repeating everyone's names. (Try it! You'll be surprised at how well you do.)

Learning names is a start, but students are probably even more interested in you than in their classmates; so give them a chance to ask questions of you. Sometimes I have asked for one or two students to act as interviewers for the class, asking questions they think the other students would like to ask.

Even if you remembered all of the students' names in the "Name Game," you may not recall them later; so it is helpful to supplement the memory in your head with an external memory. I ask a former student who has a camera to take a picture of each student. At the next class meeting I ask students to write their names, phone numbers, e-mail addresses, and other information on the photos for me. The "other information" might include previous experience relevant to the course, interests, distinctive characteristics that will help me remember them, possible major field, and so on.

Having established some freedom of communication, you can then go on to assess students' expectations and goals, and let them know what yours are. One technique for doing this is problem posting.

PROBLEM POSTING

Problem posting is a method of getting students involved and active that can be used in classes of all sizes. For this first class meeting you might say, "Let's see what problems you'd like to tackle during the course. What sorts of concerns do you think we might deal with?" or "What are your expectations for this course?" or "What goals do you have for this course?" or "What have you heard about this course?"

You might ask students to write for a minute their response to the question and then ask them what they have written. Your task then becomes that of recorder, listing responses on the board, overhead, or electronic smartboard. To make sure you understand, you may restate the response in your own words. If you feel that some response is ambiguous or too general, you might ask for an example, but you must be ready to accept all contributions, whether or not you feel they are important. It is crucial that the atmosphere be accepting and nonevaluative. Students should feel that you are genuinely interested in what they have to contribute.

By the end of the problem posting the class normally has become better acquainted, has become used to active participation, has taken the first step toward developing an attitude of attempting to understand rather than competing with one another, has reduced the attitude that everything must come from the teacher, has learned that the teacher can listen as well as talk (and is not going to reject ideas different from his or her own), and, I hope, has begun to feel some responsibility for solving its own problems rather than waiting for them to be answered by the instructor.

INTRODUCING THE SYLLABUS

Your syllabus will provide some of the answers to the concerns raised in the problem posting. In presenting the syllabus you give the students some notion of the kind of person you are. The syllabus is a contract between you and your students. But a contract cannot be one-sided. Thus it is important to give students time to read and discuss it. Give them a chance to have input and to be sure that they understand what you expect. Help the students understand the reasons for the plan you have presented, but if they have good reasons for changes, accept them. The students are, of course, interested in course requirements, but they are at least as much interested in what kind of person you are. One important issue is fairness.

Testing, Grading, and Fairness

Promoting the notion that you are objective or fair can best be handled in connection with marks and the assignment of grades (see the chapters "Assessing, Testing, and Evaluating" and "The ABC's of Assigning Grades"). A large part of the students' motivation in the classroom situation is (perhaps unfortunately) directed toward the grades they hope to get for the course. The very least that students can expect of you is that their marks will be arrived at on some impartial basis. Thus give some time to discussing this section of your syllabus. Try to help the students understand how grading and testing are tied to course goals.

The simplest way to show students that you are objective and fair is to let them know that you are willing to meet and advise them. Let them know they can tell you if they are likely to have special difficulties because of health or personal issues. Indicate your office hours. In addition, students appreciate it if you are willing (and have the time) to spend a few minutes in the classroom after each class, answering specific questions. Such queries most often concern questions of fact that can be answered briefly and would hardly warrant a trip to your office at a later time. If time permits, adjournment to a convenient snack bar or lounge may give students with special interests a chance to pursue them and get to know you better. If you teach an evening class, schedule some evening time to see students.

The first class is not the time to make sure students understand your inadequacies and limitations. Frankly admitting that you don't know something is fine after the course is under way, but apologies in advance for lack of experience or expertise simply increase student insecurity. They need to feel that you are competent and in charge even if you are shaking in your boots.

INTRODUCING THE TEXTBOOK

To continue with the discussion of the first meeting of the class, we turn now to the presentation of the textbook. Explain the features that led you to choose it. Describe how students can learn from it most effectively. Since disagreement between the teacher and the text is inevitable, the students have a right to know what they are supposed to do about such discrepancies on examinations. By facing the situation squarely, you can not only escape from the horns of this dilemma but also turn it to your advantage. Explain that rival interpretations stand or fall on the basis of pertinent evidence and plan to give your reasons for disagreeing with the textbook. This procedure will accomplish two things: (1) it will give the student the notion that your opinions are based on evidence, and (2) it will frequently point out current problems in theory that often have great appeal for the serious student.

ASSESSING PRIOR KNOWLEDGE

The most important characteristic determining student learning is prior knowledge. Thus you need to get some sense of the diversity of your class's background. You might simply ask questions like "How many have had more than X previous courses in this subject?" or you might give a short, noncredit test of relevant knowledge sometime during the first few class sessions. For students who lack sufficient background, you might advise that they transfer to the needed courses, or if this isn't feasible, you can at least suggest materials for their own self-study that would help them keep up with the other students. For those with very high scores, you might suggest that they skip your course and go on to a more advanced course, or at least suggest supplementary materials that would be enriching and challenging.

In a diverse class, adult students or students from other cultures may feel at a disadvantage relative to students who have had previous courses that are relevant. Reassure them by pointing out that a diversity of experiences not directly related to the course can enrich class discussion and contribute to learning.

QUESTIONS AND REACTIONS

Even in a large lecture it seems wise to interrupt these first descriptions of the course for student questions. Some of the questions will be designed as much to test you as to get information. Often the underlying questions are

- "Are you rigid?"
- "Will you really try to help students?"
- "Are you easily rattled?"
- "Are you a person as well as a teacher?"
- "Can you handle criticism?"

Ask students to take two minutes at the end of class to write their reactions to the first day (anonymously). This accomplishes two things: (1) it indicates your interest in learning from them and starts building a learning climate in which they are responsible for thinking about their learning and influencing your teaching; and (2) it gives you feedback, often revealing doubts or questions students were afraid to verbalize orally.

WHAT ABOUT SUBJECT MATTER?

Many instructors dismiss class early on the first day. As the preceding sections indicate, I think the first day is important even though the students have had no prepared assignment. I like to give at least some time to subject matter. Typically I give at least a brief overview of the course, indicate some of the questions we'll try to answer, and perhaps introduce a few key concepts. Either on the first day or during the second class period, I ask students to fill in concepts on a concept map (a diagram of key concepts and their relationships).

But there is a limit to what you can do. The balance between content and other activities is one that different teachers will decide in different ways. My only admonition is to use the time. The first day is important, and by using it fully you communicate that you take class periods seriously. By the end of the class period, students should feel, "This is going to be an exciting course."

IN CONCLUSION

By the end of the first day, students will have

1. A sense of where they're going and how they'll get there.
2. A feeling that the other members of the class are not strangers, that you and they are forming a group in which it's safe to participate.
3. An awareness that you care about their learning and will be fair.
4. An expectation that the class will be both valuable and fun.

Supplementary Reading

▨ B. G. Davis, *Tools for Teaching*, 2nd ed. (San Francisco: Jossey-Bass, 1993), Chapter 3.

▨ Baron Perlman and Lee McCann, "The First Day of Class," *American Psychological Society Observer*, 2004, 17(1), 13–14, 23–25.

Basic Skills
for Facilitating
Student Learning

4 Reading as Active Learning

While professors like to think that students learn from professors, it seems likely that students often learn more efficiently from reading than from listening. The chapter "Teaching Students How to Become More Strategic and Self-Regulated Learners" describes skills and strategies to improve learning and retention from reading. The journals and papers described in the chapter "How to Enhance Learning by Using High-Stakes and Low-Stakes Writing" illustrate one way to get students into the library and reading primary sources. Nonetheless textbooks are still a basic tool for teaching most courses, and you can teach students to be active readers of textbooks.

TEXTBOOKS

For decades the demise of the textbook has been eagerly predicted by advocates of each of the new panaceas for the problems of education. First television, then teaching machines, then the computer—each was expected to revolutionize education and free students and teachers from their longtime reliance on textbooks. But each of the new media has settled into its niche in the educational arsenal without dislodging the textbook. In fact, the greater availability of a wide variety of printed materials is probably as important as the technological revolution.

The introduction of open-stack libraries, paperback books, inexpensive reprint series, and the photocopier has given the college teacher the opportunity to choose from sources varying in style, level, and point of view. Many teachers are substituting paperback books, reprints, and collections of journal articles for the textbook as the sources of the basic information needed by students.

Yet learning is facilitated by organization. Without organization, facts and concepts become subject to interference and are quickly forgotten and inaccessible. With input from field experience, discussion, paperbacks, reprints, the World Wide Web, and other sources, the student needs, more than ever, some frame of reference within which to assimilate the bloomin', buzzin' confusion of points of view present in a modern course. Ideally, the textbook can provide such a structure.

If individual differences are to be attended to, students need an opportunity to learn in laboratory settings, field experiences, discussion, lectures, or reading from diverse sources. Textbooks are an important part of the teacher's compendium of tools, and the newer teaching methods and aids supplement rather than supplant reading. In fact, a goodly part of higher education is education in how to read—how to read poems, how to read social science, how to read legal briefs, how to read the literature of our culture and our professions.

HOW DO YOU GET STUDENTS TO DO THE ASSIGNED READING?

The main reason students come to class unprepared is that they don't see what difference it makes. In many courses, textbook assignments and lectures are independent parts of the course, sometimes overlapping, sometimes supplementary, but often not perceived as interdependent. Thus the first strategy for encouraging reading is frequent use of the phrase "As you read in your textbook assignment for today, . . ." or the question "What was your reaction to [the author of the textbook]'s discussion of . . . ?"

A second strategy is to have students write a one-minute paper at the beginning of occasional class periods on "The most important idea (or two or three ideas) I got from the assignment for today." Alternatively, you can have students write a question—either something they would like explained or something that was stimulated by the reading.

Probably the surest strategy is to announce that there will be a brief quiz on the assignment. Let's hope that once we have formed in our students the habit of reading the assignments, they will develop enough intrinsic motivation that the quizzes become unnecessary.

The basic problem often may be found in the meaning of the word *read*. To many, "read" is simply to pass one's eyes over the words as one does in reading a story. One has completed the assignment when one has reached the end of the assignment.

We need to teach students how to read—how to read with understanding, how to think about the purpose of the author, about relationships to earlier learning, about how they will use what they've read.

Research on Learning from Reading

A number of classic studies have compared printed materials with lectures, and the results—at least with difficult materials—favor print (Hartman, 1961).

Study questions intended to guide the students' reading are often helpful. Marton and Säljö (1976b) found that questions designed to produce more thoughtful, integrative study were more effective than questions of fact.

Nevertheless, study questions do not automatically guarantee better learning. Students sometimes tended to look only for answers to the questions while disregarding the other content of the chapter (Marton & Säljö, 1976a). Andre (1987) reviewed studies of study questions and concluded that questions generally do aid learning and that higher-level questions, rather than low-level factual questions, increase the effectiveness of student processing of the reading. Similarly, Wilhite (1983) found that prequestions focusing on material at the top of the organizational structure facilitated learning, especially for the less able

Examples of Study Questions to Encourage Thought

Your assignment for Monday is to study the next chapter, "Memory." Here are some study questions:

1. How would you apply the idea of "depth of processing" to your learning from this chapter?
2. How does the limited capacity of working memory affect your learning in lecture classes?
3. How is the approach taken by researchers in memory like, and how is it different from, that taken by the researchers in learning you studied in the last chapter?

students. You need questions that get students to *think* about the material. One way to encourage thoughtful reading is to ask students to write a half-page answer to a thought-provoking question and to bring multiple copies to class to share with peers in small groups. Discussion after the students have read one another's papers is usually lively.

Teaching Students to Learn More from Reading

As you will see in the chapter "Assessing, Testing, and Evaluating," students' study methods and learning are influenced by the sort of test questions they expect. Thus many students can read thoughtfully if tests require deeper understanding and thinking. But other students faithfully read and reread regardless of the type of assignment, memorizing definitions and facts without thought of the goal of the author and the relationship of this reading assignment to their previous learning. You can help by discussing with the students why you chose the reading and how they should read it.

There is ample evidence that students benefit from specific instruction in selecting main ideas, asking themselves questions, looking for organizational cues, and attempting to summarize or explain what they have read. Particularly in introductory classes you will help learning if you make explicit reference to your goal in assigning a particular chapter and discuss ways in which students can best achieve that goal

(McKeachie et al., 1985; Weinstein & Mayer, 1986). Suggest that your students

1. Look at topic headings before studying the chapter.
2. Write down questions they would like to answer.
3. Make marginal notes as they read.
4. Underline or highlight important concepts.
5. Carry on an active dialog with the author.
6. Comment on reading in their journals. (See the chapter "How to Enhance Learning by Using High-Stakes and Low-Stakes Writing.")

For a fuller description of ways to help students become better learners, see the chapter "Teaching Students How to Become More Strategic and Self-Regulated Learners."

IN CONCLUSION

1. Reading is an important tool for learning.
2. To facilitate learning, a teacher needs not only to choose appropriate reading materials but also to help students learn how to read them effectively.
3. Despite the availability of photocopies, coursepacks, paperbacks, and the World Wide Web, textbooks are still useful tools for teaching.
4. If material students need to learn is in print, in a form conveniently accessible for them, they may learn more efficiently from reading than from listening to you.

Supplementary Reading

T. M. Chang, H. F. Crombag, K. D. J. M. van der Drift, and J. M. Moonen, *Distance Learning* (Boston: Kluwer-Nijhoff Publishing, 1983), Chapter 4.

R. G. Crowder and R. K. Wagner, *The Psychology of Reading: An Introduction,* 2nd ed. (New York: Oxford University Press, 1992).

J. Hartley, "Studying for the Future," *Journal of Further and Higher Education,* 2002, *26,* 207–227.

F. Marton, D. Hounsell, and N. Entwistle (eds.), *The Experience of Learning* (Edinburgh: Scottish Academic Press, 1984).

Facilitating Discussion: Posing Problems, Listening, Questioning

A *ctive learning* is the buzz word (or phrase) in contemporary higher education. The prototypic teaching method for active learning is discussion. Discussion methods are among the most valuable tools in the teacher's repertoire. Often teachers in large classes feel that they must lecture because discussion is impossible. In fact, discussion techniques can be used in classes of all sizes. Generally, smaller classes *are* more effective, but large classes should not be allowed to inhibit the teacher's ability to stimulate active learning—learning experiences in which the students are *thinking* about the subject matter.

Discussion techniques seem particularly appropriate when the instructor wants to do the following:

1. Help students learn to think in terms of the subject matter by giving them practice in thinking.

2. Help students learn to evaluate the logic of and evidence for their own and others' positions.

3. Give students opportunities to formulate applications of principles.

4. Develop motivation for further learning.

5. Help students articulate what they've learned.

6. Get prompt feedback on student understanding or misunderstanding.

Why should discussion be the method of choice for achieving such objectives? The first justification is a very simple extrapolation of the old adage "Practice makes perfect." If instructors expect students to learn how to integrate, apply, and think, it seems reasonable that students should have an opportunity to practice these skills. To help students learn and think, you need to find out what is in their heads. Discussion can help.

A LITTLE BIT OF THEORY

Research in cognitive psychology has found that memory is affected by how deeply we process new knowledge (see the chapter "Teaching Students How to Become More Strategic and Self-Regulated Learners"). Simply listening to or repeating something is likely to store it in such a way that we have difficulty finding it when we want to remember it. If we elaborate our learning by thinking about its relationship to other things we know or by talking about it—explaining, summarizing, or questioning—we are more likely to remember it when we need to use it later. This may help relieve your anxiety about covering the material. In lectures teachers cover more material, but research shows that most of the material covered does not get into the students' notes or memory (Hartley & Davies, 1978). Classic studies over the last five decades have repeatedly shown that, in discussion, students pay attention and think more actively.

Because many students are accustomed to listening passively to lectures, in introducing discussion you need to explain why and how discussion will help them construct knowledge they can find and apply when needed.

PROBLEMS IN TEACHING BY DISCUSSION

In discussion groups the instructor is faced with several problems:

1. Getting participation in the discussion.
2. Making progress (or making the student aware of the progress) toward course objectives.
3. Handling emotional reactions of students.
4. Listening to the students supportively.

This chapter should help you cope with each of these problems.

STARTING DISCUSSION

After a class has been meeting and discussing problems success-fully, there is little problem in initiating discussion, for it will develop almost spontaneously from problems encountered in reading, from experiences, or from unresolved problems from the previous meeting. But during the first meetings of new groups, you need to create an expectation that something interesting and valuable will occur.

Starting Discussion with a Common Experience

One of the best ways of starting a discussion is to refer to a concrete, common experience through presentation of a demonstration, film, role play, short skit, or brief reading. It could be a common experience of all students or an issue on campus or in the media, or you can provide the experience. Following such a presentation it's easy to ask, "Why did _____?"

Such an opening has a number of advantages. Because every-one in the group has seen it, everyone knows something about the topic under discussion. In addition, by focusing the discus-sion on the presentation, the instructor takes some of the pressure off anxious or threatened students who are afraid to reveal their own opinions or feelings.

However, you will not always be able to find the presentation you need to introduce each discussion, and you may be forced to turn to other techniques of initiating discussion. One such technique is problem posting, which was discussed in the chapter "Meeting a Class for the First Time."

Starting Discussion with a Controversy

A second technique of stimulating discussion is through disagreement. Experimental evidence is accumulating to indicate that a certain degree of surprise or uncertainty arouses curiosity, a basic motive for learning (Berlyne, 1960). Some teachers effectively play the role of devil's advocate; others are effective in pointing out differences in points of view.

I have some concerns about the devil's advocate role. I believe that it can be an effective device in getting students to think actively rather than accept passively the instructor's every sentence as "Truth." Yet it has its risks, the most important of which is that it may create lack of trust in the instructor. Of course, instructors want students to challenge their ideas, but few want their students to feel they are untrustworthy, lying about their own beliefs.

Two other dangers lurk in the devil's advocate role. One is that it will be perceived as manipulative. Students may feel (with justification) that the instructor "is just playing games with us—trying to show how smart he is and how easily he can fool us." It can also be seen as a screen to prevent students from ever successfully challenging the instructor.

Yet the devil's advocate role can be effective. Its success depends a good deal on the spirit with which it is played. Linc Fisch (2001) handles this problem by donning a T-shirt with "Devil's Advocate" on the front. My own compromise solution is to make it clear when I'm taking such a role by saying, "Suppose I take the position that _____" or "Let me play the role of devil's advocate for a bit."

In any case the instructor should realize that disagreement is not a sign of failure but may be used constructively. When rigid dogmatism interferes with constructive problem solving following a disagreement, the instructor may ask the disagreeing students to switch sides and argue the opposing point of view. Such a technique seems to be effective in developing awareness of the strengths of other positions.

As Maier (1963) has shown in his studies of group leadership, one barrier to effective problem solving is presenting an issue in such a way that participants take sides arguing the apparent solution rather than attempting to solve the problem by considering data and devising alternative solutions. Maier suggests the following principles for group problem solving:

1. Success in problem solving requires that effort be directed toward overcoming surmountable obstacles.

2. Available facts should be used even when they are inadequate.

3. The starting point of the problem is richest in solution possibilities.

4. Problem-mindedness should be increased and solution-mindedness should be delayed.

5. The "idea-getting" process should be separated from the "idea evaluation" process because the latter inhibits the former.

Starting Discussion with Questions

The most common discussion opener is the question, and the most common error in questioning is not allowing students time enough to think. You should not expect an immediate response to every question. If your question is intended to stimulate thinking, give the students time to think. Five seconds of silence may seem an eternity, but a pause for 5 to 30 seconds will result in better discussion. In some cases you may plan for such a thoughtful silence by asking the students to think about the question for a few seconds and then write down one element that might help answer the question. Such a technique increases the chance that the shyer or slower students will participate, since they now know what they want to say when the discussion begins. In fact, you may even draw one in by saying, "You were writing vigorously, Ronnie. What's your suggestion?"

Factual Questions.   There are times when it is appropriate to check student background knowledge with a series of brief factual questions, but more frequently you want to stimulate problem solving. One common error in phrasing questions for this purpose is to ask a question in a form conveying to students the message "I know something you don't know and you'll look stupid if you don't guess right."

Application and Interpretation Questions.   Rather than dealing with factual questions, formulate discussions so as to get at relationships, applications, or analyses of facts and materials. Solomon, Rosenberg, and Bezdek (1964) found that teachers who used interpretation questions produced gains in student comprehension. A question of the type "How does the idea that _____ apply to _____?" is much more likely to stimulate discussion than the question "What is the definition of _____?" The secret is not to avoid questions or to lecture in statements, but rather to listen and to reflect on what is heard. Dillon (1982), a leading researcher on questioning, advises that once you have defined the issue for discussion, keep quiet unless you are perplexed or didn't hear a comment. Questions are tools for teaching, but as Dillon demonstrated, they sometimes interfere with, as well as facilitate, achievement of teaching goals. What happens depends on the question and its use.

Problem Questions.   A question may arise from a case, or it may be a hypothetical problem. It may be a problem whose solution the instructor knows; it may be a problem that the instructor has not solved. In any case it should be a problem that is meaningful to the students, and for the sake of morale, it should be a problem they can make some progress on. And even if the teacher knows an answer or has a preferred solution, the students should have a chance to come up with new solutions. The teacher's job is not to sell students on a particular solution, but rather to listen and to teach them how to solve problems themselves. Don't be afraid to express your own curiosity, question, or "what if . . ." wonder about a topic. Ask the students what they think. It is better to be an open-minded, curious questioner than the font of all knowledge.

Suppose you ask a question and no one answers, or the student simply says, "I don't know." Discouraging as this may be, it should not necessarily be the end of the interaction. Usually the student can respond if the question is rephrased. Perhaps you need to give an example of the problem first; perhaps you need to suggest some alternative answer and ask the student what evidence might or might not support it; perhaps you need to reformulate a prior question. More often than not, you can help the students discover that they are more competent than they thought.

Other Types of Questions.   *Connective and causal effect questions* involve attempts to link material or concepts that otherwise might not seem related. One might, for example, cut across disciplines to link literature, music, and historical events or one might ask, "What are the possible causes of this phenomenon?"

Comparative questions, as the name suggests, ask for comparisons between one theory and another, one author and another, one research study and another. Such questions help students determine important dimensions of comparison.

Evaluative questions ask not only for comparisons but for a judgment of the relative value of the points being compared; for example, "Which of two theories better accounts for the data? Which of two essays better contributes to an understanding of the issue?"

Critical questions examine the validity of an author's arguments or discussion. Television, magazines, and other media provide opportunities for using critical or evaluative questioning. For example, "An eminent authority states thus and so. Under what conditions might that not be true?" Being so critical that students feel that their reading has been a waste of time is not helpful, but presenting an alternative argument or conclusion may start students analyzing their reading more carefully, and eventually you want students to become critical readers who themselves challenge assumptions and conclusions.

Starting Discussion with a Problem or Case

One of the biggest problems in teaching by discussion is focus. Getting the discussion headed in the right direction and keeping it there requires that both students and the instructor be focused on the same questions. One of the better methods for producing focus is to use a problem or a case study as the main topic of discussion. The chapter "Problem-Based Learning" discusses problem-based learning and the case method in more detail, but what follows here are some general ideas about working with problem-based discussions more efficiently.

Breaking a Problem into Subproblems

One of Maier's (1952) important contributions to effective group problem solving, as well as to teaching, is to point out that groups are likely to be more effective if they tackle one aspect of a problem at a time rather than skipping from formulation of the problem, to solutions, to evidence, to "what-have-you," as different members of the group toss in their own ideas. In developmental discussion the group tackles one thing at a time.

One of the first tasks is likely to be a *clarification of the problem.* Often groups are ineffective because different participants have different ideas of what the problem is, and group members may feel frustrated at the end of the discussion because "the group never got to the real problem."

A second task is likely to be: *What do we know?* or *What data are relevant?*

A third task may be: *What are the characteristics of an acceptable solution?*—for example: What is needed?

A fourth step could be: *What are possible solutions?* and a fifth step may be to *evaluate these solutions* against the criteria for a solution determined in the previous step.

The developmental discussion technique can be used even in large groups, since there are a limited number of points to be made at each step regardless of the number of participants. Maier and Maier (1957) have shown that developmental discussion techniques improve the quality of decisions compared with freer, more nondirective discussion methods.

Socratic Discussion

The "classic" (and I do mean *classic*) discussion technique is the Socratic method. In television, novels, and anecdotes about the first year of law school it is usually portrayed as a sadistic, anxiety-producing method of eliciting student stupidity, and even when I place myself in the role of slave boy taught by Socrates in the *Meno,* I feel more like a pawn than an active learner.

Perhaps this is why I've never been very good at Socratic teaching; nonetheless I believe that it can be used as an effective method of stimulating student thinking, and it can have the quality of an interesting game rather than of an inquisition. The leading modern student of Socratic teaching is Allen Collins, who has observed a variety of Socratic dialogues and analyzed the strategies used (1977; Collins & Stevens, 1982).

Basically, most Socratic teachers attempt to teach students to reason to general principles from specific cases. Collins (1977) gives 23 rules, such as the following:

1. Ask about a known case. For example, if I were trying to teach a group of teaching assistants about student cheating, I might say, "Can you describe a situation in which cheating occurred?"

2. Ask for any factors. "Why did the cheating occur?"

3. Ask for intermediate factors. If the student suggests a factor that is not an immediate cause, ask for intermediate steps. For example, if a teaching assistant says, "Students feel a lot of pressure to get good grades," I might say, "Why did the pressure for grades result in cheating in this situation?"

4. Ask for prior factors. If the student gives a factor that has prior factors, ask for the prior factors. For example, "Why do students feel pressure to get good grades?"

5. Form a general rule for an insufficient factor. For example, "Do all students who feel pressure cheat?"

6. Pick a counterexample for an insufficient factor. For example, "Do you think these students cheat on every test?"

7. Form a general rule for an unnecessary factor. For example, if a teaching fellow suggests that cheating occurs when tests are difficult, I might say, "Probably the pressure to cheat is greater when tests are difficult, but does cheating occur only on difficult tests?"

8. Pick a counterexample for an unnecessary factor. For example, "Is cheating likely to occur on college admissions tests, such as the SAT?"

9. Pick a case with an extreme value. For example, "Why is cheating minimized on SAT tests?"

10. Probe for necessary or sufficient factors.

11. Pose two cases and probe for differences. For example, "Why is there more cheating in large classes than in small ones?"

12. Ask for a prediction about an unknown case.

13. Trace the consequences of a general rule. For example, if the teaching assistants conclude that cheating will occur when tests are difficult and are not well proctored, I might say, "Engineering classes are considered difficult, and I understand that there is little cheating even though tests are unproctored." (The school has an honor code.)

In general, the rules involve formulating general principles from known cases and then applying the principles to new cases. Even if one does not use the Socratic method to its fullest, the questioning strategies described in Collins's rules may be generally useful in leading discussions.

BARRIERS TO DISCUSSION

One of the important skills of discussion leaders is the ability to appraise the group's progress and to be aware of barriers or resistances that are blocking learning. This skill depends on attention to such clues as inattention, hostility, or diversionary questions.

Barriers to Discussion: Why Students Don't Participate

- Student habits of passivity
- Failure to see the value of discussion
- Fear of criticism or of looking stupid
- Push toward agreement or solution before alternative points of view have been considered
- Feeling that the task is to find the answer the instructor wants rather than to explore and evaluate possibilities

A primary barrier to discussion is the students' feeling that they are not learning. Occasional summaries during the hour not only help students chart their progress but also help smooth out communication problems. A summary need not be a statement of conclusions. In many cases the most effective summary is a restatement of the problem in terms of the issues resolved and those remaining. Keeping a visible record on the chalkboard of ideas, questions, data, or points to explore helps maintain focus and give a sense of progress. Asking students to summarize progress and what now needs to be done helps them develop as learners.

Another common barrier to good discussion is the instructor's tendency to tell students the answer before the students have developed an answer or meaning for themselves. Of course, teachers can sometimes save time by tying things together or stating a generalization that is emerging. But all too often they do this before the class is ready for it.

When you oppose a student's opinions, you should be careful not to overwhelm the student with the force of the criticism. Your objective is to start discussion, not smother it. Give students an opportunity to respond to criticisms, examining the point of view that was opposed. Above all, avoid personal criticism of students.

And perhaps the most common barrier is our own discomfort. We are not dispensing knowledge and not in control. It is all too easy to slip back into our old methods of teaching.

WHAT CAN I DO ABOUT NONPARTICIPANTS?*

In most classes some students talk too much, and others never volunteer a sentence. What can the teacher do?

Unfortunately, most students are used to being passive recipients in class. Some of your students may come from cultures

---

*Some students who are reluctant to participate orally will participate in a computer conference or by e-mail. Mano Singham of Case Western Reserve University asked students to identify themselves as talkers or listeners and then to discuss in each group how they could develop the skills of the other group. See *The National Teaching and Learning Forum,* February 2004, *8*(2).

whose norms discourage speaking in class. To help students become participants I try to create an expectation of participation in the discussion section. You can start to do this in the first meeting of the course by defining the functions of various aspects of the course and explaining why discussion is valuable. In addition to this initial structuring, however, you must continually work to increase the students' awareness of the values of participation. Participation is not an end in itself. For many purposes widespread participation may be vital; for others it may be detrimental. But you want to create a climate in which an important contribution is not lost because the person with the necessary idea did not feel free to express it.

What keeps a student from talking? There are a variety of reasons—boredom, lack of knowledge, general habits of passivity, cultural norms—but most compelling is a fear of being embarrassed. When one is surrounded by strangers, when one does not know how critical these strangers may be, when one is afraid of the teacher's response, when one is not sure how sound one's idea may be, when one is afraid of stammering or forgetting one's point under the stress of speaking—the safest thing to do is keep quiet.

What can reduce this fear? Getting acquainted is one aid. Once students know that they are among friends, they can risk expressing themselves. If they know that at least one classmate supports an idea, the risk is reduced. For both these reasons the technique of subgrouping helps; for example, you can ask students to discuss a question in pairs or small groups before asking for general discussion.

Asking students to take a couple of minutes to write out their initial answers to a question can help. If a student has already written an answer, the step to speaking is much less than answering when asked to respond immediately. Even the shy person will respond when asked, "What did you write?"

Rewarding infrequent contributors at least with a smile helps encourage participation even if the contribution has to be developed or corrected. Calling students by name seems to encourage freer communication. Seating is important too. Rooms with seats in a circle help tremendously.

Getting to know the nonparticipant is also helpful. For example, I have found that it is helpful to ask students to write a brief life history indicating their interests and experiences relevant to the course. These autobiographies help me to gain a better knowledge of each student as an individual, to know what problems or illustrations will be of particular interest to a number of students, and to know on whom I can call for special information. One of the best ways of getting nonparticipants into the discussion is to ask them to contribute in a problem area in which they have special knowledge.

The technique of asking for a student's special knowledge deals directly with one of the major barriers to class discussion—fear of being wrong. No one likes to look foolish, especially in a situation where mistakes may be pounced upon by a teacher or other students. One of the major reasons for the deadliness of a question in which the teacher asks a student to fill in the one right word—such as, "This is an example of what?"—is that it puts the student on the spot. There is an infinity of wrong answers, and obviously the teacher knows the one right answer; so why should the student risk making a mistake when the odds are so much against the student? And even if the answer is obvious, why look like a pawn of the teacher?

One way of putting the student in a more favorable position is to ask general questions that have no wrong answers. For example, you can ask, "How do you feel about this?" or "How does this look to you?" as a first step in analysis of a problem. Students' feelings or perceptions may not be the same as yours, but as reporters of their own feelings, they can't be challenged as being inaccurate. While such an approach by no means eliminates anxiety about participation (for an answer involves revealing oneself as a person), it will more often open up discussion that involves the student than will questions of fact. Problem posting, the technique discussed in an earlier chapter as a method for establishing objectives during the first day of class, is an example of a discussion technique minimizing risk for students. It can be useful in introducing a new topic at the conclusion of a topic, or for analysis of an experiment or a literary work. An added advantage is that it can be used in large as well as small groups.

Another technique for reducing the risk of participation for students is to ask a question a class period before the discussion and ask students to write out answers involving an example from their own experience. Similarly, one can ask students to bring one question to class for discussion. This helps participation, helps students learn to formulate questions, and also provides feedback for you.

Finally remember that out-of-class learning is often more important than that in class. E-mail, computer conferencing, and other interactive technologies can support active learning, discussion, and debate.

All of these techniques will still not make every student into an active, verbal participant. Two group techniques can help. One is buzz groups; the other is the inner circle technique.

Buzz Groups—Peer Learning

One of the popular techniques for achieving student participation in groups is the buzz session. In this procedure, classes are split into small subgroups for a brief discussion of a problem. Groups can be asked to come up with one hypothesis that they see as relevant, with one application of a principle, with an example of a concept, or with a solution to a problem. In large classes I march up the aisles saying, "Odd," "Even," "Odd," "Even" for each row and ask the "odd" row to turn around to talk to the "even" row behind, forming themselves into groups of four to six. I tell them to first introduce themselves to one another and then to choose a person to report for the group. Next they are to get from each member of the group one idea about the problem or question posed. Finally they are to come up with one idea to report to the total class. I give the group a limited time to work, sometimes five minutes or less, occasionally ten minutes or more, depending on the tasks. Peer-led discussions need not be limited to five or ten minutes or even to the classroom (see the chapter "Active Learning").

The Inner Circle or Fishbowl

In using the inner circle technique I announce that at the next class meeting we are going to have a class within a class, with several of the students (6 to 15) acting as the discussion group and the others as observers. If the classroom has movable chairs, I then arrange the seating in the form of concentric circles. I am impressed that students who are normally silent will talk when they feel the increased sense of responsibility as members of the inner circle.

THE DISCUSSION MONOPOLIZER*

If you have worked on nonparticipation effectively, the discussion monopolizer is less likely to be a problem, but there will still be classes in which one or two students talk so much that you and the other students become annoyed. As with nonparticipation, one solution is to raise with the class the question of participation in discussion—"Would the class be more effective if participation were more evenly distributed?"

A second technique is to have one or more members of the class act as observers for one or more class periods, reporting back to the class their observations. Perhaps assigning the dominant member to the observer role would help sensitivity.

A third possibility is to audiotape a discussion, and after playing back a portion, ask the class to discuss what might be done to improve the discussion.

A fourth technique is to use buzz groups with one member chosen to be reporter.

Finally, a direct approach should not be ruled out. Talking to the student individually outside class may be the simplest and most effective solution.

HOW CAN WE HAVE A DISCUSSION IF THE STUDENTS HAVEN'T READ THE ASSIGNMENT?

It's hard to have a discussion if students haven't studied the material to be discussed. What to do?

One strategy is to give students questions at the end of one class, asking them to get information on the questions before the

---

*Be sensitive to the fact that the most common monopolizer is the teacher. In our research, our observers reported that in a typical discussion class the teacher talked 70 to 80 percent of the time. Have an observer check your percentage.

next class. You can ask students to evaluate the validity of different Internet sources providing relevant information. You might even give different assignments to teams of students. Another strategy is to ask students to bring one or more questions on the assignment to be turned in at the beginning of the next class.

If there are extenuating circumstances, you (or a student who is prepared) can summarize the needed points. Alternatively, you can give students a few minutes to scan the material before beginning the discussion. If used often, however, such strategies may discourage out-of-class preparation.

If the problem persists, present it to the students. What do they suggest? One likely proposal is a short quiz at the beginning of class—which usually works. However, you'd like to have students motivated to study without the threat of a quiz. Usually the quiz can be phased out once students find that discussion really requires preparation and that the assignments are more interesting as they develop competence.

HANDLING ARGUMENTS AND EMOTIONAL REACTIONS

In any good discussion conflicts will arise. If such conflicts are left ambiguous and uncertain, they, like repressed conflicts in the individual, may cause continuing trouble. You can focus these conflicts so that they may contribute to learning.

- Reference to the text or other authority may be one method of resolution, if the solution depends on certain facts.

- Using the conflict as the basis for a library assignment for the class or a delegated group is another solution.

- If there is an experimentally verified answer, this is a good opportunity to review the method by which the answer could be determined.

- If the question is one of values, your goal may be to help students become aware of the values involved.

- Sometimes students will dispute your statements or decisions. Such disagreements may often be resolved by a comparison of the evidence for both points of view, but since teachers are human, they are all too likely to become drawn into an argument in which they finally rest on their own authority. To give yourself time to think, as well as to indicate understanding and acceptance of the students' point, I suggest listing the objections on the board. (Incidentally, listing evidence or arguments is also a good technique when the conflict is between two members of the class.) Such listing tends to prevent repetition of the same arguments.

- In any case it should be clear that conflict may be an aid to learning, and the instructor need not frantically seek to smother it.

- If you're having problems with a particular student, check the chapter "Dealing with Student Problems and Problem Students."

The Two-Column Method

Another of Maier's (1952) techniques, the two-column method, is a particularly effective use of the board in a situation in which there is a conflict or where a strong bias prevents full consideration of alternative points of view. Experimental studies (Hovland, 1957) suggest that when people hear arguments against their point of view, they become involved in attempting to refute the arguments rather than listening and understanding. Disagreement thus often tends to push the debaters into opposite corners, in which every idea is right or wrong, good or bad, black or white. The truth is often more complex and not in either extreme.

The two-column method is designed to permit consideration of complications and alternatives. As in problem posting, before the issues are debated, all the arguments on each side are listed on the board. The leader heads two columns "Favorable to A" and "Favorable to B" or "For" and "Against" and then asks for the facts or arguments that group members wish to present. The instructor's task is to understand and record in brief the arguments presented. If someone wishes to debate an argument presented for the other side, the instructor simply tries to reformulate the point so that it can be listed as a positive point in the debater's own column. But even though an argument is countered or protested it should not be erased, for the rules of the game are that the two columns are to include all ideas that members consider relevant. Evaluation can come later.

When the arguments have been exhausted, discussion can turn to the next step in problem solving. At this point the group can usually identify areas of agreement and disagreement, and in many cases it is already clear that the situation is neither black nor white. Now the issue becomes one of *relative* values rather than good versus bad. When discussion is directed toward agreements, some of the personal animosity is avoided, and some underlying feelings may be brought to light. The next stages of the discussion are thus more likely to be directed toward constructive problem solving.

Challenges and disagreements may be an indication of an alert, involved class. But the instructor should also be aware of the possibility that they may be symptoms of frustration arising because the students are uncertain of what the problem is or how to go about solving it.

Emotional Reactions

Although conflicts may arouse emotions, emotions may also arise because a topic touches a particular student in a vulnerable spot. You may notice during a discussion that one student is near tears or that a student is visibly flushed and angry. This poses a dilemma for you. You want to be helpful, but you also must have respect for the student's feelings. What should you do?

A lot depends on your knowledge of the student. If you say, "Joe (Jo), you seem to have some feelings about this," will the student be embarrassed?

If you don't wish to call attention to the student at the moment, you might say before the end of the class period, "Joe (Jo), would you stop by for a moment after class?" You could then say, "You seemed to be upset when we discussed _____. Would you like to come to my office to talk about it?"

Sometimes the best thing to do is simply wait to see if the student brings the feelings out in the discussion. If the student seems angry, I wouldn't ordinarily say, "Why are you so angry?" but if you know the student well and the class is a small one in which there is a good deal of acceptance of one another, that might be appropriate. So what will work depends on the student, the class, and your relationship with the student. Whatever the case, try to be understanding and nonconfrontational. Keep cool. This, too, will pass.

TEACHING STUDENTS HOW TO LEARN THROUGH DISCUSSION

I have already implied that classes don't automatically carry on effective discussions. To a large extent students have to learn how to learn from discussions just as they have to learn how to learn from reading. How can this occur?

First, they need to understand the importance of discussion for learning. Expressing one's understanding or ideas and getting reactions from other students and the teacher makes a big difference in learning, retention, and use of knowledge.

What skills need to be learned? One skill is clarification of what the group is trying to do—becoming sensitive to confusion about what the group is working on and asking for clarification.

A second attribute is the students' development of a willingness to talk about their own ideas openly and to listen and respond to others' ideas. It is important for students to realize that it is easy to deceive themselves about their own insights or understandings and that verbalizing an idea is one way of getting checks on and extensions of it. Teachers can encourage development of listening skills by asking one group member to repeat or paraphrase what another said before responding to it, and repeatedly pointing out the purpose and values students gain from discussion.

A third skill is planning. Discussions are sometimes frustrating because they are only getting under way when the end of the class period comes. If this results in continuation of the discussion outside the class, so much the better, but often learning is facilitated if students learn to formulate the issues and determine what out-of-class study or follow-up is necessary before the group breaks up.

A fourth skill is building on others' ideas in such a way as to increase their motivation rather than make them feel punished or forgotten. Often students see discussion as a competitive situation in which they win by tearing down other students' ideas. As Haines and McKeachie (1967) have shown, cooperative discussion methods encourage more effective work and better morale than competitive methods.

A fifth attribute is skill in evaluation. If classes are to learn how to discuss issues effectively, they need to review periodically what aspects of their discussion are proving to be worthwhile and what barriers, gaps, or difficulties have arisen. Some classes reserve the last five minutes of the period for a review of the discussion's effectiveness.

A sixth attribute is sensitivity to feelings of other group members. Students need to become aware of the possibility that feelings of rejection, frustration, dependence, and so on may influence group members' participation in discussion. Sometimes it is more productive to recognize the underlying feeling than to focus on the content of an individual's statement. One way of helping students develop these skills is to use student-led discussions preceded by a training meeting with the student leader.

STUDENT-LED DISCUSSIONS

In pioneering experiments in educational psychology and general psychology, Gruber and Weitman (1962) found that students taught in small, student-led discussion groups without a teacher not only did at least as well on a final examination as students who heard the teacher lecture, but also were superior in curiosity (as measured by question-asking behavior) and in interest in educational psychology.

TAKING MINUTES OR NOTES, SUMMARIZING

One of the problems with discussion is students' feeling that they have learned less than in lectures where they have taken voluminous notes. Thus I like to summarize our progress at the end of the period or ask students to contribute to a summary. Better yet, use the last five to ten minutes for getting feedback. For example, ask students to write a summary of the issues discussed, the pros and cons, and their conclusions.

ONLINE DISCUSSIONS

E-mail, listservers, computer conferences, and other online experiences extend the opportunities for discussion. They also provide practice in writing. They can facilitate cooperative learning. The impersonality of e-mail may reduce the inhibitions of those who are shy in the classroom, but research suggests that it may also reduce inhibitions against rudeness. Thus, in initiating an online discussion, remind your students that respect for others and rational support for arguments are just as important online as in the classroom.

You also need to be clear about your expectations for participation. I have used online discussions off and on since it first became possible to do so, but my success has been variable. If I simply recommend use of the opportunity, a few students who love computers participate, but their discussions often have little to do with the course. I tried posting questions, topics, or problems, and that helped some, but many students still did not participate. One of my teaching assistants, Richard Velayo, tackled this problem for his dissertation. He found that what worked best was to require discussion of a question each week.

IN CONCLUSION

Teaching by discussion differs from lecturing because you never know what is going to happen. At times this is anxiety-producing, at times frustrating, but more often exhilarating. It provides constant challenges and opportunities for both you and the students to learn. When you can listen for several minutes without intervening, you will have succeeded.

Supplementary Reading

▒▌ C. C. Bonwell and T. E. Sutherland, "The Active Learning Continuum: Choosing Activities to Engage Students in the Classroom," in T. E. Sutherland and C. C. Bonwell (eds.), "Using Active Learning in College Classes: A Range of Options for Faculty," *New Directions for Teaching and Learning,* no. 67, October 1996, 3–16.

▒▌ S. D. Brookfield and S. Preskill, *Discussion as a Way of Teaching: Tools and Techniques for Democratic Classrooms* (San Francisco: Jossey-Bass, 1999).

▒▌ A. Collins, "Different Goals of Inquiry Teaching," *Questioning Exchange,* 1988, 2(1), 39–45.

▒▌ J. T. Dillon, *Teaching and the Art of Questioning* (Bloomington, IN: Phi Delta Kappa Educational Foundation, 1983).

▒▌ B. S. Fuhrmann and A. F. Grasha, *A Practical Handbook for College Teachers* (Boston: Little, Brown, 1983), Chapter 6.

How to Make Lectures More Effective

The lecture is probably the oldest teaching method and still the method most widely used in universities throughout the world. Through the ages a great deal of practical wisdom about techniques of lecturing has accumulated. Effective lecturers combine the talents of scholar, writer, producer, comedian, entertainer, and teacher in ways that contribute to student learning. Nevertheless, it is also true that few college professors combine these talents in optimal ways and that even the best lecturers are not always in top form. Lectures have survived despite the invention of printing, television, and computers.

Is the lecture an effective method of teaching? If it is, under what conditions is it most effective? I will tackle these questions not only in light of research on the lecture as a teaching method but also in terms of analyses of the cognitive processes used by students in lecture classes.

RESEARCH ON THE EFFECTIVENESS OF LECTURES

A large number of studies have compared the effectiveness of lectures with other teaching methods. The results are discouraging for those who lecture. Discussion methods are superior to lectures in student retention of information after the end of a course; in transfer of knowledge to new situations; in development of problem solving, thinking, or attitude change; and in motivation for further learning (McKeachie et al., 1990).

Similarly, print offers advantages over lecture. Students can read faster than lecturers can lecture, and they can go back when they don't understand, skip material that is irrelevant, and review immediately or later. Lectures go at the lecturer's pace, and students who fall behind are out of luck. But don't despair; lectures can still be useful.

WHAT ARE LECTURES GOOD FOR?

- Presenting up-to-date information (There is typically a gap between the latest scholarship and its appearance in a textbook.)
- Summarizing material scattered over a variety of sources
- Adapting material to the background and interests of a particular group of students at a particular time and place
- Helping students read more effectively by providing an orientation and conceptual framework
- Focusing on key concepts, principles, or ideas

Lectures also have motivational values apart from their cognitive content. By helping students become aware of a problem, of conflicting points of view, or of challenges to ideas they have previously taken for granted, the lecturer can stimulate interest in further learning in an area. Moreover, the lecturer's own attitudes and enthusiasm have an important effect on student motivation. Research on student ratings of teaching as well as on student learning indicates that the enthusiasm of the lecturer is an important factor in effecting student learning and motivation. You may feel that enthusiasm is not learnable. Clearly some people are more enthusiastic and expressive than others, but you can develop in this area just as in others. Try to put into each lecture something that you are really excited about. Notice how your voice and gestures show more energy and expressiveness. Now try carrying some of that intensity and animation over into other topics. Like other learned behaviors, this takes practice, but you can do it. Murray (1997) showed that enthusiastic teachers move around, make eye contact with students, and use more gestures and vocal variation, and that teachers could learn these behaviors. Both research and theory support the usefulness of enthusiastic behaviors in maintaining student attention.*

The lecturer also models ways of approaching problems, portraying a scholar in action in ways that are difficult for other media or methods of instruction to achieve. You can say, "Here is how I go about solving this kind of problem (analyzing this phenomenon, etc.). Now you try it." One of the advantages of live professors is the tendency of people to model themselves after other individuals whom they perceive as living, breathing human beings with characteristics that can be admired and emulated. So lectures can be effective—but sometimes more effective in stimulating our own learning and thinking than in stimulating that of the students!

A LITTLE BIT OF THEORY

The preceding section has included a good bit of theory of learning and motivation, but I want to be more explicit about one aspect of the cognitive theory of learning and memory. As I noted in the preceding chapter, memory depends heavily on the learner's activity—thinking about and elaborating on new knowledge. A key difference between modern theories of memory and earlier theory is that earlier theory thought of knowledge as single associations, in some ways like tucking each bit of

---

*Don't feel that you have to show high energy every minute. There will be times when calm, quiet, slow speech may be needed—times when you may need to wait and reflect before responding.

knowledge into a pigeonhole. Now we think of knowledge as being stored in structures such as networks with linked concepts, facts, and principles. The lecture thus needs to build a bridge between what is in the students' minds and the structures in the subject matter. Metaphors, examples, and demonstrations are the elements of the bridge. Providing a meaningful organization is thus a key function of the lecture. Our research (Naveh-Benjamin et al., 1989) showed that students begin a course with little organization but during a course develop conceptual structures that more and more closely resemble those of the instructor.

PLANNING LECTURES

A typical lecture strives to present a systematic, concise summary of the knowledge to be covered in the day's assignment. Chang, Crombag, van der Drift, and Moonen (1983, p. 21) call this approach "conclusion oriented." While there are times when this is useful, more often you need to teach students how to read and understand the assignments themselves. Your job is less knowledge dispensing than teaching students how to learn and think.

I was a conclusion-oriented lecturer for 30 years. Now more of my lectures involve analyzing materials, formulating problems, developing hypotheses, bringing evidence to bear, criticizing and evaluating alternative solutions—revealing methods of learning and thinking and involving students in the process.

One of the implications of the theoretical approach I have taken is that what is an ideal approach to lecturing early in a course is likely to be inappropriate later in the course. As noted earlier, the way students process verbal material depends on the structures that not only enable them to process bigger and bigger chunks of subject matter but also give them tacit knowledge of the methods, procedures, and conventions used in the field and by you as a lecturer. Intentionally or not, you are teaching students how to become more skilled in learning from your lectures.

Because this is so, one should in the first weeks of a course go more slowly, pause to allow students with poor backgrounds time to take notes, and give more everyday types of examples. Pausing to write a phrase or sketch a relationship on the chalkboard will not only give students a chance to catch up but also provide visual cues that can serve as points of reference later. Later in the term, students should be able to process bigger blocks of material more quickly.

Adapting to the differences in students' knowledge from the beginning to the later stages of a course is but one example of the principle that one key to good lecturing is an awareness of the audience, not only in lecturing but in preparing the lecture. In every class there is student diversity—not only in background knowledge but also in motivation, skills for learning, beliefs about what learning involves, and preferences for different ways of learning (learning styles). Using multimedia will help you reach all students more effectively (Mayer, 2003).

PREPARING YOUR LECTURE NOTES

One of the security-inducing features of lectures is that one can prepare a lecture with some sense of control over the content and organization of the class period. In lectures the instructor is usually in control, and this sense of controlled structure helps the anxious teacher avoid pure panic.

But no matter how thoroughly one has prepared the subject matter of the lecture, one must still face the problem of how to retrieve and deliver one's insights during the class period. If one has plenty of time and is compulsive, one is tempted to write out the lecture verbatim. Don't! Or if you must (and writing it out may be useful in clarifying your thoughts), don't take a verbatim version into the classroom. Few lecturers can read a lecture so well that students stay awake and interested.

At the same time, few teachers can deliver a lecture with no cues at all. Hence you will ordinarily lecture from notes. Most lecturers use an outline or a sequence of cue words and phrases. Try forming your notes as a series of questions.

Day (1980) studied lecture notes used by professors at over 75 colleges and universities. She notes that extensive notes take the instructor out of eye contact with students so that students fall into a passive, nonquestioning role. Day suggests the use of graphic representations to increase teaching flexibility and spontaneity.

Tree diagrams, computer flowcharts, or network models enable a teacher to have at hand a representation of the structure that permits one to answer questions without losing track of the relationship of the question to the lecture organization. Pictorial representations using arrows, faces, Venn diagrams, or drawings that symbolize important concepts may not only provide cues for the instructor but can also be placed on PowerPoint or the board to provide additional cues for students.

Color coding your notes with procedural directions to yourself also helps. Because I try to get student involvement, I have a tendency to run overtime; so I put time cues in the margin to remind me to check. I also put in directions to myself, such as

- "Put on board." (usually a key concept or relationship)
- "Check student understanding. Ask for examples."
- "Ask students for a show of hands."
- "Put students in pairs to discuss this."

Whatever your system, indicate *signposts* to tell students what is ahead, *transitions* that tell students when you are finishing one topic and moving to the next, *key points* or *concepts,* and *links* such as "consequently," "therefore," and "because."*

Allow time for questions from students, for new examples or ideas that come to mind during the lecture, and for your own misestimation of the time a topic will require. If perchance you finish early, let the students use the remaining time to write a summary. Finally, use your notes to prepare a handout with a structure that students can use for filling in their notes and asking questions.

ORGANIZATION OF LECTURES

In thinking about lecture organization, most teachers think first about the structure of the subject matter, then try to organize the content in some logical fashion, such as building from specifics to generalization or deriving specific implications from general

---

*These four types of signposts are discussed in George Brown, *Lecturing and Explaining* (London: Methuen, 1978).

principles. Too often we get so immersed in "covering" the subject that we forget to ask, "What do I really want students to remember from this lecture next week, next year?"

Some common organizing principles used by lecturers are cause to effect; time sequence (for example, stories); parallel organization such as phenomenon to theory to evidence; problem to solution; pro versus con to resolution; familiar to unfamiliar; and concept to application.**

Leith (1977) has suggested that different subjects are basically different in the ways in which progress is made in the field. Some subjects are organized in a linear or hierarchical fashion in which one concept builds on a preceding one. The logical structure of one's subject should be one factor determining the lecture organization, but equally important is the cognitive structure in the students' minds. If we are to teach our students effectively, we need to bridge the gap between the structure in the subject matter and structures in the students' minds. As is indicated in all of the chapters in this book, you are not making impressions on a blank slate. Rather our task in teaching is to help students reorganize existing cognitive structures or to add new dimensions or new features to existing structures. Thus the organization of the lecture needs to take account of the student's existing knowledge and expectations as well as the structure of the subject matter. Analogies linking new ideas to similar ones that students already know can help. Remember that what you are trying to do is get an organization into your students' heads that will help them fit in relevant facts and form a base for further learning and thinking.

The Introduction

One suggestion for organization is that the *introduction* of the lecture should point to a gap in the student's existing cognitive structure or should challenge or raise a question about something in the student's existing method of organizing material in order to arouse curiosity (Berlyne, 1954a, 1954b). There is a good deal of research on the role of prequestions in directing attention to features of

---

**Stories not only interest students, they also aid memory. If you can make your story a mystery, you'll hold attention (see Green, 2004).

written texts. Prequestions in the introduction of a lecture may help students to discriminate between more and less important features of lectures. For example, before a lecture on cognitive changes in aging, I ask, "Do you get more or less intelligent as you get older?" and "What is a fair test of intelligence for older people?" Such questions may help create expectations that enable students to allocate their cognitive capacity more effectively. If students know what they are expected to learn from a lecture, they learn more of that material (sometimes at the expense of other material; Royer, 1977).

Another approach is to begin with a demonstration, example, case, or application that captures attention. In many fields it is possible to begin some lectures with presentation of a problem or case from a current newspaper or television show, then ask students how they would think about it in the light of this course, or alternatively illustrate in the lecture how experts in this field would think about it.

The Body of the Lecture

In organizing the *body* of the lecture, the most common error is probably that of trying to include too much. The enemy of learning is the teacher's need to cover the content at all costs. When I began lecturing, my mentor told me, "If you get across three or four points in a lecture so that students understand and remember them, you've done well." Lecturers very often overload the students' information processing capacity so that they become less able to understand the material than if fewer points had been presented. David Katz (1950), a pioneer Gestalt psychologist, called this phenomenon "mental dazzle." He suggested that, just as too much light causes our eyes to be dazzled so that we cannot see anything, so too can too many new ideas overload processing capacity so that we cannot understand anything.

Use the board, an overhead projector, or PowerPoint to give the students cues to the organization of the lecture. Going to the board to construct an outline or to write key words is useful in three ways:

1. It gives a *visual* representation to supplement your oral presentation. Using a diagram or other graphic representation will help visualization.

2. Movement (change) helps retain (or regain) attention.

3. It gives students a chance to catch up with what you've said (perchance to think!).

Using Examples. Move from the concrete to the abstract. To link what is in your head with what is in the students' heads, you need to use examples that relate the subject to the students' experience and knowledge. I am not as effective a teacher today as I was decades ago because I do not know the students' culture and am thus limited in finding vivid examples of a concept in students' daily lives. Since no single example can represent a concept fully, you usually need to give more than one example. Concept formation research suggests that examples differing from one another are likely to be most effective if you point out the essential features of the concept exemplified in each example. If you can find a cartoon or funny story that illustrates your point, humor helps maintain interest. But the danger is that students will remember the humor and not the concept, so repeat the concept. And, most important, give students a chance to give examples.

Periodic Summaries Within the Lecture. From our knowledge of students' note-taking behavior we know that students would be better able to learn from lectures if there were periodic summaries of preceding material. These give students a chance to catch up on material covered when they were not tuned in and also give them a check on possible misperceptions based on inadequate or misleading expectations. Repeat main points once, twice, thrice, during the lecture. Such summaries can help make clear to students transitions from one theme to another, so that they are aided in organizing the material not only in their notes but in their minds. In fact, you might try thinking of your lecture as two or more minilectures separated by short periods for questions, discussion, or writing.

Checking Student Understanding. Although it may seem irrational to cover material when students are not learning from it, one should not underestimate the compulsion one feels to get through one's lecture notes. A remedy for this compulsion is to put into the lecture notes reminders to oneself to check the students' understanding—both by looking for nonverbal cues of bewilderment or of lack of attention and by raising specific questions that will test the students' understanding.

Most lecturers recognize that they need to check student understanding periodically; so they ask, "Any questions?" and after three to five seconds without response assume that everyone understands. Not so! If you really want to know, give students a minute to write down a question, then have them compare notes with students sitting near them before asking for questions. You'll get some.

Once you have used this procedure a few times, so that students have found that questioning is not dangerous, you can simply say, "What questions do you have?"

The Conclusion.   In the conclusion of the lecture, one has the opportunity to make up for lapses in the body of the lecture. Encouraging students to formulate questions or asking questions oneself can facilitate understanding and memory. By making the oral headings visible once again, by recapitulating major points, by proposing unanswered questions to be treated in the reading assignments or the future lectures, and by creating an anticipation of the future, the lecturer can help students learn. One good (and humbling) technique is to announce that you will ask a student to summarize the lecture at the end of the period. Another—less threatening—is to have students spend three minutes writing a summary of main points. Either method helps the process of elaboration, which is critical for memory.

Having suggested all this, I must admit that my own greatest problem as a lecturer is that I never seem to be ready for the conclusion until it is already past time to dismiss the class.

HOW CAN LECTURES BE IMPROVED?

The message of this chapter is that one way of improving lectures is to think about how students process lectures. What are students trying to do during a lecture?

As one looks at students at a lecture and observes their behavior, the most impressive thing one notices is the passive role students have in most classrooms. Some students are having difficulty in staying awake; others are attempting to pass the time as easily as possible by reading other materials, counting lecturer mannerisms, or simply doodling and listening in a relatively effortless manner. Most students are taking notes. Ideally, many students are attempting to construct knowledge by linking what the lecturer says with what they already know.

Attention

One of the factors determining students' success in information processing is their ability to attend to the lecture. Attention basically involves focusing one's cognitions on those things that are changing, novel, or motivating. Individuals have a limited capacity for attending to the varied features of their environment. The individual's total capacity for attention may vary with the degree of activation or motivation. At any one time, part of the capacity may be devoted to the task at hand (in this case listening to the lecturer), part may be involved in taking notes, and part may be left over to shift primary attention to distractions or daydreams when boredom occurs.

Hartley and Cameron's (1967) review of the research on attention of students during lectures reports that attention typically increases from the beginning of the lecture to ten minutes into the lecture, decreases after that point, and picks up toward the end.

What Can Be Done to Get Attention?

In determining how to allocate attention, students use various strategies. Any lecturer knows that one way of getting attention is to precede the statement by the phrase, "This will be on the test." In addition, students listen for particular words or phrases that indicate to them that something is worth noting and remembering. Statements that enumerate or list are likely to be on tests and thus are likely to be attended to.

Changes in the environment recruit attention. The ability of changes to capture attention can work to the advantage of the lecturer. Variation in pitch, intensity, and pace of the lecture; visual cues such as gestures, facial expression, movement to the board; the use of demonstrations or audiovisual aids—all of these recruit and maintain attention to the lecture.

Auditory attention is directed to some extent by visual attention. Distracting movements in the classroom are thus likely to cause students to fail to recall what the lecturer has said. On the positive side, students' comprehension is greater when the students can see the speaker's face and lips (Campbell, 1999). Look at your audience; eye contact helps communication.

Motivation is important in holding student attention. Linking lectures to student interests, giving examples that are vivid and intriguing, building suspense toward resolution of a conflict—these are all techniques of gaining and holding attention.

All of these devices will help, but recall the Hartley and Cameron finding that students' attention tends to wane after a few minutes. The best device for maintaining attention is to break up the lecture rather than trying to hold attention for an hour or more. Student activities such as problem posting, the minute paper (described later in this chapter), pairing, or small-group activities can reactivate students' attention.* If you spot signs of drowsiness or fidgeting, ask students to stand up and stretch. Bligh's research summary indicated that the gain in learning after such a break more than compensates for any learning that might have occurred in the time taken for the break (Bligh, 2000).

TEACHING STUDENTS HOW TO BE BETTER LISTENERS

We assume that listening is an innate skill, but you can train your students to be better listeners. For example, you might begin by asking students to write for one minute on "What do I hope to get out of this lecture?" or "What was the most important point in the reading assignment for the day?" Then explain how this strategy will help them to be more effective listeners in any lecture. Both of these strategies act as a "warm-up," focusing attention and activating relevant prior knowledge.

---

*Brown and Atkins (1988, p. 29) list these and other student activities to get students' attention and thinking during lectures.

Another useful strategy is to ask students to listen to you (for 5 to 15 minutes) without taking notes and then to write a summary. You might then ask them to compare their summaries with those of one or two classmates sitting near them.

A related strategy is to tell students that you will give them five minutes at the end of the lecture to summarize the main points of the lecture for someone sitting near them. At the end of the class period, ask them what effect this had on their listening to the lecture, and point out that they can use this approach to lectures even if they summarize them only in their own notes.

HOW DO STUDENTS PROCESS THE CONTENT OF A LECTURE?

Let's assume that students are allocating attention appropriately to the lecture. This alone, however, does not ensure that the content of the lecture will be understood, remembered, and applied appropriately. Even though students are trying to meet the demands of the situation, they may differ in the ways they go about processing the words that they have heard.

Marton and Säljö (1976a, 1976b) and other researchers at the University of Göteborg have described differences in the way students go about trying to learn educational materials. Some students process the material as little as possible, simply taking as many verbatim notes as they can. This would be described by Marton as a "surface approach." Other students try to see implications of what the lecturer is saying, relate what is currently being said to other information either in the lecture or in their own experience and reading, and try to understand what the author intended. They elaborate and translate the instructor's words into their own. They may question. This more thoughtful and more active kind of listening is what Marton and Säljö refer to as "deep processing."

Experienced students can probably vary their strategies from verbatim memory to memory of concepts, depending on the demands of the situation. Generally, deep processing better enables students to remember and use knowledge for thinking and further learning. Pointing out relationships, asking rhetorical questions, or asking questions to be answered by class members are ways of encouraging deeper processing. You can also ask for examples of how students apply concepts to their own experiences, thus encouraging all students to realize that it is important to try to think about how concepts relate to oneself.

SHOULD STUDENTS TAKE NOTES?

Note taking is one of the activities by which students attempt to stay attentive, but note taking is also an aid to memory. *Working memory*, or *short-term memory*, is a term used to describe the fact that one can hold only a given amount of material in mind at one time. When the lecturer presents a succession of new concepts, students' faces begin to show signs of anguish and frustration; some write furiously in their notebooks, while others stop writing in complete discouragement. Note taking thus is dependent on one's ability to maintain attention, understand what is being said, and hold it in working memory long enough to write it down. Studies of student notes show, not surprisingly, that students fail to get most of the lecture content into their notes, and some of the notes are wrong. However, research supports two values of note taking. One is that the notes provide an external memory which can be reviewed later; the other is that note taking involves elaboration and transformation of ideas, which aids memory (Hartley & Davies, 1978; Peper & Mayer, 1978). But note taking has costs as well as benefits. Student note-taking strategies differ. Some students take copious notes; others take none. We know that cognitive capacity is limited; that is, people can take in, understand, and store only so much information in any brief period of time. Information will be processed more effectively if the student is actively engaged in note taking—analyzing and processing the information rather than passively soaking it up—but taking notes takes capacity that may be needed for comprehension if material is difficult. Thus, encourage students to take *fewer* notes and to listen carefully when you are introducing new, difficult material. They can then fill in their notes after class.

Students' ability to process information depends on the degree to which the information can be integrated or "chunked." No one has great ability at handling large numbers of unrelated items in active memory. Thus when students are in an area of new concepts or when the instructor is using language that is not entirely familiar to the students, students may be processing the lecture word by word or phrase by phrase and lose the sense of a sentence or of a paragraph before the end of the thought is reached. This means that lecturers need to be aware of instances in which new words or concepts are being introduced and to build in greater redundancy, as well as pauses during which students can catch up and get appropriate notes.

Snow and Peterson (1980) point out that brighter students benefit more from taking notes than less able students. For students with less background knowledge, note taking takes capacity needed for listening and comprehending, so they simply miss much of what is being said. This is not simply a matter of intelligence; rather, a student's ability to maintain materials in memory while taking notes and even to process and think about relationships between one idea and other ideas depends on the knowledge or cognitive structures the student has available for organizing and relating the material.

Hartley's research, as well as that of Annis (1981) and Kiewra (1989), suggests that a skeletal outline is helpful to students, but that with detailed notes students relax into passivity. It is better simply to provide an overall framework, which they can fill in by selecting important points and interpreting them in their own words. Because student capacity for information processing is limited and because students stop and go over a confusing part of a lecture again, you need to build more redundancy into your lectures than into writing, and you need to build in pauses where students can catch up and think rather than simply struggle to keep up.

One can train students to write better notes by collecting student notes, evaluating the degree to which they summarize, translate, and show relationships as opposed to simply representing more or less verbatim accounts, and reporting back to the class suggestions for improvement.

HOW TO GET STUDENTS ACTIVELY THINKING IN A LECTURE SITUATION

As we have seen, a major problem with the lecture is that students assume a passive, nonthinking, information receiving role. Yet, if they are to remember and use the information, they need to be actively engaged in thinking about the content presented. One easy and effective device is the "minute paper" (Wilson, 1986). The minute paper is, as its title indicates, a paper literally written in a minute (or it can be a two-minute or three-minute paper).* Announce at the beginning of the class period that you will interrupt your lecture midway through the period so that the students may write a one-minute paper on a topic derived from the lecture or that you will ask them at the end of the lecture to write the most important thing they have learned. Even better, you can ask them also to write the most important thing they learned from the previous week's lecture.

In the chapter "Teaching Large Classes" I describe other activities to stimulate thinking. The chapters "Facilitating Discussion" and "Active Learning" also describe methods for getting discussion in large classes.

Since many students feel that the best way to learn is to listen to an expert, you will need here (as in other departures from lecturing) to explain why active thinking is vital for effective learning.

THE LECTURER AS A PERSON

Lectures are often given to large groups of anonymous students. As I've said earlier, their motivation is affected by their sense that you are an interesting fellow human being who *cares* about their learning. Talk to students who come to class early. Ask students their names and try to remember some.

---

*The minute paper was invented by University of California physics professor Charles Schwartz.

IN CONCLUSION

What is the role of the lecturer in higher education? To communicate the teacher's enthusiasm about the subject.

The lecture is also sometimes an effective way of communicating information, particularly in classes where variations in student background, ability, or interest make feedback to the lecturer important. We have also shown that the organization and presentation of lectures may influence their effectiveness in achieving application of knowledge or in influencing attitudes. Discussion, however, is likely to be more effective than lecturing in achieving higher-level cognitive and attitudinal objectives, and combinations of lecture and discussion may be optimal.

Becoming conscious of what is going on in the students' heads as we talk; being alert to feedback from students through their facial expressions, nonverbal behavior, and oral comments; adjusting your strategies in reference to these cues—these will help you learn and help students to learn more effectively.

Be yourself!

Supplementary Reading

The most comprehensive book on lecturing is Donald Bligh's *What's the Use of Lectures?* (San Francisco: Jossey-Bass, 2000).

A very practical guide for lecturers is George Brown's classic paperback, *Lecturing and Explaining* (London: Methuen, 1978).

Barbara Davis's *Tools for Teaching*, 2nd ed. (San Francisco: Jossey-Bass, 1993), gives practical tips on preparing, delivering, and personalizing lecture classes.

Jerry Evensky's chapter "The Lecture," in L. Lambert, S. L. Tice, and P. Featherstone (eds.), *University Teaching* (Syracuse, NY: Syracuse University Press, 1996), is excellent. I like his statement "You should not think of the lecture as the passive period to be relieved by 'Now we're going to do active learning.'"

The paper by James Hartley and A. Cameron, "Some Observations on the Efficiency of Lecturing," in *Educational Review*, 1967, *20*(1), 30–37, is a classic.

7 Assessing, Testing, and Evaluating: Grading Is Not the Most Important Function

When we think about evaluating learning, most of us think about examinations—multiple-choice tests, essay tests, oral examinations, perhaps performance tests. Currently there is much interest in other methods of assessment. In this chapter I begin with suggestions for conventional testing and then suggest other methods of assessing student learning.

Let me start with nine assertions:

1. What students learn depends as much on your tests and methods of assessment as on your teaching, maybe even more. What is measured is often what ends up being valued, so be sure your measures reflect what you want the students to learn.

2. Don't think of tests simply as a means for assigning grades. Tests should facilitate learning for you as well as for your students.

3. Use some nongraded tests and assessments that provide feedback to the students and you. The CATs (Classroom Assessment Techniques; Angelo & Cross, 1993) methods for

gathering information about student learning can be a real boon to you and the students. They provide several ways of gathering information and providing feedback while learning is still in progress.

4. Check your assessment methods against your goals. Are you really assessing what you hoped to achieve: for example, higher-order thinking?

5. Some goals (values, motivation, attitudes, some skills) may not be measurable by conventional tests. Look for other evidence of their development.

6. Assessment is not synonymous with testing. You can assess students' learning with classroom and out-of-class activities.

7. After the course is over, students will not be able to depend on you to assess the quality of their learning. If one of your goals is continued learning, students need practice in self-assessment. Peckham and Sutherland (2000) showed that developing accurate student self-assessment requires training and practice. Peer assessment of one another's papers helps develop assessment skill and improves performance (Gibbs, 1999).

8. Don't rely on one or two tests to determine grades. Varied assessments will give you better evidence to determine an appropriate grade.

9. To summarize: assessment is *not* simply an end-of-course exercise to determine student grades. Assessments can be learning experiences for students. Assessment throughout a course communicates your goals to students so that they can learn more effectively; it will identify misunderstandings that will help you teach better; it will help you pace the development of the course; and, yes, it will also help you do a better job of assigning grades.

Since grades in many courses are determined to a great degree by test scores, tests are among the most frustrating aspects of the course to many students and arouse a great deal of overt and covert aggression. If teachers attempt to go beyond the usual practice of asking simply for memory of information from the textbook or lectures, they are immediately deluged with the complaint, "These are the most ambiguous tests I have ever taken!"

PLANNING METHODS OF TESTING AND ASSESSMENT

The first step in assessment of learning is to list your goals for the course. Once you have specified objectives, you can determine which kind of assessment is appropriate for each objective. Later in this chapter, you'll find ideas for assessing learning other than within class tests. Be open to trying something different if you're the person who gets to choose the assessment strategies. Also consider using some variety in assessing learning. Not every student can show understanding on high-stakes tests; some students might do better on written assignments or on projects or shorter assessments.

In those instances when you choose to use an in-class test, it is still a good idea to determine what level of objective you're targeting. You can look over the items that you normally write and categorize them according to cognitive level or type. You'll probably be surprised to find out how many of your test items pile up in certain categories. The major error in teacher-made tests is to ask questions about the things that are easiest to measure.

One way of maintaining a balance is to construct a grid, listing objectives along the side of the page and content areas along the top. If you then tally items as you write them, you can monitor the degree to which your test adequately samples the objectives and content desired. You can also use this kind of grid before you write the actual items. By laying out how many items or what percentage of the items you want to fall in certain categories or to test certain content, you can speed up your test writing while improving your coverage. If you're having a hard time balancing content coverage in exams, this is one way to make sure you emphasize higher-level thinking along with basic information.

Because some course examinations emphasize recall of facts, many students demand *teaching* that emphasizes memorization of facts. One student wrote on a slip evaluating me, "The instructor is very interesting and worthwhile, but I have rated him low because he doesn't give us enough facts. The sort of job I get will depend on my grades, and I have little chance of beating other students out for an A unless I can get a couple of pages of notes each period."

Students may object at first to tests requiring them to think, but if you emphasize that the tests will measure their abilities to use their knowledge, you can greatly influence their goals in the course. This is indicated by a student comment we received: "More of the course should be like the tests. They make us apply what we've learned." Marton and Säljö (1976b) showed that questions demanding understanding rather than memory of detailed facts resulted in differing styles of studying for later tests and better retention. Foos and Fisher (1988) showed that tests requiring inferences enhanced learning more than those requiring memorized knowledge.

Admittedly it is more difficult to devise measures of complex, higher-level objectives. Yet the very effort to do so will, I believe, have an influence on student motivation and learning. Moreover, consideration of these objectives may help you break out of the conventional forms of testing. For example, in my classes in introductory psychology, the desired goals include developing greater curiosity about behavior, awareness of dimensions of behavior that might ordinarily be ignored, and increased ability to describe and analyze behavior objectively. To get at this I have sometimes used a film or videotape as a stimulus, and the test questions have to do with students' reactions to the film; or I have asked students to leave the classroom for 15 minutes and then return and report on some interesting behavior they observed. I have brought in scientific journals and asked students to find an article of interest and to write their reactions to it. I have asked for analyses of newspaper items to get at the degree to which students can read critically. Using materials with somewhat greater apparent relevance to course objectives than that of typical test items is more fun for the students taking the test—and more fun to grade.

ALTERNATIVE TESTING MODELS

Group Testing

Given the prevalence of group work in classes these days, some instructors have begun to administer group tests as well. Since the students have been encouraged and actually required to study and work in groups while learning, the logic is that asking them to perform in an individual situation on the test contradicts what they have learned about peer support. Although I may not agree with that logic, I do agree that taking a test in a group situation is a good learning experience for the same reasons that collaborative learning is a good teaching method: students learn a lot from one another and from having to explain their own answers.

The most common method for this strategy is to have the students initially take the test on their own. Then after turning their copy in, they get into a group (usually the one they've been working with all semester) and go through the test again to come up with a group response to the test. It is amazing how much energy there is during this activity! It has the advantage of giving the students immediate feedback on their test performance by comparing their responses to their groupmates', and it also corrects any misconceptions right away—something that we can't do very easily in a regular test situation. Grades are a combination of individual test performance and group test performance.

There are many concerns about this strategy, most of them having to do with grading and with difficulties posed by room configurations. There is also the possibility of one student dominating the group's responses to the test. These are the same problems that arise whenever group work is suggested, and they must be at least acknowledged. Achacoso and Svinicki's (2005) descriptions of group testing by a couple of different instructors in different settings may inform your understanding of this trend.

Online Testing

Another new trend in testing is the use of testing online. In this model students take their tests on a computer, either their own or at a testing center. There are almost as many varieties of this strategy as there are instructors. Achacoso and Svinicki (2005) provide examples of different online testing strategies.

The advantage of online testing is that it can allow an instructor to give a customized test to each student through the miracles of technology and a large database of questions. Given what you know about computers, I'm sure you can imagine all the clever ways that the technology can modify, randomize, customize, and evaluate a student's test. For example, there is one format that calibrates the difficulty of each subsequent item based on whether the current item was answered correctly. This particular mode is being used with the large standardized placement tests, such as the GRE or LSAT. That's probably a little too fancy for a regular classroom test, but future developments in software may make it possible for individual instructors to design such systems just as we can now design online tutorials much more easily.

Another advantage of the online testing idea is that the instructor can include simulations that are interactive. Such questions would provide a much better test of student understanding than the static problems that can be included in paper-and-pencil tests.

The difficulty with such testing is maintaining testing integrity. Unless the test is administered under secure conditions—for example, in a computer lab or testing facility—the instructor may not be able to ensure that the person submitting the test is really the designated student or whether the student is making inappropriate use of support materials during the test. Many institutions are considering the feasibility of providing large computer-based testing centers, and it will be interesting to see whether such efforts are scalable to the kinds of large classes in which they might be the most useful.

OTHER METHODS OF ASSESSING LEARNING

Performance Assessment (Authentic Assessment)

Over two decades ago, Alverno College instituted a student-centered curriculum and performance assessment plan that has become a significant model for American colleges and universities. Faculty members construct learning situations in which they can observe student performance and judge the performance on the basis of specified criteria. The faculty has defined developmental levels in each of several abilities that students are expected to achieve. Since no one situation is sufficient for assessing a complex ability, the assessment plan stresses multiple modes of assessment related to real-life contexts. In addition, faculty actively train students in methods of self-assessment, an important outcome if students are to continue learning when there are no longer teachers around to evaluate their work (see Alverno College Faculty, 1994; Mentkowski & Loacker, 1985; Mentkowski & Associates, 2000).

Many other college teachers are using methods of evaluating learning that are more authentically related to later uses of learning than are conventional tests. For example, in chemistry, mathematics, and engineering courses instructors now use fewer standard abstract problems that can be solved by algorithms and more problems that describe situations in which more than one approach could be used and in which alternative solutions are possible. Such "authentic" assessments are particularly appropriate for service learning situations.

Simulations (on computers or role-played), hands-on field or laboratory exercises, research projects, and juried presentations (such as are used in music, art, and architecture) are also methods related more closely to later use of learning. Paper-and-pencil tasks may require similarity judgments, sorting, or successive choices or predictions following sequential presentation of information about a case, scenario, or situation.

Graphic Representations of Concepts

An organized framework of concepts is important for further learning and thinking. Graphic representations of conceptual relationships may be useful both for teaching and for assessing learning. Our research group (Naveh-Benjamin & Lin, 1991; Naveh-Benjamin et al., 1989; Naveh-Benjamin et al., 1986) developed two methods (the "ordered tree" and "fill-in-the-structure," or FITS) that we use to assess the development of conceptual relationships during college courses. In both of these methods the instructor chooses a number of concepts and arranges them in a hierarchical structure like that depicted in Figure 7.1 (which shows an example used in my Learning to Learn course). For the FITS task the instructor gives the students a copy of the basic structure with some concepts missing. The students are then asked to fill in the blanks.

FIGURE 7.1   A Fill-in-the-Structure (FITS) Example

Fill in the blanks from the list below. (12 points)

a. Attention
b. Chunking
c. Elaboration
d. Encoding
e. Expectancy
f. Extrinsic
g. Information processing
h. Means-end analysis
i. Memory
j. Motivation
k. Planning
l. Recognition
m. Retrieval
n. Schema
o. Self-efficacy
p. Self-regulation
q. Working backward
r. Working memory (STM)

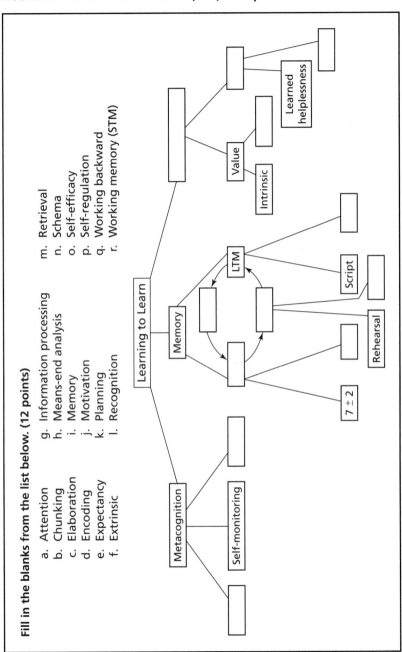

Journals, Research Papers, and Annotated Bibliographies

Journals, research papers, and reports come closer to the goals of authentic assessment than do most conventional tests. Journals are particularly useful in helping students develop critical reflection and self-awareness (MacGregor, 1993; Rhoads & Howard, 1998; Connor-Greene, 2000). The chapter "How to Enhance Learning by Using High-Stakes and Low-Stakes Writing" deals with such writing in detail. Annotated bibliographies can be a useful preparation for writing as well as a tool for assessment. Moreover, annotated bibliographies can be a resource for the whole class (Miller, 1998). Evaluating these products can be improved if you use the rubric method described earlier in this chapter.

Portfolios

Traditionally used in art and architecture classes, portfolios are becoming popular in a variety of subjects and at all levels of education. Although there are many types of portfolios, they basically are used to highlight work that individual students have accomplished over a period of time. A portfolio might include early as well as later examples in order to demonstrate progress, or a portfolio may be simply a presentation of the student's best work or, better yet, the student's own descriptions of how the work helped his or her development. In mathematics or science a portfolio might consist of problems or lab reports representing various course topics written up to show the student's understanding. Portfolios in other courses might include entries from journals describing reactions to reading, classroom experiences, or learning occurring outside the classroom; papers; notes for presentations to the class; and other materials. A portfolio helps both the students and the instructor see how students have progressed. Students report increased self-awareness, and I frequently find evidence of learning (or the lack of it) that I otherwise would have missed. Palomba and Banta (1999) provide a thorough discussion of the use and pragmatics of portfolios.

Peer Assessment

Even if you use the best assessment and grading procedures, some students will be frustrated with their grades. You can prevent some aggression if you help students develop skills in self-assessment. As mentioned earlier, this takes practice, but a lot of instructors are beginning to incorporate peer assessment into their classes (Topping, 1998). In these instances, students learn about the criteria used for assessing their work, and they learn to apply those criteria to their work before they turn it in, a real benefit for the instructor. Some instructors have developed computer-based peer reviewing systems (called "calibrated peer review") that involve students grading other students' work online using a carefully refined rubric given by the instructor (Robinson, 2001; Davies, 2000).

On a more modest level you can have your students evaluate one another's work in hard copy. After collecting tests or papers, redistribute them randomly with a rubric for evaluation. Encourage the students to write helpful comments as well as an evaluation. After students evaluate the papers they were given, ask them to exchange with a neighbor, evaluate the paper given to the neighbor, and then compare notes on their evaluations.

What you do next will probably depend on the size of your class. In a small class I collect the papers and evaluations and evaluate them before returning them to the evaluators and students evaluated. If the class is larger, I ask the class to discuss the process, what problems they encountered, and what they learned.

Assessing Group Work

As teachers use more and more team projects and cooperative learning, one of the frequently asked questions is "How can I assess group work?" First let's be clear about what we're assessing. You might be assessing student learning in the form of papers or products produced by the group or by members of the group. Or you might be assessing the way in which students worked together in the group, focusing on group process and teamwork more than on content learning.

To measure how much content each student has learned, I sometimes ask group members to write individual reports. Students are told that purely descriptive parts, such as the research design, may be the same on all papers but that parts representing thinking are to represent the students' own thinking—although students are encouraged to read and discuss each other's papers before submitting them. I sometimes include an exam question relevant to the group projects; currently I ask each group to submit a single report, which I evaluate.

To evaluate individual contributions to the group, I also ask each student to turn in a slip of paper listing the members of his or her group and dividing 100 points in proportion to each member's contribution. Almost all groups apportion the points equally because I monitor the group's progress and try to get problems solved before the final product. In addition, students understand that the grade will be lowered for any student whose contribution is perceived to be less than that of other group members. Thus on a 100-point project I might give only 50 points to a student whose contributions were 10 percent or less as judged by his or her teammates. In most such cases I would have been aware of the problem earlier and discussed it with the group and the student, but even then I try to talk with the student before assigning the lower grade.

Another strategy is to ask group members to simply describe the work contributed by other members without assessing its value. This allows them to be nonjudgmental, leaving the judgment calls up to me. Group members' descriptions of each member's contribution can be compared to get a more accurate picture of what each individual contributed.

Some instructors develop group rating forms that list the key group contributions that each member is expected to make. Each group member evaluates the other members according to those criteria. I've found it very useful to include the students in the process of identifying those key contributions. At the beginning of a group-oriented project, I have a class discussion about what constitutes good group work. Once we all agree on the behaviors that fit that designation, I draw up a contract that all the students agree to. The peer assessment and my assessment of each student's work are then based on those criteria. Because they have contributed to defining the criteria, the students have a pretty clear idea about what is expected of them.

Classroom Assessment

The primary purpose of assessment is to provide feedback to students and teacher so that learning can be facilitated. *Classroom assessment* is the term popularized by Pat Cross and Tom Angelo to describe a variety of nongraded methods of getting feedback on student learning. I described minute papers in the preceding chapter. Problem posting (discussed in the chapter "Meeting a Class for the First Time") and the two-column method (in the "Facilitating Discussion" chapter) are ways of getting feedback as well as of facilitating student learning. Angelo and Cross (1993) describe a variety of classroom assessment techniques. Regular use of such formative assessment may change the way students view what should happen in class. My own students consistently report how much they valued these regular assessments.

IN CONCLUSION

1. Learning is more important than grading.
2. Tests and other assessments should be learning experiences as well as evaluation devices.
3. Providing feedback is more important than assigning a grade. You can use nongraded evaluation as well as evaluation for assigning grades.
4. Try to assess the attainment of all your objectives, even if some objectives (such as increased motivation for learning) are not appropriate criteria for grades.
5. Avoid evaluation devices that increase anxiety and competition.

Supplementary Reading

Paul Ramsden's chapter "Assessing for Understanding," in his book *Learning to Teach in Higher Education* (London: Routledge, 1992), presents a wise perspective on assessment and gives examples from chemistry, anatomy, materials technology, engineering, history of art, statistics, medicine, and physics.

500 Tips on Assessment by Sally Brown, Phil Race, and Brenda Smith (London: Kogan Page, 1996) is a marvelous compendium of useful suggestions on all types of assessment, ranging from self-assessment through group assessment, multiple-choice tests, and assessment of performance, lab work, and dissertations.

Graham Gibbs discusses modern methods of assessing learner-centered courses in his book *Assessing Student-Centered Courses* (Oxford: Oxford Centre for Staff Development, 1995). Chapters give case studies illustrating assessment of group work, projects, journals, skills, and portfolios.

Assessment Matters in Higher Education, edited by Sally Brown and Angela Glasner (Buckingham, UK, and Philadelphia: Society for Research into Higher Education and Open University, 1999), describes innovative approaches to assessment and current United Kingdom practices in a variety of disciplines. There is an entire section on peer assessment and self-assessment. (I suspect that the pun in the title was intentional.)

Assessment Essentials: Planning, Implementing and Improving Assessment in Higher Education by Catherine Palomba and Trudy Banta (San Francisco: Jossey-Bass, 1999) is a fine resource on all manner of assessment strategies and the rules that guide their use.

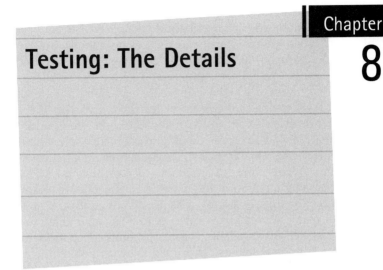

Testing: The Details

If your assessment plans call for the use of in-class testing (and they probably will), you can do a lot to make sure that the test you design serves the assessment purposes you had in mind. In this chapter, I'm going to get down to the nitty-gritty details of writing a test. Not all the details will fit every testing situation, but the planning and execution of most tests will follow this decision process.

WHEN TO TEST

Because tests are so important in operationalizing goals and influencing student methods of learning, I give an ungraded quiz during the first week and a graded test after the third or fourth week of a 14-week semester. To reduce the stress I weight early tests very little in determining the final grade. An early test gets students started—they don't delay their studying until the conventional midterm examination—and it will help you to identify problems early while they are still remediable. Thus early tests should demand the style of learning you expect, and they need to be constructed carefully even though their purpose is more motivational and diagnostic than evaluative.

I usually also give midterm and final examinations, but the amount and frequency of tests should depend on the background of your students. In a first-year course in an area new to students, frequent short tests early in the term facilitate learning, as demonstrated in the Personalized System of Instruction (Keller, 1968). Generally, however, I want to wean students from studying for tests, so that they will become lifelong learners able to evaluate their own learning. This implies less frequent testing as learners become more experienced. It probably also implies questions requiring broader integration and more detailed analysis as learners advance. For this reason my tests are all cumulative; that is, they cover material previously tested as well as material learned since the last test. Give students a chance to comment on the dates of tests or other assessments. They may know of potential conflicting events that could influence due dates.

CONSTRUCTING THE TEST

In planning your tests you may want to use a mix of different types of questions in order to balance measurements of the varied goals of education. The following sections describe the strengths and weaknesses of each type of question, as well as offer tips on constructing items.

Choosing the Type of Question

The instructor who is about to give an examination is in a conflict situation. The administration of an examination consists of two time-consuming procedures: (1) construction of the examination and (2) grading. Unfortunately, it appears to be generally true that the examinations that are easiest to construct are the most difficult to grade and vice versa.

Teachers often base their choice of question types solely on class size, using multiple-choice tests for large classes, short-answer questions for medium-sized classes, and essay questions for small classes. Class size is certainly an important factor, but your educational goals should take precedence. Your goals almost always will require the use of some essay questions, problems, or other items requiring analysis, integration, or application.

Problems. In mathematics, science, and some other disciplines, a test typically consists of problems. The value of problems depends on the degree to which they elicit the sort of problem-solving skills that are your goals. Some problems are too trite and stereotypic to have much value as indicators of whether students understand the steps they are following. In other cases the answer depends to such a large extent on tedious calculations that only a small sample of problems can be tested. In such cases you might provide calculations leading up to a certain point and ask students to complete the problem, or you might use a multiple-choice question about the proper procedure—for example, "Which of the following problems can be solved by procedure x?" Or you might have students set up the problem without actually calculating the final answer. Many instructors who have problem solving as their goal say that setting the problem up correctly is more than half the battle yet students often jump right to a formulaic response. If the grade is based solely on problem setup, students will pay more attention to it. Many teachers use problems that may be solved in more than one way or that have more than one satisfactory answer. In this case special emphasis in both teaching and grading should be on justifying the solution strategy rather than on the specific answer. This has the advantage of focusing students' attention on the process rather than on the product.

Short-Answer Items. Here is an example of a short-answer item: "Give one example from your own experience of the concept of elaboration." In responding, a student might describe an experience of explaining a concept to another student or of thinking about the relationship of a fact to a general principle. Such a question is restricted enough that it is not often difficult to judge whether the expected answer is there. Furthermore, such questions can be presented in a format that allows only a small amount of space for the answer. The student tendency to employ the "shotgun" approach to the examination is thus inhibited.

Short-answer questions permit coverage of assigned materials without asking for petty details. Unfortunately, many short-answer questions test only recall of specific facts. Short-answer questions, however, can do more than testing recall. If you are trying to develop skill in analysis or diagnosis, for example, you may present case material or a description of an experiment and ask students what questions they would ask. You can then provide additional information that they can use in an analysis. Or a short-answer question can ask students to solve a problem or propose a hypothesis relevant to information learned earlier. An example is the following question from a course on the psychology of aging:

1. Given the *differences* in ways in which men and women experience middle age, and the fact that depression rises as a psychiatric symptom in middle age, how might the *causes* of the depression differ for men and women at this time in life?

Essay Items. Although the short-answer examination is very useful in certain situations, I recommend that, if possible, you include at least one essay question on examinations in most college courses. Experiments indicate that students study more efficiently for essay-type examinations than for objective tests (d'Ydewalle et al., 1983; McCluskey, 1934; Monaco, 1977). Thus in addition to the values of essay tests as evaluation devices, you should take into consideration their potential educational value as stimuli to students' reflection about conceptual relationships, possible applications, or aspects of thinking. One strategy is to pass out several questions the week before the test and tell students that these are the sorts of questions you will use—that, in fact, you may even use one of these very questions.

Where the tests can be returned with comments, essay examinations may give students practice in organized, creative thinking about a subject and an opportunity to check their thinking against the standards of someone with more experience and ability in the field. Johnson (1975) demonstrated that when marginal comments on earlier tests emphasized creativity, creativity on the final exam was improved.

In large classes where time is limited and in classes where the writing itself is not the point of the question, you can format the answer sheet to break a long, complex answer into its critical components, each of which has a space for an answer. For example, in my class the last problem on every exam is a case to which the students must apply whatever theory we have been studying. So at the top of the sheet, there is a short description of the scenario. Then there is a space headed "In five sentences or fewer, describe your proposed solution to this scenario based on theory X." About two inches farther down the sheet there is another instruction: "In the spaces below connect the components of your solution to three aspects of theory X that are relevant and explain their relevance." That is followed by three spaces, each headed like this:

aspect one: (space)

connection to your solution and why: (space)

This considerably speeds up my grading time because rather than searching through a long essay organized (I hope) by the student, I can at a glance see if the student has provided a reasonable solution and tied it to the theory. I'm not "giving away the answer" because the prompts are fairly broad; I'm simply imposing a little organization on the answer to make my grading easier. And maybe students learn something about structuring an answer efficiently, too.

Finally, if you read the examinations yourself (or at least some of them), you get some excellent information on what students are learning. Of course the teacher can also learn from students' responses to objective tests, but the impact on the teacher of what students are learning seems to be greater and more vivid in reading essay tests.

True-False Items.   Although true-false examinations are rather easy to make up, I don't ordinarily advocate their use. Toppino & Brochin (1989) showed that students tend after the test to remember the false items as being true—an outcome not conducive to achieving your objectives. If you do use true-false items, ask students to explain their answers. This will encourage reflection and help you understand why there were some common misunderstandings.

Multiple-Choice and Matching Items.   It is improbable that most teachers can adequately measure all their objectives with a test made up entirely of multiple-choice questions. Matching questions are similar to multiple-choice in that the student must discriminate between the correct answer and other choices. Nonetheless, for some purposes multiple-choice items are useful. They can measure both simple knowledge and precise discrimination. They can measure ability to apply concepts or principles; they can assess elements of problem solving. But they are not likely to assess organization of ideas, conceptual relationships, or many of the skills involved in higher-order thinking.

Good multiple-choice questions are difficult to construct. (The greater your experience in their construction, the more you realize how long it takes per item to construct a reasonably fair, accurate, and inclusive question.) Because of this difficulty, the construction of such items is probably not worthwhile unless they will be administered to several hundred students, either in a single year or in successive years. Some books that can help you write high-quality items, if you are so inclined, are referenced at the end of this chapter. The box that follows contains hints for their construction that you won't find in an official measurement book.

Even if you don't pretest the items on students, it is worthwhile to have someone take the test before it is in its final form. If you can persuade a skilled test taker who doesn't know the subject matter to take the test, you will probably be surprised at how many he or she gets right simply from cues that you provided in the questions.

How Many Questions Should You Use?

Obviously the number of questions depends on the type and difficulty of each question. I prefer to give tests without a time limit, but the constraints of class scheduling usually require that you clear the classroom so that the next class can begin. Thus you must plan the length of the exam so that the slowest students have time to finish before the end of the period. As a rule of thumb I allow about 1 minute per item for multiple-choice or fill-in-the-blank items, 2 minutes per short-answer question requiring more than a sentence answer, 10 or 15 minutes for a limited essay question, and a half-hour to an hour for a broader question requiring more than a page or two to answer. You can get a rough

Constructing Multiple-Choice Items

1. Teachers' manuals that accompany many textbooks contain multiple-choice items. You should not rely on a manual as the source of all your questions, because the manual probably will not contain many good questions and may cover only textbook material. You need to assess what students have learned in class as well as their understanding of what they have read.

2. A second source of multiple-choice items is the students themselves. They are not a particularly satisfactory source of test questions, because only about 10 percent of the items thus written will be usable. However, this technique is a useful pedagogical device because it gets the students to read their assignments more analytically. It also gives the instructor a good index of what the students are getting out of the various sections of their reading, and it gives you a chance to remind them of the goals of the course going beyond recall of details.

3. There are statistical methods for evaluating questions, but the best suggestions for improvement come from students themselves in their discussion of the test. It seems almost criminal to waste this experience with items; therefore I recommend a permanent file.

4. If you have a problem but no good distractor (incorrect alternative), give the item in short-answer or essay form and use the students' own responses for alternatives for a later use of the item in multiple-choice form.

5. Multiple-choice questions typically have four or five alternatives. Rather than wasting your and your students' time with extra alternatives that don't test a discrimination that is important, use only as many alternatives as make meaningful discriminations. Costin (1972) showed that three-choice items are about as effective as four-choice.

6. For measuring understanding, I like questions that require the student to predict the outcome of a situation rather than questions that simply ask the student to label the phenomenon.

7. Multiple-choice items need not stand alone. You can use a sequence of related items to measure more complex thinking.

8. Grouping items under headings will improve student performance (Marcinkiewicz & Clariana, 1997).

estimate of time requirements by simply timing how long it takes to actually read the items without answering them. That can serve as a minimum time requirement. If you ask someone else to take the test as suggested above, time that person, too.

ADMINISTERING THE TEST

Handing out a test should be a simple matter. Usually it is, but in large classes, simple administrative matters can become disasters. It is hard to imagine how angry and upset students can become while waiting only ten minutes for the proctors to finish distributing the test forms. And if this doesn't move you, imagine your feelings when you find that you don't have enough tests for all of the students. (It has happened to me twice—deserving a place among my worst moments in teaching!)

How can you avoid such problems?

1. If you are having tests duplicated, ask for at least 10 percent extra—more if the test is administered in several rooms. (Some proctor always walks off with too many.) This gives you insurance against miscounting and against omitted or blank pages on some copies.

2. Unless there is some compelling reason to distribute the tests later, have your proctors pass out the tests as students come into the room. This protects students from mounting waves of panic while they wait for the tests to be distributed.

3. Minimize interruptions. Tell students before the exam that you will write announcements, instructions, or corrections on the board. Some exam periods are less a measure of achievement than a test of the students' ability to work despite the instructor's interruptions.

AFTER THE TEST

Grading Essay Questions

I recommend that you use essay questions because of their powerful effect on the way students study, but there is a drawback. Instructors don't grade essay tests very reliably. One problem is that standards vary. First papers are graded differently than later papers. A paper graded immediately after several poor papers is graded differently than one graded after several good papers.

There are nine procedures you can initiate to improve your evaluation of essay examinations—but they entail work.

1. Establish a rubric or set of criteria—not just a list of facts to be included. Are you looking for integration, for analysis, for rational arguments for and against a conclusion? Be prepared to modify your criteria as you find student responses that you hadn't thought of. Learning to create a good grading rubric is worth the effort because it can help you write good questions, maintain reliable grading of answers, and, if shared with the students, help students understand how their answer was graded. Walvoord (1998) has an excellent book on how to create rubrics based on "primary trait analysis."

Creating a good rubric through primary trait analysis involves laying out the key aspects of the response that figure into the grade. For example, on a given essay question, the analysis might list four main points that must be included in the answer, plus criteria for a clean argument and criteria for good writing itself. Then each "trait" is described along a scale of acceptability. Here is an example of a scale for the trait of "solid argumentation":

> Best answer (100% credit)—An answer at this level provides clear statements of the thesis or theses being asserted in a logical order that builds to the final conclusion. Each thesis is accompanied by sufficient reasonable evidence to support it. Each thesis also considers and counters reasonable arguments against it. The theses stand together and are internally consistent with one another.
>
> Acceptable answer (80% credit)—An answer at this level provides fewer theses but still provides reasonable and primary ones in light of the conclusion. There is evidence offered for each thesis, although possibly overlooking some minor supporting assertions. Several of the more obvious counterarguments are raised and refuted. The order is logical and builds to the conclusion. Transitions between theses are present but ordinary.
>
> Unacceptable answer (no credit)—Any two or more of the following characteristics constitute an unacceptable answer. The answer contains many errors of assertion and omission. No evidence is given

or the evidence given is incorrect or unrelated to the assertion. No attempt or a weak attempt is made to introduce and refute counterarguments. The order of presentation is not logical or convincing. The conclusion is not justified by the arguments.

Creating this type of rubric helps you clarify for yourself what you want in an answer. It also increases the reliability of grading across graders and across time within a single grader's work.

2. Read exams without knowledge of the name of the writer.

3. Read all or several of the examinations in a preliminary fashion to establish some notion of the general level of performance.

4. If you're unsure of what to expect, first read briefly through a random sample of answers. Then, having identified papers of differing levels of excellence, compare them to determine what the distinguishing features are. You will find some characteristics that were not in your original criteria. Now set up the criteria you will use, but don't be rigid. Give students credit when they come up with creative answers that don't fit the rubric.

5. Write specific comments on the papers. One of the problems in using essay exams and in assigning term papers is that students feel that the grading represents some mysterious, unfathomable bias. The more helpful comments you can write on the paper, the more students will learn. I am finding that computer technology is a big help in my grading of papers. I use the editing software available in common word processing programs to read and mark the papers that my students submit in electronic format. I can give a lot more feedback because I'm not limited by how much I can squeeze into the margins, and I can type a lot faster than I can write by hand. In addition the students can probably read my typing better than my handwriting. (There is more about this in the chapter "How to Enhance Learning by Using High-Stakes and Low-Stakes Writing.")

6. Develop a code for common comments. For example, you might want to use a vertical line alongside paragraphs that are particularly good or "NFD" for "needs further development." Or you can identify the most commonly occurring errors with numbers. When you grade, you can put the number next to the error

on the paper and give students the numbered list of errors for reference. They may learn something from reading the whole list even if they didn't make any of those errors.

7. Don't simply give points for each concept or fact mentioned. Doing that just converts the essay into a recall test rather than a measure of higher-level goals of integration and evaluation. Developing rubrics like those described earlier can be helpful in increasing reliability of grading. However, don't use them mechanically. Your overall impression may be as valid.

8. If possible, do your grading in teams. My teaching assistants and I gather after administering a test. We bring in draft model answers for each question. We discuss what we expect as answers for each question. We then establish two- or three-person teams for each essay question. Each team picks 8 to 12 test papers, which are circulated among the team members. Each team member notes privately his or her grade for the question. Team members then compare grades and discuss discrepancies until they reach consensus. A second group of tests is then graded in the same way, with grades compared and discrepancies discussed. This procedure continues until the team is confident that it has arrived at common criteria. From this point on, each member grades independently. When a team member is not sure how to grade a paper, it is passed to another team member for an opinion.

We stay with the grading until all the papers are done, but we make a party of it to alleviate fatigue and boredom. Funny answers are read aloud. Sandwiches are brought in from a delicatessen. Teams help other teams for a change of pace or to balance the workload.

If you don't have a team, try to develop your own strategies for maintaining motivation. If you begin to be bored, irritated, or tired, take a break. Or before beginning, pull out the answers of some of your most interesting students and read those when you begin to feel dispirited. Take notes to use in discussing the papers in class. Also take separate notes for yourself on what seem to be common problems that you need to correct in your teaching in the future.

Grading papers is still time consuming but does not become the sort of aversive task that makes for procrastination and long delays in providing feedback to students.

9. Before you get ready to give the tests back, it really pays to do a short analysis of overall student performance on each item. You can short-circuit a lot of student complaints by identifying items that were troublesome and knowing why. Once the students recognize that you are making a good-faith effort to identify or remediate poorly worded items, they are more likely to give you the benefit of the doubt. You also have the advantage of having at your fingertips solid data on each question so that if a student challenges a question after the test, you will know whether there is any merit to that challenge and be able to respond immediately and authoritatively.

Helping Yourself Learn from the Test

Often we get so wrapped up in the pure mechanics of correcting and grading tests that we overlook the fact that measures of student performance not only can diagnose student weaknesses but also can reveal areas in which our teaching has failed to achieve its purposes. The item analysis process described earlier is especially helpful with this. Once you've achieved some ease with the grading process, look back at the papers to see what they reveal about problems in student understanding. There may be some things about which the entire class seems a bit shaky; in addition there may be areas of difficulty experienced by certain subgroups of students—perhaps those with background knowledge or experience different from that of the rest of the class. In short, think about what *you* need to do as well as about what the *students* need to do.

Assigning a Grade

The papers have been corrected, errors noted, comments written. Now you have to worry about grading. I say more about grading in the chapter "The ABC's of Assigning Grades," but for the moment let's consider grades given on a test when you are expected to convert a number of points into a letter grade such as A, B, C, D, or F.

You could grade on a "curve"—a practice also called "norm-referenced grading" because each student is compared to the norm of the rest of the class, the "normal" curve. For example, in grading on the curve one might give the top 10 percent of the scores A's, the next 25 percent B's, the next 35 percent C's, the next 20 percent D's, and the bottom 10 percent F's. However, grading based on *relative* achievement in a given group may encourage an undesirably high degree of competition. Grading on the curve stacks the cards against cooperative learning because helping classmates may lower one's own grade.

Grading on the curve also discourages the teacher from helping less able students because any student who moves up a grade moves another student down. It increases student anxiety because a student can't interpret his or her grade without information about the overall performance of the class. Even so, many teachers prefer to grade on a curve—some because they are not sure what standards are appropriate, others because they fear that they will be accused of contributing to grade inflation if most students reach high standards of achievement. The latter is a bugaboo that persists despite evidence that grades have not gone up in the last two decades (Adelman, 1999).

A modified curving system is what I call the "gap" system. Like the curve, gap grades compare students to one another by setting grade cutoffs where there are gaps in the frequency distribution of the students' grades. So, for example, my students' grade distribution might be as shown in Table 8.1.

Notice that there is a "gap" in the grade distribution between 88 points and 82 points. If I put the cutoff for an A at 88, then there is a visible difference between the performance of the top group and the second group. (When you don't have big gaps in the distribution, you can look for low points where there is a drop in the number of students at successive levels.) You can even establish some general levels where you'd expect the grade cutoffs to be and then locate the gap nearest to those levels.

In the scenario I just described, students getting 82 points can see that they really performed differently from students getting 89, in contrast with systems where only one point separates an A from a B. Students also are much less likely to argue for more points because the number of points that they would have to talk you out of to get the next highest grade is so large.

Alternatively, and in my opinion preferably, you can grade in terms of percentage of a possible score. This is called "criterion-referenced grading" because each student is compared to a set

Score	Number at That Score	Score	Number at That Score
100	1	89	1
99	0	88	1
98	1	87	0
97	2	86	0
96	3	85	0
95	3	84	0
94	4	83	0
93	4	82	2
92	3	81	3
91	2	etc.	
90	1		

TABLE 8.1   Sample Distribution of Grades

criterion. Thus if a test has 150 possible points, I would tell the students:

> If you make 140 or over (93%+), I'll guarantee an A.
>
> 135 to 139 (90%+), A−
>
> 131 to 134 (87%+), B+
>
> 125 to 130 (83%+), B
>
> 120 to 124 (80%+), B−, etc.
>
> If everyone gets over 140 points, everyone will get an A, and I'll be very pleased if you all do well.

I tell the students that I may grade more generously than the standards I have announced, but I promise not to be tougher than announced. As it turns out, my distribution of grades has not turned out to be more generous than that of my colleagues—which may indicate that I'm not teaching as effectively as I'd like.

My "percentage of possible points" system is fairly easy to apply but lacks the educational value of criteria or standards tied more directly to course goals. Royce Sadler (1987) describes the use of exemplars and verbal descriptions of quality to set standards for grading.

Returning Test Papers

Remember that tests are important tools for learning and that discussion of a test is a worthwhile use of class time. You might begin by asking students what they learned from the test.

Were students accurate in their assessment of how well they did? (Helping students learn to assess their own learning is a worthy objective.) You don't need to discuss every question, but when there are common errors, try to find out why the error occurred and suggest strategies for avoiding such problems in the future (see Schutz & Weinstein, 1990).

Students do learn from their corrected papers (McCluskey, 1934). Although you may not wish to spend class time quibbling over some individual items, you should make known your willingness to discuss the test individually with students who have further questions.

On multiple-choice questions that many students missed, I recommend this sort of procedure: Read the stem of the item and each of the choices. For each of the incorrect choices give your reasons for regarding it as incorrect. This procedure gives you the jump on the chronic criticizer. It is more difficult to maintain that a given choice is right under these circumstances than it would be if you said nothing about the various alternatives and students could argue that the correct alternative was not completely correct.

There will still be cases in which a legitimate argument arises. If some ambiguities have gotten through the screening process and an item really is capable of two equally correct interpretations, admit it and change scores. But remember that you can't escape aggression simply by changing scores, because every time you admit a new right answer, the students who originally had the question right are likely to feel injured. That's the advantage of having done the item analysis mentioned earlier. You'll head off problems that might arise during class discussion.

For essay tests I try to describe what I expected in a good answer and the most common inadequacies. I may read an example of a good answer (without identifying the student), pointing out how it met the criteria, and I might construct a synthetic poor answer to contrast with the good one.

Dealing with an Aggrieved Student

What about the student who comes to your office in great anger or with a desperate appeal for sympathy but no educationally valid reason for changing the test grade? First of all, listen. Engaging in a debate will simply prolong the unpleasantness.

Ask the student to think aloud about what he or she was thinking when answering the questions that he or she is unhappy about. Once you have heard the student out, if you have decided not to change the grade, try to convert the discussion from one of stonewall resistance to problem solving. Try to help the student find alternative modes of study that will produce better results: "What can we do to help you do better next time?" Encourage the student to shift from blaming you toward motivation to work more effectively. Ask the student to summarize what he or she plans to do before the next test.

My colleague Deborah Keller-Cohen asks students coming to see her with complaints about grades to write a paragraph describing their complaint or point of view. She declares her willingness to go over the test of anyone who brings in such a paragraph, noting that she may change the grade either positively or negatively. She reports that this technique has a calming effect, resulting in fewer unfounded complaints and more rational discussion with students who do come in.

Although these suggestions may save the instructor some bitter moments, they cannot substitute for the time (and it takes lots) devoted to the construction of good tests.

What Do You Do About the Student Who Missed the Test?

In any large class some students are absent from the test. Their excuses range from very legitimate to very suspicious, but making that discrimination is not always easy.

Makeup tests can involve a good deal of extra work for the instructor. If you devise a new test, you may have trouble assigning a norm with which to grade the makeup comparable to grades on the original test. If you use the same test that the student missed, you cannot tell how much the student has learned about the test from students who took it at the scheduled time. I simply average marks from the tests the student did take to determine the grade, counting the missed test neither for nor against the student.

Another strategy is to drop the lowest score or missed test out of all the tests a student takes. (This, of course, presumes you have enough exams during the semester that one can be dropped.) This also lowers test anxiety because the stakes on any one test are lower. Depending on how strongly you feel about final exams, you could allow students to use the final as the test they drop if they've taken all the other exams and are satisfied with their grade. You'd be surprised what an incentive that is for working diligently during the semester.

IN CONCLUSION

1. Consider using both graded and ungraded tests and moving from more frequent tests to less frequent.
2. Select question types that target your educational goals.
3. Develop grading strategies for essay questions so that you won't shy away from using them.
4. Be prepared to address students' complaints about test scores in a way that helps them learn.
5. Learn from the test yourself.

Supplementary Reading

Effective Grading: A Tool for Learning and Assessment by Barbara E. Walvoord and Virginia Johnson Anderson (San Francisco: Jossey-Bass, 1998) does a good job of describing how to create grading rubrics for all manner of written assessments.

Constructing Test Items: Multiple-Choice, Constructed-Response, Performance, and Other Formats, 2nd ed., by Steven J. Osterlind (Boston: Kluwer

Academic Publishers, 1998), is a fairly complete discussion of the process of writing different types of test items. It may be a bit long on detail, but the guidelines for item construction are solid and fairly straightforward.

The following resources are drawn from the ERIC Digest series. This is a series of short summaries of research and best practices provided online for educators in a searchable database.

- www.ericfacility.net/databases/ERIC_Digests/index.

- Childs, R. (1989). *Constructing Classroom Achievement Tests*. ERIC Digest. ERIC Clearinghouse on Tests Measurement and Evaluation. ED315426.

- Grist, S., and others (1989). *Computerized Adaptive Tests*. ERIC Digest No. 107. ERIC Clearinghouse on Tests Measurement and Evaluation. ED315425.

- Kehoe, J. (1995). *Basic Item Analysis for Multiple-Choice Tests*. ERIC/AE Digest. ERIC Clearinghouse on Assessment and Evaluation. ED398237.

- Kehoe, J. (1995). *Writing Multiple Choice Test Items*. ERIC/AE Digest. ERIC Clearinghouse on Assessment and Evaluation. ED398236.

Tests from the Students' Perspective

It's not surprising that our students get so concerned about tests and other assessments. More is riding on their performance than just a grade in the class. All kinds of things depend on a student's grade point average, many of them with no apparent relationship to scholarly achievement. For example, in some areas, students with good grades get lower car insurance rates! Maybe the insurance companies figure that you must be home studying all the time to get such good grades, so you're not as likely to have an accident!

On a more serious note, no one is totally comfortable with being assessed and, rightly or wrongly, students often equate grades with self-worth. We owe it to them to help them maximize their potential for good performance by dealing with some of the things that might get in the way.

REDUCING STUDENT FRUSTRATION
AND AGGRESSION

Most beginning teachers find the aggression that students direct against them after a test very disturbing. It is likely to impair the instructor's rapport with the class and may actually be a block to learning. Thus strategies for reducing the aggression seem to be worthwhile.

The most obvious solution to the problem is to reduce students' frustration when taking tests. You can do this by emphasizing the contribution the course can make to students' long-range goals. Explaining how and why you test as you do will also help. A nongraded practice test will provide guidance. Periodic assessments of learning (not necessarily graded) to help students assess their own progress and to help you identify problems, as well as frequent explanations of why and how you test and assess learning, should reduce students' anxiety and frustration about testing.

Yet no matter how much you emphasize long-range goals, the tests will in large measure determine what students do. Do you want them to memorize details? Then give the usual memory-of-details test. But if you want more, make your objectives clear, and make sure that your tests measure the attainment of those objectives. If you used the Bloom Taxonomy of Educational Objectives or Biggs's SOLO Taxonomy as suggested in the chapter "Countdown for Course Preparation," remind the students of these levels before each test. McNett and colleagues (2000) use the Bloom taxonomy as a framework throughout their courses. The levels of thinking described in the taxonomy are discussed early in the course and referred to when research papers or other assignments are made and evaluated.

Test instructions should indicate whether students are to guess, what the time limit is, and any other directions that define the nature of the expected responses. Students taking a multiple-choice examination have a right to know whether there is a penalty for guessing. For the typical classroom examination, there is no point in a correction for guessing. Emphasizing in the multiple-choice test introduction that students should choose the *best* answer may help prevent lengthy discussion with students who dream up a remote instance in which the correct alternative might be wrong.

Research by McKeachie and colleagues (1955) and by Smith and Rockett (1958) demonstrated that on multiple-choice tests the instruction "Feel free to write comments," with blank space by each question for the comments, results in higher scores, especially for anxious students. A problem with this strategy is that students these days have been taught to make notes to themselves on the test, so you may find yourself reading a lot of stuff not really written to you. Here is how I have solved this problem and the problem of students who want to explain every item. I allow students to explain their choices for up to three questions. They star the question that they want to elaborate on; then on the last page of the test, called the "explanations page," they write their thoughts and indicate why they answered the way they did. This process greatly reduces their anxiety and saves me grading time. It also forces them to pick their battles; they can't simply write everything they know for every question in hopes that the correct answer is in there somewhere.

HELPING STUDENTS BECOME TEST-WISE

Particularly in the case of multiple-choice examinations, I have found that a good morale builder is spending 15 minutes or so the day before the first test telling students how to take a test of this sort and familiarizing them with the format. Some of the points that I make in such a lecture follow.

Taking Multiple-Choice Tests

The student taking a multiple-choice examination is essentially in the same position as a poker player. The object is to get into a position where you are betting on a sure thing. If this is impossible, at least make your bet on the choice where the odds are in your favor. In poker, you are in the strongest position if you know exactly what your opponent has; in the examination situation, you are in the strongest position if you know the material. There is no substitute for study. Nevertheless, you are not likely to be absolutely certain of all the right answers, and when you are not, certain techniques may help.

What I recommend to the student is this. First go through the examination and answer all of the items you know. In addition to getting a certain amount of the examination done without spending a lot of time on single, difficult items, you probably will find that going through the complete test once in this way will suggest the answers to questions that might have been difficult had they been answered in numerical order. When you have gone through the test once in this fashion, go through it again and answer any questions whose answers are now obvious. Usually there will still be a few unanswered questions. It is in connection with these that certain tricks may be useful.

If the item is multiple choice, don't simply guess at this stage of the game. See whether it is possible to eliminate some of the choices as incorrect. In a four-choice multiple-choice item, the probability of getting the answer right by pure guesswork is one in four; if you can eliminate two of the choices, your chances improve to 50-50. So take advantage of the mathematics of the situation.

After completing the examination, go through the whole thing again to check your choices to make sure that you still regard them as correct and to make sure that you made no clerical errors when recording them. In this connection, it is worthwhile to point out to students the common misconception that when you change your answers, you usually change from right answers to wrong ones. Mueller and Wasser (1977) reviewed 18 studies demonstrating that most students gain more than they lose on changed answers.

Taking Essay Tests

My instructions for essay exams are simpler.

1. Outline your answer before writing it. This provides a check against the common error of omitting one part of the answer.

2. If a question completely baffles you, start writing on the back of your paper anything you know that could possibly be

relevant. This starts your memory functioning, and usually you'll soon find that you have some relevant ideas.

3. If you are still at a loss, admit it, write a *related* question that you can answer, and answer it. Most instructors will give you at least a few points more than if you wrote nothing.

4. Write as well as you can. Even if I intend not to grade on writing ability, my judgment is negatively influenced when I have to struggle to read poor handwriting or surmount poor grammar and sentence structure. Moreover, because I believe that every course is responsible for teaching writing, writing always enters into my grading.

Why Teach Test Taking?

Is it wise to give students these tips? The answer to this question depends on your purposes in giving an examination. If you want to test for "test-taking" ability, you will not want to give students such hints. At any rate, this orientation seems to have the effect of conveying to students the notion that you are not trying to "outsmart" them and are instead interested in helping them get as high a grade as their learning warrants.

Helping Students Learn from a Test

The most important function of testing is *not* to provide a basis for grading. Rather, tests are an important educational tool. They not only direct students' studying but also can provide important corrective feedback. The comments that you write on essay tests are far more important than the grade.

What kind of comments are helpful? First of all, rid yourself of the usual teacher's notion that most inadequacies are due to a lack of knowledge, and that improvement would result simply from supplying the missing knowledge. Rather, you need to look for cues that will help you identify the students' representations of knowledge. Usually the students' problems arise from a lack of ability to see relationships, implications, or applications of material. There is always some discrepancy

Coping with Test Anxiety

Many students struggle with test anxiety because of the high-stakes testing they experienced in the past and the emphasis on grades they're experiencing now. A student may know the material but blank out during the test and be unable to show what he or she knows. If my students are having such problems, I can do several things to help:

1. I can lower the stakes of any given test. By having several assessments of learning, I can lower the overall importance of any one test and thereby lower students' anxiety about their performance on it.

2. I can offer "second chances" to students who experience difficulties while taking a test. This means allowing them after the test to earn back some of the points they missed. I describe this process later in this chapter. This is a good learning strategy, and more important for test-anxious students, it relieves some of the pressure and therefore some of the anxiety.

3. I already mentioned the strategy of allowing students to explain their answers more thoroughly on the test itself. This also removes some of the pressure that comes with uncertainty about a particular answer.

4. Prior to the test day I familiarize students with what the test will actually look like, the kinds of questions, any special procedures they'll need to follow, and how I'll grade the test. This removes a lot of the unknowns associated with the test, which are a big source of anxiety.

5. I offer ideas about studying and about getting physically ready for the test, relaxation strategies (taking deep breaths, putting down the pencil and flexing your fingers, and so on). Sometimes I even coach students to think about what they're saying to themselves that contributes to their anxiety—for example, "I've *got* to get an A" instead of "I'm going to do OK."

between the structure of knowledge in the student's mind and that in the instructor's. Students construct their own knowledge based on their individual past experiences and their experiences in the course. Thus comments on essay items are most likely to be helpful if they help students find alternative ways of looking at the problem rather than simply noting that something is wrong.

Comments that provide correction and guidance may not achieve their purpose if students become so discouraged that they give up. Thus teachers need to consider the motivational as well as the cognitive aspects of comments. Misconceptions need to be identified, but not in overwhelming number. Encouragement and guidance for improvement should set the overall tone. Feedback that helps students see their progress helps build self-efficacy and motivation for further learning. You can even allow students to earn back a small portion of the points they missed by writing an analysis of items they missed. By focusing their attention on the difference between their understanding and the most accurate interpretation of a question, you can head off the persistence of misconceptions. I do recommend that you put a limit on how many questions you allow them to correct; otherwise, some of the more compulsive students will want to correct everything and in the process will miss the point of the activity.

After you return the test, you can also ask students to write a short account of what they learned from the test. What did they do well in preparing? What do they need to do to improve?

IN CONCLUSION

1. Teach students not only the content to be tested but also how to take tests.
2. Be sure the type of test you create is in line with your goals.
3. To combat frustration, let students know how and why you test, and provide adequate instructions.
4. Help students to learn from the test.

Supplementary Reading

▥ C. E. Weinstein and L. Hume, *Study Strategies for Lifelong Learning* (Washington: American Psychological Association, 1998). The American Psychological Association Division 15 has a whole series of publications on helping students improve their learning. Access them through the APA Publications site.

▥ D. Sadker and K. Zittleman, "Test Anxiety: Are Students Failing Tests—Or Are Tests Failing Students?" *Phi Delta Kappan,* 2004, *85*(10), 740.

The entire September 2004 issue of *Anxiety Stress and Coping* is devoted to test anxiety and research on it, including how to cope with it.

Chapter 10

What to Do About Cheating

It may be hard for you to believe that your students would ever cheat—"Maybe other students cheat, but not mine!" Unfortunately, studies of cheating behavior over several decades invariably find that a majority of students report that they have cheated at some time (McCabe & Trevino, 1996). A recent Google search on "cheating in college" turned up over 400,000 pages! Most students would rather not cheat, but the pressures for good grades are so intense that many students feel that they, too, must cheat if they believe that other students are cheating. In my experience the most common excuse given by a student caught cheating is that other students were cheating and the teacher didn't seem to care, at least not enough to do anything to prevent or stop cheating. Many students thus feel less stress when an examination is well managed and well proctored.

WHO CHEATS?

If you think that cheating is confined to students who are in academic trouble you would be wrong. The Educational Testing Service, which sponsored a campaign to discourage academic cheating (www.glass-castle.com/clients/www-nocheating-org/adcouncil/research/cheatingfactsheet.html, ETS, published 1999, accessed July 2004) provided the following data:

Cheating among high school students has risen dramatically during the past 50 years.

Today above-average college-bound students are cheating.

Between 75 and 98 percent of college students surveyed each year report having cheated in high school.

Profile of college students more likely to cheat: business or engineering majors, those whose future plans include business, fraternity and sorority members, younger students, students with lower GPAs or those at the very top. Men are more likely to report that they have been cheating than are women.

In 1996 Donald McCabe and Linda Trevino provided a discussion of longitudinal trends in cheating based on their own research involving 6,000 students at 31 campuses. The authors found that cheating was very prevalent across the board in their sample. They reported that "two out of three students admitted to having engaged in at least one of 14 questionable academic behaviors" (p. 30).

The advent of technology has made cheating easier. Kim McMurtry, writing for the online journal *T.H.E. Journal Online* (2001), describes how easy it can be. Students can copy and paste, find whole papers available online for a price, or commission a specialist to create a paper made to order. This last travesty was described in an ABCNEWS.com article (2004) that described the success of a young entrepreneur, "Andy," who can make up to a thousand dollars a week writing papers for students who "want to go out and party, not do their schoolwork." All Andy needs is a topic, 25 minutes on the web, and "two hours rewriting each sentence downloaded from the Internet in order to beat Web sites like turnitin.com." He can even tailor the level of writing to what the commissioning student might reasonably be expected to earn (A or B).

WHY DO STUDENTS CHEAT?

The research on this question is alarmingly consistent. The most significant factor in a student's decision to cheat is peer influence (McCabe, Trevino, & Butterfield, 2001). McCabe and Trevino (1996) report that students don't believe they'll get caught because instructors are indifferent to their activities. Gerdeman (2000) reports students' belief that if they do get caught they won't be punished severely even if the institution has policies for dealing with such misconduct. In today's high-stakes testing environment, where there is such a strong emphasis on grades, students believe there is a large reward for success at any cost (Whitley, 1998). Certainly they see on the news successful cheaters in the real world constantly getting away without severe penalties.

HOW DO STUDENTS CHEAT?

1. Students pass information to a neighbor; for example, they may loan a neighbor an eraser with the answer on the eraser.
2. Students use notes written on clothing, skin, or small note cards.
3. Students store answers in calculators or cassette recorders used during the exam.
4. Students peek at a knowledgeable neighbor's exam (sometimes seated in groups around the best student in the fraternity).
5. Students use tapping, hand code, cell phones, instant messaging, or other communication.
6. Students accuse the teacher of losing an exam (that they never turned in).
7. Students pay someone else to take an exam or write a paper for them.
8. Students copy or paraphrase material for a paper without acknowledging the source.

PREVENTING CHEATING

"OK, so we want to prevent cheating. What can we do?"

If it's true that cheating comes from some of the causes just mentioned, then there is a lot of proactive action that you can take to prevent it or discourage it from happening. Researchers are fairly consistent in many of their recommendations. Here are a few that I've gleaned from the now extensive literature on cheating in college (Gerdeman, 2000; McMurtry, 2001; Pulvers & Diekhoff, 1999; plus web sites from teaching and learning sites at many of the major universities around the country such as the University of Illinois and the University of California at Santa Barbara). They're fairly consistent with my own practices.

An obvious first answer is to reduce the pressure. While you can't affect the general academic atmosphere that puts heavy emphasis on grades, you can influence the pressure in your own course, for example, by providing a number of opportunities for students to demonstrate achievement of course goals, rather than relying on a single examination. A second answer is to address the issue in your syllabus or have a discussion on the topic early in your course.

A third answer is to make reasonable demands and write a reasonable and interesting test. Some cheating is simply the result of frustration and desperation arising from assignments too long to be covered adequately or tests requiring memorization of trivial details. In some cases cheating is simply a way of getting back at an unreasonable, hostile teacher.

A fourth answer is to develop group norms supporting honesty. I frequently give my classes a chance to vote on whether or not we will conduct the tests on the honor system. I announce that we will not use the honor system unless the vote is unanimous, since it will not work unless everyone feels committed to it. If the vote is unanimous, I remind the students of it on the day of the exam and ask whether they still wish to have the test under the honor system. I haven't collected data on the success of this approach, but I've never had a complaint about it. Although only a minority of classes vote for the honor system, a discussion of academic dishonesty is itself useful in helping students recognize why cheating is bad. I've taken to having the students sign a pledge of academic integrity prior to each exam. I think it reminds them of my expectations and reinforces the impression that I care.

Fifth, if some students are not doing well in the course, talk to them and find out what has gone wrong and what they can do to improve. Try to reduce the stress that leads to cheating. If there are stresses originating beyond your course, suggest counseling.

What else can be done?

One principle is to preserve each student's sense that he or she is an individual with a personal relationship both with the instructor and with other students. Students are not as likely to cheat in situations in which they are known as in situations in which they are anonymous members of a crowd. Thus, if a large course has regular meetings in small discussion or laboratory sections, there is likely to be less cheating if the test is administered in these groups than if the test is administered en masse. Moreover, if the test is given in their regular classroom, they may perform better because of the cues to their original learning (Metzger et al., 1979).

Even in small groups, cheating will occur if the instructor seems unconcerned. Graduate student teaching assistants often feel that any show of active proctoring will indicate that they do not trust the students. There is certainly a danger that the teacher will appear to be so poised to spring at a miscreant that the atmosphere becomes tense, but it is possible to convey a sense of alert helpfulness while strolling down the aisles or watching for questions.

The most common form of cheating is copying from another student's paper. To reduce this I usually ask to have a large enough exam room to enable students to sit in alternate seats. I write on the board before students arrive, "Take alternate seats." Some students fail to see the sign, so in large exams you not only need two proctors at each door passing out exams but at least one more to supervise seating.

In the event that you can't get rooms large enough to permit alternate seating, you probably should use two or more alternate forms of the test. Houston (1983) found that scrambling the order of items alone did not reduce cheating. Since I prefer to have items on a test follow the same order as the order in which the material has been discussed in the course, I scramble the order of items only within topics and also scramble the order of alternatives. I typically write separate sets of essay questions for the two tests. It is difficult to make two tests equally difficult, so you probably will want to tabulate separate distributions of scores on each form of the test.

Whether you use one form or two, don't leave copies lying around your office or the typist's office. One of our students was nearly killed by a fall from a third-floor ledge outside the office where he hoped to steal the examination, and janitors have been bribed to turn over the contents of wastebaskets thought to contain discarded drafts of the test.

PREVENTING PLAGIARISM IN THE INTERNET AGE

Some plagiarism is simply the result of ignorance. Explaining what plagiarism is and indicating why it is a *serious* offense not only may prevent the naive student from plagiarizing but also may deter the intentional plagiarist.

Word processing and electronic submission of documents can both encourage and suppress plagiarism if you know how to exploit them. Although it may be easy for students to copy or purchase essays online, many commercial services accept a paper electronically and compare it with either a huge repository of other student papers from around the country or with a wide swath of Internet and other literary sources to see whether the student plagiarized the paper. Sometimes the mere existence of this service and students' awareness that you're using it will suppress plagiarism. Another strategy is to require a student to submit all of his or her notes along with the paper.

Kim McMurtry (2001) suggests that to foil electronic dishonesty, you make all your assignments unique to that semester's class. A specific assignment tailored to something particular in the class will make it hard for a student to find an already composed paper. She also suggests that you request students to be able to present an oral summary of their paper or a letter of transmittal in which they describe how they wrote the paper, what difficulties they had, the main thesis and arguments they considered, and so on. Aside from making it hard for a student to find a premade paper, these would be good instructional suggestions for learning. McMurtry recommends that you have your students submit electronic copies of their papers so that you can create your own database of papers against which to compare new submissions.

As you can imagine, some students are a lot more technologically sophisticated than we are, and that makes it easy for them to use the technology to their advantage. Also, the technology changes so fast that most people cannot keep up with it. In an interview with John Ydstie of National Public Radio (May 21, 2002), Donald McCabe of Rutgers University said that students view the Internet in a "fundamentally different way." According to McCabe, students seem to feel that because the Internet is public, there is no need to cite it as a reference. He also said that "a lack of defined standards for Internet use" may be contributing to the problem.

Those in the field who study electronic teaching and learning have suggested many ways to use technology to your own advantage. For example, computer testing allows you to create a unique exam for each student from a bank of similar questions, thus making it hard for students to copy from one another. You can control access to course assignments through the use of secure log-ins and passwords to discourage others from "stealing" materials and to provide a "paper" trail of who was online when. McMurtry (2001) also suggests that you acquaint yourself with what's out there on the Internet that might be misused by your students. If your students believe you are as savvy about the use of electronic resources as they are, that belief might be enough of a deterrent that you never actually have to enforce the rules— the topic of the next section.

HANDLING CHEATING

Despite preventive measures, almost every instructor must at some time or another face the problem of what to do about a student who is cheating. For example, as you are administering an examination you note that a student's eyes are on his neighbor's rather than on his own paper. Typically you do nothing at this time, for you don't want to embarrass an innocent student.

But when the eyes again stray, you are faced with a decision about what to do.

Most colleges have rules about the procedures to be followed in case of cheating. Yet instructors are often reluctant to begin the procedure. The reasons for instructor reluctance vary. Sometimes it is simply uncertainty about whether or not cheating really occurred. Students' eyes do wander without cheating. Answers may be similar simply because two students have studied together. "If the student denies the charge, what evidence do I have to support my accusation?"

Again, unwillingness to invoke the regulations concerning cheating may be based on distrust of the justice of the eventual disposition of the case. Cheating is common in colleges; many teachers have been guilty themselves at some stage in their academic careers. Thus most of us are understandably reluctant to subject the unfortunate one who gets caught to the drastic possible punishments that more skillful cheaters avoid. Such conflicts as these make the problem of handling a cheater one of the most disturbing of those a new teacher faces.

Unfortunately I've never been completely satisfied that I handle the problem adequately; so my "advice" should, like the rest of the advice in this book, be regarded simply as some ideas for your consideration rather than as dicta to be accepted verbatim. However, much of what I'm going to say is backed up by most writers in this field.

First, let me support the value of following your college's procedures. Find out what they are and what legal precedents may affect what you should do. Even though it may not have been long since you were taking examinations yourself, your role as a teacher requires that you represent established authority rather than the schoolboy code that rejects "tattlers." Moreover, your memories of student days may help you recall your own feelings when you saw someone cheating and the instructor took no action.

Further, student or faculty committees dealing with cheating are not as arbitrary and impersonal as you might expect. Typically, they attempt to get at the cause of the cheating and to help students solve their underlying problems. Being apprehended for cheating may, therefore, actually be of real long-term value to the students.

Finally, following college policies protects you in the rare case in which a student initiates legal action against you for an arbitrary punishment.

There still remain cases where the evidence is weak and you're not quite sure whether or not cheating actually occurred. Even here I advise against such individual action as reducing a grade. If you're wrong, the solution is unjust. If you're right, you've failed to give the student feedback that is likely to change his behavior. In such cases I advise talking to the student and calling the head of the committee handling cheating cases or the student's counselor. It's surprising to find how often your suspicions fit in with other evidence about the student's behavior. Even when they don't, advice from someone who has additional information about the student will frequently be helpful.

Finally, let's return to the case of the straying eyes. Here you haven't time for a phone call to get advice; your decision has to be made now. Rather than arousing the whole class by snatching away the student's paper with a loud denunciation, I simply ask the student unobtrusively to move to a seat where he'll be less crowded. If he says he's not crowded, I simply whisper that I'd prefer that he move. So far no one's refused.

IN CONCLUSION

1. Prevention is preferable to punishment.
2. Dishonesty is less likely when students feel that the teacher and other students know them and trust them than in situations in which they feel alienated and anonymous.

Supplementary Reading

■I S. F. Davis, C. A. Grover, A. H. Becker, and L. N. McGregor, "Academic Dishonesty: Prevalence, Determinants, Techniques, and Punishments," *Teaching of Psychology*, 1992, *19*(1), 16–20.

■I J. McBurney, "Cheating: Preventing and Dealing with Academic Dishonesty," *APS Observer*, January 1996, 32–35.

One might assume that it would be un-British to cheat. But Stephen Newstead, Arlyne Franklyn-Stokes, and Penny Armstrong found that

British students are not much different from Americans in this respect. Their article "Individual Differences in Student Cheating," *Journal of Educational Psychology,* 1996, *88,* 229–241, is consistent with American data.

A particularly interesting set of recommendations comes from the web site "On the Cutting Edge" of the National Association of Geoscience Teachers, which provides workshops for faculty in the geological sciences (serc.carleton.edu/NAGTWorkshops/index.html).

The Center for Academic Integrity at Duke University, Durham, North Carolina (www.academicintegrity.org/cai_research.asp), can provide a lot of information and sponsors workshops and research on academic integrity. They also have a searchable database of 700+ articles on this topic.

The ABC's of Assigning Grades

11

Grading is almost always in the news. Grade inflation, grading leniency, contract grading, mastery grading—all of these stimulate heated discussion and cries of dismay. My own ideas about grading have become somewhat clearer as I have talked to my teaching assistants about grading policies. That may explain why I am not overly emotional about each of these issues.

First let's agree that grades are fundamentally a method of communication. The question then becomes, What does the professor intend to communicate to whom? When we put grading into this context, four things become apparent:

1. Evaluation is a great deal more than giving a grade. In teaching, the major part of evaluation should be in the form of comments on papers, responses to student statements, conversations, and other means of helping students understand where they are and how to do better. A professor giving a course grade is communicating to several groups—individual students, professors teaching advanced courses, graduate or professional school admissions committees, prospective employers, and so on.

2. What professors communicate by a grade depends on the meaning of the grade to the person reading it—the effect that it has on that person.

3. Professors cannot change the meaning of grades unilaterally. The students' interpretations will be colored by their previous experiences with grades, and they are likely to be disturbed, or to feel that they are being misled, when a professor uses grades in new ways. This explains the strong emotional reaction to so-called grade inflation and to practices deviating from traditional meanings.

4. The meaning of A's, B's, and C's has changed over the last 50 years. In the mid-1900s, C was the average grade. Today, B is more typical. This is not a problem as long as those who assign and interpret grades understand the current meaning. Whether they do is open to debate.

What are grades used for? I suggest that the person reading a grade typically wants information with respect to some decision involving a judgment about the student's *future* performance. Mastery systems of grading, pass-fail grading, and other alternative systems are resisted because they may not be efficient conveyors of information useful for predicting future performance. The accompanying box describes how three groups—students, professors, and employers—use grades.

DO GRADES PROVIDE INFORMATION USEFUL FOR DECISION MAKING?

One of the arguments against conventional grading is that grades do not provide useful information for the major purposes for which they are usually used. Teachers assume that grades have some informational and motivational value for students. Critics, however, argue that the threat of low grades is often a crutch used by poor teachers. Moreover, a heavy emphasis on grades is likely to reduce motivation for further learning and may even result in

What Do Students, Professors, and Employers Want from Grades?

Students

Students want to be able to use grades to assist them in making decisions such as the following:

1. Will I do well if I take additional courses in this field?
2. Should I major in this field? Does it represent a potential career in which I'm likely to be successful?
3. Do I have the skills and ability necessary to work independently in this field—learning more, solving problems, ability to evaluate my own work?

Professors

Professors advising a student or making admissions decisions expect grades to tell them:

1. Does this student have the motivation, skills, knowledge, and ability needed to do well in advanced courses (insofar as the type of problems dealt with in the earlier course are relevant to the demands of the advanced courses or program)?
2. What kind of person is this? What does the pattern of grades tell us about this student's ability and work habits?

Employers

Prospective employers want to use grades to assist in decisions about whether a student is likely to do well on the job.

1. How well will the student be able to solve on-the-job problems related to the area of his or her coursework?
2. Does the overall pattern of grades indicate that this individual is the sort of person who will do well in our organization?

From this analysis it seems evident that grades are used not only as a historical record of what has happened but also as information about what a student can do in situations outside the class for which the grade was awarded. For employers and graduate admissions committees, the grade is not so much historical as potentially predictive.

poorer achievement by the students who are most motivated by grades. In fact, those who achieve the most tend to have moderate grade motivation and high intrinsic motivation (Lin et al., 2003).

What about information for employers? Probably most human resources psychologists would agree that the best predictor of success on a job is successful performance on a similar job. For a young person entering the job market, the only previous employment has been in low-level part-time jobs. The employer's decision must then depend largely on other information, such as interviews, letters of recommendation, biographical data, family background, and test scores. Each source is only partially adequate. Insofar as the new job requires some expenditure for training, it seems likely that grades—representing the result of skills applied in study, learning, and problem solving—will add some useful albeit incomplete information. Grades might also be used by others as a surrogate measure of a strong work ethic, persistence, and flexibility in adapting to a wide range of situations. (I'm not saying that is an accurate interpretation of grades, however.)

Because grades are commonly used in combination with other variables, no one should expect grades always to correlate with success for the students who are selected. It is a simple mathematical truism that when we use several selection criteria—each of them having some validity—we should expect low positive, zero, or even negative correlations between any one selection variable and the ultimate criterion of performance. This outcome occurs because we balance criteria against one another. We select some people who are low in some important attributes because they have high grades, and we select others despite low grades because they are high in other important attributes. The common criticism that grades don't predict later performance is largely invalid because most of the studies cited were carried out in situations where grades and other predictors had already been used in selection.

CAN WE TRUST GRADES?

The information value of the grades we assign is heavily influenced by the methods used to evaluate learning. In the chapter "Assessing, Testing, and Evaluating," I described several ways of measuring student learning, from the typical in-class tests to out-of-class papers and authentic assessments. For grades to be truly useful, they need to be based on what the measurement field refers to as valid and reliable methods.

Assessments that are *valid* measure what they say they measure. For example, the best way to measure students' ability to structure a persuasive argument is to have students create their own unique argument on a topic and deliver it in either written or oral form. It is not answering multiple-choice questions about the parts of an argument. It's not even critiquing someone else's argument. When we grade argumentation skills with real argument-development activities, we have the most valid measurement and probably the best predictor of future argumentation success. The farther away from that situation we get, the less valid the measurement becomes.

One thing we should look for when using grades is how valid the measures to generate them were. Lots of instructors give or take away points for student actions that have little or nothing to do with measures of student learning. For example, they make deductions for late papers or failures to follow instructions. Although these are possibly valid surrogates for qualities such as personal responsibility, maturity, or professional behavior, they are not valid measures of what a student has learned. Including them in an assignment grade lowers the overall validity of that grade. I'd be tempted to have a totally separate grade category called something like "demonstrated responsibility" or "diligence" that would be used to measure things such as tardiness, late assignments, or inattention to class policies. These would be separate from the quality of the work itself yet still part of the overall evaluation of a student. I suspect that in many cases that type of measure would be as good a predictor of future success— perhaps even a better one.

Another important quality of an assessment is its reliability. An assessment that is *reliable* produces fairly consistent results either across time or across multiple graders. Multiple-choice tests, for example, are very reliable because no subjective judgment influences grading; the answer is either right or wrong. Essay tests and papers are less reliable unless you use a rubric to grade them. If you have a reliable measure, everyone's grade indicates a very specific performance, and all individuals whose performance is the same get the same grade.

What does all this mean for you as the person giving the grades? It means that in order to communicate accurately with all the consumers of those grades, you need to be sure that the bases for your grading are both valid and reliable. If you can do that, then they can believe you when you provide them with evidence of student performance.

Of course, in reality, there are no grade police out there trying to make us all conform to the same exact standards. As a profession we have to police ourselves. It's up to us to uphold our standards, not to keep grades from becoming inflated but rather to give honest grades that truly communicate what a student has achieved.

CONTRACT GRADING

In contract grading, students and instructors develop a written contract about what the student will do to achieve given grade levels. Contracts typically specify papers to be written, books to be read, projects to be completed, and so forth. When linked to appropriate standards, contracts can be very useful. However, if students gain points not for achievement but rather for carrying out activities that *should* be conducive to achievement, there may be wide differences in achievement among students who complete the contract. Some do the minimum necessary, whereas others do excellent work. If contract grading is used, criteria for *quality* are needed (see Table 11.1). Such criteria are described in the chapter "Testing: The Details," in the discussion of rubrics for grading.

COMPETENCY-BASED GRADING

In competency-based, mastery, performance-based, or criterion-referenced systems, the students' grades are based on the achievement of specified competencies. This system focuses both teachers and students on course objectives and eliminates the negative effects of competition. In principle such systems should be an improvement over more conventional systems of

	Pro	Con
Contract	Commitment to contract motivates students. May be individualized.	May reward quantity rather than quality.
Competency	Ties grade to course goals. Encourages teacher and student to think about goals.	May be difficult to operationalize.
Both	Reduce student anxiety about competition and grades. Encourage student cooperation.	

TABLE 11.1   Contract Versus Competency Grading

assigning grades. However, there are two problems in implementing competency-based grading:

1. Developing appropriate and comprehensive definitions of the competencies desired
2. Developing adequate criteria for assessing the achievement of each competency

Any assessment involves only a sample of the behaviors that define the competencies desired. But in competency-based or performance assessment systems, there is an attempt to use evidence from more authentic samples of the students' demonstration of the desired competencies in learning situations as well as in separate assessment sessions. The more limited the definition of the achievements that the students should "master" is, the less valid a test or grade is in its ability to assess the students with respect to other problems, other concepts, or other generalizations in the total domain.

Letting students turn in papers or book reports over and over again until they do them correctly is a fine teaching technique. However, the student who writes an acceptable book report after ten trials is probably less able to write a new report acceptably than is the student who does it right the first time. Here it might be possible to have a separate measure of time or chances to completion to indicate two different aspects of a student's performance. Getting things right the first time might be worth something under such a system.

Nonetheless, mastery learning has positive features. It forces the teacher to think about goals, and it focuses students' learning. Such a focus results in better retention (Kulik, Kulik, & Bangert-Drowns, 1988).

ASSIGNING GRADES

Because to many students grades represent a fearsome, mysterious dragon, anxiety can sometimes be reduced by encouraging the students to participate in planning the methods by which grades will be assigned. Students usually can recognize the instructor's need to conform to college policy in grade distribution, and the dragon seems less threatening if they have helped determine the system by which they are devoured (or rewarded).

Some instructors go so far as to let students determine their own grades or to have groups of students grade one another. I like the idea that students should develop the capacity for self-evaluation, but I recognize that many students resist this procedure, either through modesty or through fear that they'll underrate themselves. If you use it, I suggest thorough discussion of the plan with students and an agreed-upon, well-defined set of criteria that all students should use.

Whether or not students participate, you need to be clear about your criteria. Examples of previously graded work may be helpful. Asking students to hand in their own estimates of their grades may help you to motivate them better and may also develop their abilities for self-evaluation.

In general, motivation is not helped simply by high grades; nor is it helped by tough standards. Students are most motivated when they feel that they can achieve success with a reasonable effort (Harter, 1978).

By keeping students informed during the course about where they stand, you help them control much of the anxiety they feel when the grading system is indefinite and unstructured. Sometimes it may seem easier to fight off grade-conscious students by being very indefinite about grades, but student morale is better when the students know the situation with which they must cope.

Whatever your grading strategy, being more generous in assigning grades to tests and papers than in the final distribution of grades guarantees visits from aggrieved students. One way in which you get yourself into this position is by providing opportunities for students to omit questions on an exam, to throw out the lowest test grade, or to submit extra work for a higher grade.

Any of these procedures can have some educational justification, but you need to be able to convince administrators or colleagues that the pattern of grades you assign is appropriate for the achievement of your students.

GRADING ON THE CURVE (NORM-REFERENCED) VS. GRADING AGAINST A PRESET STANDARD (CRITERION-REFERENCED)

In the chapter "Assessing, Testing, and Evaluating," we talked about grading a test on the curve. Now we extend our discussion to final course grades. One of the persistent controversies in college teaching is whether to grade "on the curve" or against an absolute standard. These two positions are probably not as far apart as the argument would indicate. Even teachers who grade on the curve are influenced in setting their cutoff points between grades by their feelings about whether the class was a good or a poor one. Similarly, teachers who do not grade on the curve set their standards in line with what previous experience leads them to regard as reasonable accomplishment in the course. As I indicated earlier, I believe that grading on the curve is educationally dysfunctional. If possible, your grades should, both in the students' eyes and in actuality, be more nearly based on absolute standards than on relative standing in a particular class.

The use of an absolute standard becomes easier if you formulated your major and minor objectives and tested their achievement. Travers (1950b) proposed one set of absolute standards:

- A: All major and minor goals achieved.
- B: All major goals achieved; some minor ones not.
- C: All major goals achieved; many minor ones not.
- D: A few major goals achieved, but student is not prepared for advanced work.
- E or F: None of the major goals achieved.

Ideally I should be able to list my goals for the course and at the end of the course assess each goal in such a way that I could use such a criterion-based system. In fact, however, my tests, papers, journals, research studies, and other elements of the assessment of learning are seldom pure measures of a single goal. For example, my tests assess knowledge and understanding of the major concepts and facts as well as ability to apply and think with these concepts. To separate out each component would be almost impossible. Consequently, I assign points to each test, paper, and other assignment, and I give grades on the basis of the total percentage of points earned by the student over the term. This strategy at least avoids the detrimental effects of grading students' performances relative to one another and probably approximates the outcomes described by Travers.

There is a larger, more philosophical issue lurking behind the great norm-referenced versus criterion-referenced grading debate. The issue is what grades mean. Is the purpose of the grade to identify the "best" students in a group (norm referencing), or is it to indicate what each student has achieved (criterion referencing)? Both are legitimate positions and can be and are argued for vociferously. There are no pat answers to the choice. For example, there are many times when we have to allocate limited resources or awards to only the best of a group. In those instances it makes sense to use intragroup comparisons. But what if everyone in the group does poorly or does really well? Do we pick "the best of a bad lot" or abandon good people who in another group would be the top performers? What if the skills needed for the next class or on the job are so critical that failure to achieve an absolute level of competence could have dire consequences?

Should we pass only those who meet the standard? (Thinking of getting a shot from a nurse or doctor who was the top student in a class of klutzes, I'd much prefer that all medical personnel meet a set standard for shot giving, thank you!)

I've already indicated in the chapter "Assessing, Testing, and Evaluating" that I favor criterion-based grading, so I don't have a pat answer for this dilemma. The choice rests on factors such as these:

1. How valid is the instrument on which the grade is based? How reliable is it? It may not be appropriate to use criterion referencing if the measures are not accurate or fair.

2. How select is the group being evaluated? If the group is very homogeneous, norm referencing is inappropriate because there's not really a distribution of skills across the group.

3. How critical is the content being evaluated? If it's critical, I favor criterion referencing every time.

4. Does future work depend on this content? If it does, then criterion referencing will at least be sure that everyone who passes has the prerequisites for that future work.

There are many more things to consider, but the important point is to consider them rather than choosing blindly.

WHAT ABOUT THE STUDENT WHO WANTS A GRADE CHANGED?

If you keep students informed about their grades on tests, papers, and other graded work during the term, you will avoid most complaints. But there still may be some. My basic strategy is the same as that used in returning tests or papers: listen first and then go over the criteria used. Try to understand the student's reasoning. This may be a learning experience for both of you.

If students are worried about their grades in connection with their admission to a specialized school or because they are on probation, I may offer to write a letter to their advisor or other authorities describing their work in detail and pointing out any extenuating circumstances that may have influenced the grade. This may serve to cushion a refusal to change the grade.

In addition, of course, you may try to explain to the students the rationale of grades. Usually this doesn't seem to do much good. Both students and faculty sometimes confuse two possible criteria on which grades may be based. One is the relative amount of *progress* the student has made in achieving the goals of the course; the other is *achievement of the goals of the course* at the end of the term. In most classes, research has demonstrated a relatively low correlation between these two criteria. If you were to mark solely on progress, students who came into the course with the least background might still be the poorest students in the class at the end of the course yet get an A for their progress. Most employers, registrars, and professors interpret a grade in terms of the achievement of course goals; hence professors who grade solely on students' progress may send students into advanced courses or jobs for which they lack the requisite skills and knowledge.

Progress, however, is relevant to prediction. A student who has made a great deal of progress despite a poor background may do as well in an advanced course or job as someone with somewhat better performance at the end of the course who made relatively little progress. My own solution is to assign grades primarily for achievement of course goals (total performance), but when a student's total points or overall performance is close to the boundary between grades, I assign the higher grade if there has been much progress.

No matter how you grade, some student will be unhappy. Be sympathetic, but beware! If you begin changing grades, the jungle drums of the campus will soon spread the word. Be sure that you understand your institution's regulations with respect to grade changes. Check, too, on procedures that students may use to appeal capricious grading.

Don't finish reading this chapter with your own anxiety aroused by the dangers of grading. It is proper that good teachers should be humble as they see how great is the power they have over the happiness of their students by printing a simple A, B, C, or D. Nevertheless, one of the real satisfactions of teaching is giving a good grade to an ordinarily average student who has come to life in your course.

A List of Don'ts

These may look absurd, but they have all happened. Don't do them!

1. Keep students in the dark about what their grades are before the final examination. The shock of seeing an F as the final grade will so stun them that they'll be incapable of protest. Or, better yet, tell them they had A's all the way through the course and got an A on the final, but you're giving them B's because you have given too many A's.

2. Tell students that you really think they deserved a higher mark but you had to conform to department grading policies and had to grade them lower.

3. Tell students that their grades on the final exam were higher than their final grades in the course. (Of course they'll understand that the final examination is only one part of the total evaluation.)

4. Even though your school doesn't record pluses, tell students that their grades were D+, C+, or B+. They'll gladly accept the fact that the C−, B−, or A− was only a few points higher and will be proud that they did better than anyone else who got a D, C, or B.

5. Tell a student that grades are really very arbitrary, that you could have split the B's from the C's in many different places, and that grades are so unreliable that you really can't distinguish your top B student from your low A student. The student will appreciate the aesthetic value of your choice of a cutting point.

GRADES VS. LEARNING: SOME RELATED RESEARCH

A lot has been written about goal orientation and its effects on learning. Carol Dweck (1986) among others has discussed the finding that many learners seem to be pursuing goals that are focused on *appearing* competent rather than on actually learning anything. This is the phenomenon of goal orientation. Some students are pursuing mastery goals (they really want to learn and are what we might call non-grade-conscious); others are working primarily for a grade (called in this literature "performance oriented").

Although originally these orientations were thought to be related to some personality traits, more recent literature relates these orientations to the conditions of learning, to what rewards and punishments are in place for success. The researchers even assert that a single person can have both types of goals in the same situation but for different aspects of the task. All of us have had students whose only interest seemed to be in their grades. The research on this topic has shown that these students are usually very literal-minded, not willing to try anything new, and likely to stick to the familiar so they know they can succeed. Sometimes you run across a student who wants to learn no matter what it takes. The research literature shows that students like this are willing to risk mistakes, to interpret failures as something to learn from rather than avoid or hide. Obviously we'd all like to have the latter students rather than the former. The great thing is that we can influence which type of goals students will work toward in our classes: learning or grades. Ames (1992) and Maehr and Midgley (1991), all researchers in the area of motivation, have given some very good guidelines about how to turn students into learning oriented learners. Their recommendations* include the following:

1. Focus on meaningful activities that students can see are related to their own future. This helps them focus on becoming skillful rather than on simply earning a grade.

2. Make the learning interesting through the use of variety and novelty. The goal is to distract the students from focusing on grades by making the learning worthwhile in and of itself.

---

*These recommendations are adapted from a set created by Pintrich and Schunk (2002, pp. 238–239), who combined the findings of all these researchers into a coherent set.

3. Make the learning challenging but doable. Challenge is a big source of motivation for students, but only if there is hope of success.

4. Give learners some choice in what they are going to do. When you are able to choose, you are more likely to work toward something in which you have a vested interest.

5. Focus on individual improvement rather than on comparisons with others. This is probably the most important but most difficult thing to control. Students have a long history of comparing themselves to others with their grades.

6. Make evaluation private rather than public. This actually supports item 5. Private evaluations make it harder for students to focus on how they compare to others.

7. Recognize effort and progress. Try to get students' minds off getting the right answer as the only goal.

8. Help students see mistakes as opportunities for learning. This is best done through the way you react when a student makes a mistake. Do you criticize, or do you try to help students work through their thought processes? These two behaviors result in very different reactions by students.

9. Encourage collaborative learning. Students who are working together toward a common goal are less likely to be comparing themselves to others.

The research on student goal orientation indicates that if you can structure your class along these lines, students will be more comfortable in putting grades aside and focusing on learning because they can trust you to help them accomplish as much as they can. Perhaps that will help take the sting out of grades and as a result decrease their importance overall.

IN CONCLUSION

1. Grades are not just a communication between teacher and student; they are a decision-making tool for future professors, employers, admissions committees, and others.

2. Useful assessments are both valid and reliable.

3. Involving students in the planning of assessment methods can reduce grade anxiety.

4. Grading on the curve can have detrimental effects. Tread carefully.

5. Try to focus students on learning rather than on grades.

Supplementary Reading

What grades mean to faculty, parents, personnel directors, and students is described in O. Milton, H. R. Pollio, and J. Eison, *Making Sense of College Grades* (San Francisco: Jossey-Bass, 1986).

A fine vignette about the problem of assigning grades is Linc Fisch's "Students on the Line," in *The Chalk Dust Collection: Thoughts and Reflections on Teaching in Colleges and Universities* (Stillwater, OK: New Forums Press, 1996), pp. 132–134.

Barbara Davis describes a number of systems for determining grades and gives sensible advice in her chapter "Grading Practices," in *Tools for Teaching*, 2nd ed. (San Francisco: Jossey-Bass, 1993).

Another good resource is B. E. Walvoord and V. J. Anderson, *Effective Grading: A Tool for Learning and Assessment* (San Francisco: Jossey-Bass, 1998).

Read more about goal orientation and its relationship to grading practices in P. R. Pintrich and D. H. Schunk's *Motivation in Education: Theory, Research and Applications*, 2nd ed. (Upper Saddle River, NJ: Merrill/Prentice Hall, 2002).

With the change in instructional methods comes the need for a change in grading practices. Rebecca S. Anderson and Bruce W. Speck's "Changing the Way We Grade Student Performance: Classroom Assessment and the New Learning Paradigm," *New Directions for Teaching and Learning*, no. 74, July 1998, gives some good suggestions about new ways to grade student work.

Grading Students by Lawrence H. Cross (ERIC Digest, 10/1995). The ERIC Digests were very good summaries of research and practice provided by the ERIC Clearinghouses on different issues. The service has been discontinued, but some of the materials are still available. A site that provides access to the material is http://www.ericdigests.org.

Understanding
Students

12 Motivation in the College Classroom

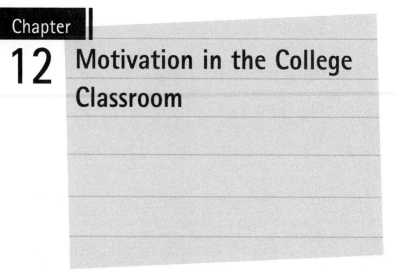

Few topics concern teachers at all levels as much as the motivation of students. We worry over the students who appear disengaged or who attend sporadically, and we often disparage those who appear to care only about grades. We delight in the students who share our passion for the subject matter, who are eager to ask intelligent questions, who view grades as informational feedback, and who not only prepare for class but seek us out to learn more. We marvel when we compare notes with a colleague and learn that these contrasting motivational profiles sometimes describe the same student—but in different courses, suggesting that motivation is something other than an abiding characteristic of an individual.

We all want students who are motivated to learn. These are the students who choose to attend class regularly, participate constructively, persist when learning is difficult, make the effort to prepare for class and to study effectively, who solicit help when they need it, and who translate all this into academic success. Knowing more

This chapter was written by Barbara K. Hofer of Middlebury College.

about how students are motivated and what you can do to structure a class that positively affects student motivation can make a significant difference in student engagement and learning. A classroom of motivated learners affects *our* motivation as well and can make teaching a more satisfying experience for the instructor.

MOTIVATIONAL THEORIES: AN OVERVIEW

Researchers typically consider three indices of motivation: choice, effort, and persistence; achievement is an outcome of these variables. Accordingly, students who are motivated to learn choose tasks that enhance their learning, work hard at those tasks, and persist in the face of difficulty in order to attain their goals. So it should be no surprise that motivation is important to consider if we want to enhance student learning. Why students vary in their motivation is a compelling question, and several theoretical frameworks help provide answers.

Some students may be driven by a high *need for achievement* (McClelland, Atkinson, Clark, & Lowell, 1953). Need for achievement may be characterized as an individual trait or disposition, and it is likely to be the outcome of early environments in which parents set high standards and valued achievement. In general, students differ from one another in the degree to which achievement for its own sake is meaningful to them, but this difference explains only one aspect of motivation, which is also considered to be contextual and malleable. A particular student may exhibit a striving for achievement on the soccer field but not in your class, or perhaps appears more motivated to achieve in some parts of your course than in others; and we have all known students who did not appear motivated at the start of a course but became deeply engaged. Moreover, classroom environment and instructional practices can foster certain types of motivation over others, as can the overall climate of an educational institution.

Autonomy and Self-Determination

Many psychologists posit that human beings have a fundamental need for autonomy and self-determination (Deci & Ryan, 2000).

In general, individuals want to be in charge of their own behavior, and they value a sense of control over their environment. We can enhance students' sense of control by offering meaningful opportunities for choice and by supporting their autonomy, which in turn enhances motivation. Quite often these opportunities for choice can be relatively simple things such as a choice of paper topics, test questions, due dates, or reading assignments, yet they go a long way toward acknowledging a student perspective.

Intrinsic and Extrinsic Motivation

Most educational researchers acknowledge that what matters is not only whether a student is motivated but also what type of motivation the student has. Instructors at the college level often complain of student preoccupation with grades, typified by the perpetual classroom question "Will that be on the test?" *Extrinsically* motivated students are likely to engage in the course for reasons of external rewards, such as grades, recognition, or the approval of others (notably instructors and parents). Individuals who are *intrinsically* motivated engage in an activity for the value of the activity itself, rather than for an external reward. Students who are intrinsically motivated are those who learn for the pleasure of learning and who have a sense of self-determination about their educational path. Intrinsic motivation has been shown to foster conceptual understanding, creativity, involvement, and a preference for challenge. Research on college student learning indicates that students with an intrinsic orientation are more likely to use cognitive strategies such as elaboration and organization, resulting in deeper processing of the material (Pintrich & Garcia, 1991).

Although the image of a classroom of intrinsically motivated learners might sound ideal, students are also driven by the desire for grades, approval, and other rewards, and understandably so. Intrinsic motivation and extrinsic motivation exist not on a single continuum but on two separate ones, and students may often have multiple goals for the same course. A student enrolled in a required course, for example, may be deeply interested in the material but may also see it as a step in her professional development and may desire to earn an A so that she will be likely to gain admission to graduate or professional school. Even students who initially appear only extrinsically motivated to take a course, perhaps viewing it merely as a requirement toward graduation, can become more intrinsically motivated if the instructor arouses their curiosity, provides appropriate levels of challenge, and offers them choices that enhance their control (Lepper & Hodell, 1989).

Although studies have indicated that external rewards may diminish intrinsic motivation by undermining self-determination (Ryan & Deci, 2000), recent research seems to support the judicious use of external rewards as a complement to other motivational approaches. Extrinsic rewards may be particularly useful when intrinsic motivation is lacking—and it is reasonable to assume that students are not always going to be intrinsically motivated to learn everything they are expected to learn during the college years. Students may also find extrinsic rewards to be productive during the early stages of learning in a new subject before they feel they can begin to master it and when the necessary nature of the tasks (such as memorizing vocabulary in a foreign language or learning a large number of terms in the sciences) may not be intrinsically interesting. There is also evidence from a study of intrinsic motivation in college undergraduates that the pursuit of grades may not be all bad (Covington, 1999), in that the attainment of grade goals can foster an increase in interest, at least among those whose goals are not driven by the desire to avoid failure.

Extrinsic rewards are most beneficial when they contain informative feedback and enable students to focus on improvement. Thus grades alone are less helpful than grades accompanied by narrative feedback that addresses specific directions for change. Taking the time to provide students with constructive feedback on papers as well as using class time when returning tests as an opportunity for further teaching can facilitate student engagement and motivation.

Expectancy-Value Theory

Students typically direct their behavior toward activities that they value and in which they have some expectancy of success

(Wigfield & Eccles, 2000). From this social cognitive perspective, motivation is viewed as the outcome of multiplying these two forces; if either one is absent, the resulting product is zero. Instructors can benefit by knowing that they need to foster both. Students need to feel that there is a reasonable possibility of success and that the work is of value. Thus even students who believe they can do well in an introductory course might not continue with the subject if they do not see that learning the material is worthwhile; likewise, even those who entered with professional ambitions dependent on the course may not persist in the field if they think that they cannot expect success. You may assume that students know the value of your field or of your particular course, but often this is not the case, and it may be worth the time to explain the relevance of what you are teaching. Fostering expectancy for success is equally important. Students benefit when instructors have high expectations for success and also provide the conditions for achieving it.

Mastery and Performance Goals

Motivated behavior is directed toward goals, and goals related to learning tend to reflect two broad types of purposes: mastery goals and performance goals (Ames, 1992). Students who adopt *mastery goals* are those whose primary desire is to understand and master the material. By contrast, students with *performance goals* are more likely to focus on their achievement relative to the performance of others. The classrooms we create may implicitly foster either type of goals, depending on grading practices, classroom climate, and other such factors, and here the faculty member can be particularly influential in affecting productive motivational beliefs.

In a class that is focused on mastery, instructors generally use criterion-referenced grading rather than normative (grading on a curve), foster a supportive climate where students can take intellectual risks, and provide opportunities for students to demonstrate improvement. A mastery orientation may be visible in classroom discussions when students ask genuine questions to which they do not already know the answers, driven by a desire to better understand the material, rather than to impress their peers and the instructor. Mistakes are viewed as an opportunity for learning.

In a class that is focused on performance, instructors often use normative grading practices (which imply that only a percentage of students are likely to succeed) and provide no opportunities for revising and improving written work. Student questions may be formulated to present the inquirer in the best light and to gain recognition and reward. In contrast to students with mastery goals, students who are ego-involved with their performance may compare grades with one another and take academic short-cuts, such as avoiding more effort than is necessary to acquire the desired grade or, as recent research indicates, engaging in academic dishonesty (Jordan, 2001).

Overall, mastery goals lead to more adaptive outcomes, for such students are likely to focus on learning, use effective cognitive strategies, and experience less performance-impeding anxiety (Pintrich, 2003). Students in highly competitive college classrooms, however—which are performance oriented by design—may find it adaptive to pursue a performance orientation (Harackiewicz et al., 1998). Faculty members thus may have considerable power in shaping goal approaches within their classrooms. Fostering a particular goal orientation begins with course design and syllabus construction, when we make choices about evaluation and grading practices and how we plan to communicate them to students. Goal orientation is also reflected in an array of teaching practices. Mastery orientation thrives in a classroom climate of warmth and acceptance where instructors support and value intellectual risk-taking and avoid comparisons among students.

Attribution Theory

When individuals need to seek an explanation for unexpected outcomes, they make attributions about the probable causes, and these attributions have motivational consequences (Weiner, 2001). In the academic sphere, this often arises when students fail to perform well on a test or get a grade that differs from what they had expected. Typical attributions are effort ("I didn't study hard enough"), ability ("I'm just not good at this subject"), or luck

("The test emphasized the material I actually studied!"). Attributions can be categorized along three dimensions: locus, stability, and responsibility, which refer respectively to whether the cause is internal or external, stable or unstable, and whether the cause is controllable or not. Students who explain their disappointments with internal, controllable attributions ("I know I didn't prepare adequately for the test") are likely to do better next time, because they believe they can affect the outcome. Students who attribute failure to stable, uncontrollable causes ("I will never understand statistics") are less likely to be motivated for improvement and understandably pessimistic about future outcomes.

Instructors can assist students in making adaptive attributions, particularly by helping them attribute failure to effort rather than ability, as well as by communicating their own positive attributions about students' capabilities to learn. When meeting with students to confer about low performance or an unexpected poor grade, you can help them reframe their thinking about the cause of their difficulties and help them gain a sense of control over future outcomes by helping them think diagnostically and rationally. Ask them to describe how they studied (or went about writing the paper), review the types of questions they missed or the most significant flaws in a paper, and help them know how to prepare or write more effectively in the future. In addition, referring students to a study skills center on your campus in order to improve their learning strategies can communicate that the problem is remediable and that they can take charge in addressing it.

Social Goals and Social Motivation

Students are obviously motivated by more than academic achievement. For example, they also have social goals that are operative in the classroom: they want to be socially responsible and to form social relationships with peers (Patrick et al., 1997; Wentzel & Wigfield, 1998). Although most studies of the relation between social goals and academic motivation and achievement have been conducted with younger adolescents, certainly no college instructor would doubt that social goals are operative in the college classroom. Enabling students to make new acquaintances in your classroom in conjunction with meeting academic goals may enhance student motivation to attend class and to participate in academic work. For example, a brief moment to discuss a question with a partner works well from a cognitive perspective because it fosters elaboration and retention and provides opportunities for clarification, but it also gives students an opportunity to get to know one another. Helping students form study groups prior to exams fosters preparation and also addresses social needs.

PUTTING MOTIVATION THEORY INTO PRACTICE

These principles can be used in many ways to structure classes that foster student motivation to learn. Here are a few suggestions:

1. When planning assignments, consider issues of choice and control. If you would like students to write two papers during the term, provide assignments during three time periods and let them choose which two to complete. This enables students to take charge of planning their work in the context of requirements from other courses and allows them to select issues of greatest interest. (This also has the advantage of spreading out the grading that you will need to do, an added bonus.) Similarly, provide a choice of topics for each assignment and consider a range of options that engage interest. Foster initiative by allowing students to propose alternative topics that meet the intent of the assignment.

2. Project your own motivation—for the subject matter and for the students. Take opportunities to describe your own intrinsic motivation for both research and teaching and your mastery orientation to learning. Too much of the literature on faculty "rewards" has focused on the extrinsic reinforcement for teaching, neglecting our own intrinsic motivation for academic work (as well as the intrinsic satisfaction of teaching). You are a powerful role model for your students as they develop their own passion and motivation for learning as well as for their future professions. Get to know your students as individuals with lives beyond your classroom.

3. Foster students' intrinsic motivation to attend class by being well prepared, making lectures and discussions interesting, varying the instructional format, inducing cognitive dissonance and stimulating thought, and adding interactive elements where appropriate. Students are more motivated to come to class when the learning experience clearly exceeds what can be copied from another's notes.

4. Foster mastery by encouraging students to revise their writing. Although it might not be reasonable for you to read drafts of every paper, you might do this for the first written assignment and then create peer review groups for additional papers. Or you can vary this process by responding to outlines for one paper and then reading drafts of opening paragraphs for the second. You can further foster mastery by uncoupling feedback and grading, so that early drafts receive written comments but no grades.

5. Adopt a criterion-referenced approach to grading rather than a normative one. Outline course requirements so that the point value for each assignment is clear from the beginning and students know what they need to do to succeed—and know that they can succeed without worrying about their standing relative to others in the course. This fosters a sense of control, creates a cooperative rather than a competitive climate, and appeals to both intrinsically and extrinsically motivated students.

6. Test frequently enough that students become accustomed to the format and have opportunities to learn from their mistakes; at the very least consider a similar format for the midterm and final. Allow students to justify and elaborate on their multiple-choice answers, which enhances control, and give partial or full credit for acceptable and reasonable justifications of alternative answers. Provide choices of essay questions to answer (e.g., "Answer five of the following six questions"). Consider providing one of the essay questions in advance, particularly one that might require more thoughtfulness and preparation.

7. When grading tests, create a frequency distribution of responses and consider dropping questions missed by a large number of students—and then reteach the material after you return the tests. This sense of shared responsibility for the

learning process heightens student awareness that you are committed more to their mastery of the material than to penalizing them for what they do not yet know.

8. Provide feedback that is constructive, noncontrolling (e.g., avoid words like "should"), and informative, thus enhancing student desire to improve and to continue to learn. View problems as something that can be addressed, not statements about an individual's worth.

9. In your supervision of teaching assistants, make the motivational implications of your instructional decisions explicit. I am indebted to Paul Pintrich, Bill McKeachie, and Scott Paris, who were extraordinary role models in their design of graduate seminars that fostered student motivation, but who also provided me with opportunities as a TA to understand the motivational structure of their undergraduate courses, which I have happily put into practice in my own teaching.

IN CONCLUSION

1. Recognize students' needs for self-determination and autonomy, and provide opportunities for choice and control.
2. Foster intrinsic motivation by arousing curiosity, providing challenge, and offering choices, and provide extrinsic rewards that contain informative feedback and focus on improvement.
3. Make the value of your courses explicit, and take time to help students understand why what they are learning matters. Teach with a sense of purpose.
4. Create conditions that enable students to expect to succeed.
5. Create a classroom environment that promotes a mastery orientation, focused on the development of understanding and mastery of material and skills, rather than on relative performance to others.
6. Foster adaptive attributions: help students value the application of effort and learning strategies, and communicate your belief in their capability.

7. Provide opportunities for students to meet social goals in ways that are compatible with academic goals—such as through constructive uses of group work and interactive lectures.

Supplementary Reading

Although the following works are directed more toward the motivational issues of K–12 schooling, the theories and many of the suggestions are useful to those who are interested in the issue of motivation in the college classroom.

■■ J. Brophy, *Motivating Students to Learn* (Mahwah, NJ: Erlbaum, 2004).

■■ P. R. Pintrich and D. H. Schunk, *Motivation in Education: Theory, Research, and Applications,* 2nd ed. (Upper Saddle River, NJ: Merrill/ Prentice Hall, 2002).

■■ D. J. Stipek, "Motivation and Instruction," in D. C. Berliner & R. J. Calfee (eds.), *Handbook of Educational Psychology.* (New York: Macmillan, 1996), pp. 85–113.

Teaching Culturally Diverse Students

Responding to the individual student may be the most important way to improve your instruction. Appreciating the unique needs and characteristics of your students sets an educational environment that will better enhance learning by each student.

Many dedicated teachers seek feedback in the classroom either by observing students' reactions or by directly soliciting comments: "How am I doing?" "Am I being clear?" "Is this too basic—do you want me to speed up?" For the most part, such feedback will enable you to accurately gauge the pace of student progress as well as the effectiveness of your approach to teaching. However, with a culturally diverse student, some basic differences in the student's and the teacher's backgrounds may cause feedback communications to fail. This chapter suggests some common cultural characteristics of some students coming from ethnic minority heritages. It highlights some illustrations of how a faculty person of a white, European American background—which I

This chapter was written by Richard M. Suinn of Colorado State University.

will refer to here as a "Western" background—may stumble in working with a student from a different cultural background.

Cultural advice can provide useful general guidelines, but those guidelines are not necessarily appropriate for all ethnic students. Keep in mind that just as "All Asians are not alike," all students within *any* ethnic group are not going to be alike—for two reasons. First, there are different nationalities and cultures even within an ethnic category. Among Asians, for instance, are Chinese, Japanese, Hmong, Korean, Vietnamese, and others (Maki & Kitano, 1989). Second, within each subgroup there may be individual differences. Varying levels of acculturation, or the fact of being raised in a nontraditional ethnic family, might invalidate the cultural premises in this chapter. For instance, to apply these suggestions to a highly acculturated, westernized ethnic student would be equivalent to employing a stereotype (Stuart, 2004).

Having offered this caution, I would like to offer some insights from a nonwhite cultural perspective. At a minimum I hope that instructors will gain a perspective that avoids the *deficit model,* the view that inadequate performance from an ethnic person automatically means the student is academically deficient, unmotivated, uninterested, or poorly prepared. Instead I will highlight new ways of understanding the communications of culturally diverse students, and I will suggest ways in which your own behavior can be adapted to enhance the students' learning environment.

CULTURE AND COMMUNICATION

Nonverbal Communication

Eye Contact.   You are giving a complicated lecture. One studen' in the audience looks at you and nods and smiles occasionally. Another student never looks at you. Instead, he continually looks down. He is not even taking notes. Which of these students is interested in the lecture? Which is listening attentively? Which is daydreaming?

The bread and butter of teaching is the act of communication as a two-way interactional process. You as the instructor usually communicate verbally. Students also communicate, not only when you ask them a question but also nonverbally, when they are listening. Nonverbal cues provide important feedback that influences your further communication.

What we observe, we interpret. And our interpretations influence our actions. Our meaning comes from our culture as Westerners. But to be culturally sensitive teachers, we must keep in mind that behaviors from different cultures have different meanings. The interpretation from a Western perspective of a student not making eye contact is that the student is inattentive, distracted, uninterested, or daydreaming. What is the consequence in your behavior? You might spend more lecture time going over the same point to arouse interest, or even talk louder (maybe the student will hear you the second time!). You might glare at the student or call him in for a conference. You might even dismiss this student as a lost cause.

Are you aware that for some ethnic groups, such as Asian Americans, African Americans, and Native Americans, looking away may be indicative of *careful attention* rather than inattention (Baruth & Manning, 1991; Garwick & Auger, 2000; Gudykunst, 1998)? It is estimated that white Americans make eye contact 80 percent of the time when listening and look away 50 percent of the time when speaking, and that African Americans make more eye contact when speaking and less when listening (Sue & Sue, 2003). In addition, among Asian cultures, staring at a person of higher status is considered rude (Sue & Sue, 2003). So eye contact or the lack thereof is not an automatic sign of attentiveness or inattention.

Nonparticipation. In the middle of your lecture, you want to know not only if the students are listening but whether they are understanding and grasping the topic. So you ask, "Have I been clear? Anyone have any questions . . . any questions at all?" And what happens is . . . nothing. No one offers a question. No one even raises a hand.

From a Western perspective, because no one speaks up and no hands are raised, you might be congratulating yourself: "All right! My presentation is clear. I must be a great teacher!" Consequently, you rapidly complete your discussion and move speedily on to the next topic. Are you aware that in some cultures it is very important to show great respect for elders or for persons with wisdom greater than one's own, and it may be considered disrespectful and insulting to raise a question? Doing so may imply that the elder (or instructor) is at fault for being unclear. Thus an ethnic student who fails to understand a teacher might blame himself or herself for being poorly prepared.

Questioning the speaker can also imply that the student is challenging the teacher. And such a challenge may be a taboo either because a challenge shows arrogance or because it disrupts harmony. Native Americans and Asian Americans value nonconfrontational interpersonal styles as a way to protect harmony in the interpersonal system. It would be unseemly to act otherwise (Lee, 1991; Swinomish Tribal Mental Health Project, 1991).

Other culturally based reasons for nonparticipation include the following:

- *A culturally ingrained value of humility.* Some cultures value modesty, not standing out in a crowd. A Japanese saying observes that "The nail that sticks out is hammered down." Another saying proclaims that Westerners place a premium "not only on knowing but on saying what you know," while the Asian "values knowledge but discourages verbalizing knowledge" (Nishida, 1996). Such a background might lead to what I call the "spotlight" effect. Like a deer that freezes in the glare of headlights, the ethnic student may freeze when the teacher focuses attention by directing a question to that student.

- *A history of distrusting the motives or intentions of others.* Students coming from experiences of racism, of being put down, and of experiencing the deficit model may feel especially vulnerable (Vontress & Epp, 1997). Out of caution, an African American student might be reluctant to volunteer or might be closemouthed when asked a question. "Am I being picked on to make me look dumb in front of the class?" a student might wonder. "Are you setting me up so you can criticize my answer and say I'm wrong again?"

What You Can Do. A better understanding of the actual meaning of student behaviors will put you in a better position to respond to nonverbal feedback. Your first step is to avoid the false assumption that lack of eye contact and nonparticipation mean lack of attention, disinterest, or boredom. Also avoid the false assumption that a lack of questions means that your presentation has been well understood.

Finding out what is going on will require gaining verbal participation from students at some point, if the nonverbal cues are not reliable indicators. This leads us to the topic of cultural aspects of oral communication.

Verbal Communication

Reluctant Speech. You stop your lecture to obtain feedback. You directly ask a student to tell you whether your lecture has been clear; or you ask whether the student has any questions; or you even ask the student to explain in his or her own words what you covered. The student gets up slowly, looks sheepish, shifts from foot to foot, keeps her head down as though she is carrying the weight of the world, and quietly offers a very brief reply . . . that leaves you wanting more. You are still in the dark about how much the student has understood your presentation.

If you were not feeling so sympathetic toward the tongue-tied student, you might feel mystified about what's going on and speculate that she is being evasive and uncooperative. But as you saw in the earlier examples, there are possible cultural explanations for the student's reluctance to verbalize much. Perhaps the student is being careful to remain respectful by not challenging or insulting the higher-status expert—you the teacher. Or perhaps the student feels the need to get away from the focus of the spotlight as quickly as possible through a brief answer. Or perhaps underlying distrust about your intentions prompts her cautiousness.

What You Can Do. How might an instructor overcome an ethnic student's reluctance to respond more extensively even to a direct prompt? There are various strategies an instructor could try yet still be sensitive to various cultural concerns.

- *Concern about insulting the teacher.* How you word your prompt can make a difference. "Is my explanation clear?" is a very difficult question for a respectful student. Instead restructure the situation so that the student's reply is collaborative rather than critical. For example, "By the way, you know I've covered this topic with so many classes that sometimes I forget how familiar this topic is to me and I leave out some important details, so you can help me . . ."

- *Concern about being in the spotlight.* Despite many years of experience as a lecturer and classroom teacher, at times I feel this discomfort, such as when I'm taking part in a discussion with a group of people I've just met. It is a feeling of embarrassment, of suddenly being aware that everyone is quiet, that all eyes and ears are focused not on the discussion leader but on me! All of my cultural sensitivities become stirred: avoid standing out, do not embarrass yourself, be modest and defer to others to take the lead, you can be seen but certainly not heard, avoid arrogance . . .

  One solution to discomfort from being in the spotlight is to shorten the exposure. Turn the spotlight off or away. Let the students know that you are going to ask a question but you want them to limit themselves to a brief reply because you want to quickly move to other students' replies to obtain a group viewpoint. This strategy shines the spotlight on any individual for only a brief moment. You might also add that students need not stand up when called on.

- *Concerns related to trust.* It takes time to build distrust and to establish trust. Individuals with difficult life experience sometimes learn to be very observant and to attribute meaning to the tone associated with statements, to the implied meaning of terms, to the signals of posture, or to other nonverbal behaviors. Often these serve as guides for survival, particularly in an unfamiliar environment. So how a teacher words a question, what tone or posture accompanies the query, and what an instructor says after the student replies—all offer information influencing trust/mistrust.

  When you ask a student to answer, could it seem as though you are issuing a challenge, or is it clear that you honestly want to know what the student has to say—no strings attached? To improve trust, carefully consider the wording of your questions, perhaps taking a bit more time to explain *why* you are asking ("So I know how to think up more examples that help make sense out of this messy topic"). Avoid abruptness not only in wording a question but in your comments following a response. Consider what you say after the student replies. Is your follow-up comment supportive, or is it a correction that implies that the student was wrong or that you didn't like the reply? A little bit of encouragement and a positive attitude will go a long way to building bridges.

Circularity vs. Linearity.   At your initial class meeting you decide to establish rapport by asking for a simple personal opinion: "Did you enjoy your vacation?"

You receive a fairly extensive response: "Well, like, you know, spent first day at home . . . My neighbor is getting another job soon. Some of us went to see *The Matrix* . . . then *Return of the King* . . . Got back yesterday . . . So, like, now I'm back with my roommate . . . Was interesting visit."

This roundabout, rambling reply might feel confusing rather than satisfying. The generic "interesting" conveys everything and nothing. But this response might represent an ethnic "circular" style of oral communication rather than a more "linear" Western one (Gudykunst, 1998). Western thought and language tend to proceed in a linear fashion. You ask a question; you expect a direct answer. "What did you have for breakfast?" "Bacon and eggs." "Where and when shall we have lunch?" "There's an excellent menu today in the student center. Let's meet there at 11:30." "How was the movie?" "Excellent! I liked the part about . . ." A linear reply to the question "Did you enjoy your vacation?" would ultimately communicate a yes or a no. Many details might be offered, but the basic question to be answered is "Did you or didn't you?"

A teacher with a Western background who hears a student's roundabout reply may think, "The student is being evasive and is avoiding my straightforward question. Is there a reason? Maybe I'm not trusted, or maybe the student had a bad experience during vacation and doesn't want to talk about it. Maybe the student did something that was shameful, maybe even criminal . . . This student rebuffs my overtures to be sociable. He is rejecting my attempts to reach out. Maybe the student just has low social skills." The teacher may be unaware of a number of cultural issues giving rise to circular communication (Gudykunst et al., 1996; Huang, 1994; Okun, Fried, & Okun, 1999; White & Parham, 1990):

- The student's reply may reflect a cultural tradition deriving from a preliterate period in which knowledge was passed on orally, storytelling was the medium for education, and lengthy tales or proverbs were used to convey information. The student begins in an indirect fashion well suited for imbedding a moral, a message, or the main answer. In this student's culture, grasping the overall theme of the "story" is more important than the meaning to be found in specific words, and general conversation may precede any serious interaction. Such seemingly superficial chatting or small talk develops a comfort level and establishes rapport (Ruiz & Padilla, 1977).

- A circular response might be another way of maintaining a respectful attitude toward the teacher-authority-expert. Carefully phrased replies avoid the impression that a student is so presumptuous as to offer advice, instruct the instructor, or even tell the teacher something the teacher does not know.

- A level of defensiveness may prompt the circular reply, as it keeps the student from being personally evaluated. Circularity may enable the student to avoid committing to a firm statement or being pinned down, but not because the student has anything to hide.

What You Can Do. Here again you can take the initiative in setting the stage for improved responsiveness from the student. Keep in mind that some of the behaviors of a culturally diverse student come from a long tradition or repeated socialization. His or her way of behaving is thus neither conscious nor intentional but rather habitual or even traditional. Thus it may require a dedicated teacher to get the best from the student.

Patience, of course, is essential. Control your own need for a quick, precise, linear response. Permit the serpentine narrative to unwind at its own speed. Listen carefully for the overtones and the hidden theme.

Beware of phrasing questions that can put the student on the spot. Develop your own version of nonlinearity (Block, 1981;

Sanchez & Atkinson, 1983). Instead of "Tell me how *you* would solve this problem?" consider asking "What might be at least one approach to dealing with this problem?" or "Suppose someone you know is facing this problem, how do you think that person would start attacking it?" or "What have you seen others do?"

MOTIVATION AND STRESS

"Why don't these students perform like they should?" "They just don't respond to encouragement like other students. Obviously, they don't care!" "I can't seem to get through to them. I know they can do better—after all, they made it this far."

Such concerns about inadequate student performance might be explained by two contributing cultural factors: differences in motivation across cultures and cultural stressors. Increasing a student's performance toward his or her potential might be enhanced through culturally appropriate incentives or through reduction of interference from certain stressors.

Cultural Differences in Motivation

There is a fundamental difference between Western and certain ethnic motivational orientations. The former emphasizes an individualistic orientation, the latter a collectivistic orientation.

Westerners tend to be spurred by goals such as individuation, independence, self-development, self-reliance—"being the best *you* can be," experiencing the satisfaction of personal achievement. Other cultures tend toward collectivism, perhaps tracing back to the era of tribes but now focused on the family unit. Within ethnic cultures goals are group goals, achievement honors the family, and personal failure is agonizing because it reflects negatively on the family (Avila & Avila, 1995; Fuligni et al., 1999; Garrett & Garrett, 1994; Gudykunst & Matsumoto, 1996). Thus appeals based on individual recognition and accomplishment might fail to motivate an ethnic student, but putting the focus on family values might be more successful.

"Family" Defined.   For various ethnic cultures, *family* means more than the nuclear family or even blood relatives. For some

Hispanics, there are terms for a type of family member, *compadrazo* or *compadre/commadre,* referring to godparents who function as family (Arredondo, 1991; Ruiz, 1995). For African Americans, family roles may be assumed not only by grandparents but even by individuals outside the household, ranging from neighbors to ministers (McAdoo, 1999).

Collectivism and Family Goals.   Calling upon family ties can be an effective approach to use with a student who requires motivational inspiration (Trusty & Harris, 1999). One underachieving Hispanic undergraduate improved his study habits when faced with the question "If you drop out, what do you think your younger brother will do with his life?" This was a more telling argument than the entreaty "You are throwing away your life unless you shape up!"—an individualistic appeal.

With family support, an ethnic student achieves great strength and feels a powerful desire to work toward goals (Vasquez, 1982). Once when discussing weekend plans, I tentatively asked a Latina graduate student if her new boyfriend's visit might distract her from attending to her assignments for the week. Her immediate and no-nonsense reply was "No way! My parents and I agreed: I have only one reason for being here . . . my studies come first. Dropping out is not an option. My boyfriend understands that!"

Family-based values can also influence what defines success (Sage, 1991). For some older-generation parents, success by their adult offspring might be finding a secure job with a steady income. Thus the value of an education is measured in those terms.

For a Native American, the collectivistic orientation may involve tribal members, who not only influence values but also offer support. Solving problems "the Indian Way" refers to seeking the wisdom of tribal members, often by returning to the reservation (Attneave, 1982; J. McDonald, personal communication, 2004; P. Thurman, personal communication, 2004).

Cultural Stressors

Keep in mind that underachievement might be caused by impaired performance due to the stressors that the culturally diverse student faces. There are several possible unique stressor conditions: the imposter syndrome, the first-generation condition, and acculturation anxiety.

The Imposter Syndrome. This is the stress caused by self-doubt as the ethnic student is aware of his or her minority status. Surrounded by majority white students who are from different sociocultural backgrounds and whose English may seem more fluent or without accent, culturally diverse students cannot help but feel different. In fact, they are at least outwardly different in physical appearance.

The imposter syndrome raises questions such as "Do I really belong?" and "Perhaps it is a mistake for me to be here" (McDavis et al., 1995). Despite all facts to the contrary, it is often difficult to avoid such a feeling. During my own career, I was successful in being elected to several important committees and boards of the American Psychological Association. Though basically confident about my abilities, I still felt discomfort at my first meeting—the vague, gnawing sense that everyone else was familiar with one another and I was the only outsider. I finally ended my unease by reminding myself that the election procedure meant that three new people were always reporting in, so there had to be two others who were in the same situation as I. Further, instead of acting as though I didn't belong, I immediately introduced myself to the others and took my place at the table as they did.

On occasion the imposter issue is worsened by accusations from others. I recall a disgruntled, unsuccessful white applicant claiming that an ethnic student took "his" place only because of affirmative action. I also remember the experience of an African American who tested at the gifted level on standardized tests normed on white children, entered a school for the gifted, and continuously confronted other students' belief that she couldn't possibly have qualified on her own.

The First-Generation Condition. "First-generation students" are the first in their families to attend school at a level higher than the level their parents attained, such as being the first admitted to college. As such they sometimes experience stress caused by lack of familiarity with the new environment—that is, university life. Entering college may be like entering a foreign country as the student faces decisions about what courses to take, misses home and family, struggles to engage with a world consisting mainly of the white majority, and tries to make sense of unfamiliar customs. The student's normal familial support system might be unable to help. Because no family members ever experienced the demands of that level of schooling, they might not understand the new pressures and strains the student is experiencing and may offer no sympathy (Fallon, 1997; Komada, 2002; Shields, 2002).

For students from an ethnic minority cultural environment, certain concepts or procedures may be difficult to grasp. Here are some that are associated with college enrollment:

- *Being on time.* Some Native Americans believe that taking the time to do things well is more important than doing things quickly but poorly. Thus the requirement to complete an assignment "on time" might initially seem to be a troublesome demand because the student is inclined to focus more on doing a complete, high-quality job (Herring, 1997; LaFromboise et al., 1994; Sutton & Broken Nose, 1996).

- *Having grades based on class participation.* The requirement to speak out in class can come into conflict with the issues I cited earlier regarding reluctance to participate.

- *Being graded on the curve.* For ethnic groups that value cooperation and collectivism (working for the common good), the idea behind being graded on a curve may be hard to comprehend, because it involves an individual competing against everyone else for an individual goal.

- *Seeking help from strangers.* Well-meaning friends might warn an ethnic student, "You're going to be at a disadvantage. Remember, no one there will want to help you succeed. So you must be tough, be prepared to deal with things yourself" (Thompson et al., 2004). Under these conditions, especially if the student feels any shyness with strangers for other reasons, it takes a strong student to ask for help from a teacher, to locate a tutor, or to identify a mentor.

Acculturation Anxiety.   I remember a Native American student whose tribal elders were hesitant about her leaving the reservation.

There was fear that she would find life more attractive elsewhere and that her core identity would be diminished through acculturation into the mainstream society.

Each of the four American ethnic minority groups has a term for group members who lose their ethnic identity through exposure to the Western culture. These are persons who have exchanged their cultural roots for an identification with the white culture. They are variously called "apples" (red on the outside, white on the inside), "bananas" (yellow on the outside, white on the inside), "coconuts" (brown on the outside, white on the inside), or "Oreos" (black on the outside, white on the inside) (LaFromboise et al., 1998; Lone-Knapp, 2000; Maruyama, 1982; Tatum, 1993; Willie, 1975). What does this imply? It represents another source of stress for the ethnic person, who now is not only coping with academic tasks and possibly adapting to a new environment, but also facing the risk of denigration from his or her own cultural group.

Educational experiences often aim at enhancing personal growth and development of new knowledge, conducting inquiry, and opening new vistas into the world at large. As personal knowledge and skill levels expand, so does the sense of self. One's identity may be solidified, expanded, or even dramatically challenged. If changes in identity were without social consequences, the transformation would be easy. However, for an ethnic student with strong traditional ties, serious discomfort can be an outcome instead. "Have I betrayed my own group?" "What am I? I am neither fish nor fowl now! And is the person I've become better or worse that what I was before?" "Am I now such a hybrid that I am an outcast from both the majority and the minority cultures?" It is easy to imagine how such a significant conflict can disrupt attention to academic studies and even raise thoughts of dropping out.

A teacher can enhance an ethnic student's learning and performance in a number of ways. The most important first step is to continue to be aware that low achievement may be due not to low ability but to motivational issues or interference from stressors. If motivation or stress is involved, then the following approaches might be useful.

Increasing Motivation

What You Can Do.   Remember that individualistic goals may not be as meaningful as collectivistic, family-oriented goals. In discussing goal setting with an ethnic student, find out how he or she came to be in school to begin with, and gain a sense of the familial values and expectations. Identify the strength of these familial ties, and determine if there are special family or community members whose opinions carry more weight. Try to differentiate between personal goals and familial goals, and be prepared to deal with conflicts between familial goals and expectations and newly developing personal desires—the student whose family expects to have "my son, the doctor" or "my daughter, the lawyer" while the student is now dreaming about being a philosophy major.

Consider inviting significant family or community persons to work with the underachieving student. This could even include problem solving.

James, an African American student, lived at home while entering his freshman year of college. As the oldest child, and now the first to attend college, James was looked up to by his family and friends. Six siblings of all ages also lived in the apartment, and the environment was lovingly described as "organized chaos." A grandmother also shared a room and helped in daily cleaning, cooking, and baby-sitting the youngest children while James's mother worked. Although James had been able to keep up with high school work, he soon discovered that in college the extra reading assignments and pressure from deadlines added new demands. Because the college campus was two hours away by public transportation, studying at home after school was the only option. However, the lack of privacy, the constant flow of activity, and the noise level were problems.

A teacher thinking along majority-culture lines would inquire about a move to a dormitory, which would provide quiet hours, have student tutors, enable being integrated into "college life," and promote individuation. However, that solution would overlook certain cultural values, beyond the issue of expenses. James would be forced to leave his major support system, his responsibility as the "man in the family," and a cultural environment that is an integral part of his current psychological development. His presence in the community and church is an inspiration to the neighborhood, a role that embarrasses him but that he recognizes as coming with the turf.

As a culturally sensitive alternative, one of James's professors, who saw the need for James to have study time, paid a visit to James's home for a conference with the entire family present. It quickly became apparent that everyone understood the problem and wanted James to be successful in his schooling. The family discussed options such as studying at a neighbor's place, but this would have been an imposition on others so it was temporarily tabled. Eventually, one solution was suggested by the grandmother. In a firm voice, she declared that henceforth all children would participate in a nightly "Help James Time." One room would be vacated and would be "James's college room" for two hours. During this period, James's grandmother, with the help of James's next oldest sibling, would arrange for each of the children activities such as story time, TV time, and outside play-time to ensure quiet. The children would rotate through the activities. A chart was posted on which James would note his study progress after each evening's session. As James completed assignments and received grades, he would share these with the family before the next "Help James Time." With this solution, James and his family eventually were able to celebrate his bachelor's degree.

Dealing with Stressors

What You Can Do.   Understanding the source of a student's stress may assist you in offering appropriate help. The imposter syndrome may have its roots in a history of racism, or it may be an issue of simply entering a new and unfamiliar setting, including new social/interpersonal settings. A mentor who believes in the student, who knows how to teach the student to use his or her strengths, and who recognizes the value of taking one step at a time can be a major positive influence.

The specter of presumption of special privilege through affirmative action may contribute to the imposter syndrome. There is no one action that would erase such feelings. However, the following argument might be valuable: If detractors interpret affirmative action as special privilege, it is equally important for them to recognize that "white privilege" also exists but goes unexamined. Because of white privilege a white person in the majority community never needs to be aware of how she or he is viewed by others when entering a store, restaurant, or class, or when boarding a bus, waving down a taxi, or standing up to express an opinion (Lawrence, 1998; Sue, 2003; Sue, 2004). Being accepted as belonging, never standing out, never worrying about below-the-surface evaluations, and not having your comfort level displaced in interactions are privileges. An ethnic person is continuously faced with looking different or sounding different and is unable to alter those facts. This person will adapt, of course, but will never fully acquire white privilege.

It is entirely legitimate for schools, businesses, and industries to set criteria for selection of personnel based on goals. Athletes are recruited; Merit Scholars are enticed into undergraduate programs; students with special life experiences, those who show evidence of high motivation and excellent work habits, or even those representing geographic diversity are offered admission to limited graduate programs. These represent opportunities, not guarantees of eventual success. To those of your students who might be vulnerable to the imposter syndrome I would quickly point out, "The door has been opened for you to enter. Whether you deserve to remain will be up to you to prove."

The first-generation condition is not unique to ethnic students, although a history of poverty, poorer educational preparation, or recent immigration might lead to more ethnic students being the first generation in college. Because these students lack information about the school environment that is likely to be a key factor in their success, any steps your school can take to increase their familiarity will help.

One useful solution is precollege visitation days, at which incoming students and their families can become familiar with the campus and procedures. Putting together a survival guide for culturally diverse students or distributing a section from an existing guidebook might provide an excellent resource. (APA has one for graduate students; see El-Ghoroury et al., 1999). Informative roundtable discussions sponsored by ethnic student services offices can be important, as well as a way of matching upper-division ethnic student mentors with new students.

Many students experience homesickness when they leave their homes to attend school elsewhere. The homesickness compounds the difficulty of sudden geographic displacement, separation from a support system of family and friends, being confronted with the unfamiliar college culture, and the stress of the immediate need to adapt to numerous new challenges.

Most students manage their initial homesickness, develop a new sense of freedom and self-confidence, and become comfortable with their new identities. As I mentioned previously, the ethnic student may also adapt quickly and discover the new "self" that emerges but may also be confronted with the identity conflict this brings. For some white students, brief visits home or even phone calls to family serve as a connection that smooths the transition. Similarly, for a culturally diverse student, making this connection can provide a refreshing energy to move forward. For some Native Americans, a powerful spiritual renewal comes from even a brief return to the reservation or tribal environment.

TAILORING YOUR TEACHING METHODS

In addition to being sensitive to cultural differences among students, you can make your classroom more welcoming and effective for ethnic minority students by your choice of teaching approaches.

Match Learning Styles

Try this exercise: Close your eyes. Using your imagination, develop a clear image in your mind of a very large plane flying over you. You are looking up at it. It's very close as it passes over you. Now stop and describe this airplane to a friend in as much detail as you can.

How did the airplane appear in your imagination? As you described it, what details were salient? Visual ("The plane had a long body with windows")? Auditory ("It roared past me")? Tactile ("I felt the wind rush by")? Have some friends repeat this exercise, and compare the results. Notice the individual differences in the way a particular sense dominates in each person.

The exercise shows you that different people experience imagery in different ways. Likewise, different students—both majority and minority—may have different learning styles. Some learn best through audio input, the typical lecture format. Some learn best through visual input, seeing the material in writing. Others learn best when they themselves write down the material or when they verbalize the material aloud in their own words. It is as if their internal wiring is different, like a VCR that has video input but also audio input. Entering an audio signal into the video input will fail and vice versa. Using the correct input produces clear results. By matching your teaching method to a student's learning style, you enhance that student's ability to grasp the information and to remember the material.

Be Concrete

Being concrete is another generic principle of teaching, but there are different ways of achieving this. You can use a demonstration/exercise, use metaphors, or use examples from students' personal life experiences. Understanding the cultural experiences of an ethnic student can help bring academic material to life in concrete ways. It is also useful to discuss the practical applications of classroom topics to satisfy the pragmatic interests of ethnic students (Reyes et al., 1999).

Enhance Performance Measurement

Earlier, I described some differences between Western and ethnic groups' concepts of time. Native Americans, we saw, value doing a task well rather than doing it quickly. Therefore, timed tests might be a poor indicator of their actual knowledge. Also the commonly used timed multiple-choice examinations rely extensively on memory skills. Useful alternatives would be take-home examinations that can measure analytic skills, creativity, and comprehension without the side issue of time.

One interesting approach is testing based on the triarchic theory of intelligence, which postulates three elements: analytic, creative, and practical. Sternberg (2003) and others (Grigorenko et al., 2002) found that measures of analytic/creative/practical knowledge predict college grade point averages more accurately than the traditional SAT verbal/math test scores, and that students taught with attention to these educational priorities perform better on traditional course examinations.

Choose Appropriate Nonverbal Behaviors

Just as the way a student speaks, listens, and stands creates an impression on you, the impact you have on your students results not only from your explicit verbal communications but also from certain nonverbal behaviors:

- *Conversational pauses.* Typically, a Westerner pauses one second before continuing to speak; therefore any longer pause signals that the speaker has finished. Native Americans pause a bit longer, four to five seconds, before completing a sentence or thought (Baruth & Manning, 1991). Failing to understand the meaning of this longer pause, a Westerner may begin to talk, thereby interrupting the conversation and communicating rudeness, disinterest or disrespect, or a dominating attitude.

- *Personal space.* Different cultural groups interact normally at different distances. The space each group prefers is known as personal space. If one person steps into another's personal space, this is experienced as an intrusion. Similarly, if too much distance is maintained during an interaction, this may be interpreted as aloofness. African Americans and Hispanics tend to stand closer to someone they are conversing with than do white Americans, and Asians tend to prefer greater distances (Jensen, 1985; Mindess, 1999). An understanding of personal-space norms is important for maintaining good interpersonal communications.

Be Accessible

Cultures can be viewed as either horizontal or vertical in their interpersonal structure. A vertical, hierarchical culture establishes high- to low-status roles associated with titles of address

(Feldman & Rosenthal, 1990; Gudykunst, 1998; Lee, 1999). The structure of Western cultures tends to be horizontal—everyone is on the same level. A student raised in a vertical culture may prefer to address you by your title and may be puzzled by your insistence on a more familiar mode of address. For students from a horizontal culture, the invitation to "Just call me Bill" or the remark "I'm Janet" confirms the desired message of equality. You can use a title to allow ethnic minority students to be comfortable, while still conveying by other actions your openness and accessibility.

A recent research study found that the dropout rate among Hispanic high school students was nearly three times higher than that of white students and two times higher than that of African American students (Fry, 2003). A study of factors associated with persistence in school identified teachers as the second most influential factor for Hispanics (Fuentes et al., 2003). Most interesting is how these teachers were described. They were seen as encouraging their students to succeed, having high expectations, and believing that their students could meet these expectations. Rather than being viewed as aloof or regimented, the teachers were described as "playful." In essence, they were seen as approachable, interested in their students, and inclined to find potential rather than deficits in the young people they teach.

It is important for you to take the initiative to be accessible and to convey genuine interest and to be welcoming in words and in behaviors. A simple greeting helps, in the classroom, in the hallways, and outside of school.

- Take time to chat. At first you may need to take the lead, avoiding the spotlight effect.
- Have consistent office hours, but encourage drop-in visits.
- Be encouraging and positive, supportive and solution oriented, and by all means listen.
- Work on problems and engage in positive reappraisal: "Persistence will work." "A step at a time is progress." "You can make it."
- Help students identify their strengths, find ways to cope and succeed, and leverage those strengths.

IN CONCLUSION

Pay attention to your students in order to learn about them and truly understand them. Be a caring person, a welcoming person, an interested person. Identify and build on strengths, and encourage them!

Supplementary Reading

▥ C. Bennett, *Comprehensive Multicultural Education: Theory and Practice,* 5th ed. (Boston: Allyn and Bacon, 2003).

▥ J. Clayton, *One Classroom, Many Worlds: Teaching and Learning in the Cross-Cultural Classroom* (Portsmouth, NH: Heinemann, 2003).

▥ P. Gorski, *Multicultural Education and the Internet: Intersections and Integrations* (New York: McGraw-Hill, 2001).

▥ W. Gudykunst, *Bridging Differences,* 3rd ed. (Thousand Oaks, CA: Sage, 1998).

▥ S. Lassiter, *Cultures of Color in America: A Guide to Family, Religions and Health* (Westport, CT: Greenwood Press, 1998).

▥ D. W. Sue, and D. Sue, *Counseling the Culturally Diverse: Theory and Practice,* 4th ed. (New York: Wiley, 2003).

14 Dealing with Student Problems and Problem Students (There's Almost Always at Least One!)

There isn't a teacher in the world who hasn't had to deal with student problems and problem students. Somehow it is reassuring to know that one is not alone in having a particular problem and that the problem is probably not due solely to one's inadequacy as a teacher. This chapter discusses some common problems that teachers at all levels face, and it suggests some strategies to try. I organized the chapter into three categories of problems, ranging from those directly related to the academic side of teaching to those stemming from the fact that we're working with humans engaged in the process of learning.

First, a word of general advice: It is human nature to perceive the problem as the student; but before focusing on changing the student's behavior, take a few moments to look at what you are doing that might be related to the student's behavior. Interpersonal problems involve at least two people.

INTELLECTUAL/ACADEMIC PROBLEMS

The problems examined in this section arise from things that affect how people learn and what happens when they have difficulties doing it.

Aggressive, Challenging Students

There are many reasons why one or more students might be inclined to be aggressive and always challenging what is said in class. The most desirable reason might be that they are interested in the topic and have a lot of prior experience or knowledge to contribute, even if that prior knowledge is actually wrong. Or they might be challenging you because there is genuine disagreement about a particular topic and they're flexing their academic mental muscles against someone (you) who is very knowledgeable in the area. You usually can tell the difference between these students and those who convey, both verbally and nonverbally, hostility toward you and the whole enterprise. Sometimes the attitude is not so much hostility as a challenge to your authority.

Faced with the first of these two alternatives, you should be pleased! Consider this a "teachable moment." By disagreeing or always adding their two cents, these students are giving you an opportunity to accomplish two very important teaching tasks. The first is to delve more deeply into the logic behind the facts and principles that sometimes pass for content in students' minds. Rather than blindly accepting everything you say, students should be trying to reconcile new information with their preconceptions. They should be asking for greater depth, more examples, more explanation. These challenging students are out in the forefront of that student push. The second teaching task that these students are allowing you to do is to model what it means to be a critical thinker in the face of challenges to your ideas. In what passes for political dissent these days, students seldom have the opportunity to see two individuals actually discuss together rather than talk past one another about a controversial point. When students challenge you, you can demonstrate scholarly debate, including careful listening, thoughtful reflection, respectful disagreement, and reasonable compromise where appropriate.

Later in this chapter, in the section on emotional problems, I discuss students who are hostile or angry about everything.

Students Who Want the Truth and Students Who Believe that Everything Is Relative

You just gave a superb lecture comparing two competing theories. A student comes up after class and says, "That was a great lecture, but which theory is right?"

All too many students feel that the teacher's task is to tell them the facts and larger truths and the student's task is to listen to the truth, learn it, and be able to give it back on exams. This conception seemed to William Perry of Harvard University to be particularly common among first-year students.

Perry (1981) suggested that individual differences in student responses to teaching may be conceptualized in terms of stages of cognitive development. Students at the earliest stages have a dualistic view of knowledge. They think that things are either true or false, right or wrong. They believe that the teacher knows the truth, and that the student's job is to learn the truth. Students in the middle stages have learned that authorities differ. They accept the idea that there seems to be no settled truth, and that everyone has a right to his or her own opinions. This stage is succeeded by the recognition that some opinions and generalizations are better supported than others, and that the student's task is to learn the criteria needed for evaluating the validity of assertions in different subject matter fields. Students in the final stages are ready to commit to values, beliefs, and goals, and to make decisions and act on their values, despite their lack of complete certainty.

Sixteen years after Perry's article was published, Barbara Hofer (1997) found that dualists were rare at the University of Michigan, where she conducted her research. Rather, college students were more likely to believe that multiple perspectives are equally valid. Students like those studied by Hofer might be the very students who challenge everything that you or any other authority says. How should you respond to the challenge?

Unfortunately we sometimes play into the hands of these students with the kinds of teaching and testing we do. If all we ever do is deliver information in a clean and neat format, if all we ever use are tests where there really is only one right answer, why should the students believe differently? Or if we don't critique ideas or give them feedback when their points are less than coherent or correct, why should they bother to think more deeply? Here is one instance where we have to shoulder some of the blame for the problem.

Perry and Hofer would agree that teachers need to help students understand how knowledge is arrived at in their own disciplines, what counts as evidence, and how to read critically and evaluate knowledge claims. For development in such epistemological beliefs, students need to debate and discuss issues in which competing ideas are challenged and defended; they need to write journals and papers that are responded to by the teacher or by peers. Most important of all, they need good models of how to think about the quandaries that are a constant in higher-level thinking and learning. As I said in the previous section, they need to see how you deal with contradictions and inconsistencies, how you solve problems when you don't have enough information, how you cope with the frustration of never being sure of the "right" answer.

Students Who Are Underprepared for the Course or Struggling

Sometimes students come into our classes without the appropriate background. Perhaps they didn't have the right prerequisites, or they didn't apply themselves diligently in their previous courses. It really doesn't do you or them any good to rail against their previous efforts or castigate them for imagined or real previous failures. That was then; this is now. What are you going to do with them now?

If the gaps in students' background can be remedied by pointing students toward supplemental or remedial resources, that's a good first step. It puts the students back in charge of their own learning, which is a good source of motivation, especially for those who are behind through no fault of their own. These days a lot of remediation can be made available electronically. Resources available on the Internet might be helpful for basic skill development, such as math skills or writing skills. Alternatively you can prepare tutorials on the most commonly occurring deficits that you've seen in students in prior semesters. Your department may even want to create a common web site that helps students with key skills needed in all courses in the discipline or that provides definitions, examples, and activities to practice the basics of the discipline. You also can put materials or alternative textbooks on reserve in the library for those students who may not have had the appropriate content in prerequisite courses. Include sample questions or old exams to help them decide whether they understand well enough to go on.

You know the value of working with someone else when you're having problems. So if you can, encourage students to form study groups to work together throughout the semester, not just when there's a test coming. The hardest part of this for students is finding a time to get together. A colleague of mine who teaches a mega-course (500 students) set up an electronic matchmaker that allows students to indicate when they're free to study and in which part of town they live. Such a system helps struggling students find others who are not struggling and are willing to help them as a way of earning extra credit (all instructor certified, of course). Another way of providing help is to set up a class discussion board where students can post questions and get responses from other students or from the instructor. If enough students ask the same question, you might create a FAQs page with the best solution to the problem and make it available to everyone, including future classes.

Some students are having trouble that requires additional help. I give quizzes and tests early in the term to help students identify and diagnose their difficulties. I invite those who do not do as well as they hoped to come in to see me. When they do, I ask them for their own assessment of the cause of their difficulty and try to offer helpful suggestions. Usually I also ask some specific questions:

"Have you missed any classes?"

"Do you study the assignments before class?"

"How do you study?" (This may lead to a discussion of learning strategies; see the chapter "Active Learning.")

"What kind of notes do you take?" (I usually ask to see them.)

"Do you discuss the class with classmates—asking questions, explaining, summarizing?"

Sometimes I refer students to other resources on campus, such as a student learning support center. I keep learning-center handouts in my office to provide to students who might need a nudge. If they see how helpful such folks can be, they might be more inclined to go and see them. I check with students later to see whether they tried any of my suggestions, and I watch later performance to see if further help is needed.

Individualized Teaching and Mentoring

Here I want to discuss interactions dealing with larger issues of students' educational and personal development. The potentially most fruitful and most appropriate interpretation of educational counseling is the one least often defined explicitly and most neglected. Even in classes of 40 to 60 students, it is difficult for the learning process to include the meeting of a maturing and a mature intellect. Too frequently students must be content to listen to lectures and pursue readings aimed at some abstract notion of "the student."

In out-of-class interactions with students or as a student's academic advisor, you can supplement course-related learning with personalized learning that facilitates individuals' adjustment to college. This is particularly necessary for first-year students, to whom new intellectual spheres are being opened, usually at a time when they have taken a big step away from their families and communities. This is likely to be a time when a great many new assumptions and new ways of dealing with important ideas need to be digested. Educational counselors, because they have no commitment to covering a specific subject matter, can provide students with an opportunity to digest and integrate the intellectual experiences they have been having. Far from being a chore to be assigned to the least successful faculty member, such a demanding responsibility is best undertaken by persons of broad intellectual interests and foundations who, at the same time, have strong pedagogical commitments.

This time, when students are making big strides toward greater independence from family and are trying to seek out models who can represent innovations of the adult role to which they aspire, is a time when there should be opportunities for close relationships with faculty members. The very characteristics of the large university throw obstacles in the way of such an experience. Educational counseling is one of the important means for achieving it. It seems probable that the most effective pattern for doing this would be for counselors to plan small-group meetings with the students assigned to them for counseling to provide an opportunity for the groups of new students coming from different parts of the state and country to exchange with each other and with a person of some intellectual maturity the impacts of their initial university experiences. A number of colleges and universities group first-year students into interest groups or seminars that meet regularly during the first term to help establish both academic and social support systems. We often think first of mentoring graduate students, but mentoring is a role you will have for students at all levels.

The problems of the older student entering college are in some ways similar to those of young first-year students despite the obvious differences in life experience. Both young and older students often feel some anxiety about their ability to carry out academic work successfully. The older students, however, may have even greater concerns about their ability to adapt to the college environment and to form helpful relationships with peers (most of whom are much younger than they and experiencing quite different social and recreational lives).

CLASS MANAGEMENT PROBLEMS

Sometimes the problems we have with students are really issues of policy or rule keeping. It's amazing how much effort some students will put into trying to get around the rules. The best way to save yourself time and effort in this area is to have fair policies that you state clearly in a readily available source (such as the syllabus or the class web site) and that you enforce consistently (but not inflexibly). Let's consider some specifics.

Attention Seekers and Students Who Dominate Discussions

In *The College Classroom,* Dick Mann (1970) and his graduate students describe eight clusters of students, one of which is "attention seekers." Attention seekers talk whether or not they have anything to say; they joke, show off, compliment the teacher or other students—they continually try to be noticed (Mann et al., 1970).

At the beginning of the term, when I am trying to get discussions started, I am grateful for the attention seekers. They help keep the discussion going. But as the class develops, both the other students and I tend to be disturbed by the students who talk too much and interfere with other students' chances to talk. What do I do then?

Usually I start by suggesting that I want to get everyone's ideas—that each student has a unique perspective and that it is important that we bring as many perspectives and ideas as possible to bear on the subject under discussion. If hands are raised to participate, I call first on those who haven't talked recently.

If the problem persists, I may suggest to the class that some people seem to participate much more than others and ask the whole class for suggestions about what might be done to give all students a chance to participate. Alternatively, I might ask two or three students to act as "process observers" for a day, to report at the end of the class or at the beginning of the next class on their observations of how the discussion went, what problems they noticed, and what suggestions they have. (I might even ask an attention seeker to be a process observer.) Another possibility is to audiotape or videotape a class and play back one or more portions at the next class period for student reactions.

If all else fails, I ask an attention seeker to see me outside class, and I mention that I'm concerned about the class discussions, and that although I appreciate the student's involvement, it would be helpful if he or she would hold back some of his or her comments until everyone else has been heard. Sometimes I phrase it like this: "The other students are starting to depend on you to do all the work, so let's make them speak up more." Put this way, the comment makes the two of us accomplices in furthering the education of the rest of the class!

Some dominant students are knowledgeable, fluent, and eager to contribute relevant information, contribute real insights, and solve problems. We prize such students; yet we must recognize the potential danger that other students will withdraw, feeling no need to participate because the dominant student is so brilliant or articulate that their own ideas and questions will seem weak and inadequate. Here subgrouping may help, with the stipulation that each student must present his or her question, idea, or reaction to the task of the group before beginning a general discussion.

In his newsletter *The University Teacher* Harry Stanton (1992), consultant on higher education at the University of Tasmania, suggests that each student be given three matches or markers at the beginning of a class. Each time students speak, they must put down one of their markers, and when their markers are gone, their contributions are over for the day. Perhaps subgroups could pool their markers or one group could borrow or bargain for an extra marker for a really good idea that needs to be presented.

Inattentive Students

Periodically I have a class in which two or three students in the back of the room carry on their own conversations. This is annoying not only to me but to students sitting near them. What to do?

First consider whether the problem is with the material rather than with the students. Is the lecture material too difficult? Too easy? Does the topic of discussion arouse anxiety? If the answer to these questions is "no" and the behavior persists despite changes in topic or level of difficulty, what next?

My first attempt is typically to break the class into buzz groups assigned to work on some problem or to come up with a hypothesis, and to move around the room to see how the groups are progressing, making sure that I get to the group including the disruptive students to see that they are working on the group task. Usually this works, and sometimes this gets the students reengaged in the class for the rest of the class period.

But suppose that in the next class period the same problem recurs? This time I might have the class write minute papers and call on one of the inattentive students to report what he or she has written, or alternatively I might call on someone seated near the inattentive group, centering activity toward that part of the classroom.

Another possibility is to announce that, because research evidence indicates that students who sit in front get better grades (you can explain why seeing an instructor's face and mouth improves attention and understanding), you have a policy of rotating seats periodically and next week you will expect those sitting in the back row to move to the front row and all other students to move back one row.

If all else fails, I might have a general class feedback discussion on what factors facilitated and what factors might have interfered with learning in the class thus far in the term. Alternatively, I might ask one or more of the students to see me outside of class to ask them about their feelings about the class and to express my concern about not being able to teach in a way that captures their attention.

Students Who Come to Class Unprepared

There are often good reasons why students come to class unprepared, but some students are chronically unprepared for no apparent reason. What can we do? Here, I'll elaborate on the suggestions made in the chapters "Facilitating Discussion" and "How to Make Lectures More Effective."

In my introductory course I try to communicate from the beginning that I expect students to read the assignments before class. I announce that on the second day of class I will give a brief quiz based on the first lecture or discussion and the assignment for the second day of class. I give the quiz and then ask students to correct their own papers, indicating that this quiz had two purposes: to start the habit of reading the assignment before class, and to give them an idea of whether or not they were getting the main points of the assignment. I give a second quiz a week later and a longer one three weeks later. By this point I hope that my students have established a routine for keeping up with their assignments.

Such a procedure assumes that students know what is expected of them. One of the most common causes of underpreparation is that students don't really know what is expected. Often instructors say something like "You might want to look at the next chapter of the book before the next class," or they state that the next lecture will be on topic X but don't indicate that this is also the topic of the next reading. Giving students some questions to think about as they study the next assignment can help, as will announcement of an activity in the next class that depends on the assignment. One of the advantages of a well-written syllabus is that it communicates your expectations. You also need to communicate expectations by frequent use of such phrases as "As your assignment for today demonstrated" or questions such as "What does X (the textbook author) say about . . . ?" or "What evidence from the assigned readings would support (or not support) your position?"

The Flatterer, Disciple, Con Man (or Woman)

If you are new or somewhat insecure, it is tempting to respond positively to anyone who tells you that you are the best teacher he or she has ever had, or who is impressed with the depth of your knowledge and wants to learn more about your special research interests. Actually, you do not need to be new or insecure; we all relish compliments and interest in our work. Often such interest is genuine and can be genuinely enriching for both you and the student, but there are students for whom such an approach is a conscious strategy for winning better grades or getting exceptions from deadlines for papers or other requirements.

The real danger presented by such students is that you will begin to mistrust all students and lose compassion for students who really need an extension of time or some other indication of flexibility. I would rather be conned a couple of times than to turn off by cold rigidity a student who is in real need. Thus my advice is to start with an assumption of honesty; nonetheless, in general, don't change the rules of the game unless you are willing to change them for everyone or unless you are convinced that there are reasonable grounds for a special exception.

Students with Excuses

I believe that it is better to be taken in by a fraudulent excuse than to be seen as unfair in response to a legitimate excuse. Nonetheless, one doesn't want to be seen as so gullible that students come to rely on excuses rather than doing their assignments. Caron and colleagues (1992) studied excuse making and in their sample found that about two-thirds of their students admitted having made at least one false excuse while in college. From these students' reports it appears that fraudulent excuses were about as frequent as legitimate ones. In most cases the excuse was used to gain more time for an assignment.

The Caron group's data do not give many clues about what one can do to prevent or detect false excuses. If the problem is one of time, you might build in checks on the progress of a paper or other assignment to reduce the tendency to put off work until the last minute. You could, for example, have students turn in an outline or bibliography sometime before a paper is due.

Sometimes I announce in the syllabus that there will be a graded series of penalties depending on how late a paper is, indicating that this tactic is to make up for the advantage that late students gain from having extra time to look up more sources, get comments and feedback from other students, and so forth. An alternative that I have not used, which might be more advantageous psychologically, is to offer a bonus for papers turned in early. It might also be wise to say in your syllabus that you want to be flexible about deadlines, you recognize that unforeseen events may prevent students from being able to meet a deadline, but in making exceptions you will require evidence supporting the request for an extension.

I think the best defense against excuses is a good offense—that is, a well-designed course that takes into consideration the fact that lives don't always run as planned. For example, in the chapter "The ABC's of Assigning Grades" I talked about the wisdom of allowing students to drop the lowest grade on a test, no questions asked. This avoids having to judge the truthfulness of student excuses for missed exams. Students rarely are willing to make excuses for continued absences without a good way to back up their claims. The message is therefore to think about ways to provide legitimate opportunities in case students mess up. If they don't, all the better for them. If they do, you've avoided having to act as judge and jury.

EMOTIONAL PROBLEMS

Now we come to the type of problems that are the most difficult for every teacher to face: those that involve emotional issues rather than the cold academic or managerial issues I've been describing up to this point.

Angry Students

Earlier I described students who are aggressive in challenging ideas. Some students, however, are actually angry at you or your authority and express their anger verbally or nonverbally in or out of class. What should you do with them?

Probably the most common strategy is to try to ignore them. This strategy often succeeds in avoiding a public confrontation and disruption of the class. But it may not result in better motivation and learning for the student, and sometimes it's hard to keep from reacting hostilely in return. Hostility would be a mistake because it doesn't provide a good model of how to deal with emotional situations, either for that student or for the rest of the class.

I try to forestall situations like this by becoming better acquainted with the student. If I have had students turn in minute papers or journals, I read the angry student's writings especially carefully to try to understand what the problem is. I may ask the student to come in to see me and discuss the paper. During this meeting I ask how the student feels about the course, what things he enjoys, what topics might be interesting to him. (I use the masculine pronoun deliberately because these students are most likely to be males, although I have also encountered hostile female students.) Sometimes you will feel in such a conversation that you have to drag each word from the student, yet the student will accept your invitation to come in for another discussion. Sometimes you may need to invite a small group of students to meet with you (including the hostile student) in order to make the situation less threatening for the hostile student who hides fear with aggressiveness. Whatever your strategy, it seems to me important to let the student know that you recognize him as an individual, that you are committed to his learning, and that you are willing to listen and respond as constructively as possible.

What about overt hostility—the student who attacks your point of view during a lecture or class discussion, or the student who feels that your poor teaching or unfair grading caused his or her poor performance on a test? First of all, *listen* carefully and respectfully. Remember that nothing is more frustrating than to be interrupted before your argument or complaint has been heard. Next, acknowledge that there is a possibility that the student may be right or at least that there is some logic or evidence on his or her side. Recognize the student's feelings. Then you have at least two or three alternatives:

1. State your position as calmly and rationally as you can, recognizing that not everyone will agree. If the issue is one of substance, ask the class what evidence might be obtained to resolve or clarify the issue. Don't rely on your own authority or power to put the student down or to make it a win-lose situation. If the issue is one of judgment about grading, explain why you asked the question, what sort of thinking you were hoping to assess, and how students who did well went about answering the question. Acknowledge that your judgment may not be perfect, but point out that you have the responsibility to make the best judgment you can, and you have done so.

2. Present the issue to the class: "How do the rest of you feel about this?" This tactic has the obvious danger that either you or the aggressor may find no support and feel alienated from the class, but more often than not it will bring the issues and arguments for both sides into the open and be a useful experience in thinking for everyone. This might be a place to use the two-column method described in the chapter "Facilitating Discussion," listing on the board, without comments, the arguments on both sides.

3. Admit that you may have been wrong, and say that you will take time to reconsider and report back at the next class session. If the student really does have a good point, this will gain

you respect and a reputation for fairness. If the student's argument was groundless, you may gain the reputation of being easy to influence and have an increasing crowd of students asking for changes in their grades.

What about the student who comes into your office all charged up to attack your grading of what was clearly a very good exam paper? Again, the first step is to listen. Get the student to state his or her rationale. As suggested in the chapter "Assessing, Testing, and Evaluating," you may gain some time to think if you previously announced that students who have questions or complaints about grading of their tests should bring a written explanation to your office of their point of view and the rationale for their request for a higher grade.

But, once again, don't be so defensive about your grading that you fail to make an adjustment if the student has a valid point. I have on rare occasions offered to ask another faculty member to read the paper or examination to get an independent judgment.

If you don't feel that the student has a valid point and your explanation is not convincing, you may simply have to say that, although the student may be right, you have to assign the grades in terms of what seem to you the appropriate criteria. If you have been clear about the rubric you use in grading, both before giving the assignment or test and when you returned the papers, grievances should be rare.

Discouraged, Ready-to-Give-Up Students

Often after the first few weeks you will spot some students who seem depressed and discouraged. Sometimes they come to class late or miss class; often their papers are constricted and lack any sense of enthusiasm or creativity. In my introductory classes, some students begin with great enthusiasm and energy and a few weeks later seem to have lost their energy. Interestingly, we spot the same phenomenon in our proseminar for beginning Ph.D. students. In both cases the transition to a new level of education brings demands greater than those students have experienced in the past. Often their familiar supports from family and friends are no longer available; they begin to doubt their own ability to achieve their goals.

There is a magic elixir for this problem that research has demonstrated to be surprisingly effective. This is to bring in students from the previous year who describe their experiences of frustration and self-doubt during their first year and report that they surmounted them and survived. The theory explaining why this works basically states that the task is to convince the discouraged students that their problems need not be attributed to a lack of ability that cannot be changed but rather is a temporary problem. By developing more effective strategies, investing more effort, or simply becoming less worried, students are likely to achieve better results (Van Overwalle et al., 1989; Wilson & Linville, 1982).

Students with Emotional Reactions to Sensitive Topics

In almost every discipline there are some topics that will arouse strong feelings in some of your students. In a psychology class the sensitive topic might be "group differences in intelligence"; in biology it might be "evolution" or "animal experimentation"; in sociology it might be "the role of birth control and abortion in population policy." Often we are hesitant to open such topics up to discussion. But if the topic is relevant and important, it is probably wise to acknowledge the sensitivity of the topic, admit that it may be hard for some members of the class to feel free to contribute their ideas, and explain why the topic is relevant to the goals of the course. Comparing alternative approaches, perhaps by using the two-column method described in the chapter "Facilitating Discussion," may help students see the complexity of the issue.

When you are conducting the discussion of a sensitive topic, it is important to stress that each student should listen to other students with respect and try to understand their positions. You might ask a student to put into his or her own words what other students have said. If feelings are running high, you might cool things off by asking students to write for a couple of minutes on one thing they have learned or one point that needs to be considered. Having students write a short essay advocating a position opposed to their own is an effective way to open their minds.

Be sure to allocate enough time for adequate discussion. Students may be reluctant to participate until they feel that it is safe to speak honestly. Such fear of rejection also suggests that you schedule controversial topics late enough in the term to ensure that students have developed trust in you and in their classmates.

Dealing with Psychological Problems

At some point you will suspect that a student needs psychological counseling. Some of the signs are belligerence, moodiness, excessive worry, suspiciousness, helplessness, emotional outbursts, or depression. Sometimes you will spot symptoms of drug or alcohol abuse. How do you get the student to the help needed?

The first step may be to get the student to talk to you. Usually you can do so by asking the student to come in, perhaps to discuss a paper or test. Typically the student is aware that things aren't going well, and you can simply ask, "How are things going?" or "What do you think is the reason for your problems?" Listen rather than intervening. After listening and expressing concern, you might then say, "What do you think you can do?" One alternative, probably the best, is to seek professional help. (Take the time to find out what is available before you need it.) If the student agrees that professional assistance might be a good idea, I've found that it helps to pick up the phone and say, "I'll call to see when they can see you." In fact, most counseling agencies will at least carry out an initial interview with any student who walks in. But the sense of commitment involved when a faculty member has called seems to make students more likely to follow through than if they simply agree that they'll go in. Even if the student does not immediately get professional help, your concern and support will be helpful, and awareness of the availability of professional help may be valuable later.

Potential Suicides

The increasing concern with suicide risk among college students prompts a few words on the early recognition of the kinds of depressed states that accompany such risks. If you were to notice a sudden falling off of a particular student's faithfulness in attending class, you might want to inquire further, especially if you noted signs of neglect of personal grooming and hygiene, lethargy, and any marked weight changes, or a facial expression atypically gloomy or distressed. Your interest in the student should include concern with any other changes he or she has been experiencing, including major separations or losses and mood states. You should listen for talk of death or references to suicide or to getting one's personal and legal affairs in order.

Your major concern should not be to reach an accurate assessment of suicide risk. A student manifesting any of these characteristics is surely troubled and should be urged to seek whatever professional counseling is available. Once I walked with a student to the clinic to be sure that he got there. On a couple of occasions when a student seemed unlikely to seek help, I asked the university health service to call the student in.

IN CONCLUSION

1. Don't duck controversy. Use it as an opportunity to model good problem-solving skills and critical thinking.
2. *Listen*, and get students to listen to one another.
3. Keep your cool. You don't have to respond immediately.
4. Paraphrase, question, and summarize, but delay suggesting alternatives until you are confident that you understand.
5. Talk to colleagues. Ask what they would do.
6. Remember that your problem students are human beings who have problems and need your sympathy and help—no matter how much you would like to strangle them.

Supplementary Reading

An excellent review of the attributional retraining research dealing with motivation of discouraged students is R. P. Perry, F. J. Hechter, V. H. Menec, and L. Weinberg, *A Review of Attributional Motivation and Performance in College Students from an Attributional Retraining Perspective*, Occasional Papers in Higher Education, Centre for Higher Education

Research and Development, University of Manitoba, Winnipeg, Manitoba, Canada R3T 2N2.

Two interesting compilations of research and thinking on problems in classrooms are Steven M. Richardson's "Promoting Civility: A Teaching Challenge," no. 77, March 1999, and John Braxton and Alan Bayer's "Faculty and Student Classroom Improprieties: Creating a Civil Environment on Campus," no. 100, 2005, in the *New Directions for Teaching and Learning* series.

In A. W. Chickering, *The New American College* (San Francisco: Jossey-Bass, 1988), the chapter by Jane Shipton and Elizabeth Steltenpohl provides a useful perspective on the broad issues faced by academic advisors. The typical schedule of 15 minutes per advisee is clearly insufficient for planning an academic program in relationship to lifelong goals.

In *Tools for Teaching* (San Francisco: Jossey-Bass, 1993), Barbara Davis offers good practical advice in Chapter 44, "Holding Office Hours," and Chapter 45, "Academic Advising and Monitoring Undergraduates."

Also see Alice G. Reinarz and Eric R. White (eds.), "Teaching Through Academic Advising: A Faculty Perspective," *New Directions for Teaching and Learning,* no. 62, 1995.

Chapter 7, "One-on-One Interactions with Students," in Anne Curzan and Lisa Damour's book *First Day to Final Grade* (Ann Arbor: University of Michigan Press, 2000), provides good advice on counseling students who have a variety of problems.

A helpful source is Mary Deane Sorcinelli's chapter "Dealing with Troublesome Behaviors in the Classroom," in K. W. Prichard and R. M. Sawyer (eds.), *Handbook of College Teaching: Theory and Applications* (Westport, CT: Greenwood, 1994).

Barbara Hofer and Paul Pintrich review the various theories about epistemological beliefs and learning in "The Development of Epistemological Theories: Beliefs About Knowledge and Knowing and Their Relation to Learning," *Review of Educational Research,* 1997, *67,* 88–140.

Adding to Your Repertoire of Skills and Strategies for Facilitating Active Learning

15 How to Enhance Learning by Using High-Stakes and Low-Stakes Writing

A LITTLE THEORY: HIGH STAKES AND LOW STAKES

Because writing is usually learned in school (where it is nearly always graded or evaluated), and because writing tends to be used for more serious occasions than speaking ("Are you prepared to put that in writing?"), most people feel writing is an inherently high-stakes activity. But writing is not *inherently* a high-stakes activity. Indeed writing is better than speaking for *low-stakes* language use—for exploration and experimentation—because writing can so easily be kept private or revised entirely before being shared with any reader. Of course we need to set high-stakes writing assignments in our college courses, but that writing will result in more learning for students and go better for us if we also exploit the resources of low-stakes writing.

Why high-stakes essay assignments? If we ask students to articulate in clear writing what they are studying, we help ensure

This chapter was written by Peter Elbow and Mary Deane Sorcinelli of the University of Massachusetts Amherst.

that they will in fact learn it. And without these carefully written papers, we can't give trustworthy final course grades—grades that reflect whether students actually understand what we want them to understand. For if students take only short-answer tests or machine-graded exams, they may often *appear* to have learned what we are teaching but they don't really understand. Besides, writing is a central skill for higher education, and students will not get good at it if they write only for English or writing teachers.

And low-stakes writing? The goal here is not so much to produce excellent pieces of writing as to increase how much students think about, understand, and learn what we are teaching. Low-stakes writing is usually more informal and tends to be ungraded or graded informally. You could describe the goal this way: we can throw away the low-stakes writing itself yet keep the neural changes it produced—the new insights and understandings.

LOW-STAKES WRITING

Kinds

The most obvious approach is to ask for comfortable, casual, exploratory writing about a question or topic, and urge students not to struggle too much to try to get the thoughts exactly right or the writing good. Make it clear that the writing is for exploring and processing course material—and will not be graded. Low-stakes writing also increases fluency and confidence in writing and helps with creativity and risk taking. These benefits are maximized if you sometimes ask for low-stakes writing in the mode of *freewriting*—asking students to write without stopping, putting down whatever comes to mind even if it doesn't make sense.

Occasions

In Class. Many teachers ask for five or ten minutes of low-stakes writing at the start of class—to help students bring to mind the homework reading they did or to explore their thoughts about the topic for today. Or in the middle of class, to ponder a particular question—especially if discussion goes dead. Or at the end of class, to summarize and reflect on what was discussed. Students will have more to say in discussion, and be less afraid to speak up, if you start with a few minutes of freewriting. Two minutes of quick freewriting after you ask a question will make all the difference in the world.

Out of Class.   Many teachers ask students to keep a journal of informal reflections on the readings and classes. The goal is to get students to process what they are studying and connect it with the rest of their experiences, thoughts, and feelings. Because students sometimes experience journal writing as an artificial exercise and resist it as useless "busy work" (especially if no one else reads it), many teachers have found it helpful to ask for weekly *letters* that students write to a classmate or friend—letters in which they reflect on the course material (see Young, 1997). Many teachers now ask students to post letters or journal entries on a class web site—or even simply have students e-mail entries to everyone using a group e-mail address.

Benefits of Low-Stakes Writing

Some faculty members are nervous about inviting students to write loosely and informally. Therefore, we feel it's important to spell out a number of the benefits:

- Low-stakes writing helps students involve themselves actively in the ideas or subject matter of a course. More minds are usually at work on the course material during low-stakes writing than during a lecture or discussion.

- Low-stakes writing helps students find their own language for the issues of the course; they stumble into their own analogies and metaphors for academic concepts. Theorists like to say that learning a discipline means learning its "discourse," but students don't really know a field unless they can write and talk about the concepts in their *own* informal and personal language. Successful parroting of the textbook language can mask a lack of understanding.

- Frequent low-stakes writing improves high-stakes writing. Students will already be warmed up and fluent before they write something we have to respond to. And when they turn in an impenetrable high-stakes essay (and who hasn't tangled up one's prose through extensive revising?), we don't have to panic. We can just say, "Come on. You can revise this some more into the clear lively voice I've already seen you using."

- Low-stakes writing helps us understand how student minds are working: how students are understanding the course material, feeling about it, and reacting to our teaching.

- There's a special application of low-stakes writing to math and science courses—and to problem solving in general: ask students to write the story of the paths their minds followed as they tried to solve a problem. These paths are interestingly idiosyncratic but instructive, and it's useful to have students share these meta-cognitive stories.

- Regular low-stakes assignments make students keep up with the assigned reading every week. This means that they contribute more and get more from discussions and lectures. Quizzes can do this job, but they invite an adversarial climate and don't bring the other benefits described here—including pleasure.

- And don't forget: low-stakes writing takes little of our time and expertise. We can require it but not grade it. We can read it but not comment on it. In many cases we don't even need to read it. Yet we can get students to read each other's informal pieces—and (if we want) discuss them.

Handling Low-Stakes Writing

There are still plenty of students who are not used to low-stakes writing—or who don't expect it in a "hard-nosed disciplinary course." They assume that all writing must, by definition, be read and graded by the teacher. So it's important to explain frankly to them why you are requiring it but not grading it. You can point out that much writing in the world gets no response at all. If it helps, you can say, "This is graded. You get 100 if you do it; 0 if you don't."

Most teachers set up a combination of different audience relationships for low-stakes writing: some is private and some is shared; some of the shared writing goes to the teacher and some only to fellow students. Sometimes students are invited to *discuss* the information and thinking they've heard in each other's low-stakes writing—but not give feedback on the quality of the writing. If you have time to give a nongraded response to some of their low-stakes writing, that can be useful, but most of us need to save most or all of our responding time for their high-stakes writing (but see the section later in the chapter on "middle-stakes writing.")

Some teachers read journals; others treat them as private and just check that students have written. Some teachers ask students to trade journals weekly with a peer—perhaps for a response, perhaps not. Letters are natural for sharing, and lots of learning comes from this sharing.

When we start a new class with students who don't trust us and who might resist writing anything we don't see, it can be useful to collect the low-stakes pieces for a few sessions. We stress that we won't grade it or comment on it—just check quickly to make sure they explored the topic. By doing this, we help them learn that nongraded or even private writing is not wasted busy work but, in fact, leads to new insights and better enjoyment of writing. Many students have never had the experience of writing with their *full attention* on their thoughts. Their writing has always been for a teacher and a grade, and therefore much of their attention has leaked away in worries about mistakes in language, spelling, or wording. After a few sessions, we can stop collecting it and let these pieces be entirely private—or just for sharing with classmates.

When students are asked to do low-stakes writing in class, it's important for the *teacher* to write too. This helps students see it as a process that adult professionals and academics use for developing their thinking.

Will low-stakes writing promote carelessness in writing? This is only a problem if teachers fail to emphasize the sharp distinction between low-stakes and high-stakes writing—and fail to insist on high standards for the latter.

HIGH-STAKES WRITING

We cannot give fair course grades unless we get a valid sense of how much students have learned and understood. For this, we need high-stakes writing. The stakes are high because the writing needs to be good and bears directly on the course grade. Most readers of this book are not trained as teachers of writing and understandably feel some apprehension about high-stakes writing—especially about devising topics, commenting, and grading. The stakes are high for teachers as well as students.

If your campus has a writing center, it can be enormously helpful with high-stakes writing. Tutors there can help students at *all stages* of the writing process: understanding the assignment; brainstorming ideas; and giving feedback on either early or late drafts. A writing center is specifically not a "copy editing service," but tutors can *help* students learn to copy edit better.

Topics and Assignments

When devising assignments, it's worth doing some strategic thinking about goals. For the obvious goal of *learning*, it's worth trying to choose topics that will lead to writing that interests the writer and will interest the reader. Thus, try to avoid assignments that ask for mere regurgitation of material from textbooks or lectures.

How about the goal that students should learn to write in the academic forms used by professionals in your field? In a graduate course, this will certainly be a goal; perhaps for majors. But a huge proportion of students in undergraduate courses in, say, physics or sociology or literature will never have to write like professional or academic physicists, sociologists, or literary critics. Perhaps you feel nevertheless that they should have *experience* with those forms and genres, even though they won't actually need to use them later. You get to decide. For ourselves, we lean away from using academic genres and styles for nonmajors.

Our goal, instead, is what is sometimes called "essayist literacy": the ability to organize an essay around a main point, to support that point with clear reasoning, and to illustrate it with apt examples. In truth, a fully academic genre with all the rituals of academic style can sometimes *get in the way of* clear exposition and argument. We think students often learn more from explaining course concepts or making an argument to readers *outside the field*. Note how much publication there is of high-quality science writing for general readers.

It is important, we believe, to insist on "standard" edited written English for final drafts. This demand does not preclude interesting or adventuresome alternative genres that don't focus so much on "essayist" structure. Here are some examples: papers written as a dialogue between two figures you are studying—or other interested parties; personal papers that start from a disagreement that came up in class discussion—that analyze the issue or take a side; fiction-like accounts of something you are studying (e.g., a certain person you are studying in a certain era—or the behavior and "motivation" of a certain molecule or enzyme); collaborative papers. Letters to the editor constitute a high-stakes assignment that is *short* but still takes careful thought; papers in the form of a collage are much easier to write but still ask for good thinking and writing (see Elbow, 2000a, 2000b).

Criteria for Evaluation

"Professor, what are you actually looking for in this paper?" Students can annoy us when they ask this question, but it's a valid one and deserves an answer—ideally on the handout stating the assignment. (Teachers often regret it when they don't put assignments on a handout.) We cannot fairly comment or grade if we're not conscious of criteria our judgments derive from. How much will we care about factors like these: correct understanding of course concepts; application of concepts to new instances; creative original insights; organization; clarity of sentences and good word choice; examples; spelling and grammar? Certain assignments will suggest other criteria (documentation; correct format for lab reports; voice). There are no right answers here—good professionals differ in their priorities—but we don't think it's fair to keep your priorities hidden.

Multiple Papers and Multiple Drafts

There are two powerful ways to improve student writing and student learning: multiple papers and multiple drafts.

We can assign several short papers rather than just one large one (usually a term paper—a "terminal paper"). Students tend to delay writing term papers, they tend to pad them, and they seldom learn from our comments since the course is over before they pick up their papers—*if* they pick them up. On short papers we can give briefer responses.

We can require students to write drafts of high-stakes papers, then get feedback, and then revise. Are we suggesting doubling our responding duties? No. Our time is limited so we need to think strategically: how can we use our response time to do the most good? (Consider the guiding principle for our better-paid medical colleagues: "At least do no harm.") If we devote most of our available time to feedback on a *draft,* we have a better chance of getting students to improve their writing *and* their understanding of course concepts. By responding to drafts, we are coaching improvement—instead of just writing autopsies on finished products that will never be improved. If we respond only to final drafts, students have a hard time using our feedback to improve future papers (especially if there are no other papers in the course—or if the next paper is quite different). But, of course, if we spend our limited time commenting on a draft, then we need to *save* time on final versions: we can save the time we need by reading through them once and grading them with a grid. Here's a simple generic grid:

	Unsatisfactory	OK	Excellent
Content, thinking, mastery of ideas	☐	☐	☐
Organization, structure, guidance for readers	☐	☐	☐
Language: sentences, wording, voice	☐	☐	☐
Mechanics (spelling, etc.) and correct citations	☐	☐	☐
Overall	☐	☐	☐

With a grid of this sort, teachers with too many students can limit themselves to reading each paper once and merely checking the boxes. The use of multiple criteria provides feedback about strengths and weaknesses—feedback notably lacking in conventional, one-dimensional grades. Because there are only three levels for each criterion, you don't have to stop and "compute a grade" for each criterion. You need only read the paper and then hold each criterion briefly in mind to see if the paper seems *notably strong* or *notably weak* in that dimension. If neither, then the verdict on that criterion is "OK." (See the discussion later in the chapter on three-level grades and twelve-level final course grades.)

Grid criteria can be added or changed to fit different genres, your priorities, or a particular writing skill you want to emphasize (e.g., research; considering both sides of an issue; skill in revising; audience awareness). It helps to use plain language for criteria. (See the chapter "Assessing, Testing, and Evaluating" for more on grids.)

Worst-Case Scenario

Teachers who have large classes or heavy teaching loads (and who have no training in the teaching of writing) will feel, understandably, that they have no time for the "luxury" of multiple papers and multiple drafts. The situation is not so hopeless, however, if we look more closely at the reality of what happens when students write for teachers. When we assign writing and get students to write, we can trust that we are helping them learn more and probably write better. But when we comment on their writing and grade it, we can't be so confident of good results. Research points up some disturbing facts. Comments by faculty members are often unclear. After all, we write most comments in great quantity—working slowly down through thick stacks of papers; it is often late at night; and we're usually in a hurry and perhaps even discouraged or downright grumpy. Almost inevitably, we write quickly and fail to read over and revise what we've written.

Even when our comments are clear, they are likely to be untrustworthy. When we write typical comments (like "You should omit this paragraph or put it later" or "This hypothesis has been discredited"), respected colleagues might well disagree with us. Grades on papers are notoriously unreliable (as students sometimes prove by turning the same paper in to different teachers). It's not surprising that many bright students are cynical about teacher response. And even when we manage to write comments that are clear, valid, and helpful, students often mis-understand them because they read through a distorting lens of discouragement, resistance, cynicism—or downright denial. And dare we acknowledge all those students who don't even read our comments—looking only at "what matters," namely the grade? (See Hodges [1994] for some research on how often our comments misfire when read by students).

So even though teachers caught in a worst-case scenario have very little "time per student," their *strategic assigning* of writing yields the biggest payoff from their limited time. They can increase learning even more by assigning *two* or more shorter papers and save responding time by using a grid instead of writing comments. Remember: grids give feedback about different strengths and weaknesses in the writing, whereas conventional grades give nothing but a number on a yea/boo meter.

To increase learning by getting students to draft and revise, teachers in a worst-case scenario will have to resort to a worst-case strategy—but it's fairly effective. Tell students openly that you don't have time to give them feedback on their drafts but that you can help them nevertheless. Set a due date for a required draft of each high-stakes paper—perhaps one week before the final draft is due. Collect the drafts (counting off severely for drafts not turned in), but just glance at each one to see that it seems to be a draft on the chosen topic. Then a week later, collect final drafts and respond with the grid. It's only fair to admit that of course this doesn't *force* them to revise. But most students will find ideas for a better paper coming to mind after they turn in their draft. Even more students will revise if you devote some class time for students to read their drafts out loud to each other in pairs or trios. (See below for more about sharing or peer feedback.)

Responding to High-Stakes Papers

Here are some specific suggestions for revising.

Response as Dialogue.   Commenting is easier and more productive if we ask students to write a brief and informal *cover letter* or *writer's log* to hand in with the draft or final version. It should answer questions like these: What was your main point—and your major subpoints? How did the writing go? Which parts feel strong and weak to you? Most important of all: What questions do you have for me as reader? And when it's a revision: What changes did you make—and why? With this cover letter, our comment is not the *start* of a conversation about the writing but rather the *continuation* of a conversation started by the student. Cover letters help us decide what to address with our comment. Often we can agree with much of what the student has said—and sometimes even be more encouraging about the essay than the student was. (Students write better cover letters if, on the first couple of due dates, we take ten minutes for writing cover letters in class and hearing a couple of examples—so we can kibitz a bit.)

On a couple of occasions when we *return* papers to students, we can continue the dialogue by taking five minutes for students to write us a short note telling what they heard us saying in our comment and how they are reacting to it. These short notes tell us when our comments are unclear or when students misinterpret us.

Read Through the Whole Piece *Before* Making Any Comments. Students can seldom benefit from criticism of more than two or three problems. We can't decide *which* problems to focus on till we read the whole paper through. When we write marginal comments while reading, we often get into trouble: wasting our time on something that turns out to be a minor issue; making a brief comment that the student misunderstands; saying something that's actually wrong ("you don't understand X" although later on it's clear that the student does understand X); or getting caught up in a little spasm of unhelpful irritation. If we settle for making straight and wavy pencil lines during our first reading (for passages that are notably strong or weak), these will serve as reminders after we have read it all and we are trying to decide what few issues to address. Even when we want to give "movies of the mind"—that is, to tell the story of our reactions as we were in the process of reading—we can usually do this more clearly and helpfully by waiting until we've read the whole piece.

Write Comments on a Separate Sheet Rather Than in the Margins. This helps us comment *as readers* about what works and doesn't and how the writing affects us—rather than falling into the trap of trying to be an *editor trying to fix the text*.

Sometimes, of course, we can say something more briefly if we put the comment in the margin, but most of us save time by writing comments on a computer—which means using a separate sheet.

Use Plain Language.   Comments about the writing are usually more effective when we use plain everyday language instead of technical terms from English or rhetoric or grammar. How much better to say "Your writing sounds distant and pompous to me in this passage" than to say "Too many passive verbs here." How would you talk about a writing weakness to a colleague in your field?

About Criticism and Encouragement.   There's an essential learning principle that is too often neglected: students can make more improvement in a weak area if we can tell them to do *more of something* they've already done—than if we tell them only *not to do* what they have done. An example:

> I often got lost as I read your paper. It has big problems with organization. But I've put straight lines along several paragraphs that hang together just fine; and also a few lines *between* several paragraphs where you linked them well and your transition works fine. Give us more of that! You've shown you can do it.

One of the most useful kinds of response is often overlooked because it seems too simple: *describe the paper* as you see it. For example, "Here's what I see as your main point: . . . . Here's what I see as your subsidiary points: . . . . Here's what I see as your structure: . . . ." This helps students learn to *see* their own writing from the outside (a difficult skill), and it tells them what got through and what didn't.

MIDDLE-STAKES ASSIGNMENTS: THINK PIECES

These are not essays and don't have to be organized around a single point, but they are more than mere freewriting. They are short exploratory pieces that ask students to think through a topic. The student needs to *work at thinking* and clean up what is handed in enough so it is not unpleasant to read. We can describe them as thoughtful letters to an interested friend. A good think piece, like a good letter, might pursue one line of thinking, then discover a problem, and finish by rethinking the matter in a different frame of reference.

If your teaching conditions permit it, consider requiring a think piece every week (say one to three pages). You can respond to each one with just a check, check-plus, or check-minus—with or without a few words from you (not about the writing but about the ideas). No think piece would be due on weeks when a high-stakes draft or revision is due. Think pieces can also function as exploratory drafts for high-stakes essays.

Think pieces help students get more out of readings, class discussions, and lectures. Topics can be completely open (e.g., "Write about something that interests you in this week's reading"). But topics can focus on particular concepts that are slippery, or can help students practice particular intellectual tasks. Examples: "Compare these two concepts from the reading." "Use this concept from the reading or lecture [e.g., the second law of thermodynamics? internalized racism?] to describe and analyze something you have encountered in your life." "Write a true or fictional story that uses the technique of flashback or unreliable narrator." "Write about this historical event from inside the head of one of the participants." Students can take intellectual and rhetorical chances because they know their grade will be fine if they throw themselves into the task. Learning is vastly enhanced if you take five or eight minutes on due dates for students to read think pieces out loud to each other in pairs or in small groups.

PEER RESPONSE

For teachers of a writing course, it's crucial to use peer response and take the considerable time necessary to teach students how to give it and receive it well. But most readers of this essay will not be teaching a writing course, so our advice is to emphasize *peer sharing* more than peer response. Students get *excellent* feedback by reading their drafts and final versions aloud to classmates. When students experience how each sentence fits in the mouth and sounds in the ear, they can usually tell which sentences work and which ones are a problem. And not just sentences: reading an essay aloud gives students an almost visceral feel for the organization and train of thinking—and when that train goes off the rails. Best of all, mere sharing—reading aloud—takes very little class time. Sharing is not just about the writing: when three students hear each other's drafts (and lots of low-stakes writing too), they are hearing different understandings of the *course content*.

Teachers and students who have not used sharing in this way will be surprised at its power—not just to help with writing and learning course material but also in building community. One warning: someone reading a piece aloud tends to feel awkward at not hearing any response, and listeners tend to feel awkward saying nothing. In truth, *listening thoughtfully and appreciatively* is the biggest help for a writer, but there's a helpful ritual for dealing with the silence: listeners say "thank you" and then move on to the next reader.

The sharing of writing can be a good occasion for discussing the content ("I don't see it the way you do. In my view . . ."). And if you want to encourage minimal peer response, here are two simple and quick responses—(1) "pointing": "Here are the words and phrases that feel effective or stick in mind"; (2) "say back" or summarizing: "Here's what I hear as your main point; and you also seem to be saying . . ." (For those who want to make a bigger commitment to peer response, see Elbow and Belanoff [2003]).

ABOUT CORRECTNESS: SPELLING AND GRAMMAR

It's not possible or appropriate for us to try to teach grammar and spelling in a college course. But we don't have to teach everything we demand (e.g., typing or word processing). The main thing students need to learn about correct mechanics is schizophrenic: it's *not* important for rough exploratory writing, but it's *crucial* for final drafts.

For high-stakes essays, we think it makes good sense to require not only clear well-organized writing but also good copy editing. Here is a useful formulation: "Your final drafts must be virtually free of mistakes." Many students can't manage this without the help of friends (or paid typists), so it's not realistic to demand that they reach this standard entirely on their own. But we can demand that they learn to get whatever help they need for good copy editing. *This* is the skill and the habit they need when they write on most other occasions they'll encounter. (Most of us ask for help in copy editing, and we get professional help when we publish.)

It doesn't make sense to penalize students for surface mistakes on in-class writing since they have no time to revise with fresh eyes and have no access to help. For exploratory think pieces written out of class, we can require what's appropriate for an informal letter to the teacher: there's no problem if there are some mistakes, but the pieces can't be annoying or hard to read because of mistakes or messiness. A few students can quickly go over and neatly correct obvious errors; others have to recopy and correct.

ABOUT GRADING

There's a whole chapter in this book devoted to the difficult matter of grading (see the chapter "The ABC's of Assigning Grades"). We'll just briefly mention a few practices that are particularly useful because of the central problem in grading a piece of writing: a conventional grade like B− is an attempt to represent with just *one dimension* the quality of a *multidimensional* performance. (A spelling test, in contrast, asks for a fairly one-dimensional performance.) In deciding on the value of a piece of writing, teachers will naturally differ about how much weight they give to the various dimensions of the performance (e.g., accuracy of course content, validity of thinking, originality, structure, sentence/word clarity, mechanics).

Grading grids mitigate this problem since they spell out individual judgments for individual dimensions. The kind of grid we illustrated *does* end up with a single dimensional "overall" verdict, but at least it *reveals* the teacher's values instead of *hiding* them as a regular grade does. For example, an "unsatisfactory" on one criterion, such as "content," might pull the overall grade down to "unsatisfactory." Grids don't get rid of the inherent subjectivity in grading (how *bad* is "unsatisfactory content"? how *good* is "excellent clarity"?), but at least they reduce it. (Research has shown repeatedly that the same paper often gets a wide range of grades from respected readers. Kirschenbaum and colleagues [1971] summarize extensive research. See also Tchudi [1997] and Diederich's classic study [1974]).

For final grades most of us are obliged to settle for a one-dimensional grade, but we can still use a grid to communicate the meaning of our grade to *students*. Here the criteria will encompass a wider array of performances, and teachers can communicate whether they are counting for dimensions such as effort, improvement, or attendance.

The grid we presented earlier in this chapter shows only three levels of quality (unsatisfactory, OK, excellent). This may seem crude; people seem to hunger for fine distinctions. But the more levels of quality we use, the more work we give ourselves, the more chances we have to be wrong (that is, to differ from how other respected readers would judge), and the more chances we have to make students disagree with us and resist our teaching. Yet of course most of us have to give a course grade with something like twelve levels of quality (counting pluses and minuses). There are many relatively simple ways to add up or average out multiple crude three-level grades to yield a twelve-level final grade.

Portfolios

The problem of using a one-dimensional grade for a multidimensional performance does not go away when it's a grade for a portfolio. But somehow the problem isn't so pressing because it's a grade for a number of multidimensional performances. With multiple writings, we get a more trustworthy picture of the student's ability or learning (thus "validity" is enhanced). And portfolios have other advantages. The grade seems fairer because students can choose a *selection* of their best writing and they are not so penalized for having started out the semester unskilled. Most of all, portfolios greatly enhance student learning because they function as an occasion for retrospective meta-thinking. For the final piece in a portfolio is typically a reflective analysis in which the student looks back at everything in the portfolio and tries to articulate what he or she has learned. For the sake of this reflection, it's helpful for students to include some low-stakes writing and at least one example of an "instructive failure."

Contract Grading

Contracts are mentioned in the chapter "The ABC's of Assigning Grades," but we want to mention a little-known hybrid or mixed kind of contract that can be very productive in certain courses. Students are given a list of *all* the course activities that the teacher thinks are important sources of learning, and students are guaranteed a course grade of B if they simply *perform* them all with good faith or decent effort. Typically this list involves things like attendance, meeting deadlines, genuinely revising drafts, giving feedback, satisfactory copy editing, and any other activities that are important for learning—such as labs or special projects. The teacher gives normal feedback on all these activities where it's appropriate—feedback about quality—but for the grade of B, judgments of quality are irrelevant. This system tends to get more students to do the work yet gives them a large foundation of safety; it reduces the degree of adversarialness in grading. Yet judgments of quality come into play for grades higher than a B.

PREVENTING—AND HANDLING—PLAGIARISM

We can't catch all plagiarism—and if we try, we'll turn ourselves from teachers into suspicious cops. It's hard to track down the sources in Internet cheating. "Using Internet search engines, DVD-based reference works, online journals, Web-based news sources, article databases, and other electronic courses, students can find information about nearly any topic and paste the data directly into their papers. Or students can take credit for documents they find or buy online, or that they get as email attachments from friends living down the hall or a thousand miles away" (Sterngold, 2004, p. 16).

The issue of plagiarism gets more complicated as a growing number of students from other countries and cultures "enter the [current U.S.] college classroom believing that truth, wisdom, and cultural artifacts such as art and literature are cultural community property, the result of years of accumulated wisdom transmitted by venerated leaders and by oral traditions, many of them religious" (Swearingen, 1999; see also McLeod, 1992). Thus it's far easier to *prevent* plagiarism than to handle it after the fact. See the chapter "What to Do About Cheating" for a fuller treatment of cheating. Here we treat only plagiarism in writing.

Despite our best efforts to prevent plagiarism, it can happen. But when we get work that looks plagiarized, we must withhold judgment in the absence of trustworthy evidence. In particular, it's no fair saying, "This work is better than you can do," for in fact most students are capable of work that's astonishingly better than what they usually turn in.

Some teachers who suspect plagiarism meet with the student right away and present their account of the situation. They try to bring samples of the student's earlier writing. If the student cited sources, they ask that he or she bring the source materials to the meeting. If the student pleads guilty, you may conclude, nevertheless, that it was not intentional plagiarism. In such a case, you can resolve the matter informally—for example, by allowing the student to rewrite the assignment rather than lowering the grade for the assignment or course.

Other teachers try first to establish definitive proof, for example, by using google.com or new software that can detect plagiarism such as turnitin.com.

Many campuses have a policy on academic dishonesty that forbids imposing any penalty at all without reporting the case to the official committee and allowing the student to appeal. This may seem bureaucratic at first glance, but there are two good justifications. Many students have been falsely accused and penalized; and not a few students have been found working out informal arrangements with teachers over and over again—convincing each teacher that they've never been involved in anything like this before. It's important to check out the procedures at your institution.

Ways to Prevent Plagiarism

- Clarify in your syllabus what constitutes plagiarism in your course. Tell students what documentation is required for essays, including use of the Internet. Tell students what is acceptable and unacceptable collaboration with other students.

- Encourage students to come to you or e-mail you if they are in doubt about citations. Try to persuade them that admitting that they don't know something is much better than making a mistake that could constitute plagiarism.

- Ask students to check their syllabi in advance to see if there are some weeks in which they have too many writing assignments due at once. Allow students to hand in an assignment early so as to balance their workload.

- Collect lots of low-stakes informal writing so students know that you know their style and voice.

- On high-stakes essays, where students might be more tempted to cheat, assign specific, idiosyncratic topics so they can't lift things from books, the Internet, or other courses. Examples: "Apply this theory to that set of data"; "Describe your reactions to X and then go on to . . ."; "Give a sympathetic summary and then a critical summary of what X writes on page 134, and then write an essay of your own reflections about it"; "Write a short story that illustrates the principles we've studied this week."

- Require drafts and revisions and cover letters that explain the revisions. Require students to hand in all previous versions and notes with every final draft.

- Write fresh topics each year so students aren't tempted to recycle papers from previous years.

- In large courses with different section leaders, have each leader make up different assignments for think pieces and essays—so students aren't tempted to copy work between sections. Circulate copies of new (and old) topics to all instructors.

- Students are less tempted to plagiarize from the Internet if you project that you are savvy and familiar with what is out there. One of our colleagues deters problems with this note in his syllabus: "Last year, we suspended paper-writing in favor of hour tests while we studied Internet plagiarism and how to detect it. Now we're ready."

IN CONCLUSION

Teachers can enhance student learning if they use a combination of high-stakes and low-stakes writing. (Most people experience writing as a high-stakes use of language—in contrast to speaking as a low-stakes use. But writing, because it is so easily kept private, is ideal for low-stakes use.) We need high-stakes writing in order to test whether students have learned what we are teaching. If we use only short-answer exams, we don't get a trustworthy picture of whether students have a genuine understanding of course concepts and how to apply them.

Low-stakes writing is for exploration and learning: there is no concern about quality or correctness. It helps students explore and figure out new ideas, connect personally with them using their own language, become more active learners, and become fluent and comfortable in writing before they have to write the high-stakes essays that determine their course grade. (And low-stakes writing takes little teacher time or skill.)

Students learn and improve more if they are assigned two or three essays, not just one, and if they have to turn in a draft of each essay for feedback before revising it.

Teachers can handle the increased demands implied by the previous point by (a) keeping the essays short; (b) giving their main response time to drafts—when these responses can actually help students improve; and (c) responding very quickly to final drafts by using a multi-criterion grid and just checking boxes—rather than writing a comment. The multiple criteria make the final grade more valid and reliable. (We provide many specific suggestions for the process of responding and grading.)

It's far more feasible to *prevent* plagiarism than to catch and prosecute it. Methods for preventing plagiarism include making essay assignments particular and idiosyncratic so that students cannot find anything written by someone else that fits the assignment; insisting on drafts of essays and then revision on the basis of feedback to those drafts (along with a process note about how they revised); and seeing lots of students' low-stakes, informal, in-class writing so we know their writing voice and they know we know it.

Supplementary Reading

P. Diederich, *Measuring Growth in English* (Urbana: NCTE, 1974).

P. Elbow, "Using the Collage for Collaborative Writing," in *Everyone Can Write: Essays Toward a Hopeful Theory of Writing and Teaching Writing* (New York: Oxford University Press, 2000), pp. 372–378.

P. Elbow, "Your Cheatin' Art: A Collage," in *Everyone Can Write: Essays Toward a Hopeful Theory of Writing and Teaching Writing*, pp. 300–313.

P. Elbow and P. Belanoff, *Sharing and Responding* (New York: McGraw-Hill, 2003).

E. Hodges, "Some Realities of Revision: What Students Don't or Won't Understand," *English in Texas*, Summer 1994, 25(4), 13–16.

H. Kirschenbaum, S. Simon, and R. Napier, *Wad-Ja-Get? The Grading Game in American Education* (New York: Hart Publishing, 1971).

Susan H. McLeod, "Responding to Plagiarism: The Role of the WPA," *WPA: Writing Program Administration*, 1992, 15(3), 7–16.

M. D. Sorcinelli and P. Elbow (eds.), "Writing to Learn: Strategies for Assigning and Responding to Writing Across the Disciplines," *New Directions in Teaching and Learning*, no. 69, February 1997.

A. Sterngold, "Confronting Plagiarism: How Conventional Teaching Invites Cyber-Cheating," *Change*, May/June 2004, 36(3), 16–21.

C. Jan Swearingen, "Originality, Authenticity, Imitation, and Plagiarism: Augustine's Chinese Cousins," in Lise Buranen and Alice M. Roy (eds.), *Perspectives on Plagiarism and Intellectual Property in a Postmodern World* (Albany: State University of New York Press, 1999), pp. 5–18.

Stephen Tchudi (ed.), *Alternatives to Grading Student Writing* (Urbana: NCTE, 1997).

A. Young, "Mentoring, Modeling, Monitoring, Motivating: Response to Students' Ungraded Writing as Academic Conversation," in M. D. Sorcinelli and P. Elbow (eds.), "Writing to Learn: Strategies for Assigning and Responding to Writing Across the Disciplines."

Active Learning: Cooperative, Collaborative, and Peer Learning

One of the recurring criticisms of higher education is that it hasn't increased its productivity at the same rate as industry. By "productivity" critics typically mean that colleges should turn out more students using fewer teachers—as if colleges were factories producing shoes, automobiles, or soap.

The bottleneck in educational efficiency is that learning to think requires thinking and communicating one's thinking through talking, writing, or doing, so that others can react to it. Unfortunately a professor can read only one paper at a time, can listen to only one student's comments at a time, and can respond with only one voice.

The problem is not one of communicating knowledge from professors to students more efficiently. Printed materials have done this very well for years, and for most educational purposes are still superior to any of the modern alternatives. The problem is rather one of interaction between the learner and teacher. Fortunately, interactions that facilitate learning need not be limited to those with teachers. Often those with peers are more productive.

PEER LEARNING* AND TEACHING

The best answer to the question "What is the most effective method of teaching?" is that it depends on the goal, the student, the content, and the teacher. The next best answer may be "students teaching other students." There is a wealth of evidence that peer learning and teaching is extremely effective for a wide range of goals, content, and students of different levels and personalities (Johnson et al., 1981). Moreover, skill in working cooperatively is essential for most vocations. Miller and Groccia (1997) found that cooperative learning produced positive results in ability to work with others as well as better cognitive outcomes. Marbac-Ad and Sokolove (2000) found that cooperative learning in biology courses resulted in higher-level student questioning.

Here are some tips that may be helpful in initiating a variety of types of cooperative learning methods:

1. Have students discuss what contributes to effective group functioning. Explain why working together is important and valuable even for students who don't like to work in groups.

2. Make sure students know what their task is; for example, if it involves out-of-class work, give teams a few minutes before the end of the class period to make plans. At this time they should also report to you what they plan to do and when and where they will meet.

3. For in-class group work, move around and listen in to be sure students are not lost and confused. Use this time to get and keep them on the right track.

4. Help students develop the skills they need for working together effectively.

---

*I use the term *peer learning* to include "collaborative" and "cooperative" learning. Some authors distinguish collaborative from cooperative learning, but both involve peer learning in which there is interdependence of students working toward a common goal. Similarities in and differences between collaborative and cooperative learning are discussed in Cooper et al. (2003).

Suggestions for Students: How to Be an Effective Group

1. Be sure everyone contributes to discussion and to tasks.

2. Don't jump to conclusions too quickly. Be sure that minority ideas are considered.

3. Don't assume consensus because no one has opposed an idea or offered an alternative. Check agreement with each group member verbally, not just by a vote.

4. Set goals—immediate, intermediate, and long-term—but don't be afraid to change them as you progress.

5. Allocate tasks to be done. Be sure that each person knows what he or she is to do and what the deadline is. Check this before adjourning.

6. Be sure there is agreement on the time and place of the next meeting and on what you hope to accomplish.

7. Before ending a meeting, evaluate your group process. What might you try to do differently next time?

PEER TUTORING

"Pay to be a tutor, not to be tutored" is the message from studies of peer tutoring. For example, Annis (1983a) compared learning of students who read a passage and were taught by a peer and students who read the passage and taught it to another student.

The results demonstrated that teaching resulted in better learning than being taught. A similar study by Bargh and Schul (1980) also found positive results, with the largest part of the gain in retention being attributable to deeper studying of material when preparing to teach. These results fit well with contemporary theories of learning and memory. Preparing to teach and teaching involve active thought about the material, analysis and selection of main ideas, and processing the concepts into one's own thoughts and words. However, this does not mean that those being tutored fail to learn. Peer tutoring also helps those being tutored (Cohen et al., 1982; Lidren et al., 1991). Hartman (1990) provides useful suggestions for training tutors. Peer tutoring need not be one on one. Group tutoring is also effective.

THE LEARNING CELL

One of the best-developed systems for helping pairs of students learn more effectively is the "learning cell" developed by Marcel Goldschmid of the Swiss Federal Institute of Technology in Lausanne (Goldschmid, 1971). The learning cell, or student dyad, refers to a cooperative form of learning in pairs, in which students alternate asking and answering questions on commonly read materials.

1. To prepare for the learning cell, students read an assignment and write questions dealing with the major points raised in the reading or other related materials.

2. At the beginning of each class meeting, students are randomly assigned to pairs, and one partner, A, begins by asking the first question.

3. After having answered and perhaps having been corrected or given additional information, the second student, B, puts a question to A, and so on.

4. During this time, the instructor goes from dyad to dyad, giving feedback and asking and answering questions.*

A variation of this procedure has each student read (or prepare) different materials. In this case, A "teaches" B the essentials of his or her readings; then asks B prepared questions, whereupon they switch roles. Research by Goldschmid and his colleagues demonstrated that the learning cell is effective in a variety of disciplines (Goldschmid, 1975; Goldschmid & Shore, 1974). Training students to generate thought-provoking questions enhances learning (King, 1990; Pressley et al., 1992). To recapture student attention and stimulate deeper processing, I often ask

---

*Students can also use the learning cell technique outside of class. My students use it in preparing for tests. A similarly structured method is "Ask to Think—Tell Why" (King, 1997).

students to think about a problem for a minute, write for a minute, and then share their thoughts with a neighbor (Think-Pair-Share). Students then feel more free to participate in a general discussion of the problem. Pairing can also be effectively used for interviews, discussion of an issue or questions, analyzing a case or problem, or summarizing a lecture or assigned reading.

TEAM LEARNING: SYNDICATE AND JIGSAW

The term *syndicate* has a faintly evil connotation in the United States, but in Great Britain and other countries, *syndicate* is used to describe a team-based system of learning that has proved to be effective. In syndicate-based peer learning, the class is divided into teams (or syndicates) of four to eight students. Each syndicate is given assignments (perhaps three or four questions). References are suggested, and members of the syndicate may divide up the readings. The findings are then discussed by the various syndicates as they meet in small groups during the regular class period. The syndicate may then make a written or oral report to the class as a whole.

I have found that I get more interesting reports when I remind students that they have probably sometimes been bored by student reports. Hence they need to plan not only the content of the report but also how to make it interesting. I'm impressed by student creativity; my students have developed graphic and audio aids, skits, class participation, and other devices for motivating their classmates.

The *jigsaw* method, first developed by Elliot Aronson, begins like the syndicate by dividing a class into groups that are given assignments. Members of each group report back to their group, which agrees on what and how to present to the rest of the class. However, instead of a presentation to the entire class, each member of the group next meets in a new task group with one member from each of the other groups. In this new task group each student is responsible for teaching the students from the other groups what his group has learned. Since every student is thus in a group in which every group is represented, all students have the opportunity to learn the essence of all the assignments.

Students often form groups to study difficult material together or to prepare for an exam. Yan & Kember (2004) interviewed students from a variety of disciplines and found that some groups collaborated to minimize the work for the individual group members. Others, however, collaborated to gain a better understanding of an issue or concept.

STUDENT CHARACTERISTICS AND PEER LEARNING

Peer learning works better for some students than for others, but learning is increased for most students and does not hurt the learning of others. In the presence of ability differences, heterogeneity may be better than homogeneity. Larson and colleagues (1984) found that cooperative learners with partners with dissimilar vocabulary scores recalled more main ideas after studying a textbook passage, not only on the passage studied cooperatively but on a passage studied individually.

WHY DOES PEER LEARNING WORK?

Motivationally, peer learning has the advantages of interaction with a peer—an opportunity for mutual support and stimulation. (One piece of evidence for the motivational value of peer learning [Schomberg, 1986] is that it reduces absenteeism.) Knowing that your teammates are depending on you increases the likelihood of your doing your work. Cognitively it provides an opportunity for elaboration—putting material into one's own words—as well as a chance to begin using the language of the discipline. It communicates that the locus of learning is in the students' heads. An effective partner can act as a model of useful strategies as well as a teacher.

Several of the effective peer learning techniques involve alternating between listening and summarizing or explaining. Structures of peer learning such as the learning cell that reduce the chance that one participant is simply a passive recipient seem likely to be better for both motivation and learning.

The task of the successful student in peer learning is to question, explain, express opinions, admit confusion, and reveal misconceptions; but at the same time the student must listen to peers, respond to their questions, question their opinions, and share information or concepts that will clear up their confusion. Accomplishing these tasks requires interpersonal as well as cognitive skills—being able to give feedback in nonthreatening, supportive ways, maintaining a focus on group goals, developing orderly task-oriented procedures, and developing and sustaining mutual tasks. It is little wonder that peer learning sometimes fails; the wonder is that it so frequently works. And it does.

Students are more likely to talk in small groups than in large ones; students who are confused are more likely to ask other students questions about their difficulties or failure to understand than to reveal these problems with a faculty member present. Students who are not confused must actively organize and reorganize their own learning in order to explain it. Thus both the confused and the unconfused benefit.

IN CONCLUSION

1. Students often learn more from interacting with other students than from listening to us. One of the best methods of gaining clearer, long-lasting understanding is explaining to someone else.

2. This does not mean that we can be eliminated or have time to loaf. More of our time will be spent in helping students work together effectively, less time in preparing lectures.

3. Cooperative peer learning is one of our most valuable tools for effective teaching.

Supplementary Reading

One of the preeminent scholars of cooperative learning in higher education is Jim Cooper, who in 1991 initiated the newsletter *Cooperative*

Learning and College Teaching, an excellent source of ideas for different ways of using cooperative learning. You can subscribe by writing:

Network for Cooperative Learning in Higher Education
Dr. James L. Cooper
HFA-B-316
CSU Dominguez Hills
1000 E. Victoria St.
Carson, CA 90747

Small Group Instruction in Higher Education, edited by J. L. Cooper, P. Robinson, and D. Ball (Stillwater, OK: New Forums Press, 2003), is a fine resource.

Other good resources are Philip Abrami's book *Classroom Connections: Understanding and Using Cooperative Learning* (Toronto: Harcourt Brace, 1995), and *Team-Based Learning: A Transformative Use of Small Groups* (Westport, CT: Praeger, 2002), edited by L. K. Michaelson, A. B. Knight, and L. D. Fink.

Two comprehensive books on cooperative learning are D. W. Johnson, R. T. Johnson, and K. A. Smith, *Active Learning: Cooperation in the College Classroom* (Edina, MN: Interactive Book Co., 1991), and B. Millis and P. Cottell, *Cooperative Learning for Higher Education Faculty* (Phoenix: ACE & Oryx Press, 1998).

Cooperative learning does not imply absence of controversy. D. W. Johnson, R. T. Johnson, and K. A. Smith describe the use and value of controversy in their book *Academic Controversy: Enriching College Instruction Through Intellectual Conflict* (Washington, DC: ASHE/ERIC, 1997).

Problem-Based Learning: Teaching with Cases, Simulations, and Games

PROBLEM-BASED LEARNING

Problem-based learning is (along with active learning, cooperative/collaborative learning, and technology) one of the most important developments in contemporary higher education. The ideas embodied in problem-based learning have a long history, ranging back at least to the use of cases in Harvard Medical School in the nineteenth century and extending through John Dewey's philosophy, Jerry Bruner's discovery learning, and the development of simulations in the 1960s. The current surge of interest stems from McMaster University, where in 1969 the medical school replaced the traditional lectures in first-year basic science courses with courses that started with problems presented by patients' cases. A chemical engineering professor at McMaster, Don Peters, developed a problem-based approach for his courses, and another engineering professor, Charles Wales of West Virginia University, had a little earlier developed a problem-based method called "guided design." In a few years, courses and curricula in various disciplines in universities all over the world were using similar problem-based methods. In this chapter, I will describe guided design, the case method, and simulations—all variants of problem-based learning.

Problem-based education is based on the assumptions that human beings evolved as individuals who are motivated to solve problems, and that problem solvers will seek and learn whatever knowledge is needed for successful problem solving. Even in cultures where students do not expect to participate actively in classes, problem-based learning can be successfully implemented; Marjorie McKinnon (1999) describes the introduction of problem-based learning at the University of Hong Kong in her article "PBL in Hong Kong." If a realistic, relevant problem is presented before study, students will identify needed information and be motivated to learn it. However, as in introducing any other method, you need to explain to students your purposes.

The steps involved in "guided design," described in the box "Steps in Problem-Based Learning," are representative of those likely to be involved in many variations of problem-based learning. Note the emphasis on assessment of constraints, costs, benefits, and evaluation of the final solution. Helping students develop skills of self-assessment is an important goal of education.

Problem-based learning does not mean that you can sit back and relax once you have presented the problem. Check on each group's progress. If you have set a time when groups must report, you may have to help a group clear up a misconception or get out of a blind alley. It's frustrating to start a problem and not have a chance to finish.

In the McMaster model of problem-based learning, students meet in small groups with a tutor who acts as a facilitator. Although the facilitator is typically a faculty member, teaching assistants or peers can also be successful if trained. Typically, after the students have presented their recommendations, classroom discussion summarizes the learning that has occurred and integrates it with students' prior skills and knowledge.

THE CASE METHOD

As indicated earlier, the case method has been widely used in business and law courses for many years and is now being used in a variety of disciplines. Generally, case method discussions

Steps in Problem-Based Learning (Guided Design)

1. State the problem and establish a goal that will be pursued in resolving it.
2. Gather information relevant to defining the problem and understanding the elements associated with it.
3. Generate possible solutions.
4. List possible constraints on what can be accomplished as well as factors that may facilitate getting a solution accepted.
5. Choose an initial or possible solution using criteria that an acceptable solution must meet. The criteria can include tangible and monetary costs and benefits, the likely acceptance of the solution by others, and discipline or other standard criteria normally applied to such problems.
6. Analyze the important factors that must be considered in the development of a detailed solution. What has to be done, who does it, when it should happen, and where the solution would be used are possible factors to explore.
7. Create a detailed solution.
8. Evaluate the final solution against the relevant criteria used earlier, to ensure that it meets at least those requirements and others that now appear to be necessary.
9. Recommend a course of action and, if appropriate, suggest ways to monitor and evaluate the solution when it is adopted.

"Steps in the Guided Design Process" by Dr. Charles E. Wales. Excerpted from *Educating Professionals*, Jossey-Bass, 1993, Chapter 8. Used by permission of the author.

produce good student involvement. Case methods, like other problem-based methods, are intended to develop student ability to solve problems using knowledge, concepts, and skills relevant to a course. Cases provide contextualized learning, as contrasted with learning disassociated from meaningful contexts.

Cases are often actual descriptions of problem situations in the field in which the case is being used; sometimes they are syntheses constructed to represent a particular principle or type of problem. For example, in medicine a case may describe a patient and the patient's symptoms; in psychology the case might describe a group facing a decision; in biology the case might describe an environmental problem. Whatever the case, it typically involves the possibility of several alternative approaches or actions and some evaluation of values and costs of different solutions to the problem posed. Usually cases require that the students not only apply course content but also consult other resources.

Finding the Right Cases

You can write your own cases, but you may be able to find cases already written that are appropriate for your purposes and are motivating for your students. For example, Silverman and colleagues (1994) have published cases for teacher education. Other cases can be found on the Internet.

Typically the case method involves a series of cases, but in some case method courses the cases are not well chosen to represent properly sequenced levels of difficulty. Often, in order to make cases realistic, so many details are included that beginning students lose the principles or points the case was intended to demonstrate. Teachers attempting to help students learn complex discriminations and principles in problem solving need to choose initial cases in which the differences are clear and extreme before moving to more subtle, complex cases. Typically, one of the goals of the case method is to teach students to select important factors from a tangle of less important ones which may nevertheless form a context to be considered. One does not learn such skills by being in perpetual confusion, but rather by success in solving more and more difficult problems.

The major problem in teaching by cases involves going from the students' fascination with the particular case to the general principle or conceptual structure. In choosing a case to discuss, the teacher needs to think, "What is this case a case *of*?"

Tips for Teaching with Cases

Usually cases are presented in writing, but you can use a videotape or you can role-play a problem situation. (Role playing is like a drama in which each participant is assigned a character to portray, but no lines are learned. The individuals portraying specific roles improvise their responses in a situation—a situation that presents a problem or conflict.)

Whatever method you use to present the problem, you should allow class time for students to ask questions about the process they are to use and to clarify the nature of the problem presented.

You should clarify ways of going about the case study, such as:

1. What is the problem?
2. Develop hypotheses about what causes the problem.
3. What evidence can be gathered to support or discount any of the hypotheses?
4. What conclusions can be drawn? What recommendations? Make it clear that there is no one right answer.

Very likely you will want to form teams (as described in the preceding chapter "Active Learning") and take time during class for the teams to agree on when to meet and to determine what they will do before their meeting. Some problems may involve work extending over several meetings in class and out of class.

When the teams report, your role is primarily to facilitate discussion—listening, questioning, clarifying, challenging, encouraging analysis and problem solving, and testing the validity of generalizations. You may want to use a chalkboard, overhead visuals, or a computer to keep a running summary of points established, additional information needed, and possible ethical or value considerations. Don't forget to include the evidence supporting alternative approaches.

If the case is one that actually occurred, students will want to find out what actually was done and how it worked out. You can have a productive discussion about how the actual process, variables considered, or strategies used differed from those in the class. Sometimes you might bring in someone working in the field so that the students can see how an expert analyzes the case, and also ask questions about what really happens in practice.

GAMES AND SIMULATIONS

An educational game involves students in some sort of competition or achievement in relationship to a goal; it is a game that both teaches and is fun. Many games are simulations; for example, they attempt to model some real-life problem situation. Thus there are business games, international relations games, and many others. Whatever the topic, the planner of the game needs to specify the teaching objectives to be served by the game and then plan the game to highlight features that contribute to those objectives.

Early educational games often involved large-scale simulations in which participants played the roles of individuals or groups in some interpersonal, political, or social situation. Now many simulations are available on computers. Research and laboratory simulations are available for courses in the sciences, and interactive social simulations can be used to teach foreign languages. Computer simulations are often more effective in teaching research methods than are traditional "wet labs."

As with other teaching methods, the effectiveness of simulations depends to some extent on the degree of instructional support or structure. Research on traditional as well as nontraditional teaching has shown that students with low prior knowledge tend to benefit from a higher degree of structure than students with greater knowledge or intelligence (Cronbach & Snow, 1977). Veenstra and Elshout's research (1995) on computer simulations in heat theory, electricity, and statistics found even more complex relationships. Structuredness made little difference for high-intelligence students; more structure enhanced learning for students with low intelligence and low meta-cognitive strategies (poor analysis, planning, evaluation, and work methods).

The chief advantage of games and simulations is that students are active participants rather than passive observers. Students must make decisions, solve problems, and react to the results of their decisions. Lepper and Malone (1985) have studied the motivational elements in computer games. They found that key features are challenge, self-competence, curiosity, personal control, and fantasy.

There are now a number of well-designed games that have been used in enough situations to have the kinks worked out. Some use computers to implement the complex interaction of various decisions. One classic example is SIMSOC (Gamson, 1966), a sociology game in which students are citizens of a society in which they have economic and social roles; for example, some are members of political parties, and some have police powers. Games like this are useful in getting students to consider varied points of view relevant to the issues addressed in the game. Like the case method, an educational game may be either too simple or complex to achieve the kind of generalization of concepts or principles that the teacher desires. The biggest barrier to the use of games is logistic. Often it is hard to find a game that fits the time and facilities limitations of typical classes. Devising one's own game can be fun but also time consuming. Nonetheless, games are potentially useful tools for effective teaching.

IN CONCLUSION

Whether one uses cases, games, simulations, or other problems, problem-based learning is a valuable part of one's armamentarium of teaching strategies. In fact, even if you don't use problem-based learning in its traditional forms, the general principle that students like to solve problems that offer a challenge but are still solvable is important. And motivation isn't the only reason to use problems. If students are to learn how to think more effectively, they need to practice thinking. Moreover, cognitive theory provides good support for the idea that knowledge learned and used in a realistic, problem-solving context is more likely to be remembered and used appropriately when needed later.

There is a good deal of research on problem-based learning in its various forms, including case methods and simulations. My summation of the results is that, compared with traditional methods of teaching, problem-based learning may sometimes result in less acquisition of knowledge but typically shows little, if any, decrement. However, retention, application, and motivational outcomes are generally superior to those in traditional methods of instruction.

Supplementary Reading

Guided design is fully described in C. E. Wales and R. A. Stager, *Guided Design* (Morgantown: West Virginia University, 1977).

Kenneth France has a nice article on using PBL in service learning: "Problem-Based Service Learning: Rewards and Challenges with

Undergraduates," in Catherine Wahlburg and Sandra Chadwick-Blossey (eds.), *To Improve the Academy*, 2004, 22, 239–250.

Donald Woods has published three useful books on problem-based learning: *Problem-Based Learning: How to Gain the Most from PBL* (written for students), *Helping Your Students Gain the Most from PBL* (written for teachers), and *Resources to Gain the Most from PBL*. All three are published by Donald R. Woods, Department of Chemical Engineering, McMaster University, Hamilton, ON L85 4LT, Canada.

For comprehensive help in using PBL, see Dave S. Knowlton and David C. Sharp (eds.), "Problem-Based Learning in the Information Age," *New Directions for Teaching and Learning*, no. 95, September 2003. Also see Maggi Savin-Baden, *Facilitating Problem-Based Learning* (Maidenhead, UK: Open University Press, 2003).

The Harvard Law and Business Schools were pioneers in using the case method. The following reference provides a good description of the methods they developed: C. R. Christensen and A. J. Hansen, *Teaching and the Case Method* (Boston: Harvard Business School, 1987).

A sophisticated description of the use of the case method in medical education as well as two experiments on activating and restructuring prior knowledge in case discussions may be found in H. G. Schmidt, *Activatie van Voorkennis, Intrinsieke Motivatie en de Verwerking van Tekst* (Apeldoorn, The Netherlands: Van Walraven bv, 1982). (Don't worry. Despite the Dutch title, the text is in English.)

The use of active learning in geography is described in M. Healy and J. Roberts (eds.), *Engaging Students in Active Learning: Case Studies in Geography* (Chettenham, UK: University of Worcestershire, 2003).

Linc Fisch's article "Triggering Discussions on Ethics and Values: Cases and Innovative Case Variations," *Innovative Higher Education*, 1997, 22, 117–134, has lots of practical tips.

Samford University has played a leading role in problem-based learning. They have a web site with a newsletter: www.samford.edu/pbl.

Hank Schmidt and Joseph Moust describe four types of problems used in PBL—explanation problems, fact-finding problems, strategy problems, and moral dilemma problems—in "Towards a Taxonomy of Problems Used in Problem-Based Learning Curricula," *Journal of Excellence in College Teaching*, 2000, 11(2), 57–72.

Technology and Teaching

A s network computing and tools for learning, teaching, and administration gain more power and accessibility, integrating technology into the educational process is becoming a major thrust for most colleges and universities. Some instructors are embracing technology whole heartedly, while others feel skeptical or left behind. Given the concerns we have heard from instructors, we believe that the essential questions of technology integration are threefold: (1) How will technology enhance teaching and learning? (2) What considerations go into teaching with technology? (3) What are the effects of technology on teaching? In this chapter, we address each of these issues.

This chapter was written by Erping Zhu and Matthew Kaplan of the University of Michigan.

HOW WILL TECHNOLOGY ENHANCE TEACHING AND LEARNING?

When instructors ground their choice of technology tools in individual course goals, personal teaching philosophy, and disciplinary values, technology tools are capable of enhancing teaching and learning. As a tool, instructional technology can serve a number of very useful functions in college and university classrooms, including the following:

1. *Providing new opportunities for enhancing student learning that otherwise would be impossible or very difficult.* For example, course management tools allow you to post notes and other resources that might be prohibitively time consuming or costly to create, especially for larger classes. Distance learning makes possible connections between students on different campuses who can work together in real time in ways that are simply impossible without technology.

2. *Addressing specific learning goals more effectively.* For example, in order to promote critical thinking, instructors in the health sciences can post electronic case studies that contain images and patient information and a set of questions that ask students to offer diagnoses and develop recommendations for patient care. Similarly, by using e-mail lists or chat functions, you can extend discussions in any discipline beyond the classroom so that students are critically engaged with course materials and there is a written record of the conversation that they can return to and review.

3. *Taking advantage of the rich information now available online.* From searchable databases such as Wilson Index and government documents and reports to technical information and primary sources, a wealth of information is now at students' fingertips. Instructors can take advantage of these resources to build in real-world applications to their courses, a strategy that promotes learning and long-term retention (Halpern & Hakel, 2003).

4. *Preparing students for life in a wired world.* Although many students now come to higher education having used technology,

they have not necessarily developed the skills to critically evaluate the information they find or the ability to use advanced applications that go beyond e-mail and surfing the web. Such skills are taking on increasing significance in the workplace and beyond, and students will benefit from exposure to a variety of technologies and a thoughtful consideration of sources of information and their validity.

There is of course no guarantee that instructional technology will accomplish these ends effectively. Just like any tool, technology can be used poorly or inappropriately. Successful incorporation of technology tools depends on the extent to which they are connected to course goals, combined with effective pedagogies, and designed to improve student learning rather than being used for their own sake.

WHAT CONSIDERATIONS GO INTO TEACHING WITH TECHNOLOGY?

The phrase "teaching with technology" may conjure up a variety of different images depending on our own experience as instructors, students, or even conference attendees. For some it might mean using PowerPoint in lectures; others may think of using a course management system like WebCT or Blackboard; and still others may think of specific disciplinary applications such as designing web-based simulations to teach skills and concepts. Although it is natural to think first of the technology tool itself as a starting point, the use of instructional technology is more likely to be effective and appropriate (that is, facilitate student learning, increase your own productivity) if it is integrated into a careful planning process that takes into account the various factors involved in teaching and learning.

From a systems approach, teaching with technology involves four major components: the students, the instructor, course content, and technology tools (see Figure 18.1). We need to attend to each component in order to make technology integration as successful as possible. *Course content* can be examined in terms of learning outcomes and the discipline being taught and how

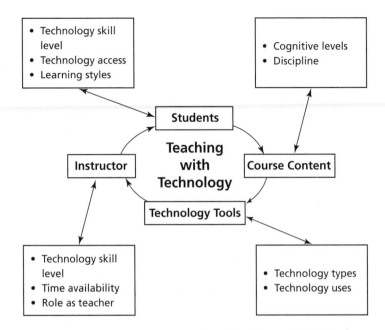

FIGURE 18.1 A Systems Approach to Teaching with Technology

technology may promote specific types of learning. As *instructors*, we can think of our own experience with technology, the amount of time we have for planning and teaching, and our view of our role in the teaching and learning process. We also need to think carefully about our *students*, their exposure and access to technology as well as their preferred learning styles. Finally, we can turn to the *technology* itself and analyze it according to its functions and relevance to our teaching. This approach to teaching and learning with technology assumes that the four component parts are interrelated and that effective changes in one part will require reconsideration of the other three as well.

Course Content

In order to use technology effectively in teaching, we must examine our course goals. What do you expect students to learn from the class? What skills and knowledge do you want them to

FIGURE 18.2   Technology and Learning Objectives

acquire by the end of the term? What teaching strategies (lecture, discussion, group work, case studies, and so on) will best help students achieve these goals? (See the chapter "Countdown for Course Preparation.") Once you have answers to these questions, you can choose the appropriate technologies to support your goals and design appropriate learning activities to incorporate that technology into your course.

To help make the connection between goals and technology tools, we can turn to the taxonomy of educational objectives developed by Benjamin Bloom (Bloom, 1956). Objectives at the lower levels of Bloom's taxonomy involve acquisition of factual knowledge or development of basic comprehension. Higher-level learning involves skills such as analysis, synthesis, and evaluation. Figure 18.2 briefly illustrates the basis for selecting technology in accordance with this taxonomy of objectives. For example, if you want students to record and remember materials effectively, you could use *Microsoft PowerPoint* to improve readability of lecture topics and post the outlines so that students have easy access to them for review and correction of their own notes. However, if you also wish to promote critical thinking through active learning during lectures, *Microsoft PowerPoint* alone may not be the best choice: presentation software can lead to a teacher-centered and student-passive mode of instruction (Creed, 1997).

To avoid placing students in a passive learning mode you will need to incorporate activities that engage students in active thinking, reflecting, and performing tasks. In this case, you might still want to incorporate PowerPoint slides, but you could use a personal response system with the Peer Instruction teaching method (Mazur, 1997) in lectures to reinforce students' understanding and engage them in thinking. With this approach, an instructor poses a conceptual question, students discuss possible answers in pairs, and then they vote electronically for the correct answer. The instructor then has immediate feedback about how well the students have understood the concept. You could also extend student thinking beyond the class by setting up an online class discussion using a web-based conferencing program.

The discipline you teach as well as the goals you set for student learning will affect your decisions about which technologies are most appropriate for a given course. In some disciplines technology is a standard part of professional work in the field, and decisions about technology integration need to take these realities into account.

The Instructor

Once you have a clear view of the course content and how technology can support your instructional goals, you will need to ask some questions about your own skills and confidence: (1) How skilled and experienced are you in using technology? (2) How much time do you have for course planning and preparation? (3) What is your role as a teacher?

If you have no or little experience using technology, it might make sense to start slowly with tools that are established and easy to use so that you build your confidence and support your students' learning. You may go to colleagues in your department or to a technology workshop to get started with software programs commonly used at your institution.

The time you have available for course planning and skill development should also influence the extent to which you undertake technology integration in your courses (see Table 18.1). The more complex and unfamiliar a particular tool is to you, the more time you will need to dedicate to course planning, development of materials and learning activities, and your own skill

Easy (little time)	Moderate (some time)	Complex (more time)
These software programs are commonly available and easy to use.	These software programs are somewhat complicated but can be learned with some effort.	Specialized software, hardware, or programming expertise are required.
Example:	*Example:*	*Example:*
■ e-mail, listserver ■ Text-based presentation (e.g., PowerPoint) ■ Course management systems (Blackboard, WebCT, CTools)	■ Instant messenger, chat, bulletin boards ■ Single digital audio or video clip ■ Text and graphic presentation (e.g., PowerPoint) ■ Web sites ■ Web conferencing	■ Multimedia presentation ■ Complex animation (e.g., Macromedia Flash) ■ Simulation/game (e.g., authoring programs, *Applets*, etc.) ■ Integrated audio/video clips ■ Streaming audio/video ■ Database creation ■ Statistical packages

TABLE 18.1 Common Technology Tools and Their Use

development. Start-up time for such activities may be greater than you expect or wish to spend on teaching. You need to be aware of this and be well prepared and ready for such a time commitment when you make the decision to integrate technology into your courses. Using technology to teach without adequate preparation and time commitment could have a negative impact on your teaching and student learning.

Many campuses now have teaching centers and offices of instructional technology with consultants who can work with you and help you plan effectively. In addition, you can look for graduate and undergraduate students who have experience working with technology and might be able to provide support and assistance.

One final issue with this component is how the instructor views his or her role in the teaching process and how technology integration can support or conflict with that view. If you see your main role in teaching as that of an expert, an authority in a given field whose main task in teaching is to convey information, you may find it disconcerting to discover that the incorporation of technology places you in the role of guide or facilitator. In some cases you may discover that your students know more about and are more comfortable with the technology than you are. It is best to think carefully about your own view of teaching and learning, how your use of technology might change the dynamics in your class, and whether you are willing to make that shift.

Students

As you adopt technology tools into your courses, you will need to consider students' previous experience with technology, their access to technology, and the variety of learning styles they bring to your course.

Many instructors report that students' comfort and experience with technology seem to increase each year. Data from national studies confirm that, overall, Americans are gaining greater access to technology. In 2002, about 61 percent of U.S. households were connected to the Internet. Access to computers in the public schools had increased to 99 percent by fall 2002 (http://nces.ed .gov/surveys/frss/publications/2004011/2.asp#one). The generation that grew up with the personal computer is now on campus and relies on the Internet in every dimension of college life.

Despite these encouraging statistics, some segments of the population are far less familiar with technology. A 2003 report suggested that the tremendous growth in the percentage of the population with Internet access stalled after 2001, possibly because of one-time users dropping their connectivity, the effects of economic downturn, or the fact that technology usage peaked at this point in time (Lenhart et al., 2003, p. 33).

Moreover, a digital divide still exists in this country, although the exact nature of the differences is shifting. As an example, we can look at the issue of Internet connectivity. In 2002, growth of Internet usage was happening most rapidly among African Americans and Latinos, although individuals from these groups were still less likely than whites and Asian Americans to be connected. Older Americans, individuals with lower incomes, and people from rural areas are also less likely to be connected. And individuals who have disabilities use the Internet at considerably lower rates: 38 percent versus 58 percent of all Americans. "Of the 62% of people with disabilities that do not use the Internet, 28% said their disability impaired or made impossible the use of the Internet" (Lenhart et al., 2003).

Thus it is important not to assume that all students have had the same exposure and access to the technology you plan to use in class. Instead, you can conduct a brief survey at the beginning of the semester to find out where your students stand. Even students who come from households where technology was present might not have spent much time with it and might not be familiar with the applications you expect them to use. To help all students succeed, you can develop a brief orientation to the technology as well as some tasks that would allow students to learn the technology and accomplish some course-specific goals. You can also seek out the office on your campus that supports students with disabilities to learn more about services they offer so that you can be proactive (in your syllabus and in introducing the technology) about discussing accommodations for disabled students. Finally, find out where students can go for help with technology questions, and tell them about the resources available.

Aside from issues of exposure and access to technology, you will want to take into consideration that students will come to your class with a variety of learning styles and preferences (Grasha & Yangarber-Kicks, 2000). For example, today's students are much more accustomed to multimedia presentations of information, multiprocessing, and multitasking (Brown, 2000). For many students, presenting information in both verbal and visual modes improves information retention and transfer (Mayer, 2001). For more information on student learning styles, see the chapter "Teaching Culturally Diverse Students."

Beyond addressing learning styles, you will need to consider how technology alters the roles students need to take on in your classes. When you use technology in teaching, students may be required to assume new responsibilities, such as monitoring their own learning goals, setting priorities, and controlling the pace of learning. Some students may not be ready or willing to take on these responsibilities. Students can even be resentful of new expectations and challenges because they are used to learning in a passive and responsive way rather than being active and taking initiative. If you take a more student-centered approach as a result of incorporating technology into your teaching, some students might see it as an abdication of responsibility rather than a positive development. As you move toward greater student involvement and autonomy, you will need to explain why you are taking this approach and build in enough structure so that students do not feel lost. The following suggestions should help:

- Discuss options for support if students encounter difficulties.

- Provide opportunities for feedback about the class so that you can make minor adjustments when problems arise.

- Be clear about your expectations for using technology and for any projects and assignments.

- Build in multiple milestones for independent or group projects so that you can check student progress.

Technology Tools

Now that we have carefully considered the context of teaching and learning, we can turn to an examination of the technology itself. One of the challenges we all confront is the need to understand the possible uses and functions of an ever-expanding array of technologies. You need to consider which applications are appropriate for your students, course content, and teaching style. Not all the tools are the same. Some can assist learning in one content area only; others are useful for a range of disciplines. Some technology tools are built with specific instructional goals in mind; others are more generally applicable.

In order to explore appropriate uses of technology, we can categorize various technology tools into groups according to function. For example, a large group of tools can be used to help students communicate and interact with each other or with the instructor. Software programs such as *Inspiration* and *PowerPoint* assist users in organizing information and displaying it in text or graphic format. Course management tools make it easy for instructors to distribute to students course materials such as a syllabus and assignments and, in some cases, to manage quizzes and student grades. Table 18.2 briefly summarizes common types of technology, provides examples, and lists possible instructional uses for each type.

Communication.　Current communication technology enables users to communicate with one another in three different modes: (1) One-to-one communication via telephone or electronic mail allows comparatively private conversations between a student and an instructor. (2) One-to-many communication via teleconference or listserver offers the means to broadcast information to a group. (3) Many-to-many communication, such as threaded electronic discussions, allows students to share information/ideas and collaborate with each other on learning tasks.

Various communication tools make it possible for students to extend class discussions beyond the class time and to reach experts beyond campus walls and collaborate on learning tasks with peers in other countries. For distance learning courses, communication tools are essential for forming online learning communities that connect distant learners at diverse locations. Students can hold group meetings or discuss course assignments and projects in asynchronous or synchronous programs. Instructors can use both programs for online office hours and for online discussions in distance learning and on-campus courses.

An example of practical application: Mark Clague, a music professor at the University of Michigan, asked students to listen to musical excerpts and discuss their reactions with each other in a "threaded" discussion in UM.CourseTools. He could thus begin the face-to-face discussion with topics that interested or perplexed the students. "The online discussion quickly became a core component of the course and its organization. . . . The threaded discussion complemented the classroom experience, encouraging a richer, more open, more respectful and thoughtful dialogue" (M. Clague, personal communication, Fall 2001). He also posts film-related questions before each film is screened, thereby allowing students to consider topics while they are watching a film and then share their thoughts immediately after viewing.

TABLE 18.2 Technology Types, Examples, and Instructional Uses

Type	Example	Instructional Use
Communication		
■ One to one	E-mail, telephone	Presenting information
■ One to many	Bulletin board,	
■ Many to many	listserver, tele-conference and video conference, web conferencing	Integrating information
	Internet relay chat (IRC)	Interacting with others and collaborating on tasks
Organization and Presentation		
■ Text	PowerPoint,	Presenting information
■ Text/graphic	Inspiration	
■ Text/graphic/ sound/animation	HTML editors	Integrating information
	Macromedia Fireworks and Flash	
	Audio/video (CD or DVD)	
	Streaming media	
Information Searching and Resource Management		
■ Information searching	The World Wide Web, the Internet	Presenting, integrating, and manipulating information
Local access	Electronic databases such as MathSci Database, Wilson Indexes, and ERIC database	
Worldwide access		
■ Information managing		
	Procite, EndNotes	
Web-based Course Management System		
■ Commercial product	Blackboard	Presenting information
	WebCT	
■ Noncommercial product	TopClass	Integrating information
	UM.CourseTools and CTools*	Interacting with others and collab-orating on tasks

*UM.CourseTools is a customizable web-based classroom management tool used at the University of Michigan. CTools is the Next Generation of CourseTools, a web-based system for coursework and collaboration at the University of Michigan.

Tips for Using E-mail and Asynchronous Online Discussion

E-mail

Set up rules for class e-mail. For example:

- Establish conventions for naming message titles and subtitles (for example, ECON 101–Assignment and ECON 101–Requesting an Appointment).

- Clarify wait time for the instructor's response (for instance, a student who sends an e-mail at 3 a.m. can't expect a timely response from the instructor).

- Ask students to use consistent attachment formats (such as saving documents in MS Word or Text format).

Keep a copy of important correspondence yourself. (Don't assume that your students will keep all the messages you send.)

Asynchronous Online Discussions

Preparation:

- Define clear goals and objectives for the online discussion.

- Organize the online conference clearly by category and topic ahead of time.

- Provide detailed instructions for students, including student roles and responsibilities.

- Establish rules for appropriate and inappropriate behaviors before starting discussions.

- Require students to log in a certain number of times each week.

- Establish clear expectations and standards for assessing student performance in the online discussion.

- Distinguish between two types of conferences: (a) formal and (b) informal ones.

- Create an outline of different types of activities for the online conferencing/discussion.

- Make online discussion/conferencing an integral part of the course. (Do not separate what is happening in the conference from what is happening in the face-to-face class meetings.)

- Establish a clear starting and ending time for each discussion topic.

(cont.)

- Direct students to technology training classes, online tutorials, and any other assistance when necessary.

Facilitation:

- Create a comfortable atmosphere for the online conferencing/discussion. For example:

  Be an active participant.

  Challenge the students without threatening them.

  Use personal anecdotes when appropriate.

  Bring your own experiences to the discussion.

  Do not dominate a discussion or let a few students dominate it.

- Ask questions at different levels (for example, knowledge, comprehension, application, analysis, synthesis, and evaluation).

- Paraphrase a message if it is not clear.

- Encourage active student participation.

- Energize the online discussion if needed (by using such techniques as role-plays, simulations, pros and cons).

- Bring closure to an online discussion (by, for example, summarizing learning points).

Organization and Presentation.   Presentation technology allows instructors to organize and present information in text, graphic, animated, or multimedia format. It is easy to prepare lecture notes or outlines in text and graphic format with software programs like *Microsoft Word* or *Microsoft PowerPoint.* The learning curve for making a PowerPoint presentation is not steep, and the time you need to learn the skills is manageable. Using digital media such as CD or DVD clips and integrating them into your presentations, however, requires specific skills. On most campuses, instructional technology labs or centers help faculty with various media projects such as digitizing film clips and creating multimedia presentations. The use of graphic presentations of abstract information and hierarchical relationships can help you explain difficult concepts. Research shows that presenting novel and difficult concepts to learners in both auditory and visual symbolic modes results in more learning than presenting information in either mode (Mayer, 1997; Mousavi et al., 1995).

For example, Linear Algebra at Virginia Tech is a large lecture course taken each year by a large number of first-year students majoring in engineering, physical science, and mathematics. Instructors redesigned the course and replaced regular class meetings with various kinds of technology-assisted learning materials, such as web-based resources, interactive tutorials, computational exercises, an electronic hypertext, practice exercises with video solutions to frequently asked questions, applications, and online quizzes. The introduction of technology and new teaching and learning methods into the course improved cost-effectiveness in teaching and also produced small improvement in student learning (http://www.center.rpi.edu/PewGrant/RD1award/VA.html).

Tips for Using PowerPoint

- Use fonts 24 points or larger for the text.
- Ensure that your slides are legible (for example, watch your color choices for type and background).
- Avoid USING ALL CAPS. (The normal use of upper and lowercase characters is easier to read.)
- Use italics or color rather than underlining to emphasize a point. (Underlining makes some characters difficult to read.)
- Limit the copy to seven words per line and eight lines per slide.
- Use the slide as a guide for presentation.
- Face the audience when showing the slide.
- Distribute a copy of the slides to students ahead of time if possible.
- Keep the room lights on and avoid showing slides in a dark room for more than 15 minutes (Dark rooms can make students drowsy.)
- Avoid putting students in a passive mode of receiving information by combining the slide presentation with chalkboard/whiteboard use or other learning activities.
- Have a backup plan in case of a power outage or equipment failure.

Information Searching and Resource Management. This technology helps users search, locate, and manage information. Instructors across the curriculum identify the set of skills associated with searching, managing, and evaluating information on the Internet as important student learning objectives. You can help students gain skills in Internet search and web site evaluation by reviewing the basics of Internet search engines and offering information or guidelines on evaluating web sites (see Table 18.3). Most university and college libraries have these kinds of resources available for students. For example, the Undergraduate Library at the University of Michigan provides "Criteria for Web Site Evaluation" at http://www.lib.umich.edu/ugl/research/evaluation/, and the University of California at Berkeley has useful information on Internet search engines and web site evaluation at http://www.lib.berkeley.edu/TeachingLib/Guides/ Internet/Evaluate.html.

When assigning students to use Internet resources for writing projects, the instructor should teach students differences between common knowledge and plagiarism and strategies to recognize and avoid plagiarism. Resources for instructors and students on academic integrity are available at most institutions. For example, the University of Michigan has a web site with extensive resources on academic integrity at http://www.lib.umich.edu/acadintegrity/. Penn State University's information technology services gather useful resources on plagiarism at http://tlt.its.psu.edu/suggestions/cyberplag/, including examples of acceptable and unacceptable paraphrases. See also the discussion of plagiarism in the Internet age in the chapter "What to Do About Cheating."

Web-Based Course Management Systems. These systems provide an instructor with a set of tools, allowing the instructor to create and manage course web sites without using HTML editors or other programming languages. A web-based course management system usually includes space for a schedule or calendar, announcements, assignments, online discussions, and resources. Some systems are built with an assessment module and a gradebook, allowing the instructor to give students online quizzes or tests. Students will find course materials in one location once the institution has adopted a course management system. Most current web-based course management systems are great for storing and

TABLE 18.3   Basics About Internet Search Engines

Types	Web Site Search	Directory Search	Meta Search
	Search web sites (full text) in a single database	Search web sites in directories organized in subjects by human beings	Search multiple databases using multiple search engines
Example	**Google**	**Yahoo**	**Vivisimo**
	http://www.google.com	http://dir.yahoo.com	http://www.vivisimo.com
	Teoma	**Librarians' Index**	**Metacrawler**
	http://www.teoma.com	http://www.lii.org	http://metacrawler.com
	Altavista	**Academic Info**	**Dogpile**
	http://www.altavista.com	http://www.academicinfo.net	http://www.dogpile.com

Tips for Using Course Management Systems

- Identify what features in a course management system you will use and why you will use them.
- Start with a few features if you are a first-time/novice user of the course management system.
- Consider how to organize and present course materials effectively through the use of a web-based course management system.
- Prepare students for the use of the course management system, and arrange student training if necessary.
- Be aware that creating web-based courses and modules requires at least as much effort and time as creating traditional courses—and maybe more.

distributing information and hosting online discussion, but they are still limited in dynamic display and manipulation of information.

Many instructors also use regular web sites for teaching. Instructors can take advantage of hyperlinks on the Internet, build a web site to distribute course materials and resources, and involve students in the development of content and also experiment with a new way of teaching and learning. For example, Valley of the Shadow project (http://valleyvcdh.virginia.edu), which appeared on the web in early 1990s, introduced a new way of learning and studying history. The technology skills required to start a simple course web site may be similar to those needed to create a PowerPoint presentation. Current HTML editors like Dreamweaver and Homesite are straightforward and easy to learn. To publish your pages on the web, you will need to find out how to access the designated spaces on the webserver of your department or institution. Once you publish the web site, the subsequent revision and addition will become very easy (see the box "Tips for Creating Course Web Sites").

You can also incorporate web site creation into student projects. Having students create their own web sites and making their work available to a larger audience can increase students' motivation for learning and raise their expectations about the

Tips for Creating Course Web Sites

1. Allow plenty of lead-time for planning the course and designing course web pages.

2. Be sure that the course web pages are functional and contents are accessible to students with disabilities.

3. Have a back-up plan for lectures (for example, print or save the web pages on your local hard drive).

4. Be well prepared for your presentation. For instance:

   ■ Check the classroom setup (browser, software, computer memory, monitor, and audio, and so on).

   ■ Verify links, especially the external links.

   ■ Check the room lighting to see whether it is suitable for both viewing the projected screen and for taking notes.

   ■ Arrange for a technical support staff to be in your classroom at the start of class to help with the setup if necessary.

   ■ Always know whom to call for help if technical problems occur.

5. Emphasize the need for filtering and interpreting information on the web when encouraging students to use online resources.

6. Remind students that only a small fraction of the whole archive of knowledge is available on the web.

quality of their work and the time they are willing to invest in a class. At the same time, such projects present challenges for both students and instructors. Students may not have strong technology skill backgrounds and may be new to using this kind of medium for class projects. Instructors also might not have much experience designing or assessing this type of project (see the box "Tips for Assigning Student Technology Projects").

In his eighteenth-century British literature courses, David Porter of the University of Michigan encourages students, working in small groups, to write and design their own web pages exploring various aspects of eighteenth-century life and culture in England. This assignment serves as the final project for the course. Students who participate in the web project find that the experience enhances their intellectual and technical skills.

Tips for Assigning Student Technology Projects

1. Define specific goals for students' web pages/projects.
2. Provide detailed guidelines for students' web pages/projects.
3. Establish clear expectations and standards for assessing students' web pages/projects.
4. Make students' web pages/projects an integral part of students' learning experience in the course.
5. Encourage students' sharing and reviewing of projects.
6. Set periodical check-in points for a semester-long technology project.
7. Arrange technology training for students if necessary.

One student noted, "Not only was this project useful in increasing my confidence with technology, but I felt that it helped me to better understand some of the novels we read, as well as the historical context in which these novels were written" (Retrieved on September 17, 2003, from http://www.umich.edu/%7Eece/about.html#comments). Figure 18.3 shows a student projects page from Porter's course web site.

Teaching at a distance can include all the technology tools listed above. In addition, distance learning courses can be delivered via videoconference systems (one- or two-way audio and video) and the Internet-based audio and videoconference software programs. For more information on distance learning courses, see the chapter "Teaching by Distance Education."

WHAT ARE THE EFFECTS OF TECHNOLOGY ON TEACHING?

Assumptions about technology and its effects vary among technology users. Some proponents of technology believe that both instructors and students can take advantage of technology to teach well and learn well if they get the right hardware and

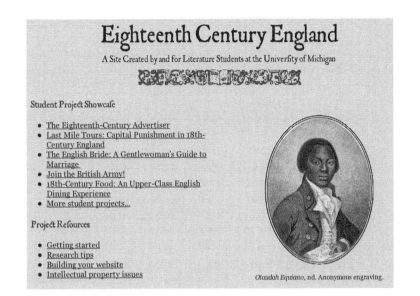

Eighteenth Century England

A Site Created by and for Literature Students at the Univerſity of Michigan

Student Projeĉt Showcaſe

- The Eighteenth-Century Advertiser
- Last Mile Tours: Capital Punishment in 18th-Century England
- The English Bride: A Gentlewoman's Guide to Marriage
- Join the British Army!
- 18th-Century Food: An Upper-Class English Dining Experience
- More student projects...

Projeĉt Reſources

- Getting started
- Research tips
- Building your website
- Intellectual property issues

Olaudah Equiano, nd. Anonymous engraving.

FIGURE 18.3   Page from "Eighteenth Century England" Course Web Site

Source: Eighteenth Century England: A Site Created by and for Literature Students and the University of Michigan. Reprinted from www.umich.edu/%7Eece/index.html by permission of Professor David Porter, Department of English, University of Michigan.

software in the classroom. Others believe that hardware and software used in the class are irrelevant to student learning. These two opposing positions actually reflect the debate of medium and message in the field of educational technology (Clark, 1994a, 1994b; Kozma, 1994). The research studies collected in *No Significant Difference Phenomenon* by Tom Russell (1999) do indicate that the vehicle—that is, the technology used for providing information—does not significantly affect student learning outcomes. However, other researchers, such as Kozma (1994), argue that we have not sufficiently used and examined the attributes and specific functions of individual technologies or explored and compared their effectiveness in instruction. We cannot, therefore, expect to find that technologies make a difference until we can exploit the unique capabilities of the medium.

Kulik conducted a meta-analysis that reviewed more than 100 controlled studies on the use of instructional technology in college courses during the 1980s and early 1990s. This meta-analysis showed that computer-based instruction made small but significant contributions to academic achievement and also produced positive, but again small, effects on student attitudes (Kulik, 2003).

For practical and useful research into teaching with technology, questions should be directed toward exploring what the best teaching and learning strategies are and how technologies best support those strategies (Ehrmann, 1995; Kozma, 1994). Some examples of faculty pursuing these types of questions can be found on the web site for the Visible Knowledge Project (http://crossroads.georgetown.edu/vkp/), which focuses in part on applying methods from the scholarship of teaching and learning to technology. The web site contains short descriptions of individual faculty projects that focus on a specific technology and its impact on student learning and attitudes. As you think about the effects of technology on teaching and learning, you need to consider the full range of changes technology has brought to a given course or curriculum. The following questions are designed to help you think about how you might evaluate the effect of technology in teaching and student learning:

- Were there any changes in teaching and learning practices as a result of the new technology? Examples of changes could include:

    Level of student engagement in learning

    Interaction between the instructor and students and among students themselves

    Ways of addressing diverse learning styles

- Did the change(s) in teaching practice and the use of technology help students achieve the course goals and learning objectives? Examples could include:

    Demonstration of student knowledge, skills, and attitudes

    Pre- and post-test results

    Comparison of student learning before and after technology was integrated

- How does the technology impact teaching and learning efficiency?

    Use of class time

    Instructor's time on course preparation and management

    Students' time on learning tasks

IN CONCLUSION

The successful integration of technology entails the careful consideration of course content, the capabilities of various technology tools, student access to and comfort with technology, and the instructor's view of his or her role in the teaching and learning process. The use of technology may change teaching methods and approaches to learning as well as attitudes, motivation, and interest in teaching and learning the subject. With careful thought and planning, faculty can take advantage of developments in instructional technology to enhance their courses, reexamine their own ideas about teaching, and promote greater student academic achievement.

Supplementary Reading

PowerPoint

- B. Brown, "PowerPoint-Induced Sleep," *Syllabus,* 2001, *14*(6), 17.

- T. Creed, *PowerPoint, No! Cyberspace, Yes,* 1999, available at http://www.ntlf.com/html/pi/9705/creed_1.htm

- D. Hlynka, "PowerPoint in the Classroom: What Is the Point?" *Educational Technology,* 1998, *38*(5), 45–48.

- R. Mason, "PowerPoint in the Classroom: Where Is the Power?" *Educational Technology,* 1998, *38*(5), 42–45.

- T. Rocklin, *PowerPoint Is Not Evil,* 1999, available at http://www.ntlf.com/html/sf/notevil.htm

- E. R. Tufte, *The Cognitive Style of PowerPoint* (Cheshire, CT: Graphics Press, 2003).

E-mail and Online Discussion

■ C. J. Bonk and K. S. King (eds.), *Electronic Collaborators: Learner-Centered Technologies for Literacy, Apprenticeship, and Discourse* (Mahwah, NJ: Erlbaum, 1998).

■ G. Collison, B. Elbaum, S. Haavind, and R. Tinker, *Facilitating Online Learning: Effective Strategies for Moderators* (Madison, WI: Atwood Publishing, 2000).

■ eModerators provides resources specifically for facilitators and moderators of online discussion at http://www.emoderators.com

■ D. Hanna, M. Glowacki-Dudka, and S. Conceicao-Runlee, *147 Practical Tips for Teaching Online Groups: Essentials of Web-Based Education* (Madison, WI: Atwood Publishing, 2000).

Teaching with the Web

■ S. Horton, *Web Teaching Guide: A Practical Approach to Creating Course Web Sites* (New Haven, CT: Yale University Press, 2000).

■ B. H. Khan (ed.), *Web-Based Instruction* (Englewood Cliffs, NJ: Educational Technology Publications, 1997).

■ G. R. Morrison, S. M. Ross, and J. E. Kemp, *Designing Effective Instruction* (New York: Wiley, 2001).

Part 5

Skills for Use in Other Teaching Situations

19 Teaching Large Classes (You Can Still Get Active Learning!)

In the middle of the twentieth century, most first- and second-year courses were taught by lecture in large classrooms or auditoriums. Over the next decades, research demonstrated that better learning occurred if students had an opportunity to discuss the material. Thus many large courses now supplement lectures with one or two hours of small-group discussion. However, with decreasing government support and increasing enrollments, more and more universities all over the world feel pressure to revert to large classes without support from small discussion groups or tutorials.

Most of this chapter deals with skills and strategies useful in large groups, whether or not they are supplemented by discussion groups. Before concluding, I discuss aspects of the teacher's role involved in supervising teaching assistants who lead discussion or laboratory groups.

If you are assigned to teach a large course, you are likely to assume that you must lecture and use multiple-choice or other easily scorable tests, but large classes need not constrain you. You don't need to lecture—at least not all the time.

FACILITATING ACTIVE LEARNING

The most commonly used method of stimulating active learning is questioning and encouraging student questioning, as discussed in the chapters "Facilitating Discussion" and "How to Make Lectures More Effective." But many other tools in your active learning kit are usable in large classes. In the chapter "Active Learning," I reported the research showing that students learn more in student-led discussions, or in learning cells, than they learn in traditional lectures. Thus you can get the advantages of a multisection course by organizing students to meet in class or out of class for discussion. Active learning does not need to be restricted to in-class activity. You can organize study groups. You can use e-mail. The chapter "Technology and Teaching" describes ways in which technology can facilitate learning both in and out of class.

Techniques such as buzz groups, problem posting, and the two-column method of large-group discussions were also described earlier. Buzz groups (described in the chapter "Facilitating Discussion") can be formed and asked to discuss how the material might be used or applied. Simply pausing occasionally to give students a couple of minutes to compare their notes can activate thinking (Ruhl et al., 1987).

It is still possible even using these techniques for students to hold back in large classes, but technology may be coming to your rescue. Recent advances in wireless technology make it possible to have every student in the class actively respond to questions and problems. In the generic system each student has a remote control handset with a keypad. The instructor projects a multiple-choice question on a screen at the front of the room. Each student selects one of the alternatives and enters that response on his or her keypad. The choice is then transmitted to a computer, all the responses are compiled, and the results are displayed in graphic format, showing how many folks chose each alternative. The instructor gets immediate feedback on how well the students were understanding the lecture content, and the students get immediate feedback on whether or not they understood. Some systems make it possible for the instructor to identify—for grading purposes later—which students are making which responses. Even if the instructor doesn't know which students made which responses, he or she can invite students to defend a given option (if they chose it) or to challenge another one. Because the students can see how many other students in the class agreed with them, they will feel more or less inclined to speak up when their option is challenged. This procedure can be done in groups, with each group's response rather than an individual's response entered on the keypad. The system can be used to take roll or simply to give the students an active learning opportunity.

Encouraging Student Writing in Large Classes

One of the most important drawbacks of large classes is the lack of student writing. Because grading essays is so time consuming, most faculty members reduce or eliminate writing assignments in a large class. Take heart! You can get some of the educational advantages of writing, and at the same time improve attention to the lecture, without being submerged by papers to grade.

The minute paper, described earlier, is one valuable tool.* At an appropriate point in the lecture, announce the paper and the topic or question you want students to address; for example, you might ask the students to summarize the major point or points made so far in the lecture. Or you might give the students a choice of topics, such as a summary, a question, an application, or an example. When the minute is up, you may either collect the papers or break the class into pairs or subgroups to review and discuss one another's papers.

If you wish, you can evaluate and comment on the papers as you would any other student papers. If the class is exceptionally large, you may announce that you'll read and return only a sample of the papers. Students can be motivated to think and write without the threat of grades, and this technique not only gets students thinking actively during the lecture but gives you feedback about what students are learning from the lecture.

The problem with evaluating these papers in a large class is the huge amount of work that it causes for the instructor. I find that after reading a sample of answers I can give generic feedback to

---

*The minute paper need not be one minute; it can be two, three, or as many minutes as needed for a particular topic.

the whole class in the form of general comments put up on the class web site. Students can then compare their efforts to these general comments. Another alternative is the calibrated peer review system, discussed in the chapter "Assessing, Testing, and Evaluating." In this system students review one another's papers online in a grand randomized sequencing. Each student's review is weighted according to a calibration system and his or her contribution to peers' papers is figured accordingly.

Similar to the minute paper is the "half-sheet response" (Weaver & Cotrell, 1985). In this technique students tear out a half-sheet of notebook paper to respond to a question or instruction such as:

"What do you think about this concept?"
"Give an example of this concept or principle."
"Explain this concept in your own words."
"How does this idea relate to your own experience?"
"What are some of your feelings as you listen to these ideas?"
"How could you use this idea in your own life?"

Both the minute paper and the half-sheet response can help initiate a large-group discussion.

Other Ways to Maintain Student Involvement

There are a variety of techniques that can help break the deadly routine of lectures day after day: debates, fishbowl, interviews.

In addition to the large-group discussion and subgrouping techniques discussed in the chapters "Facilitating Discussion" and "Active Learning," you can enliven your class with debates either between faculty members or between student teams. If you use student debaters, you need to provide a clear structure, probably using a handout describing the issue, the length of talks, opportunity for rebuttal, and the goal of the debate as a learning device. If the topic is one on which students are likely to have strong biases, you can open minds by assigning groups to argue the side opposite their initial position. You can follow the debate by dividing the class into buzz groups whose task is to find a solution or resolution that takes into account the evidence and values of both sides.

The "fishbowl" can be used in small, as well as large, classes. Tell the students that at the next class meeting you will choose six students (or any convenient number) to be "in the fishbowl." You will then conduct a discussion (based on the work to date) with the students in the fishbowl. The rest of the students are to act as observers and recorders, noting both the process and the content of the discussion. Before the end of the class period, observers will write a brief summary of the discussion and raise questions that remain or answer the question, "What would you have said that wasn't said?"

Another break in lectures can be provided by an interview— perhaps of a colleague with special expertise, someone from outside the university, or one of the students with special experience. A variant might be a dialog on a topic in which you and a colleague have somewhat different views.

Student presentations can enhance the learning and motivation of students who have special interests or expertise and can also be valuable for the other students if presentations are well done. But don't assume that this will be a chance to reduce your own preparation time. If the student simply reads a paper, the audience will be bored. So work with the student on ways of enhancing interest and attention. For some shy students, you may want to conduct the presentation as an interview.

If you plan to have a number of presentations, consider the possibility of a poster session—a method now common in scholarly conventions.

If you use these methods, some students will be frustrated. They came to hear you tell them the TRUTH, which they can then memorize for tests. To handle this frustration, two things may help:

1. Explain how active participation contributes to better understanding and memory.

2. Make sure that your students realize that your tests will require thinking, not just rote memory.

STUDENT ANONYMITY

A major problem of teaching a large class is that students not only feel anonymous, they usually *are* anonymous. And as social psychological research has shown, people who are anonymous feel less personal responsibility—a consequence not only damaging to morale and order but also unlikely to facilitate learning. Moreover, the sense of distance from the instructor, the loss of interpersonal bonds with the instructor and with other students—these diminish motivation for learning.

The larger the group, the less likely that a given student will feel free to volunteer a contribution or question. Yet the students who prefer anonymity may be the very ones who most need to find that others respect their ideas.

What can we do? The fact that with increasing class size it becomes less and less possible to know students as individuals is likely to make us feel that it is not worth trying to do anything. I think this is a mistake. In my experience the students appreciate whatever efforts you make even if they do not take advantage of them. The "Reducing Students' Feelings of Anonymity" box shows some things I've tried.

If you don't want to or can't reduce student anonymity during the class period itself, you might consider encouraging students to form study groups outside of class. At least they will have a small number of classmates whom they know and who know them. Some large-class instructors try to help students with this group formation by using technology to create a sort of mass calendar. Students who want to study at a particular time can consult the calendar and sign up to be available for studying at that time. Others who consult the calendar can see who's available when or where and get together with those other students at a time that fits their schedule.

ORGANIZATION IS THE KEY

The biggest challenges of teaching a large class are related to being organized. With a large class you can't do things very spontaneously; things have to be planned or they will flounder. What follows are some of the areas in which organization can make or break a class.

Giving Tests in Large Classes

In classes of 200 or more, unwary instructors are likely to run into problems they would never dream of in teaching classes

Reducing Students' Feelings of Anonymity

1. Announce that you'll meet any students who are free for coffee after class. (You won't be swamped.)

2. Pass out invitations to several students to join you for coffee and to get acquainted after class.

3. Pass out brief student observation forms to several students at the beginning of class and ask them to meet with you to discuss their observations.

4. Circulate among early arriving students to get acquainted before class starts.

5. Use a seating chart so that you can call students by name when they participate.

6. During your lecture, move out into the aisles to solicit comments.

7. If you can't use regularly scheduled discussion sections, set up an occasional afternoon or evening session for more informal discussion of an interesting question or for review before an examination.

8. Have students fill out an autobiographical sketch with name, hometown, year in college, and what they hope to get out of the course (Benjamin, 1991).

9. Create a set of flash cards with students' names on one side and their pictures on the other. Study them during odd moments, like when standing in lines.

10. When students are working in groups regularly, you can learn the names of all the students in the group as a set. Then remembering any one student's name may trigger recall of all of them.

with an enrollment of 20 to 30. Most of these problems are administrative. For example, course planning almost inevitably becomes more rigid in a large class because almost anything involving the participation of the students requires more preparation time.

Perhaps you're used to making up your tests the day before you administer them. With a large class this is almost impossible. Essay and short-answer tests that take relatively little time to construct take a long time to score for 200 students; so you may spend long hours trying to devise thought-provoking objective questions for a part of the test. But once you've made up the questions your troubles are not over, for secretaries require a good deal of time to make several hundred copies of a test. Thus spur-of-the-moment tests are almost an impossibility, and by virtue of the necessity of planning ahead for tests, other aspects of the course also become more rigid.

As I indicated in the chapter "Assessing, Testing, and Evaluating," essay examinations are superior to typical objective examinations in their effect on student study and learning. Thus you are likely to regret the loss of the opportunity to give essay tests in a large group. But this loss is not inevitable. To some extent it can be compensated for by greater care in the construction of objective test items. But it is also possible to use essay items without increasing your load beyond reason. In a 500-student lecture course, I regularly included an essay item on the final examination with the stipulation that I would read it only if it would affect the student's letter grade for the course. Since the majority of the students were fairly clearly established as A, B, C, or D students on the basis of other work and the objective part of the final examination, the number of essays I needed to read was not excessive. My subjective impression was that knowledge of the inclusion of an essay item did affect the students' preparation for the exam.

Making Outside Reading Assignments

The testing problem is just one of several factors structuring the conduct of large classes. Another is the assignment of readings in the library. With a small group you can assign library work with little difficulty, only making sure that the materials needed are available and, if necessary, reserved for the class. With a class of several hundred students a library assignment without previous planning can be disastrous. The library's single copy of a book or journal is obviously inadequate. Thus a library assignment must be conceived far enough in advance (usually several months) that enough copies of the book can be obtained, and the librarian can prepare for the fray.

Once again technology can come to the rescue. Some institutions have been able to establish "electronic reserve" systems as a replacement for the library reserves we're all so familiar with. In these systems, the instructor can put an electronic copy of the reading material on the library's computer. Students who are enrolled in the course for which that material is assigned can access it electronically either in the library itself or from any computer with Internet access. Because only students in the class have access to the material, some level of security is preserved and copyright is protected. My students have been particularly enthusiastic about this new system because it allows them to avoid having to make several trips to the library in hopes of being able to get the paper copy. They also can store a copy on which they take notes and save it without using extra printing.

Communicating with Large Classes

Of course, the most important aspect of teaching a large class is being able to maintain up-to-date communication with such a lot of people. Being certain that every student has the latest word on class or assignment changes, deadlines, and exams can be challenging. I can't stress enough the value of having a class web site for a large class. Operating as information and communication central for the class, the web site is available to students 24/7, so you don't have to be. In addition most course management software systems have group e-mail functions that allow you to send out a single notice to the entire class in a single e-mail. Course web sites will always have the latest word on course organization and the latest versions of any course handouts, so you will not need to constantly reannounce changes during class time. As students start asking questions via e-mail or on a class discussion board, you can gather all the similar questions together and post answers to them on the web site, where students learn to look first for answers to their questions before coming to you. My own university made it a policy that e-mail and class web sites should be considered official communication formats of the university.

Technology also helps you with managing office hours. For example, you can have an electronic appointment scheduler for students who want to visit you during office hours. A student checks the calendar, finds an open spot that matches his or her schedule, and registers for that time slot. Or you can hold "virtual office hours" by being available online at announced times. Any student who wants to "chat" can log in and ask questions from a distance. You have the advantage of being able to continue working from anywhere your computer is because it will announce that someone is online and wants to chat.

COORDINATING MULTISECTION COURSES

In any multisection course taught by several different instructors, the problem of coordination inevitably arises. The first approach to coordination is enforced uniformity of course content, sequence of topics, testing, grading, and even anecdotes. Such a procedure has the advantage that students who later elect more advanced courses can be presumed to have a certain uniform amount of background experience. It also is efficient in that only one final examination must be constructed, only one course outline devised, and students can transfer from section to section with no difficulty in catching up.

The disadvantage of this approach is that such uniformity often makes for dull, uninteresting teaching. If the teaching assistants are unenthusiastic about the course outline, they are likely to communicate this attitude to the students. If the course can be jointly planned, this may make for greater acceptance, but may also take a great deal of time.

A second approach to this problem is to set up completely autonomous sections, with all the instructors organizing and conducting their sections as they wish. The effectiveness of giving teaching assistants autonomy depends on how well you train and supervise them.

TRAINING AND SUPERVISING TEACHING ASSISTANTS

Your responsibility begins well before the first class meetings, for your teaching assistants need to know what you are expecting in terms of attendance at lectures, participation in weekly planning and training sessions, testing and grading, office hours, and such. At my institution we have a checklist of possible TA responsibilities. At the beginning of the semester the TA and the supervising professor sit down together and work through their expectations and work assignments. Both sign and get a copy of the checklist so that there is no confusion later about what was expected and when.

Even more important than the formal requirements are the aspects of preparing the teaching assistants for meeting their first classes, establishing a good working relationship with their students, and developing the skills needed for leading discussions, answering questions, and carrying out other teaching responsibilities. Here are some suggestions for assisting teaching assistants:

1. Hold weekly meetings to discuss teaching problems and plans.

2. Collect feedback from students early in the term.

3. Observe classes and discuss your observations with the TA.

To get student feedback, you can use simple open-ended questions, such as:

"What have you liked about the class so far?"
"What suggestions do you have for improvement?"

Visiting classes or videotaping can provide useful information about nonverbal characteristics of the teacher and reactions of the students. But observation or videotaping takes time. If you have time, visit classes, but if you are short of time, there is little evidence that videotaping or observation results in significantly greater improvement in teaching than consultation on student ratings collected early in the term (and perhaps repeated a little later). So if you're short of time, invest it in consultation.

IN CONCLUSION

Class size is important.

When taught appropriately, small classes are likely to be better than large classes for achieving long-term goals, such as retention and use of knowledge, thinking, and attitude change.

Nonetheless, when dealing with large classes, you can come closer to the outcomes of small classes by

1. Providing discussion sections taught by trained teaching assistants.

2. Using teaching methods that facilitate active, meaningful, learning.

The fact that in a large class you will probably spend some of the time lecturing does not mean that students can now slip into passivity. What is important in active learning is active *thinking*. The techniques discussed in this and preceding chapters can produce active thinking and learning even in large lecture halls.

Supplementary Reading

Because almost every large university now has a program for training teaching assistants, there was a biennial meeting on training, and the papers from the meeting were typically published. The first volume is still one of the best:

▓ J. D. Nyquist, R. D. Abbott, D. H. Wulff, and J. Sprague (eds.), *Preparing the Professoriate of Tomorrow to Teach: Selected Readings in TA Training* (Dubuque, IA: Kendall/Hunt, 1991).

For teaching large classes:

▓ Jean MacGregor, James L. Cooper, Karl A. Smith, and Pamela Robinson (eds.), "Strategies for Energizing Large Classes: From Small Groups to Learning Communities," *New Directions for Learning and Teaching*, no. 81, May 2000.

▓ C. Stanly and M. E. Porter (eds.), *Engaging Large Classes: Strategies and Techniques for College Faculty* (Bolton, MA: Onker Publishing, 2002).

▓ R. J. Sternberg (ed.), *Teaching Introductory Psychology: Survival Tips from the Experts* (Washington, DC: American Psychological Association, 1997).

20 Laboratory Instruction: Ensuring an Active Learning Experience

In the sciences, laboratory instruction permits learners to experience phenomena directly as well as understand how new knowledge is constructed. Although laboratory instruction derives from the revered apprenticeship model for learning practical arts, it is certainly not limited to the traditional "wet laboratories" of the physical and natural sciences. From practicum experiences in psychology and education to studios in the fine and performance arts, instructors create learning environments where students can ask questions and seek answers modeled on the way in which professionals do their work. Historically, the latter, performance-based disciplines do an intrinsically better job of engaging students in authentic work (drawing, writing, acting) than the sciences do in getting students to do scientific inquiry and investigation.

Laboratory teaching assumes that firsthand experience is superior to other methods of developing the same skills. Laboratory instruction also rightly presumes that the next generation of

This chapter was written by Brian P. Coppola of the University of Michigan.

practitioners will be motivated by an opportunity to participate in practice. The prevailing rhetoric of "learning by doing" characterizes the passionate attachment that faculty have to this form of teaching. The attributes of research, such as hands-on, "mind's-on" work and individualized experimental design and decision making combined with collaborative tasks, should all theoretically contribute positively to learning. Frequently, though, introductory laboratory instruction in the sciences does not rise above validating results that are repeated year in and year out all over the country by students using rote and lock-step, or "cookbook," procedures.

Authentic, research-based laboratory information is hard earned, emerges over extended periods of time, and would appear to be inefficiently gained in comparison with abstractions presented orally, in print, or digitally. Thus one would not expect laboratory instruction to have an advantage over teaching methods whose strength is in rapidly transmitting large amounts of factual information. Rather one might expect the difference to be revealed in retention, in ability to apply learning, or in actual skill in experimental design, observation, or manipulation of materials and equipment. Unfortunately, few research studies have attempted to measure these kinds of outcomes, a bad situation that is made worse by the lack of consensus about what the goals of laboratory teaching are.

STYLES OF LABORATORY INSTRUCTION

In an attempt to define different instructional goals and their corresponding methodologies, Domin (1999) created a taxonomy of laboratory instruction styles that, though originally based in chemistry, hold up well across many disciplines. Explicit analogies with other areas are not provided here, for they are beyond the scope of this chapter. However, it is important to note that these methods are not simple, neutral choices. Students' early laboratory experiences, which are strongly influenced by instructional design, are often the critical gateway for the level of experience or self-confidence that influences their decisions to persist (or not) in the sciences, particularly in the cases of women and underrepresented minorities (Seymour & Hewitt, 1997; Eccles, 1994). Instructional designs that favor cooperative environments with individual accountability, opportunities for creative design and expression, and chances for reflection and analysis all contribute to positive, motivating experiences that, in turn, favor persistence and continuation.

Domin's categories are expository instruction, inquiry instruction, discovery instruction, and problem-based learning.

Expository Instruction

The most popular and most criticized of Domin's instruction styles, expository instruction features verification of preordained results and an emphasis on manipulation skills, and it asks students to follow exactly prescribed directions (or "cookbook" procedures). A prelaboratory session sets out what is to be observed and how to do it. Postlaboratory sessions review and recapitulate the information. In general, the goal for this kind of instruction is for students to develop manipulative or kinesthetic skills. In a typical activity used both in high school and in college, students might all receive a block of aluminum and be asked to follow an exact procedure for determining its density, the value of which is provided. Students follow precise directions, often filling in a worksheet with numerical values according to a prescribed script. The presumption is that a student who has successfully followed the procedure and arrived at the expected answer has also learned something about measurement and how it is done.

Expository instruction can be done on a large scale with minimal engagement by the instructor, it is largely impervious to variation in who does it, and it minimizes cost, space, and equipment. Unfortunately, it also may be true that almost no meaningful learning takes place (Hofstein & Lunetta, 1982).

Inquiry Instruction

In inquiry instruction, without a predetermined outcome, students are asked formulate their own problem from the information at hand; in doing so, they mimic the process of constructing knowledge. The density activity might begin with a question posed to the students who have been given different-sized samples of the same metal: "What is the relationship between mass and volume in this material?" Different procedures for measuring volume are provided, and the results derived from these different methods are compared. Students have more choice in design and more responsibility in making sense of their results, and they must generally face more directly the importance of reproducibility in making measurements. Follow-up questions are either posed by the teacher ("Is density an intrinsic or extrinsic property?") or elicited from the students ("Is the density of all metals the same?").

Inquiry instruction is a compromise between closed- and open-ended instruction favored by national recommendations (National Research Council, 2000). In a practical sense, it is difficult to keep inquiry laboratories vital because it is difficult to conceal the details of the solutions to these problems from one generation of students to the next without a great deal of effort. Also, the drive to make the teaching process easier can slowly turn these inquiries into exposition.

Discovery Instruction

In discovery instruction, also called "guided inquiry," the teacher constructs an instructional setting with a prescribed outcome in mind and directs students toward that outcome. Discovery instruction seeks to make knowledge more personal for students and thereby more highly owned. Adapting the density experiment to discovery mode might begin with a prelaboratory discussion in which the exercise is introduced by a question: "What measurements can be made to determine the physical properties of materials?" The students are encouraged to make predictions, formulate hypotheses, and then design experiments. All the while, the instructor controls the discussion, steering students toward the information from prior classes, including different mass-to-volume relationships as potentially useful quantities. The instructor also uses these opportunities to evaluate the experimental designs suggested by the students, motivating them with the sense of ownership and curiosity about the undetermined result, and inevitably guides the discussion toward the preplanned experiment. Students work individually or in groups, with enough variation in their activities for the class to pool their results. Afterward, the discussion led by the instructor moves the class to the intended lesson. Discovery-based instruction can invest the student in his or her own learning and can result in deeper understanding (Horowitz, 2003).

Problem-Based Learning

Problem-based learning (PBL) creates a context for students to generate their own questions, but it does so with strong fore-grounding by the instructor (Albanese & Mitchell, 1993). PBL is popular across many disciplines. An instructor crafts and selects evidence and then presents the case study to the students, who in turn uncover what the faculty member has in mind as the root lessons.

Meta-lessons about doing research can be abstracted and returned as a PBL framework for collaborative, open-ended exercises (Coppola, 1995). The density activity would begin with black enamel paint concealing the color of a group of differently shaped metal pieces. Wenzel's (1995, 1998) analytical chemistry program is noteworthy for its emphasis on framing a term-long investigation, often addressing a problem of high community interest (such as air quality) as the context for students to develop authentic investigative, procedural, and communications skills. The significant aspects of PBL include the following:

1. *An organizing question that students can understand is posed.* They are then expected to design experiments to solve the question. In this case, each student gets a different piece of metal; instead of asking students to identify the metal, which is far outside of their experience to design, the instructor asks them to determine who else in class has the same metal as they do.

2. *The problem cannot be answered by the work of an individual acting alone.* It requires the class to make group decisions about the experiments they carry out, how they are going to share the information, and what the standards of reasonable comparison need to be. The class might select density as the property to measure. Students will need to decide on units of measurement,

how many trials must be done, and what will constitute "the same" and "different."

3. *Multiple and equally valid strategies can be used to solve the problem* (Mills et al., 2000). The students might request to do chemical tests on other samples of the metals in order to collect data. They might choose hardness, malleability, color (after scraping), or some combination of these after initial groups have been made.

4. *Experimental procedures are a means to an end.* Exposition and inquiry both have roles in carrying out an individual's work. Procedures for carrying out a known process should be able to be followed. Yet the purpose for collecting information (density) remains focused squarely on the goal (who has the same?) rather than on the measurement for its own sake.

5. *Communication and comparison are key.* Students need to decide how to share their data and how they will make their conclusions. Samples may be exchanged and tested independently if there are outlying data points or if some students have a hard time reproducing their experiments.

6. *Follow-up work is implied by the results.* Inquiry inevitably leads to new questions. Once the relative identification is made and the students have grouped themselves according to the convergence of measured properties, new questions can be posed or elicited: "What are the identities of these metals?" "Is this information enough, or is other information needed?"

Relative identification is a widely applicable strategy for making problems. In chemistry, one might ask who has the same solid, liquid, mixture, or concentration of acid. In mathematics, one might ask who has numbers in the same type of series. In psychology, one might ask who has the same personality type; in the history of art, who has a painting from the same period; and in English, who has a paragraph with the same structure.

Inquiry, discovery, and problem-based activities are a better way than exposition to accomplish instructional goals because they are more engaging, permitting higher ownership and self-regulation of learning. Some formal heuristics developed for learners in these types of laboratory settings have demonstrated success. One of these is POE (Predict-Observe-Explain [Champagne et al., 1980]); another is the MORE (Model-Observe-Reflect-Explain [Tien et al., 1999]) method, which was developed for formal laboratory modules. Case studies are a kind of PBL that begins by posing questions based on a news headline ("Two would-be chemists die in explosion while attempting to make methamphetamine") and turning the case into a structured activity (Bieron & Dinan, 2000).

STUDIO INSTRUCTION BRINGS TOGETHER THE ARTS AND SCIENCES

Many colleges have tried to work within the confines of traditional lab and lecture times, but St. Edwards University (Austin, Texas) set aside the traditional class structure and uses two four-hour lab periods so that students are able to "act as scientists and learn as a scientist learns" (Altmiller, 1973). The University of North Carolina at Charlotte's inquiry-based "intimately meshed" lecture and lab (DiBiase & Wagner, 2002) and North Carolina State University's cAcL$_2$ (concept Advancement through chemistry Lab-Lecture) active learning environment (Oliver-Hoyo et al., 2004) are other examples. A group of four chemistry departments—at California Polytechnic Institute (Bailey et al., 2000), Rensselaer Polytechnic Institute (Apple & Cutler, 1999), California State University at Fullerton (Gonzalez, 1999), and the State University of West Georgia (Khan et al., 2003)—adopted the studio teaching method, inspired in part by the studio in the RPI physics department (Wilson, 1994). In general, adopting studio instruction has also involved remodeling the physical space in order to accommodate these pedagogical changes. The University of Michigan has experimented with the question of bringing this nontraditional instructional style into a traditional setting in order to lower the barrier for others who might not wish (or be able) to make the capital investment (Gottfried et al., 2003).

In a studio, learning and practice are intimately integrated and take place in the same space, so that transitions between theory and practice are unhindered. In the sciences, a studio implies an environment where students have access to concepts, problem solving, and experiments in the same space and practice and theory are inseparable; interactive, hands-on experiences deliver fast results; and students use the results from one inquiry to design and carry out the next one. As in an art class, studio instruction in the sciences focuses on the artifacts created by students as the basis for discussion and further work. The studio teaching method is especially appealing because it does not limit itself to a single type of best practice. Instead it allows mixing and matching of proven ways of teaching chemical concepts.

The breaking of the tradition of centralized authority in teaching and learning coincides with society's demands for increasing the diversity of people who are prepared to do (or understand) science and technology. This is fortunate, because many believe that this increase can be accomplished by designing classrooms that foster success both broadly and inclusively. Seymour and Hewitt (1997) showed that "the most effective way to improve retention among women and students of color, and to build their numbers over the longer term, is to improve the quality of the learning experience for all students—including non-science majors who wish to study science and mathematics as part of their overall education." They also found that while almost all students value collaborative learning, students from underrepresented groups "appreciate it more and miss it when [it is] unavailable."

TURNING NOVICE RESEARCHERS INTO PRACTICING SCIENTISTS

The goals for upper-level laboratories may be quite different from those for lower-level laboratories, where professional development for a specialized work force makes sense. As illustrated above, traditional verification laboratories can be adapted to more inquiry and open-ended activities. Adaptation can be further extended to capture an even closer flavor of research. Milestones for this process include the following:

1. *Defining the higher-level goals to be derived from the exercise.* In preparatory chemistry, one of the prescribed criteria is how long a set of reagents is to be stirred together before the reaction is

considered to be complete. Monitoring the reaction process while it is occurring and deciding when it is done is a high-level skill that is precluded by providing this information. Instead of providing a complete "cookbook" recipe to follow, the instructor can truncate or rewrite the procedure in order to make this activity an instructional goal.

2. *Moving from the known as a precedent for exploring the unknown.* In preparatory chemistry, it is customary to test out a new procedure on a model compound, perhaps even repeat the procedure on a substrate reported in the literature, before proceeding to the new and unfamiliar substrate. The research literature is a wellspring of information for adapting and creating new laboratory exercises. If the instructor selects from the recent research literature a new methodological procedure that appears to be amenable to the time and material constraints of the teaching laboratory, the substrates reported in the literature can be purchased and the recent scientific results used with students. Students become quite engaged when they are handed a copy of a journal article and have access to the substrates. Selecting procedures that can be extrapolated to new, unreported substrates allows students to do actual research and integrates exploring the unknown into the lesson (Coppola et al., 1997).

3. *Freeing up time for students to design and carry out new experiments.* In many cases, students can suggest new questions about and adaptations of experiments they have performed. With careful supervision for safety considerations, such as writing out a proposal and having it subjected to formal approval, students can pursue their own work.

4. *Higher-level students doing fundamental experimental design and carrying it out.* The features of research can be explored with simple problems of which students take nearly complete ownership. This requires extra time and resource support in order to work more individually with students, but this is appropriate for upper- or lower-level honors students. First-year chemistry honors students, for example, can be directed to select a two-step synthetic sequence that represents any part of the subject matter they have studied in the course. They then need to do library or online

research to find a proper precedent, make a proposal, keep material costs below a prescribed level, and submit this for approval. Safety data and procedural issues should be included. Upper-level students who have access to better instrumentation or other physical resources can be asked to generate a more open-ended question derived from their entire undergraduate program. Not only can they prepare a proposal, but class members can be asked to peer review and critique each other's work. After the work is completed (or attempted), the results can be made public via web publication or poster sessions to which other students and faculty respond (Henderson & Buising, 2000).

Laboratory instruction also raises an opportunity to incorporate issues that are naturally aligned with practice, such as laboratory safety, which ranges from the manipulation of concentrated chemical substances to human-subjects issues. Increasingly, formal discussion of research ethics concerning practices such as data handling, laboratory management, authorship, and peer review is being encouraged for beginning and advanced students alike (Coppola, 2000; Kovac, 1999; Sweeting, 1999).

LINK TO COGNITIVE DEVELOPMENT

Instructors can help students develop important thinking and learning skills in laboratory courses that complement the instructional goals for other types of teaching and learning. One set of these skills is described by the Modified Reformed Science Teacher Behavior Inventory (MR-STBI) (Sutman et al., 1998), namely,

1. The use of lower- and higher-level divergent questions.
2. Group-centered cooperative group activities.
3. Activities designed to assist students to reevaluate scientific (mis)conceptions.
4. Laboratory results that are integrated with theories from other disciplines.
5. Instructor-generated discussion related to the laboratory observations.

6. Use of collected data as a primary source of postlaboratory student/teacher interactions.

7. Instructor's use of process terminology (such as *classify, analyze, predict,* and *create*).

8. Instructors encouraging students to engage in meaningful discussion with each other.

9. Instructors encouraging clarification of students' initial responses.

10. Instructors' supervision of laboratory activities by moving from group to group.

WHAT RESEARCH SAYS

Individual studies make differential claims about the efficacy of one kind of laboratory instruction over another (Arce & Betancourt, 1997; Higgenbotham et al., 1998), but there is no general consensus about how one design advantages itself over another. Gains have been observed when students process information in the manner of experts in a laboratory that has an authentic design (Coppola et al., 1997). Such students are more intrinsically motivated by the course, and they develop better strategies for meaningful learning. Finally, despite positive findings that support the use of inquiry to teach concepts, changing methodology alone is not a panacea. Without carefully planning to integrate the entire student population, and without serious commitment from instructors and institutions, reform-based efforts can backfire, favoring the students who are more immune to deficiencies of their instructional environment, and may actually increase achievement gaps—typically disadvantaging exactly those students whom we wish to interest and motivate (Von Secker & Lissitz, 1999; Von Secker, 2002).

IN CONCLUSION

Laboratory instruction is a complex activity that needs to be examined closely and systematically. However, perhaps because expository instruction is so poor at promoting engaged and deeper learning, nearly any strategy that promotes more active learning and decision making by students is observed to produce learning gains. As is so often true, not only must the goals that one has for an instructional intervention be explicit, but their alignment with the instructional methodology must be carefully managed.

Supplementary Reading

N. A. Glasgow's *New Curriculum for New Times: A Guide to Student-Centered, Problem-Based Learning* (Thousand Oaks, CA: Corwin Press, 1998) is an easily read and adaptable introduction.

V. L. Lechtanski's *Inquiry-Based Experiments for Chemistry* (New York: Oxford University Press, 2000) provides useful, explicit translations of standard experiments to inquiry-based methods.

L. C. McDermott and the Physics Education Group at the University of Washington, *Physics by Inquiry,* vol. 1 and vol. 2 (New York: Wiley, 1996) provide the best examples of instructional laboratory design based on disciple-centered educational research.

Student-Active Science (http://active.hampshire.edu/index) is a rich and multidisciplinary resource maintained by leaders in the field.

21 The Teacher's Role in Experiential Learning

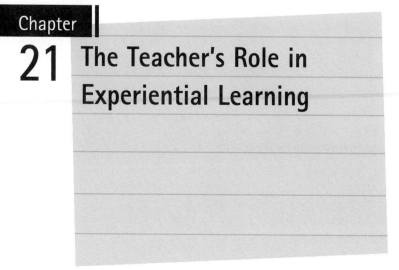

Beyond the perimeter of the classroom and the compressed efficiency of the textbook lies the potential to provide students direct engagement with the untidy but compelling subject matter of many fields of study. When students sense they are finding out something that is important and useful for themselves, using their own powers of observation and interpersonal skill, everything changes. And not only for the students.

At first glance, this looks pretty straightforward. We want our students to get some hands-on experience. We want to find a setting where this can happen. We want to be sure that they "really learn something," which usually means that we hope they will integrate the concreteness of the field setting with the prevailing concepts and propositions of our department or specialized area of study.

However, several questions emerge. Why would we want to do this, in our own course? What are the likely positive and

This chapter was written by Richard D. Mann of the University of Michigan.

negative outcomes for the students and for ourselves as teachers? How might adding such an experiential component to our course, or to our department's overall offerings, change the way the faculty and the students see themselves and each other? And when and how did experiential learning emerge on the landscape of American education?

HISTORY OF EXPERIENTIAL LEARNING

One of many educational innovations associated with the 1960s, experiential learning and the more specialized form within that called service learning came from students' increasing insistence that what they learn be relevant, applicable, and closely connected to their values. But if we take as an example Project Outreach, which a group of us started in the Psychology Department at the University of Michigan in 1965, it seems that the roots of this innovation trace even more directly to the cadre of young faculty and graduate teaching assistants. They wanted a way to teach that expressed their political and humanitarian concerns in two significant ways.

It was the era of the civil rights movement, the Great Society, and community mental health, and these young educators were trying to shape their careers so as to be of service in these and other such contexts. They were seeking ways to learn and teach in much closer proximity to the "real world." They were also preoccupied with transforming the primarily top-down structures of the classroom into something more mutual, something that enhanced rather than disdained the students' own yearnings for relevance and immediacy.

The questions that these efforts raised were not new, and Project Outreach was modeled on numerous innovations in previous decades. The teachers' questions are no less germane today: How will I define who I am in my role as teacher? Are there roles or facets of my overall life as a teacher that I wish to give greater priority? And how do I view the students? Are there strengths and potentials within the students that I can choose to emphasize?

SIX POSSIBLE ROLES

In *The College Classroom* (Mann et al., 1970) my research colleagues and I teased out six quite different aspects of how we define ourselves and our students through a schema we called the Teacher-As Typology. Experiential learning and the kind of field- or service-oriented pedagogy we associate with such learning represent a particular set of answers to these questions. The six facets of the teacher's self-definition that we isolated for scrutiny were the teacher as (1) formal authority, (2) expert, (3) socializing agent, (4) facilitator, (5) ego ideal, and (6) person. I'd like to begin our survey of field-oriented learning by exploring first the seeming polarity of the teacher as expert and the teacher as facilitator.

The Teacher as Expert

When we wonder what legitimizes our status as the paid instructors of our students, we often turn first to the assertion that we know more than they do. We have presumably developed a particular expertise, and over time they will, we hope, incorporate some of the elements of our knowledge, perspective, and even the questioning and curiosity that befit our kind of expert. When we plan and execute an experiential course or part of a course, our expertise comes under pressure in three distinct ways. First, we are called to organize the content material of the course in ways that interact effectively with the students' direct experience. Eyler and Giles (1999) found that students show far greater gains in knowledge and conceptual sophistication when the field experience and the content material are well integrated with one another.

The second shift in the role of teacher as expert comes when the challenge to our expertise shifts from our command of "the literature" to the accumulated knowledge typical of those who have worked long and hard in the various field settings. Even as course organizers, we are called on to find good settings and good field supervisors and to possess or develop a familiarity with the client population. For some academics, this can be quite a stretch, and a sense of partnership, even apprenticeship vis-à-vis the numerous effective practitioners, can often ease the sense of unfamiliarity that might arise at first.

The third pressure on the teacher as expert derives from the considerable likelihood that the concepts, typologies, and assertions of the academic wing of a discipline might prove to be difficult to apply, not terribly salient or useful, or even countered by what the students see for themselves in the field setting. Finding ways to reframe the academic content and coping with the unpredictability and challenges of the field setting can be daunting or exciting. It will always be an uneven process, and in the end whether experiential learning takes hold in a teacher's course planning may depend on identifying some of the other changes in role that may open up new and satisfying possibilities.

The Teacher as Facilitator

It goes without saying that facilitator forms a part of the teacher's role in every mode of teaching, not only in experiential education. Every time we enable students to find ways to challenge the prevailing view on some topic or the conventional interpretation of a poem or document, we are hoping that the joys of discovering their own voices will be part of what the students gain from their effort. However, it is especially true in a field setting that students appear, on the basis of observation and self-report, to develop a sense of mastery that accumulates from all the conversations, observations, and testable hunches that come along. And so too are they made aware of the many obstacles that need to be overcome before this mastery can flourish: their social anxiety in a strange environment, their initial tendency to prejudge and stereotype, their limited capacity to handle the most difficult moments. To normalize and help reduce students' anxiety, to guide them past their conventional or defensive reactions to people whose lives are far removed from their own, calls for time when the students can unpack their experience without fear of criticism or shaming. It is in these conversations that their reactions and tentative proposals for problem solving can be encouraged and worked with productively.

Many experiential learning courses and field opportunities bring into the cohort of educators not only the practitioners who may orient and supervise the students but, in addition, a group of experienced students who have gone through the course and return now to serve as group leaders in small, trust-building discussions connected to a particular setting. They can offer tips, commiserate over the frustrations of bureaucracy, and reward the courageous steps all students must take in order to serve and learn at the same time, which is no small feat.

The Teacher as Person

The social distance between teacher and student is typically much narrower in a field setting. Formerly relatively anonymous members of a large lecture class, suddenly the students are known by name, coached to surmount specific difficulties, and brought to experience the personal side of working in a team and working with a client. Each step a student takes toward apprehending the group leader, field supervisor, or course instructor as another fallible, complex human being is a usually much-appreciated step toward being fully present not as "just another student" but as a person. All the social skills students have brought to the new situation enter the roster of what they have to offer. They can now give and receive recognition and support, smiles and laughter. The teacher as person encounters the student as person, which is not a goal for its own sake but a natural, valuable adjunct to the whole process of coming to care what happens and to respond with all one's talents and humanity.

The Teacher as Ego Ideal

Beyond the teacher as expert, as facilitator, and as person is another crucial teaching function that most of us seldom mention, except when we recall with gratitude our favorite, most influential teachers. Then the teacher is added to that list of characters who serve as *ego ideals*—models and exemplars. It isn't exactly students' appreciation of the teacher's cognitive mastery or group skills or personality that define this facet of teaching. It is, rather, the flash of recognition that here is someone who is living a life one might wish to live. The one attribute that correlates most highly with students' overall evaluation of the teacher is what students call "enthusiasm." The teacher's focus, sense of being present, and evident love of the task at hand speak to some students' most pressing questions: Is there a way to be in the world that works? A way that works for me? Can I watch how someone maneuvers through the specific challenges of life and learn from his or her example, not necessarily what career to choose but how to be fulfilled in any career? The opportunity to view an exemplar at work abounds in the experiential learning setting. To watch how skillful ward attendants ease patients past a stormy crisis, to sense that they are drawing on more than accumulated concepts and techniques, that it is their whole maturity of character one is being affected by, offers a student a glimpse of the deeper developmental agenda that, in the end, matters most of all.

The Teacher as Formal Authority: Options for Assessing Field Learning

If we compare the demands and pleasures of teaching in this sort of format with those in the more traditional modes of classroom teaching, two facets of the teacher's role stand out because they are not so easy to carry out and to rationalize. The grade sheet shows up in the instructor's mailbox whatever the format. But how can one fairly and usefully assess the quality of a student's work in the field? The teacher as formal authority—the person who sets up the syllabus, maintains decorum, and sends the evaluations over to the registrar's office—has a unique problem when it comes experiential learning. At least three ways to solve the problem have emerged over the years.

The Exam Option.   In the first solution, especially when the field experience is ancillary to the textbook/lecture part of the course, you can simply ask questions on the exam to assess the students' comprehension of these additional sources and see whether the students emerged from the field with a firmer grasp of the course fundamentals. Especially in a "high-integration" service-learning course, in which the assigned readings and lectures serve to clarify and enlighten the students' field experience and vice versa, the more students learn in one part, the more they profit from the other. But you would not have to compromise the usual criteria of excellence in the course. One negative aspect to this arrangement is that some students may complain that their investment of energy and reflection seemed, in the end, not to count for much in their final grade, almost as if they had been tricked into paying too much attention to the fieldwork.

The Growth and Reflection Option.   A second grading strategy is to directly assess the quality of the student's performance in the field and assign some weight to it for the final evaluation. The most common forms of such evaluation are tied to assignments that have great value in and of themselves, such as having the students keep weekly journals. Coming up with a satisfactory rating system or evaluation of student journals has been tried with varying success, as one would expect, and with some of the familiar pitfalls. Questions invariably arise. With so many important components of success, such as compliance with agency authority (or not), effective social skills put into action (or not), perceptiveness and compassion used in responding to the reality of the people being worked with (or not), the weighting of these diverse components for assessing all students becomes problematic.

And then too: Are you grading progress in any or all of these components, or an overall or final level of attainment? For some students, the most important consequence of the field experience may take the form of a breakthrough, a sudden awareness of just how unhelpful their prior assumptions had proven to be when they tried to understand or work with people. These giant steps are hard to credit but equally hard to ignore. Such growth spurts are not usually noted in, say, a calculus class, but perhaps we are dealing with a different sort of learning here. Similarly, do we give an A to the students for whom the setting was basically home base (an environment they had lived or worked in before), who seemed not to progress beyond their initial high level of performance, and who remained fixed in their sense that they had little to learn? Finally, as if these were not problems enough, the fact that students feel far more involved, typically reporting that they are learning a lot more than in "regular" classes, and the fact that field staff and experienced group leaders tend to agree that rewarding the students' dramatic outpouring of energy only makes sense, the specter of what some take to be grade inflation is almost unavoidable. Can a project succeed so well that all 10 or 100 students get some sort of A? It seems likely, but the impact of this outcome on the rising GPA of all students tends to reverberate all through the academic system.

Pass-Fail Option.   The third solution to the grade issue is to dodge all of these complexities by scanning for utterly unsatisfactory performances and then coding student outcomes only as pass-fail. This works better in a stand-alone course such as Project Outreach at Michigan, but even there it has its drawbacks. Remarkable performances are lumped in with every other outcome, but this may be mitigated by glowing letters of recommendation and the option of further work as a group leader. Even with the pass-fail option and the unavailability of an easy A, students still enroll in Project Outreach and other such courses in large numbers. Jerry Miller (1993) fashioned a fuller description of the ongoing history of such issues in Project Outreach.

The Teacher as Socializing Agent

A final aspect of the teacher's role concerns the future—the teacher's function of being a gatekeeper for students who are "going on" in a field, or who wish to. Teachers are typically engaged in recruiting promising prospects for their specialty or discipline and advising the various admissions committees about how they have come to view a particular applicant. These are the functions of the teacher as socializing agent. Sometimes it seems equally natural to play the gatekeeper for neighboring disciplines and professions with similar prestige and value to society. But experiential and service learning exposes talented students to the allure of careers that don't require graduate training or the kind of research and scholarship that define the academic training process—for instance, the promising anthropology student who decides to pursue a career in health care. The tension created by sensing that one's academic discipline may be "losing good people" is not necessarily a matter of urgent concern for every teacher. In fact, one outcome of expanding the role of socializing agent may be to vastly increase the number of career paths being followed by one's students that stir a sense of pride and accomplishment in the teacher. Somewhere between the obscure goal of preparing students for "citizenship" and the familiar funneling of the best students into graduate school there is a complex, honorable role to be played by the educator who fashions a bridge to the world of lifelong service and effective engagement.

OUTCOMES

Do students manifest the kinds of gains and satisfaction that we hope for in experiential learning? Outcome research demonstrates that the students are satisfied with what they feel they have learned and grateful for this opportunity to flex their muscles in a field setting. Eyler and Giles's (1999) empirical study of the effect of service learning across a number of disciplines shows that students gain in both high-level cognitive functioning and in their positive sense of themselves, their appreciation for the diversity of others, and their conviction about the importance of service. Particularly when their field experience is effectively integrated into the concepts and insights of the academic field, students emerge with a greater capacity both to carry out a complex analysis of field situations and to form plans that are realistic and well grounded in the academic discipline. Their increased capacity for critical thinking is apparent, but from this and other outcome research it is not so easy to demonstrate that the students master the more concrete academic material more effectively.

IN CONCLUSION

The most dramatic and evidently satisfying outcome for the students lies in the domain of the teacher as facilitator, person, and even ego ideal. Learning for oneself, learning what human capacities, such as empathy and initiative, one has yet to master but then making progress along those lines, is tremendously invigorating. Greater personal access to field workers and professors is usually appreciated, leaving students feeling more adult and more valued than in their other classes. These are typically high-morale teaching situations. And the challenge becomes how to channel all this energy into synthesizing the student's direct experience with the conceptual, research-driven side of the course in a way that values both mastery and reflection.

Supplementary Reading

Jeffery Howard provides helpful guidance for anyone planning a new experiential course in his *Service-Learning Course Design Workbook,* issued in Summer 2001 as a companion volume to the *Michigan Journal of Service Learning.*

A thoughtful discussion of what kinds of learning and development emerge from this form of education is found in Morris Keeton's *Experiential Learning* (San Francisco: Jossey-Bass, 1976).

A wide-ranging discussion of important pedagogical issues is found in David Kolb's *Experiential Learning* (Englewood Cliffs, NJ: Prentice Hall, 1984).

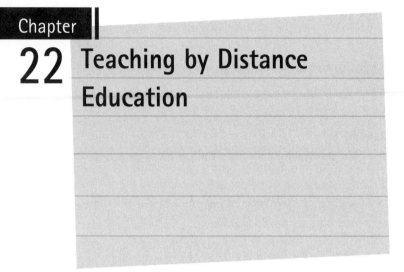

22 Teaching by Distance Education

D istance education presents one of the most challenging and satisfying forms of teaching. Instead of your efforts evaporating behind you as you grapple with the uncertainties of day-to-day teaching encounters, you can (indeed, must) take the time to think your teaching through, get it right, and then record it for the benefit of many. Distance teaching is an extended act of imagination. Without students around you to observe and respond to, you must construct the entire teaching and learning process in your head. The shift from conventional lecturer to distance teacher is like switching from street performer to playwright. You can no longer develop your act by trying out new lines and dropping the ones that bomb. You have to put yourself on the line—make your investment up front, by plotting the intellectual progress of your students through a series of imagined maneuvers that you hope will achieve the learning desired.

Distance education encompasses an enormous range of teaching systems whose common feature is that students learn from teachers without having to travel to meet them. A distance education

This chapter was written by Andrew Northedge of The Open University.

package may involve a few hours of study or several hundred. It may be delivered online or as a mail package containing texts and a CD-ROM or DVD. It may be studied entirely independently or be backed up by peer and tutor support through online conferences, telephone link-ups, or face-to-face meetings. Distance education is also developed in very different contexts. I, for example, work within a distance education mass-production system at the UK Open University. I might work full-time with a team of eight lecturers and over ten support staff to produce a 600-hour course for 5,000 students a year. By contrast, smaller distance education packages are often produced by one or two lecturers working around the edges of an existing teaching load, with a lot less support.

SKETCHING OUT THE SHAPE OF A COURSE

Whatever form it takes, distance education is constructed from a variety of elements, each of which needs careful planning and design. To give some perspective, let me walk you through a hypothetical example. Let's say you have to produce a 90-hour course, with 6 hours of study per week over 15 weeks. You look for a suitable textbook around which to build the course but decide instead to bind together your own collection of readings from different sources. You also decide to bring the course to life with case studies of real people talking about their experiences (opting for the cheapness and simplicity of audio rather than video). Experience tells you that students progress better with peer and tutor support, so you opt also for an online conference. Regarding assessment, you decide you will use a mix of computer-graded multiple-choice assignments and written assignments marked by a tutor. To bring all this together, you will need to write a study guide. You might develop it in the form of a printed text, a CD-ROM, or a web site. For our purposes here, it doesn't matter which.

As with any course, you begin by thinking what ideas and knowledge you want to teach. You set aside the first and last weeks for introductory and review purposes, and two other weeks for assignment writing. Then you divide the subject into broad topics that you allocate over the 11 remaining weeks. Because students are working in isolation, you decide to provide additional support with assignment writing, working with numerical data, and organizing their studies. You now produce a rough draft of course *objectives and outcomes* (see the chapter "Countdown for Course Preparation") and begin to consider how you might set about delivering them within your six hours a week.

Table 22.1 models how your course might be structured. Working up from the bottom of the table, we see that every week presents six hours of work. You have decided on two written assignments: one in week 5, about one-third of the way through the course, to ensure that students start internalizing the ideas of the discipline by putting them to use; then a longer one in week 12, near the end of the course but with enough time for work to be marked, returned, and discussed in the online conference. You put a multiple-choice assignment in week 2, so that students get early feedback on whether they are picking up the right messages, another in week 9, and a longer one in week 15 to keep students studying right up to the end of the course. You decide that, to succeed, the online conference must make a substantial contribution to the course, so you allocate 15 hours, giving more time in the early weeks to help generate collective momentum. You place online sessions to enable support in preparing for written assignments and feedback after marking them, but avoiding the assignment weeks, when students will be distracted. Three hours of audio material are divided into six half-hour segments, supplied on a CD-ROM. The first five present case material; the sixth has an expert reviewing the subject. (Actually 15- to 20-minute segments might be preferable, as recorded case material can require intensive listening and time-consuming analysis. However, this would have messed up the table.) Studying the collection of readings takes up 27 hours, nearly a third of the course—the amount varying from week to week. Similarly, working with the study guide occupies just over a third of the course, the weekly time varying according to the tasks being tackled. To clarify these tasks, we need another table (Table 22.2), this time showing the main teaching and learning activities.

Working up from the bottom of Table 22.2, you have decided to provide study skills support at four points in the course: "getting started" in week 1, "reviewing progress" after the first written assignment, "reflecting on strategy" in week 8, and "reviewing personal development" at the end. These half-hour activities will be incorporated within the flow of the study guide. So will the number skills exercises, which you have spread across the course

TABLE 22.1 Weekly Study Hours for a 15-Week Course

Modes of Study	Week Number															Total Hours
	1	2	3	4	5	6	7	8	9	10	11	12	13	14	15	
Study guide	3.5	2	3	2	2	3	1	3.5	2	2.5	1.5		2.5	2	2.5	33
Collection of readings	1	1.5	1.5	2		2.5	3	2.5	1.5	3	2.5		3	2	1	27
Audio material	0.5		0.5			0.5				0.5			0.5		0.5	3
Online conference	1	2	1	2			2		2		2			2	1	15
Multiple-choice assignment		0.5							0.5						1	2
Written assignment					4							6				10
Total	6	6	6	6	6	6	6	6	6	6	6	6	6	6	6	90

TABLE 22.2 Weekly Study Hours Represented as Teaching and Learning Activities

Teaching and Learning Activities	Week Number															Total Hours
	1	2	3	4	5	6	7	8	9	10	11	12	13	14	15	
Framing* (study guide and conference)	2.5			0.5	0.5			0.5			0.5				2.5	7
Teaching narrative (study guide)	1	1.5	1.5	1.5		1.5	1	1	1.5	2	0.5		0.5	1.5	1	16
Case studies (study guide and CD-ROM)	1		1.5			2		1.5		1			1.5	0.5		9
Independent reading	1	1.5	1.5	2		2.5	3	2.5	1.5	3	2.5		3	2	1	27
Online group activity (conference)		2	1	1					2		1					7
Working on assignments		0.5			4				0.5			6			1	12
Writing support (study guide and conference)			0.5	1			2				1.5			2		7
Number skills (study guide)		0.5			1				0.5				1			3
Study skills (study guide)	0.5				0.5			0.5							0.5	2
Total	6	6	6	6	6	6	6	6	6	6	6	6	6	6	6	90

*See explanations of "framing" and "teaching narrative" in the text discussion of this table.

to encourage a steady buildup of skill and confidence. (In weeks 2 and 9 multiple-choice assignments on the number work give an added incentive.) Support for preparing the first written assignment consists of an activity in the study guide in week 3, followed in week 4 by a tutor-led online activity. In week 11, there is similar preparation for the second written assignment, both in text and online. Online postmortems on assignments fall in weeks 7 and 14. The next row shows assignment work (multiple-choice and written assignments). The row above shows that you have allocated half the online conference time for structured online activities. These are bunched with an initial burst over three weeks early on, then two later sessions. (The "Independent reading" row replicates the "Collection of readings" row in Table 22.1.) The case studies are presented primarily through the audio material on the CD-ROM, but each is set up in the study guide, along with activities and discussion. The case studies in weeks 8 and 14 are not audio based.

The top two rows of Table 22.2—"Framing" and "Teaching narrative"—represent the heart of the course. Here the skilled and imaginative distance teacher makes it all happen. By "framing," in row one, I mean "putting in context"—painting the big picture of what the course is all about (the teaching narrative is discussed in the next section of this chapter). We can only ever make sense within frames of reference, and a recurring problem in education is that teachers fail to realize the extent to which students do not share their frames of reference. Consequently, students comprehend little and soon switch off. In distance education, because students and teachers do not meet and are all the more likely to be thinking at cross-purposes, framing is a vital opening maneuver. This does *not* mean talking in grand abstractions. It means starting where the student is and using strong examples to establish the issues the course is setting out to address. For example, after half an hour of preliminaries ("Hello, this is week 1 of a 15-week course," and so on) you might plunge into an exercise using the audio case material to introduce the big themes of the course. These might then be taken up and discussed within the online conference (after initial logging on and introductory rituals have been accomplished). It is important to excite imaginations from the earliest moments. As this book emphasizes throughout, students learn only when they are actively thinking. Having "hooked" them, you will make them ready to grapple with details about how the course works, its various components, and the study activities they will be managing over the weeks ahead. This broad framing needs to be reinforced at times during the course. (Notice the extra portions in weeks 4 and 5, in the buildup to the first written assignment.) In the final week, course review activities constitute the other end of the framing process: closure.

DEVELOPING A TEACHING NARRATIVE

The purpose of the initial framing is to launch a flow of shared meaning, jointly generated by teacher and students (through writing and reading, respectively)—a flow that must then be maintained throughout the course. The teaching and learning process works only because human beings are able to make meaning together, allowing teachers to lend students the capacity to construct meanings they cannot yet achieve unaided. But whereas in a classroom you can share "live" meaning face-to-face within the frame of reference of your common surroundings, with distance education you have to resort to other, more "literary" devices, such as stories, pictures, diagrams, and vivid examples. Without these meaning carriers, your explanations are wasted on students. They simply cannot make your arguments work in *their* heads. If you link these meaning carriers together, you create a *teaching narrative* that drives and supports your students' thinking as they work through the course.

It's like writing a play. You must have an opening scenario that captures your audience's attention, whatever kind of day they had at home or work. (Distance students usually lead busy lives.) This scenario must pose questions that make your audience curious. (Make your introduction lead up to a short list of *core questions* that your course addresses.) Then there must be incidents that bring in new characters, issues, and questions. These take the form of *examples, case studies*, and *activities* through which you develop a "plot," leading up to a final denouement. Thus, although you first conceive of your course as a sequence of theoretical expositions, you need for teaching purposes to rethink it as a series of cases and activities that do the job of delivering the theoretical argument.

These then need to be linked within an overall *story line,* so that students carry their developing thoughts along with them as they address each new case. When courses work like this, students get very involved and learn deeply; indeed, they carry on learning in nonstudy hours and after the course is over.

Achieving this, however, depends on sensitivity to your audience. First, you must be clear who they are. (Write down a description of them.) Then try to imagine them as you write. (Think of someone you know who might take the course.) How can you make your case study so thought provoking that students skip the TV serial and resist family gossip? How can you challenge everyday assumptions and explanations? How can you design a really intriguing activity that is satisfying to complete? (Avoid treating your student as either a moron or a genius—neither "Write down what I just said" nor "Write notes on how you would redesign local government.") Include only activities that are carefully framed and focused and develop your plot. Otherwise, students will soon take to skipping them. (Try writing your own answer to an activity; then refine the task so that it leads directly to that answer and doesn't waste students' time.) And always pick up the thread afterward, so the activity leads directly into the next plot development. Finally, *summarize periodically,* so that students keep track of the plot and can orient themselves for the next advance. (Succinct bulleted points in propositional form impose an excellent discipline, forcing you to be explicit about what you believe has been established.) All this constitutes the *teaching narrative* through which your study guide site gives coherence and dynamism to the course.

MAKING THE COURSE MANAGEABLE

You need to keep the course within bounds. Student dropout is a major issue in distance education. It is so easy—no loss of lifestyle or identity. They just stop, and the most common reason given is feeling overwhelmed by the *workload. Teachers* always underestimate this. They forget that reading takes many times longer with an unfamiliar subject (3,000 words an hour is good going if a text is challenging your ideas). Teachers also forget to add together all the components of the course—hence the two tables shown earlier. Students can set aside only so many hours per week. If you unthinkingly demand more, you simply force them to drop course elements arbitrarily or to drop out altogether. Nor is it simply a matter of quantity; it is also a question of clarity and organization. At all times it must be obvious what to do next (simple, explicit instructions; work schedules; calendars). And the course should provide a regular rhythm of study, so students can establish a routine. Naturally their patterns of study will vary greatly, but it is much easier to develop a strategy for fitting study into a busy life when a course has a clear and regular structure.

The other major stumbling block is *difficulty*. Teachers tend to be wildly optimistic about what students can handle. You can, however, bring difficulty levels down dramatically.

- Choose the *familiar* rather than the strange (for instance, when selecting examples and case studies) so that students can apply existing concepts and frames of reference and build on them.

- Work with the *concrete* rather than the abstract so that students' thoughts are not reliant solely on half-formed and loosely organized conceptualizations.

- Keep your treatment of the topic *simple*. Avoid side issues and cross-references until students have a base from which to comprehend them.

- Use *everyday language* as much as possible.

When teaching requires you to go to the difficult end of one of these dimensions, strive toward the easy end of the other three.

IN CONCLUSION

This chapter offers a first glimpse of distance teaching. If you are seriously involved, you will certainly need to read more. However, I must at least mention the following:

- *Assessment*. Spread it across the course as far as your budget will allow. Little and often keeps students motivated and *moving* in the right direction. It is easy to get a long way off track when studying in isolation.

- *Teaching through assignment marking.* This is a skilled activity. Comments on assignments provide the only personalized teaching that distance education students receive. If you employ others to mark assignments, they will need training.

- *Feedback systems.* Distance teachers never see the puzzlement in students' eyes. It is essential to have materials tried out during development by colleagues or, better still, by potential students, and to gather feedback systematically once a course is running. Otherwise you will waste a lot of time and money.

- *Keep it simple and direct.* If you follow only one rule, this is it.

Supplementary Reading

Distance teaching is a very broad subject. Where you start reading depends on what type of distance education you are concerned with and what aspect you are interested in. For an introduction to the basics of designing distance materials, you could try either of these:

- Fred Lockwood, *The Design and Production of Self-Instructional Materials* (London: Kogan Page, 1998).

- Derek Rowntree, *Preparing Materials for Open, Distance and Flexible Learning* (London: Kogan Page, 1993).

If you are particularly interested in online education, try these:

- Greg Kearsley, *Online Education: Learning and Teaching in Cyberspace* (Belmont, CA: Wadsworth Thomson Learning, 2000).

- Rena M. Palloff and Keith Pratt, *Building Learning Communities in Cyberspace: Effective Strategies for the Online Classroom* (San Francisco: Jossey-Bass, 1999).

If you want a broader view of distance education, try these:

- Desmond Keegan, *Foundations of Distance Education,* 3rd ed. (London: Routledge, 1996).

- Otto Peters, *Learning and Teaching in Distance Education: Analyses and Interpretations from an International Perspective* (London: Kogan Page, 1998).

You can follow up the theme of framing and teaching narrative, try these:

- A. Northedge, "Organising Excursions into Specialist Discourse Communities: A Sociocultural Account of University Teaching," in G. Wells and G. Claxton (eds.), *Learning for Life in the 21st Century: Sociocultural Perspectives on the Future of Education* (Oxford: Blackwell, 2001).

Part 6

Teaching for Higher-Level Goals

23 Teaching Students How to Become More Strategic and Self-Regulated Learners

For many years, the study of student learning was divorced from the study of teaching. Good teaching practices were assumed to be universals that did not depend on individual differences among students or on teaching students how to study, learn, and think about course content. But these are exciting times for college instructors and students because findings in educational and cognitive psychology have changed our views of the teaching/learning process and provide both conceptual and practical information about the ways that students learn and how instructors can use this information to inform their teaching practices. We now know that it is the interaction of good instructional practices with students' strategic use of learning strategies and skills, motivational processes, and self-regulation that results in positive learning outcomes (Weinstein et al., 2000). However, many college students do not know what to do to learn the content in

This chapter was written by Claire Ellen Weinstein of the University of Texas at Austin, Debra K. Meyer of Elmhurst College, Jenefer Husman of Arizona State University, Gretchen Van Mater Stone of Shenandoah University, and Wilbert J. McKeachie of the University of Michigan.

all the different content domain areas that they study in college. All instructors have some implicit or explicit conceptions or theories about what it means to learn and think in their own discipline. Helping students become aware of these conceptions is an important aspect of teaching. As students learn subject matter they also need to learn something about the skills involved in learning that subject matter. For example, students need to know how to reason through problems in engineering, how to read math texts, and how to identify important information about a particular literary work. Therefore, it is important that you use effective instructional practices for presenting content information as well as effective instructional practices for fostering the development and elaboration of both general learning strategies (such as previewing a textbook chapter) and content-specific learning strategies (such as how to learn and understand mathematical formulas).

In the following sections, we discuss strategic learning and address several ways you can help develop students' learning-to-learn strategies and skills in the college classroom by increasing students' self-awareness, teaching domain-specific strategies, connecting new ideas with existing knowledge, modeling and teaching learning strategies, and providing feedback on these learning strategies. We also highlight the instructor's role in helping students become more strategic and self-regulated in technology-rich instructional environments.

WHAT ARE THE CHARACTERISTICS OF STRATEGIC LEARNERS?

Most college instructors can easily recall strategic learners they have seen in their own courses. These learners approach instructional activities and tasks with a high degree of confidence that they can succeed, as well as a good idea of how to try to complete them. Strategic learners are diligent and resourceful in pursuit of a learning goal and do not give up easily, even in the face of difficulty. They understand that learning and studying are active processes largely under their own control. Strategic learners know when they understand new information and, perhaps even more important, when they do not. When they do encounter problems studying or learning, they use help-seeking strategies such as getting help from the instructor or teaching assistant, their classmates, or a student learning center. They also understand that studying and learning are systematic processes, again, largely under their own control (Paris et al., 1983; Pintrich & De Groot, 1990; Pressley & McCormick, 1995; Schunk & Zimmerman, 2003; Weinstein, 1994; Zimmerman, 1990, 1994, 2001).

Although we are all familiar with students who are strategic learners, it is still helpful to take a systematic look at some of the characteristics of these students. Understanding these characteristics is essential for deriving instructional strategies to help students be more strategic in pursuing their academic goals in your course and throughout their academic careers.

THE IMPORTANCE OF GOALS AND SELF-REFLECTION

How can you help students to become more effective learners? We know that strategic learners need to be able to set and use meaningful goals to help them learn and to help them generate and maintain their motivation for studying (Schunk & Ertmer, 1999). We can help students become clearer about their goals by encouraging them to set useful goals for our classes. Unfortunately, many students are not clear about their educational goals in general or about their goals for specific courses. Not every course holds the same interest value for every student, but usually there are at least some aspects of the course that each person can perceive as useful. Providing your students with opportunities to identify how the material presented in your courses might be useful to them as they strive to reach their own educational, personal, social, or occupational goals can enhance motivation as well as cognitive effort (Husman et al., 2000). Even a brief class discussion about upcoming topics and how these topics might relate to students' present or future interests can help. Asking students to write a brief paragraph or two about a topic and why it might be relevant to them now or in the future is another way to establish perceived relevance.

It is important to remember that we cannot give students goals—they must own their goals. However, with goal ownership comes responsibility. Students need to learn how to set, analyze, and use goals and how to respond to goal achievement and failure. Students also should learn how to implement strategies that will help them negotiate emotional responses to achieving or not achieving their goals (Boekaerts et al., 2000; Schutz & Davis, 2000). It is also important to assist students in establishing process rather than product goals. Even simply reminding students that the goal of the exercises or projects you assign to them is to gain mastery of the content will help support effective self-evaluation. Students are more likely to evaluate their success on the pieces of a project if they have goals for each of those pieces (Schunk & Ertmer, 1999)

INCREASING STUDENTS' SELF-AWARENESS

Students who are aware of their learning goals tend to reflect on what it takes to learn. Thinking about thinking, or knowing about knowing, has come to be known as meta-cognition (Flavell, 1979; Pintrich, in press; Zimmerman, 1995). Meta-cognitive processes include knowledge about oneself as a learner, knowledge about academic tasks, and knowledge about strategies to use in order to accomplish academic tasks. Awareness about oneself as a learner helps students to allocate their personal resources, or the resources that are available in their academic institution such as group study sessions, tutoring programs, and learning centers. If students do not anticipate needing help with a potentially difficult course, or if they do not monitor their own comprehension closely, it is unlikely that they will take advantage of available resources. It will also be difficult for them to judge the personal resources they will need, such as extra study time or more opportunities for review and consolidation of the material before a test (Entwistle, 1992; Winne, 1996).

Increasing student self-awareness is imperative for effective strategy instruction. If students attribute their successes or failures to luck, an easy test, or innate ability, then there is no need for effort, time management, or learning strategies (for a review see Pintrich & Schunk, 1996). Therefore, college instructors should provide opportunities for students to reflect on the general characteristics of their approaches to, and on their specific actions toward, academic tasks. You may want to survey students to promote self-awareness of strategies by asking them questions such as the following on the first major assignment or test:

1. How many hours do you spend a week studying for this course?
2. Are you up-to-date on course assignments and readings?
3. How do you take notes or study while reading the textbook?
4. How do you take notes in class? Do you review your notes? When? How?
5. Do you stop periodically and check to see if you are understanding the material?

Self-reflection is important for self-regulation, which Zimmerman (1989) defines as "the degree that (students) are metacognitively, motivationally, and behaviorally active participants in their own learning" (p. 4). As college faculty, we should increase student self-awareness of learning strategies and teach students when and how to use strategies (Svinicki et al., 1995; Weinstein et al., 2000).

USING EXISTING KNOWLEDGE TO HELP LEARN NEW THINGS

College professors have long known that teaching an introductory course is often more difficult than teaching an advanced course in the same area. Although many explanations for this finding have been offered, most of them involve the students' lack of prior knowledge. It is all but impossible to think analytically or solve problems in an area without relevant knowledge. In addition, thinking about relevant knowledge also strengthens new learning by generating meaningful relations, or bridges, to new information. For example, if students think about what they already know concerning the economic causes of World War I, this can help them understand the economic causes of the Second

World War. Strategic learners understand the role of relevant prior knowledge and can use this knowledge to help themselves learn new things (Alexander & Judy, 1988).

We tend to use prior knowledge in one of two main ways: to create direct relations and to create analogical relations. When we create direct relations, we directly relate our prior knowledge to what we are trying to learn. For example, comparing and contrasting the causes of the two world wars involves direct relations. However, there are times when we do not have directly applicable prior knowledge but we do have knowledge in an area that is somehow similar and may help us to understand the new information, ideas, or skills we are trying to learn. For example, we use analogies to help us relate familiar and new things that share some key characteristics but are very different in other ways. Using a post office to explain aspects of computer storage, referring to social disagreements as a way to explain conflicts in organizations, and using the structure of a bird to explain design elements of an airplane are all ways we use analogies to help students build meaning for new concepts that may, at first, seem dissimilar.

TEACHING DOMAIN-SPECIFIC AND COURSE-SPECIFIC STRATEGIES

College faculty teach students not only content but also modes of thought, and strategies for learning and thinking about the content in their courses (Donald, 1995). Different instructional means may result in students having the same amount of knowledge but not the same organization and understanding needed for different applications using this new knowledge. Comparisons of college teaching methods typically find few significant differences in tests of knowledge. There are, however, differences between teaching methods in retention, application, and transfer (Donald, 1995).

Greeno (1991, 1997) suggests that general ways of thinking about the material need to be taught along with content because they are prerequisites to understanding content. Students who have no general modes of thinking for understanding science may be as lost in a biological science course as a student attempting to use conventional English narrative structures to understand the biology textbook. Thus, instructors have to consider ways of thinking not only as results of instruction but also as prerequisites for instruction. In addition, you must find ways of helping students transition from existing knowledge structures in their minds to more accurate or advanced knowledge structures.

Besides developing methods to provide students with instruction concerning the ways of thinking within your content domains, you should also provide direct instruction concerning strategic learning approaches for the tasks that are specific to your content area. You can impact your students' strategic learning by helping them understand the nature and requirements of academic tasks in your course. As you assign a variety of academic tasks throughout the course, you need to define clearly how each assignment relates to course learning goals so students can approach tasks strategically. There are two levels at which we should address strategies: the domain of the course (e.g., how to think and write like a psychologist) and the course-specific materials and pedagogy (e.g., how lectures and labs are organized, how collaborative problem solving is structured).

Many college students approach all their courses in the same way; therefore we must explicitly teach learning strategies that are domain-specific to our courses. For example, different disciplines have different discourse structures, different forms of argument, and different ways of approaching and solving problems. The domain differences between our course and our students' other courses should be clearly established. To be self-regulated learners, students must learn strategies that are appropriate for the domain (Alexander, 1995; Boekaerts, 1995). College faculty have found that cognitive modeling, thinking out loud, and demonstrating the use of texts in a self-regulated manner are ways to provide opportunities for students to learn about domain-specific strategies (Coppola, 1995). Most students cannot write like a scientist unless they are taught scientific writing. Domain-specific approaches to learning are especially critical in introductory courses. Therefore, you should consider activities such as these:

1. Previewing the textbook and its text structure.
2. Providing anonymous examples of student work to illustrate both DO's and DON'Ts.
3. Giving sample items from previous tests as practice.
4. Being clear about terminology that has domain-specific meaning.

In addition to learning strategies that are applicable to the domain of the course, students must learn strategies that are effective with the instructor's methodological and material choices. When modeling the use of the course textbook as a domain-specific strategy, the instructor also can explicitly outline how the text complements or supplements the lecture or lab materials. As we introduce students to new approaches (e.g., problem-based learning or writing-across-the-curriculum techniques), it is important to also introduce them to the skills needed to successfully participate in our methods and enhance their confidence in applying these skills (Bridges & Hallinger, 1996). Therefore, faculty should help students approach their courses strategically by outlining their individual instructional approaches and materials. For example:

1. As you deliver your first couple of lectures, take notes on the overhead to emphasize what you consider to be the important points.
2. Before you begin a specific pedagogical approach, such as the case study method, take time to explain the method and the skills necessary to use it successfully.
3. Use some simple everyday examples of the approach you will be using so students can focus on the process rather than having to focus on both the content and the process.

We must remember that as faculty we can be models of self-regulated learning (Pintrich, 1995). Therefore, we should strive to model discipline-specific thinking processes and course-specific strategies for learning in our classrooms. If an instructor models self-regulation and provides feedback and guidance concerning the students' self-regulation, the instructor can have a significant affect on students' self-regulation (Zimmerman & Schunk, 2001).

We have said that strategic learners can take much of the responsibility for helping themselves study effectively and reach their learning goals. For these students, a core component of strategic learning is their repertoire of cognitive learning strategies (Weinstein & Mayer, 1986; Weinstein et al., 2000). Cognitive learning strategies are goal-directed approaches and methods of thought that help students to build bridges between what they already know or have experienced and what they are trying to learn. These strategies are used to help build meaning in such a way that new information becomes part of an organized knowledge base that can be accessed in the future for recall, application, or problem solving. Research has shown that one of the hallmarks of expertise in an area is an organized knowledge base and a set of strategies for acquiring and integrating new knowledge (Chi et al., 1988).

The simplest forms of learning strategies involve repetition or review, such as reading over a difficult section of text or repeating an equation or rule. A bit more complexity is added when we try to paraphrase or summarize in our own words the material we are studying. Other strategies focus on organizing the information we are trying to learn by creating some type of scheme for the material. For example, creating an outline of the main events and characters in a story, making a timeline for historical occurrences, classifying scientific phenomena, and separating foreign vocabulary into parts of speech are all organizational strategies. Some learning strategies involve elaborating on, or analyzing, what we are trying to learn to make it more meaningful and memorable. For example, using analogies to access relevant prior knowledge, comparing and contrasting the explanations offered by two competing scientific theories, and thinking about the implications of a policy proposal are examples of elaboration strategies.

As instructors, we can all have a tremendous impact on helping students to develop a useful repertoire of learning strategies. One of the most powerful ways for teaching these strategies is through modeling. By using different types of strategies in our teaching, we can expose students to a wide variety of strategies in different content areas. However, it is not enough to simply use strategies in our teaching. It is also necessary to teach students how to do this on their own when they are studying. For example, after paraphrasing a discussion in class, point out what you did and why you did it. Briefly explain to the students what paraphrasing is and why it helps us to learn. You also could explain that it helps us to identify areas that we might not understand. If we have trouble paraphrasing something we are studying, it probably means we have not yet really learned it.

Finally, you should provide students with opportunities over time to practice and reflect on their uses of different learning strategies. As Pintrich (1995) noted, modeling the ways in which to learn strategically in our courses is necessary but not sufficient. We must structure opportunities for students to practice using these strategies. We also need to ask students not only *what* they think, but *how* they think, and *if* this was the most effective process for them. Guided practice with feedback is a powerful way to teach students how to learn because it provides students with opportunities to practice strategies and evaluate them to see which ones are or are not useful.

Testing practices also influence students' use of learning strategies. Rote memory questions such as "According to the author the shortage of teachers depends on three factors. Which three?" produce surface-level processing, whereas deep-level processing can be induced by questions such as "Explain the meaning of the following quotation—'Too many poor teachers will drive good ones out of the market.'" According to Pressley and McCormick (1995) one of the most powerful ways to influence the degree to which students use deep rather than surface strategies is through test demands. Students are more willing to learn to use deep processing strategies when it is evident to them that these types of strategies help them to meet the demands of the test or other evaluative procedures.

METHODS FOR CHECKING UNDERSTANDING

Strategic learners must be skillful self-regulators who periodically check on the usefulness of their learning methods by monitoring their progress toward learning goals and subgoals (Schunk & Zimmerman, 2003). Without checking actively on their progress, many students may think that they understand when in fact they do not. Often students do not realize there are holes in their understanding until they receive their grade on a test. This is because the test is the first time they were asked to check on their new knowledge in a way that would identify gaps or misunderstandings. Strategic learners know that the time to check on understanding is before taking a test or other formal assessment measure. Checking on understanding and looking for gaps in knowledge integration should be an ongoing activity present in every studying and learning context.

Checking our understanding can be a simple as trying to paraphrase or apply what we have been trying to learn. In fact, many homework or project assignments are designed to help students identify gaps in their knowledge or areas of misunderstanding so that they can be corrected. Getting past these problems helps students to deepen their understanding of a topic. Many of the learning strategies we discussed earlier also can be used to test understanding. For example, trying to paraphrase in our own words what we are reading in a textbook is a good way to help build meaning, but it also helps us to identify gaps or errors in our understanding. If we try to apply our knowledge and have difficulty using it, or if we try to explain it to someone else and cannot do it, we would also know that we have some comprehension problems. Monitoring our comprehension is an important part of strategic learning that fosters self-regulation. Only if we know we have a problem in our understanding or a gap in our knowledge can we do something about it.

A very useful method for checking understanding and helping to teach a variety of learning strategies is the use of cooperative learning. Cooperative learning is a method that builds on peer tutoring. We have long known that in many traditional tutoring situations the tutor, not the student receiving the tutoring, benefits the most. While processing the content for presentation, the tutor is consolidating and integrating his or her content knowledge. At the same time, the tutor is also learning a great deal about how to learn. The tutor needs to diagnose the tutee's learning problem, or knowledge gap, in order to help the tutee overcome it. Refer to the chapter "Active Learning" for a more complete discussion of the benefits of cooperative learning within "learning cells."

KNOWING HOW TO LEARN IS NOT ENOUGH— STUDENTS MUST ALSO WANT TO LEARN

Strategic learners know a lot about learning and the types of strategies that will help them meet their learning goals. However, knowing what to do is not enough. Knowing how to do it is still not enough. Students must want to learn if they are to use the knowledge, strategies, and skills we have addressed so far. It is the interaction of what Scott Paris and his colleagues have called skill and will that results in self-regulated learning (Hofer et al., 1998; Paris et al., 1983; Pintrich & De Groot, 1990). Many students know much more about effective study practices than they use. Just as in the case of an overweight person who is an expert in weight loss techniques, knowledge is not always sufficient for action. We all have many different potential goals and actions competing for our attention and resources at any point in time. Which goals we select and how much effort we put toward the goals we have selected is at least partially determined by our motivations. Strategic learners know how to learn, but they also want to be effective learners. It is the interaction of skill and will that gives direction to their actions and helps them to persist at tasks even in the face of obstacles.

One way to enhance students' perceptions of their competence is by giving performance feedback that focuses on strategic effort and skill development. Simply telling students that they did well does not really focus on their role in the performance. Telling a student, "This is great! I can really see the effort you put into this," says a lot more. Talking directly about students' strategic efforts and the skills they are developing helps them to focus on their role in the learning process. Remember, a key component of strategic learning is believing that you can play an active role. If students do not believe they can make a difference, they will not use many of the effective strategies we have been discussing. Many students listen to strategy instruction and believe the strategies are very useful—but not for them! Our task is to help students understand that they can take more responsibility for their own learning. Remember that motivation results from a number of interacting factors (Murphy & Alexander, 2000;

Pintrich & De Groot, 1990). As we discussed earlier in this chapter, establishing the potential usefulness of new learning helps to generate interest and direction for students' learning activities. The chapter "Motivation in the College Classroom" includes a more complete discussion of the effects of motivation on learning.

PUTTING IT ALL TOGETHER—EXECUTIVE CONTROL PROCESSES IN STRATEGIC LEARNING

We have discussed both skill and will as important components of strategic learning. A third essential component is the use of executive control processes, or self-regulation (see Weinstein, in press). These control processes are used to manage the learning process from the beginning (setting the learning goal) to the end result. Strategic learners use executive control processes to (1) organize and manage their approach to reaching a learning goal, (2) keep them on target and warn them if they are not making sufficient progress toward meeting the goal in a timely and effective manner, and (3) build up a repertoire of effective strategies that they can call on in the future to complete similar tasks, thereby increasing their learning efficiency and productivity (Paris & Paris, 2001; Weinstein, 1988). When students are facing new and unfamiliar tasks, they must do a lot of planning to help identify potentially effective methods to achieve their goals for task performance. Unfortunately, many students simply adopt a trial-and-error approach to learning, or they try to adapt other familiar strategies they have used for different tasks to the current one. Students do not realize that this approach is often neither effective nor efficient. The time invested in generating, following, monitoring, and perhaps modifying a plan is a good investment for reaching learning goals now and in the future. As we develop expertise, we do not need to dwell on developing a plan for each task we face. Generating and evaluating plans for reaching learning goals helps build up an effective repertoire that we can call on in the future when similar learning needs arise.

Several instructional approaches emphasize how college instructors can help students generate, maintain, and evaluate their learning methods—that is, self-regulate their learning within college coursework. For example, Zimmerman and Paulson (1995) reported a four-phase sequence to teach self-monitoring skills. Such skills are essential for checking understanding and assessing the effectiveness of strategies. When self-monitoring is successful, the student not only learns more but also develops better strategies. In addition, students' successes increase their self-efficacy in the course and their motivation to learn. As college instructors, we must be careful not to overemphasize one stage of learning (such as planning over implementation). Thus another important aspect of learning is the use of volitional strategies. For example, Trawick and Corno (1995) outlined a volitional training plan that includes specific instructional activities, modeling, role playing, record keeping, and instructor and peer feedback. They emphasized that faculty need to teach volitional skills in addition to cognitive and motivational strategies. Finally, in addition to learning how to learn course content and learning how to control motivation and volition, Boekaerts (1995; Boekaerts & Niemivirta, 2000) emphasized that students must also learn "emotion control"—the management of emotions and levels of arousal while learning.

College faculty can help facilitate self-regulated learning by encouraging students to share examples of successful approaches to learning with each other. Guided discussions about what is and is not working help students refine their own methods and get ideas for other potential approaches. They also focus students' attention on the importance of not simply working hard but also working strategically to meet their goals. Discussions of self-regulated learning should emphasize the need to change strategies in different contexts and for different purposes. Working strategically should be addressed as a challenging endeavor, cognitively, motivationally, and affectively. The students' success in meeting these challenges is among the intrinsic rewards of learning and teaching.

We have discussed many ways to help students become more strategic, self-regulated learners in classroom learning contexts. Now we turn our attention to some of the special strategies and skills students need in online or technology-rich learning contexts.

WHAT INSTRUCTORS CAN DO TO HELP THEIR STUDENTS SUCCEED IN ONLINE LESSONS AND COURSES

The online revolution has begun in earnest, and we all have much to be excited about as it spreads to all levels of education. However, we cannot let our euphoria over this new instructional medium and the exciting educational possibilities it offers cloud our perceptions of the challenges inherent in online instruction from a student's perspective. E-learning offers tremendous control to the learner of both the instructional resources and the technical tools provided in these learning environments. In the hands of a student prepared to take responsibility for using these tools to enhance learning, they can indeed be powerful tools. But in the hands of students who have difficulty with strategic learning, such as problems with managing time, meeting commitments, and maintaining motivation, online learning can offer many challenges. As indicated by reports of dissatisfaction and poor retention and completion rates (Carr, 2000; Frew & Weber, 1995; Nessler, 1999), many online learners often are unsuccessful. Although portions of this problem may be attributable to poorly designed materials, or novelty, or computer phobias, it is also becoming apparent that many students simply do not know how to learn and, perhaps even more important, how to manage their learning in online instructional settings. With the rapid and exponentially expanding growth of online courses, it is imperative that instructors and course designers help students develop the self-regulation and skills needed to intelligently exercise learner control. The following suggestions are derived from research and applied literatures examining these issues:

1. Teach students about the special instructional features of instructional programs, such as glossaries, self-tests, multimedia material, and supplementary information.
2. Teach them how to *use* the special instructional features of the program.
3. Teach students about the special technical tools available, such as chat rooms, contacting the instructor, and getting help.

4. Teach them how to *use* the special technical tools.

5. Provide instruction in critical self-regulation areas, including

   a. *Time management:* The flexibility of time and location is a distinguishing characteristic between online courses and traditional classroom-based courses. Traditional courses have a regular class time and classroom; online learning often allows for flexibility in both study times and places. Many online learners can schedule their study times at their convenience and can log on anywhere computer and Internet access is available. This flexibility gives online learners much more choice and autonomy than traditional classroom learners. However, if they have problems with time management, they are much more likely to put off their work more than they should and fall behind in their studies.

   b. *Generating and maintaining motivation:* Online learners have a greater responsibility for generating and maintaining their motivation over time. The absence of direct instructor and peer pressure, and a study environment often full of competing tasks, such as spending more time with friends and family or at work, often make it difficult for students to commit to completing their coursework.

   c. *Self-testing:* In online courses it is critical that students monitor their own understanding and progress through the material. In traditional classrooms this function is often carried out by the instructor, but in online learning contexts students must know how to use the feedback they are getting on their progress and to use self-testing to monitor their understanding on an ongoing basis.

   d. *Managing anxiety:* If learners in online courses are uncertain about what they are supposed to do in a course or experience an unexpected problem, they may feel frustrated about online learning. In addition, learners with insufficient computer skills often feel anxious about online learning. Finally, the text-based nature of online communication requires students to communicate through writing that might be distressing for those students who do not have the ability to express themselves effectively in writing.

6. Help students create a management plan for successfully completing an online lesson or course. This plan should be checked frequently and revised when necessary. The critical steps in the plan include

a. Setting one or more goals.

b. Reflecting on the personal resources they will need to reach each goal.

c. Brainstorming and creating a plan of attack to reach each goal.

d. Selecting the methods they will use to accomplish their plan.

e. Implementing their plan.

f. Monitoring (on an ongoing basis) the success and timeliness of their plan.

g. Formatively evaluating their progress.

h. Modifying, if necessary, their methods or even their goals.

i. Summatively evaluating the outcomes to see whether they want to use this plan again in the future or whether they need to modify or discard it.

IN CONCLUSION

Teaching strategic learning is more than an investment in your students' future learning; it also is an investment in the present. Strategic learners are better able to take advantage of your instruction and their studying activities. The time you invest will come back to you in enhanced student understanding and performance, as well as increased motivation. It is also important to remember that all of us have goals for what we hope the students in our classes will learn. In today's rapidly changing world, the ability to acquire or use knowledge and skills is more important than compiling a static knowledge base. There is an old Talmudic expression that loosely translates like this: "If you feed a person a fish, you have fed them for a day, but if you teach them how to fish, you have fed them for a lifetime!" As college instructors our task is to provide edible fish (content knowledge), but our task is also to teach our students how to fish (learning how to become strategic learners in our field).

Supplementary Reading

B. K. Hofer, S. L. Yu, and P. R. Pintrich, "Teaching College Students to Be Self-Regulated Learners," in D. H. Schunk and B. J. Zimmerman (eds.), *Self-Regulated Learning: From Teaching to Self-Reflective Practice* (New York: Guilford, 1998), pp. 57–85. This entire book is worth reading but might get a little technical for the beginner in this area. However, this chapter is focused on college students and therefore worth spending time on.

P. R. Pintrich (ed.), "Understanding Self-Regulated Learning," *New Directions for Teaching and Learning*, no. 63, June 1995, has chapters on the theories behind this important concept and the practical applications to a variety of settings, disciplines, and students.

C. E. Weinstein, J. Husman, and D. R. Dierking, "Self-Regulation Interventions with a Focus on Learning Strategies," in M. Boekaerts, P. Pintrich, and M. Zeidner (eds.), *Handbook of Self-Regulation* (San Diego: Academic Press, 2000). Another fairly complete discussion of the whole self-regulation concept.

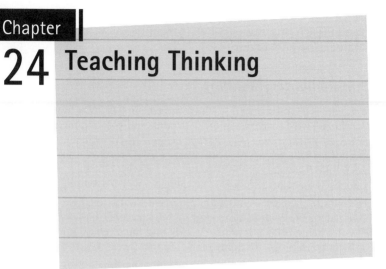

Historу credits Plutarch with the observation that "the mind is not a vessel to be filled but a fire to be kindled." This statement elegantly captures differing attitudes of educators about their overarching objectives in higher education. "Filling vessels" has been the dominant strategy that most college students experience. However, in the last few decades, widespread dissatisfaction with the performance of college graduates has produced new pressures for higher educators to adopt Plutarch's perspective. Barr and Tagg (1995) described and promoted this paradigm shift with their differentiation of *content-centered instruction* and *learner-centered instruction*.

Content-centered teachers share important facts and concepts with students and show limited attention to the process. Many content-centered teachers believe that merely exposing students to the ideas of the discipline will facilitate changes in students' thinking over time. Content-centered teachers often credit students' innate intelligence as responsible for their academic success and therefore believe that it doesn't make much sense to

This chapter was written by Jane S. Halonen of the University of West Florida.

invest valuable class time in concentrating on process instead of in exploring the important "stuff" of the discipline.

In contrast, learner-centered teachers embrace the responsibility for fostering changes in students' thinking skills. They believe that students' grappling with ideas will lead to more meaningful and enduring learning. Factual knowledge rapidly deteriorates unless the ideas can be meaningfully encoded or practiced with some regularity (Eriksen, 1983). Consequently, learner-centered teachers regularly turn to active learning strategies to engage students in process. Cognitive scientists report that when students think about material in more meaningful ways, underlying brain structures will change to promote more enduring learning (Leamnson, 2000).

Neuroscientific findings further support the pressures for curriculum reform, new pedagogical strategies, and accountable performance by college educators. As a consequence, most colleges and universities now routinely promise the improvement of students' thinking as an explicit goal of the mission. Improving thinking is sometimes couched in terms of objectives to promote critical thinking or problem-solving skills (Halpern, 1996).

Most academic programs have responded to increased demands for accountability by crafting a coherent curriculum in which thoughtful sequencing of thinking and learning experiences can maximize student gains. Students can be supported as they move from simpler learning challenges, such as getting introduced to basic concepts in the discipline, through the complex performance demands that might be required in a capstone course. They can move from novice to baccalaureate-level expert, and programs can capture the quality of their instruction through a well-designed assessment plan that reflects the journey.

Any given course can provide a context in which students can learn to think better, and any course can make a contribution to students' cognitive evolution, particularly when faculty set expectations for how students should think within the discipline. Many teachers have found the use of systematic frameworks can help them design learning experiences that can be pitched to the right level of cognitive complexity. Perhaps the most enduring framework was originally developed nearly a half century ago.

SETTING GOALS FOR THINKING

Benjamin Bloom and his colleagues (1956) collaborated on the development of a popular framework to improve an instructor's ability to teach thinking, regardless of the discipline. Bloom's taxonomy became a foundation for teaching across all levels. The original work suggested that thinking skills could be subdivided and sequenced in terms of sophistication. Some skills represent *lower-order* thinking, including knowledge, comprehension, and application. The *higher-order* skills required greater complexity and effort, including analysis, synthesis, and evaluation. Bloom and his colleagues suggested that a thoughtful course design that relied on the taxonomy for guidance could clarify assignment expectations and enhance student performance. The taxonomy became a widely used tool for teachers developing test questions and promoting more complex thinking skills.

Recently, Anderson, Krathwohl, and colleagues (2001) revised Bloom's taxonomy to improve its pedagogical utility and accuracy. Anderson's team recognized that "knowledge" was not really a process, as originally proposed in the taxonomy, but the context in which thinking takes place. They differentiated the various kinds of knowledge (factual, conceptual, procedural, and metacognitive) that learning encompasses. They changed the first level of the taxonomy from "knowledge" to "remember." Throughout the revised taxonomy, Anderson and his colleagues developed more outcome-oriented language to assist teachers in developing workable objectives and learning activities. For example, they changed "evaluation" to "evaluate" to stress the action by using appropriate verbs rather than nouns. (See Figure 24.1 for other examples.) As in the original taxonomy, Anderson's team retained the hierarchical design in which each skill level builds on the prior level, but they reorganized the sequence of higher-order skills. In Anderson's revision, "create" (formerly "synthesis") assumes the status of the most complex thinking skill, followed by "evaluate," reversing their original relationship in Bloom's sequence.

Unfortunately, the constraints of testing formats used with large classes often prompt teachers to limit themselves to lower-order objectives. Multiple-choice tests tend to emphasize remembering and understanding. Skilled item writers can use multiple-choice

The revision retains the hierarchical nature of thinking skills, but offers a new sequence in the hierarchy and emphasizes action verbs to promote more effective design of test questions and assignments.

Higher-Order
Skills

Create
Reorganize elements into a new pattern, structure, or purpose
(*generate, plan, produce*)

Evaluate
Come to a conclusion about something based on standards/criteria
(*checking, critiquing, judging*)

Analyze
Subdivide content into meaningful parts and relate the parts
(*differentiating, organizing, attributing*)

Apply
Use procedures to solve problems or complete tasks
(*execute, implement*)

Understand
Construct new meaning by mixing new material with existing ideas
(*interpret, exemplify, classify, summarize, infer, compare, explain*)

Lower-
Order
Skills

Remember
Retrieve pertinent facts from long-term memory
(*recognize, recall*)

FIGURE 24.1   Anderson, Krathwohl, and Colleagues' (2001) Revision of Bloom's Taxonomy

Source: Anderson, L. W., & Krathwohl, D. R. (Eds.). (2001). *A taxonomy for learning, teaching, and assessing: A revision of Bloom's taxonomy of educational objectives.* New York: Longman.

tests to tap higher-order objectives; however, these items are much more difficult to create. Familiarity with Bloom's taxonomy or Anderson's revision can help produce a more systematic approach to teaching thinking skills. Beginning courses in a discipline will emphasize lower-level thinking skills but should not be devoid of higher-order challenges. As students progress in their majors, they should face more complex thinking demands. Research papers, structured class discussions, and original presentations can facilitate the development of higher levels of thinking when instructors frame their directions properly. Students can analyze and evaluate concepts, incorporating them into a coherent viewpoint, which should improve their ability to benefit from what they have learned and to generalize their learning to new situations. Emphasizing higher-order skills will enhance students' cognitive complexity (cf. Perry, 1970). Advanced courses that only develop and test lower levels of thinking simply shortchange students by limiting their conceptual development and thinking practices.

IMPROVING THINKING QUALITY

1. Be explicit in your syllabus that your goal will be to help students improve their thinking, especially learning to think "like a _____" (historian, psychologist, biologist, and so on). Describe what constitutes successful thinking in the discipline as explicitly as you can.

2. Share the revised Bloom model with students during the orientation to the course, to clarify your goals for their cognitive development. This strategy can reduce complaints that you are trying to be "tricky" when your test items are tapping higher-level skills.

3. Provide ample opportunities to practice thinking during class. The results of grappling with ideas will have more enduring impact than mere exposure to ideas.

4. Model thinking skills. Think out loud when you answer student questions.

5. Don't answer every student question yourself. Turn student questions into opportunities for all of the students to think their way to a satisfying answer.

6. Show excitement about all aspects of thinking: good questions, odd questions, partial answers, and unsolvable problems.

7. Acknowledge examples of good student thinking. When an example is off target or poorly developed, ask the class to collaborate to improve the response.

8. Ask students to judge the quality of their own contributions. Encouraging self-assessment can promote greater autonomy in thinking.

9. Design challenges that will appeal to diverse learning styles. Some students will require more reflection time before they can express their thinking confidently.

10. Give yourself permission not to cover all of the content. Select from the relevant content to promote the thinking goals that you have in mind.

IN CONCLUSION

Learning thinking skills is not easy, but students will not make progress without specific training. Along with specific discipline-based strategies that sharpen their thinking skills, students need to develop habits of reflection—of thinking about their experience, their successes and failures, their plans and purposes, their choices, and their consequences.

Teaching thinking skills also is not easy. Teachers need to commit to the importance of building thinking into course design, to provide plenty of practice opportunities, and to offer developmental feedback to achieve their desired outcomes.

Supplementary Reading

John Dewey's classic *How We Think* (Boston: Houghton Mifflin, 1998), written over a half-century ago, underlies much of the work since his time and is still fresh and helpful today.

David Levy's book *Tools of Critical Thinking* (Boston: Allyn and Bacon, 1997) deals with many of the biases and errors in everyday thinking and includes excellent exercises to help students become better thinkers.

One aspect of good thinking is reflection. See Jean MacGregor (ed.), "Student Self-Evaluation: Fostering Reflective Thinking," *New Directions for Teaching and Learning*, no. 56, 1993.

Also helpful in teaching thinking are the following:

- D. F. Halpern and associates, *Changing College Classrooms: New Teaching and Learning Strategies for an Increasingly Complex World* (San Francisco: Jossey-Bass, 1994).

- E. Langer, *The Power of Mindful Learning* (Reading, MA: Addison-Wesley, 1997).

- M. Mentkowski and associates, *Learning That Lasts: Integrating Learning, Development, and Performance in College and Beyond* (San Francisco: Jossey-Bass, 2000).

- R. J. Sternberg and E. L. Grigorenko, *Teaching for Successful Intelligence* (Arlington Heights, IL: Skylight Professional Development, 2000).

Chapter 25

The Ethics of Teaching
and the Teaching
of Ethics

Imagine you're teaching a course at the introductory level, one that is required of all students who want to proceed on to major in your department. And let's suppose that after the first exam a student whose performance was much below standard approaches you and offers you a considerable sum of money if you'll change a grade on the exam so the student can pass. What is the ethical thing to do in this situation?

Now imagine the same situation, but instead of offering you money, the student pleads for an opportunity to retake the exam because of extenuating circumstances during the first test administration. Now what is the ethical choice?

Next imagine the same situation, but this time you are the one who notices that a student who has been working hard in your class and whom you expected to do very well has instead failed the exam miserably. How does this situation compare with the others from an ethical standpoint?

The first scenario seems fairly straightforward, a definite violation of ethics if you were to accept the money to change the grade. The second example is not as straightforward. To what extent should the student be allowed an opportunity that is not available to all the other students? Does providing that opportunity constitute unethical behavior? Or is it just unfair? Or is there a difference? In the third instance, to what extent should your assessment of a student's abilities counter actual performance? Where do you draw the line in helping students?

The most difficult questions that teachers face often have nothing to do with the content of the course or the way it is presented. They focus instead on the ethical issues of teaching, how we relate to our students, to our institution, to our discipline, and to society at large. What are our responsibilities to each constituency, and what do we do when responsibilities conflict? Unfortunately there are no easy answers to these questions. I raise them here as food for thought because you *will* face them sometime in your teaching career.

This chapter addresses the issue of ethics in teaching. What do we mean by "ethics in teaching"? In recent years, more and more has been written about the topic as the teaching mission of the university comes under increasing scrutiny (Cahn, 1994; Fisch, 1996; Lewis, 1997; Matthews, 1991; Strike, 1988). It seems only proper that those who currently teach and those who aspire to a faculty career be introduced to the concept.

What is an ethical question in teaching? Ethical questions are sometimes defined in terms of right and wrong (Strike, 1988); in terms of cultural norms such as honesty and promise keeping (Smith, 1996); or as "general guidelines, ideals, or expectations that need to be taken into account, along with other relevant conditions and circumstances, in the design and analysis of teaching" (Murray et al., 1996, p. 57).

In general, *ethical standards are intended to guide us in carrying out the responsibilities we have to the different groups with whom we interact*. Ethics violations can occur when we are tempted to act contrary to those standards. Ethical dilemmas occur when multiple responsibilities conflict or have more than one right answer (Strike, 1988). It is often surprising to consider all the different things that can cause ethical problems for instructors. They range from the obvious bribe attempt previously described, to failure to present all legitimate sides of an issue adequately, to accepting remuneration for extra tutoring for a class with which one is already connected.

In a 1991 research study of psychologists teaching at academic institutions, Tabachnick and colleagues reported reactions to various ethical questions involved in teaching at the college level. Respondents were asked to report how frequently they engaged in a wide range of various activities and the extent to which those activities were ethical or unethical. The activities included things as drastic as sexual harassment and more mundane activities such as teaching materials that the instructor had not yet fully mastered.

The behavior *most often* engaged in was teaching when not adequately prepared, although it was not a consistent pattern for most people. The authors attributed this behavior more to heavy workloads and rapid advances in the field than to the shirking of responsibilities. The rarest of behaviors were those related to sexual harassment. Whether this study is an accurate reflection of behavior or of reluctance to report such behavior is impossible to tell. Also rare were actual sexual encounters with students.

Perhaps the most interesting sources of ethical conflicts for the Tabachnick study group were a result of the conflicting roles of mentor/sponsor and evaluator. For example, over two-thirds believed that allowing a student's likability to influence a grade was unethical, but over two-thirds reported doing it at some point anyway. The same sort of dilemma is seen when instructors interact socially with students. On the one hand, the interaction with faculty is reported as vital to student growth by Pascarella and Terenzini (1991); on the other, it raises the possibility of conflict.

In a more recent study (Braxton & Bayer, 1999), a national sample of faculty in higher education was asked to rate the acceptability of a range of violations of teaching standards, such as "The instructor insists that the student take one particular perspective on course content" or "The instructor does not introduce new teaching methods or procedures." The researchers identified 126 different behaviors that a teacher might engage in and asked the participants to rate how strong a sanction each behavior should bring. The authors then identified two levels of sanctions that they felt were present in the data. The most serious sanctions were for those norms they labeled as inviolable. These included seven clusters: condescending negativism, inattentive planning, moral turpitude, particularistic grading, personal disregard, uncommunicated course details, and uncooperative cynicism.

The second set of clusters was labeled "admonitory norms"—behaviors that, though inappropriate, didn't evoke as strong a reaction from the participants. These included advisement negligence, authoritarian classrooms, inadequate communication, inadequate course design, inconvenience avoidance, insufficient syllabus, teaching secrecy, and undermining colleagues. When these clusters were compared across institutional types and disciplines, only two were identified by all groups of faculty as inappropriate: moral turpitude and authoritarian classrooms. Demographic characteristics of the respondents did not make a difference in what they felt was inappropriate behavior. The final conclusion by the authors was that there were four values that seemed to undergird the judgments of the participants: respect for students as individuals, equal consideration for all students, an obligation to prepare for teaching, and an obligation to participate in the governance and life of the institution. If you find these results intriguing, you might want to respond to the original survey yourself and compare your responses with those of the national sample. The survey, College Teaching Behaviors Inventory, can be found in Braxton and Bayer's 1999 book reporting their findings.

Values like these are becoming more and more common in discussions about teaching in higher education (Markie, 1994; Carr, 2000). In fact, the American Association of University Professors provided a statement of professional ethics dealing with the responsibilities of faculty members that highlights what AAUP considers to be the special responsibilities of individuals in an academic position (AAUP, 1987). A similar set of principles was developed by the Society for Teaching and Learning in Higher Education (STLHE) and distributed to faculty in Canadian institutions (Murray et al., 1996). Perhaps these standards can help highlight what a faculty member should consider when making personal choices.

RESPONSIBILITIES TO STUDENTS

Both the AAUP guidelines and the STLHE guidelines recognize that one of a faculty member's first responsibilities is to the students. The specifics that follow illustrate the broad range of impact that faculty can have on student lives.

To Encourage the Free Pursuit of Learning

The primary purpose of teaching is to encourage learning; therefore the first ethical responsibility an instructor has is to that goal. All that we do to prepare and conduct well-designed instruction is part of that responsibility. The ethical instructor knows the content to be learned, the students who will do the learning, and the methods that could be used to foster the learning. The STLHE guidelines state this explicitly in their first and second principles: content competence and pedagogical competence (Murray et al., 1996). In a discussion of the ethics of teaching psychology, Matthews (1991) interprets the American Psychological Association's professional standards as they apply to teaching and cites the issues of responsibility and competence as two key contributors to encouraging learning. In her interpretation, faculty members are responsible for remaining current and presenting accurate and balanced views of the field, an idea also related to the concept of scholarly behavior discussed later in this chapter.

There are many ways an instructor might violate these standards. Here are two examples:

- Most obvious is to fail in our duties in class preparation. One can't always be in top form, but just as we expect students to come to class prepared, we must make the same effort. This is one of the most commonly occurring violations reported by the sample (Tabachnick et al., 1991) and was identified as a key admonitory norm by Braxton and Bayer (1999).

- A second, less obvious way is failing to remain current both in the content area and in instructional methods that foster learning. Although it is unlikely that faculty would not be current in the content, it is very likely that faculty will not have kept up with research into better instructional methods.

A second part of this responsibility is to protect and encourage the autonomy of our students so that eventually they no longer need our constant guidance. The STLHE guidelines list this as the fourth of their eight principles: "to contribute to the intellectual development of the student" (Murray et al., 1996). If students are to develop into thinking individuals, we must structure our interactions with them in such a way as to both model and support independent thinking, even when this means they might end up disagreeing with us.

To Demonstrate Respect for Students

Ethical instructors also respect the "otherness of students" (Churchill, 1982)—that is, the individual and independent nature of the students and the fact that students are at different stages of their lives than are the instructors. For example, instructors need to be aware of the special needs of their students, whether those be cultural, physical, or based on background (Matthews, 1991). This also means respecting students' goals, their choices, and their value as individuals (Strike, 1988), another key value listed by Braxton and Bayer (1999).

The most obvious venue for this particular principle is in the interactions we have with students in and out of class. During class, the way we respond to students' questions and comments should convey the idea that everyone's participation is welcome and respected. How we respond to a student's question affects more than just the student who asked it. And outside of class, the way we greet students who come to office hours or see us in the halls speaks volumes about the level of respect we have for them. We show respect by being available when we say we will be, by keeping promised appointments, by being willing to listen to students' concerns, by giving as much thought and preparation to our interactions with undergraduates as we do to those with graduate students and colleagues.

An example of a not-so-obvious need to respect students as individuals is discussed in an article by Grauerholz and Copenhaver (1994) about the use of experiential teaching methods, especially those that involve a great deal of self-disclosure by students. The choice of instructional strategies such as journaling and small-group problem sharing may violate your students' rights and be harmful as well as unethical unless done with a great deal of care and concern for the students' well-being. To guard against the possibility of harm, here are some suggestions on how to structure the experience. For example, you should carefully choose strategies and make their purpose clear to your students. It might also be appropriate to allow alternative ways of satisfying the learning requirement for those who do not feel comfortable with these methods. Use of such teaching methods raises the issue of trust because when students trust an instructor, they are more willing to engage in self-examination. Making self-examination safe for students is reason enough to be sure that your relationship with students is one of trust and respect.

Similar issues of trust arise during the discussion of sensitive topics, such as race, sexual preference, and religion. When faced with a potentially sensitive situation, you can

- Provide early disclosure of the potentially sensitive nature of the topics.

- Make sure that students understand what is being presented as fact and what as opinion.

- Offer extra time outside of class to those students who need to discuss the topics and their reactions to them (Koocher & Keith-Spiegel, 1998).

I have advised faculty to draw up a set of "rules of engagement" for sensitive topics that could spark heated debate in class. These rules would specify how these debates would be conducted and would include such things as cooling-down activities, the obligation to be able to state the other person's position before attacking it, and the avoidance of personalizing arguments. If such guidelines are provided early in the course, students can feel more comfortable when sensitive topics are raised.

This does not mean that the topics will be avoided, because that would be a violation of the first of our guidelines: open inquiry. One can see how this conflict would raise ethical dilemmas for teachers, especially in disciplines where sensitive topics are the norm rather than the exception.

To Respect Confidentiality

The issue of self-disclosure leads to another large component of respect: the belief that students have a right to privacy in their dealings with us. Not only does this principle have the weight of ethics behind it, but in many cases it also carries the weight of law. Here, however, we are speaking of less egregious violations of privacy, such as discussing a single student's situation with some-one who does not have a legitimate interest in that student's case. Practices such as leaving student papers out so that they can be retrieved at the students' convenience might be a violation of this principle because that means students have access to their peers' work (Murray et al., 1996). At my institution, the posting of grades in a public place in any way that would allow an individual's grade to be identified by others is prohibited.

To Model the Best Scholarly and Ethical Standards

A teacher, whether by accident or by design, is more to students than a content expert. The teacher is a model of all that it means to be a scholar, a thinking person. We teach not only what we know but also what we are. Part of the ethics of teaching is to realize this responsibility and to become the best models we can be, which requires some serious self-reflection on our personal standards of scholarship and living. Clark Kerr (1994), in a discussion of ethics in the academic culture, supports this struggle when he says that we are obliged to present a variety of perspectives, our own as well as others', so that the facts can be judged for themselves. This does not imply that you must always take a dispassionate stance; but even, or perhaps especially, when you feel strongly about an issue, it is necessary to demonstrate by your actions that intelligent people can disagree and still remain rational. Giving students the ability to differentiate emotion from reason is an especially important responsibility of instructors, according to Hanson (1996). As she says, "Teachers who can nimbly convey the strengths of a position they in fact oppose, who can clearly display the weaknesses in a position they in fact embrace, are *modeling* a critical engagement from which students may learn their most important lessons" (p. 35).

To Foster Honest Academic Conduct and to Ensure Fair Evaluation

Perhaps the most obvious ethical problems arise in the area of evaluation of student learning, a point echoed in both the AAUP guidelines and those from the STLHE. Instructors are the arbiters of entrance into the profession and are therefore responsible for seeing to it that standards are upheld. However, we are also responsible for guaranteeing that all are given a fair chance of demonstrating their abilities. When we allow academic dishonesty to go unheeded, we violate the rights of all the students who are abiding by the rules. If we fail to establish an evaluation system that accurately assesses the students' progress, we are abdicating our responsibilities to both the students and the profession.

The most important type of fairness for students is interactional fairness (how individuals are treated), followed by procedural fairness (the degree to which there is impartiality in how grades are determined and performance is evaluated), and finally outcome fairness (the degree to which grades and other outcomes reflect performance) (Rodabaugh, 1996).

The conflicts most often occur when this standard of fairness is pitted against the first responsibility of respecting the individual and fostering independence. The examples that opened this chapter speak to this issue. How important is it that all students be evaluated in the same way? Are we being fairer if we maintain standards and vary conditions of evaluation or if we use individual standards according to the special situation of each student? Which factors are legitimate considerations? There is no agreement on these issues. The best we can do is to continue to discuss and deliberate, alone and in groups, because the conditions under which we operate today will not be the same as those in the future.

To Avoid Exploitation, Harassment, or Discrimination

One of the variables that should be at the forefront of our thinking about the ethics of teaching is the great power discrepancy between teacher and students. Whether we like it or not, whether we seek it or not, by virtue of our position alone we are invested with a great deal of power over the lives of our students. To make matters worse, many students invest us with even more power than we are entitled to. For this reason, both the AAUP and the STLHE guidelines list one or more principles concerning harassment, exploitation, and discrimination.

Abuse of this power is at the base of many of the ethical traps that lie strewn across our paths as teachers. The very special nature of the relationship between teacher and student is all too easy to abuse (Smith, 1996). The most blatant examples of unethical behavior, those most frequently mentioned in written codes of ethics, deal with exploitation or harassment of various types: sexual, racial, religious, even intellectual. The most egregious of these (and possibly the most debated) is sexual harassment in the form of improper relationships between instructors and students. Braxton and Bayer (1999) list this as the one inviolable norm that retained its importance regardless of type of institution surveyed or discipline represented by the respondent. It could be held forth as the most important norm they identified. The area of the proper relationships between teachers and students is particularly difficult for graduate students, who are both teachers and students. Because of their age they occupy a place between their own students and their own professors. Thus they can be either harasser or harassed. Intimate relationships between teachers and students are generally considered inappropriate at least. The best decision for an instructor or a student is to keep the relationship on a professional level as long as the power imbalance exists.

But there are plenty of other forms of exploitation that occur in academia. For example, requiring students to engage in class activities that are unrelated to the educational purposes of the course but that serve our personal ends is an abuse of power. Making derogatory comments about population subgroups is an obvious example of harassment.

Another area of ethical problems involves receiving special considerations or benefits as a result of being in a position of authority. For example, is it a violation of ethics to adopt a less-than-adequate book simply because of an incentive made available by the publisher? How legitimate is it to accept an invitation to a party or other event as the guest of a student in your class? Does it matter if that student is no longer in your class? Does it matter if the event is somehow connected with the student's academic program—for example, a dinner honoring that student's work? We must be aware that by our position alone we will sometimes be put in a compromised situation in all innocence on our part or the student's.

THE TEACHING OF ETHICS

There is an aspect of this topic that seems to span all the ethical areas just discussed: the teaching of ethics and values. You can see how violation of this central question can occur in all sorts of ways. It might be violated when we fail to present all reasonable sides of an issue or fail to allow students to explore a topic in depth. It might happen when we judge students on the basis of their beliefs rather than their achievement. It might happen when we grade students' work for its conformity to our own perspective rather than for its representation of whatever position it supports. The question here is, should we teach values? Or by teaching values do we violate the ethical standards just described? I believe that we have no choice: we *will* teach our values, if not through direct instruction then through our behavior.

Valuing is as natural as thinking or breathing. We automatically make value judgments about our experiences. "This was good, that was bad; this is beautiful, that's ugly." You have already made judgments about the value of this book. Our students are continually valuing. It would be strange if their college experiences had no impact on that valuing process.

"But," you say, "isn't it a misuse of our position if we indoctrinate students with our values?" True. Probably our avoidance of explicit attention to values results from our concern about the evil of indoctrination. But there are two aspects to my answer.

The *first* is that I would have no compunction about indoctrination with respect to such values as honesty and respect for other individuals as human beings. We cannot teach our students well if they plagiarize papers, fake laboratory results, or cheat on examinations. We cannot carry out effective classroom discussions without an atmosphere of respect for others' feelings or a sense of shared humanity. In a multicultural society like ours there is a special need for thinking seriously about values—how we differ and what we share. Certainly we want our students to value learning.

The *second* is that we can help students to become more sensitive to values issues, to recognize value implications, to understand others' values, without indoctrination. Even with respect to fundamental values (such as honesty), student discussion, exploration, and debate about their implications are more useful than simple advocacy. Open consideration of the complexity of value issues is probably less subversive than disregarding values altogether. What values should we teach?

Those who say we should be taking a neutral stance on values typically are restricting their definition of values to sociopolitical ones. Very few would dispute the fact that we are concerned about honesty, respect for others, and rationality. A major goal of education presumably is to increase students' skills in critical, rational thinking. We want students to value rational thought, but not at the exclusion of other ways of knowing and thinking. In considering problems in society or in their everyday lives, our graduates will, I hope, look for evidence rather than react on the basis of unreasoning prejudice; they will be aware of the implications of their values but not let their values close their minds. Particularly in social science courses we ask our students to ask "What is the evidence?" before jumping to conclusions. Even those who point out that "rationality" has sometimes been defined in ways that confirm power relationships present rational arguments and evidence for their position. Our greater sensitivity to the issues raised by feminist and other critics is itself a tribute to rationality.

The big question in teaching is what to do about controversial social and political values. Here it seems to me that we are not privileged to demand acceptance of our own values, as I think we are privileged to do with respect to requiring academic honesty. But this does not imply avoiding values issues. Too often we communicate—by the way we handle touchy material—that you don't rock the boat by taking a position. In avoiding controversial issues we communicate the notion that it may be all right to talk about these things in dormitories or in other places but not in educational settings where rational arguments and the complexities of the issue are more likely to be salient. The apple of temptation for us as teachers is that we may too easily accept affirmation of values that we share, letting students get away with simply stating a position with which we agree, without asking for rational support, as we might for a position that conflicts with our own.

On the other side, however, is the problem of dealing with those with whom we disagree. There is the danger that we will yield to the temptation of demolishing the student with the force of our logic, but arguing can also be a way of showing respect. Remember that the power you have in your role as teacher may make it difficult for the student to muster a strong defense. Take it easy until students trust you enough to argue without fear of retribution. It is all too easy to intentionally, or unintentionally, coerce students into overt agreement.

Perry (1970, 1981) described the development of Harvard students as progressing from the dualistic belief that things are either true or false, good or evil, through a stage of relativism in which they feel all beliefs are equally valid, to a stage of commitment to values and beliefs that are recognized to be incomplete and imperfect but are open to correction and further development. We may not all reach Perry's highest stage, or we may reach it in some areas but not in others, but Perry suggests that as teachers and members of the community of learners, we have the responsibility not only to model commitment and open-mindedness but also to share our own doubts and uncertainties.

How Can We Teach Values?

We exemplify and communicate our values in what we teach and in the way we teach. Teaching values does not mean neglecting knowledge. Knowledge is a powerful sword to protect students from biased, emotional appeals.

Probably every teacher, whether in the arts, the sciences, or the professions, tries to teach students that it is not enough simply to respond to material or performance as good or bad, but rather to be able to back up one's judgment with evidence that is reasonable in terms of the standards of that discipline. We communicate that value by our comments on papers, our reactions to student comments or performance, and ultimately by our grades. So we have a group of values that we accept and either explicitly or implicitly communicate to our students through our behavior as teachers.

Our values also affect our course planning. We begin with the goals we take for the course. Who should determine those goals? Is this something to be determined by the university, by the department, by the instructor, or should students be involved? Personally, I have faith that in a situation in which students and faculty members participate jointly, our decisions will come out with reasonable values, reasonable content, and reasonable coverage—all the things that we worry about when we're thinking about how to set up a course. A cooperative approach exemplifies the value of respect for others. Asking students to write or discuss their goals for the course involves thinking about values. Asking them at the end of the course to think about what goals they have achieved and how these are related to their long-term goals sensitizes students to values issues.

If we want students to change, they have to have a chance to express their ideas and values in words or actions and see how they work. They need reactions not only from teachers but also from peers and others who share or oppose their positions. They need to trust the teacher's good will and good sense. They need to feel that the class is a community in which each will be accepted despite differing views.

Cooperative peer learning can contribute to building community and often has a positive effect on attitudes and values. Cooperation is itself an important value in our culture, and success in learning how to work cooperatively with other students on a project or other learning experience is likely to have a positive impact on students' value for cooperation as well as on building the kinds of support and trust necessary for frank discussion of values issues.

We know that students remember the content of our courses better if they elaborate the content by relating it to other knowledge—if they question, explain, or summarize. Such elaboration is important in the values area as well. And it's important that the discussion and experiences be in places where there is mutual respect and support. Values are not likely to be changed much simply by passively listening and observing a lecturer. Change is more likely in situations in which the teacher and the students reflect, listen, and learn from one another.

Modeling Values

We model our values and those of our discipline in almost every class. Perhaps most important is the model of ethical behavior we provide. Clearly, sarcasm, favoritism, and failure to respect the diversity of students' cultures, values, and attitudes represent a negative model. But avoiding unethical behavior is not enough. How do we handle legitimate requests for exceptions from a policy printed in our syllabus? Do we weigh individual needs or are we rule-bound? How do we handle students with handicaps or learning disabilities? When a student comment is wrong or inappropriate, do we make it clear that we are criticizing the idea and not the person?

What about the ethical decisions we face in preparing and conducting the course? Do we give proper credit to the sources we use? Are our assignments and learning assessments dictated by student learning or by our own need to save time? Are we conscientious about preparation and attendance at class? Are we ethical in our use of licensed software?

MAKING ETHICAL CHOICES

The array of possibilities for ethical decisions seems endless. How, then, can we avoid stumbling somewhere along the line? Although there are no easy answers, there may be some ways of thinking about our actions as professionals that will maximize the possibility of acting ethically. Some very interesting strategies are suggested by several authors in a book on ethical dimensions of teaching edited by Fisch (1996), and the reader is pointed in that direction. Here, however, I draw the following principles for evaluating one's actions from two sources, the first five from Brown and Krager (1985) and the last from Schön (1983):

1. *Autonomy.* Am I acting in ways that respect freedom and treat others as autonomous?

2. *Nonmalfeasance.* Am I causing harm through either commission or omission?

3. *Beneficence.* Do my actions benefit the other person rather than myself?

4. *Justice.* Do I treat those for whom I am responsible equitably?

5. *Fidelity.* Do I uphold my part of any relationship?

6. *Acting consciously.* What are the assumptions on which I base my actions, and are they valid?

IN CONCLUSION

It is a great privilege to be a teacher. But all great privileges carry great responsibilities as well. Many of those responsibilities are subtle, thrust on us by the expectations of others rather than sought by us. Keeping those six principles in mind won't solve all the ethical dilemmas you face as a teacher, but they might give you a way to reflect on them alone and with other teachers. Teach your students to reflect both in and out of class. That reflection should never stop, because conscious reflection on values is perhaps the cornerstone of the ethics of teaching and the teaching of ethics.

Supplementary Reading

▦ American Association of University Professors, "Statement on Professional Ethics," *Academe*, 1987, 73(4), 49.

▦ S. M. Cahn, *Saints and Scamps: Ethics in Academia*, 2nd ed. (Totowa, NJ: Rowman & Littlefield, 1994).

▦ D. Carr, *Professionalism and Ethics in Teaching* (New York: Routledge, 2000).

▦ L. Fisch (ed.), "Ethical Dimensions of College and University Teaching: Understanding and Honoring the Special Relationship Between Teachers and Students," *New Directions for Teaching and Learning*, no. 66, 1996.

▦ W. L. Humphreys, "Values in Teaching and the Teaching of Values," *Teaching-Learning Issues*, no. 58 (Knoxville: Learning Research Center, University of Tennessee, 1986).

▦ C. Kerr, "Knowledge Ethics and the New Academic Culture," *Change*, 1994, 26(1), 8–16.

▦ M. Lewis, *Poisoning the Ivy: The Seven Deadly Sins and Other Vices of Higher Education in America* (Armonk, NY: M. E. Sharpe, 1997).

▦ P. Markie, *A Professor's Duties: Ethical Issues in College Teaching* (Totowa, NJ: Rowman & Littlefield, 1994).

▦ D. Schön, *The Reflective Practitioner* (San Francisco: Jossey-Bass, 1983).

Self-reflective learning involves much consideration of values. See Jean MacGregor (ed.), "Student Self-Evaluation: Fostering Reflective Learning," *New Directions for Teaching and Learning*, no. 56, 1993.

Joseph Lowman has a helpful discussion of how to handle controversial issues in his book *Mastering the Techniques of Teaching* (San Francisco: Jossey-Bass, 1984).

Lawrence Kohlberg's book *Essays on Moral Development* (San Francisco: Harper & Row, 1981) is a good resource for thinking about moral issues.

Parker Palmer provides a thought-provoking resource for teaching values in *The Courage to Teach: Exploring the Inner Landscape of a Teacher's Life* (San Francisco: Jossey-Bass, 1993).

G. Collier, "Learning Moral Judgment in Higher Education," *Studies in Higher Education*, 1993, *18*(3), 287–297, provides a discussion of why and how to teach values in college classrooms, including the use of group discussion and films and literature.

L. Moore and D. Hamilton, "The Teaching of Values," *New Directions for Student Services*, no. 61, Spring 1993, pp. 75–86. This interesting article in an interesting issue shows how academics and student affairs can work together in teaching values.

A. Colby, T. Ehrlich, E. Beaumont, and J. Stephens raise the issue of helping undergraduates become productive contributing members of the society in *Educating Citizens: Preparing America's Undergraduates for Lives of Moral and Civic Responsibility* (San Francisco: Jossey-Bass, 2003). The book is one of the many products of the Carnegie Foundation for the Advancement of Teaching dealing with the larger issues of higher education.

Part 7

Lifelong Learning
for the Teacher

26 Vitality and Growth Throughout Your Teaching Career

I have just completed my 58th year of teaching psychology at the University of Michigan. I am not as effective as I was 50 years ago because I don't know the students' culture well enough to build good bridges between the course content and what is in their heads. But I continue to be exhilarated going to class and to feel upbeat when I leave. And I continue to pick up new ideas to try out in next term's class. Teaching is still fun for me. One of my students commented on the student rating form, "Dr. McKeachie comes to class everyday as if there were no place on earth he'd rather be." I am depressed that some faculty members (a minority) don't continue to develop and enjoy their teaching. What can be done to foster continued development and enjoyment?

Part of my answer lies in motivation research and theory. Human beings have survived as a species because we are learners. We enjoy learning; we become curious when we confront something more complex than we are accustomed to; we like to confront and master challenges; we take pleasure in becoming and feeling competent.

Human beings are also a social species. We are stimulated by interaction with other human beings; in times of stress, we rely on social support; we learn from one another. Recent primate research suggests that we are also naturally altruistic. We get pleasure from helping others.

Teaching is thus an ideal career. There is infinite complexity and challenge. Each class is different, each student is unique, and there is always more to learn. New developments in our discipline, new research and theory about learning and teaching, new technology, and creative new ideas for teaching continually emerge. Our roles often shift as changes in curriculum (such as an emphasis on interdisciplinary team teaching) occur or as new technology presses us to develop new skills. There are never-ending opportunities to grow in competence and understanding.

And teaching is both an intellectual and a social activity. Each term, students come up with new questions, stimulate new insights. Classes offer ever-changing interpersonal dynamics. Getting to know and like each new group provides a continuing source of satisfaction and stimulation. And it is particularly rewarding when former students speak warmly of how we have made a difference in their lives.

The human interactions also offer challenges. There are always some students who seem to be uninterested, some who are confrontational, some who seldom appear. Trying to find out more about the reasons for their behavior, getting to know them better, finding their interests and trying to relate the course material to their interests and goals, involving them in teamwork with other students, demonstrating that you are committed to their learning—all of these may fail, but when something works, what satisfaction!

From the standpoint of motivation theory, it is thus clear that teaching offers great potential for continued vitality, growth, and satisfaction. But these do not come automatically. It is easier for some than for others. Enthusiasm for one's subject matter, an outgoing personality, a commitment to teaching well—these give one a big head start. But good teaching consists of learnable skills, and all your good qualities may go for naught if you teach at a level over the students' heads, are disorganized, evaluate student performance erratically, or lack the skills to implement your good intentions.

And those who are not naturally bubbling over with enthusiasm, outgoing, or even sure that they want to teach can still become effective teachers. In fact, developing as a teacher is a recursive activity. As you develop some skills and strategies that work, they generate positive reactions; this in turn increases your confidence and liking for your students; and that in turn generates more reflection and thinking about teaching as well as interest in developing additional skills, which continues the positive cycle.

HOW CAN YOU DEVELOP EFFECTIVE SKILLS AND STRATEGIES?

The easy answer is "Practice, practice, practice." Practice is important, but just as in sports or music, if one is practicing the wrong technique, one is not likely to improve. Psychologists would add to the "practice" maxim "Practice with feedback—knowledge of results." Moreover, there are additional complications.

1. What should one practice? If I have never heard or seen a particular method in use, such as team learning, I cannot practice it until I have read about it, heard about it, or seen it used. Thus the developing teacher needs to learn about possibly useful skills and strategies.

2. Methods of teaching differ in their difficulty. Which should I try first? As I indicated in the first few chapters of this book, there are a number of useful techniques that are easy to implement and are likely to work well the first time you try them. I advocate using such techniques as problem posting, minute papers, and the two-column method as techniques for stimulating attention and active learning early in the term, explaining their value for learning. These are low-risk, high-payoff, easy-to-use strategies that will help both you and the students build confidence that the class will be a useful learning experience. If you are lecturing or leading discussions, they can help activate student interest and attention. And using them gives you a chance to practice your lecturing or discussion skills in smaller segments.

3. How can I continue to perfect my skills? Here is where practice with feedback comes in. How can we get good feedback on what works and what doesn't?

Now let's examine in more detail how one can learn about what methods or strategies to use and how to get feedback.

LOOKING FOR NEW IDEAS, NEW METHODS, AND ALTERNATIVE STRATEGIES FOR HANDLING PROBLEMS

There are three possibilities: reading, hearing, and seeing.

Reading

I mention this first because you have been reading this book, which was written on the premise that most faculty members have learned how to learn from reading. At the end of each chapter are suggestions for other books or sources that can provide additional insights or suggestions. In addition to the more general resources to which we have referred, there are journals in each discipline dealing with teaching and education in that discipline. Subscribing to such a journal or to one of the newsletters or journals dealing with teaching, such as the *National Teaching and Learning Forum, The Teaching Professor, College Teaching, Change, New Directions for Teaching and Learning,* and *Innovative Higher Education,* will provide regular stimulation to think of new ideas.

Journals dealing with research on learning and teaching are also important sources. *Educational Psychologist, Journal of Higher Education, British Journal of Educational Psychology, Journal of Educational Research, Journal of Educational Psychology,* and similar journals can help you avoid falling for the latest fad as well as stimulate you to think about implications for your own teaching.

Hearing, Discussing

Peers are among the best sources of ideas. Talking about teaching with colleagues can be an invaluable source of ideas as well as provide emotional support when a class hasn't gone well. The colleagues need not be in one's own discipline. You will often get interesting ideas from teachers in other disciplines. I often give workshops on teaching for faculty members from a variety of fields. I am kept humble by the typical comment on feedback sheets: "The best thing about the workshop was getting ideas from faculty members in other fields who have similar interests and problems."

National and international conferences, such as the International Conference on Improving Learning and Teaching, as well as the disciplinary conventions, also have sessions that provide opportunities for learning.

Seeing, Experiencing

One of the best ways to learn a new skill is to see it performed. As you talk to your colleagues about teaching, ask if they would mind if you observed a class to see how they actually use a particular method. Faculty development centers frequently sponsor workshops in which you can see and experience particular methods of teaching or uses of technology. Videotapes demonstrating various methods of teaching are also available.

HOW CAN YOU GET AND USE FEEDBACK TO CONTINUE TO IMPROVE YOUR TEACHING?

Feedback from Student Performance

We haven't taught well if students haven't learned; so the ultimate test of our teaching is evidence of learning. Unfortunately, just as students blame the instructor if they fail to learn, we blame the students for not learning. "The students weren't willing to work." "The class wanted to be entertained rather than taught." "These students should never have been admitted to college. They are simply not prepared for college work."

But, as I have said previously, everyone can learn. Our task is to facilitate learning, and if our students are not learning we have not motivated them, presented material at an appropriate level, arranged activities that would promote effective learning, or taught the students how to learn more effectively.

All too often we pay attention to mistakes, poor papers, and items that were missed on examinations as the basis for assigning grades but fail to think about how we might have better taught the material that was missed. Asking a colleague to look over a few student papers will not only help determine whether your expectations were unreasonable but also result in suggestions for ways of presenting the particular area in which students are not performing well. In every discipline there are some concepts or skills that seem to be particularly difficult to teach. Often, experienced teachers have strategies for overcoming these difficulties. When I team-taught the beginning statistics course with an expert, I learned how to do a better job of teaching standard deviation, which had been difficult for me to get across to my students in the past.

Feedback from Peers

In the preceding paragraphs I have indicated the value of peer feedback on papers and in team teaching. But probably the most common form of feedback from peers is based on classroom visitation. As Centra (1975) demonstrated, classroom observation by peers is a very unreliable source of evidence for decisions about promotion or merit pay. If you know that an observer's judgment is going to affect your career, it is likely that you will either be so anxious that you will not perform at your normal level or that you will put on an especially good performance for the observer's benefit.

Even when the observer is not there to obtain evidence for our personnel files, we are likely to be concerned about what kind of impression we will make. Consequently, the choice of the observer and the nature of the observation are important considerations. Clearly we want an observer who will be helpful and whom we can trust. Bob Wilson at Berkeley found that retired faculty members were particularly helpful, not only because of their experience in teaching the discipline, but also because they were not involved in personnel decisions. Campbell Crockett, former dean at the University of Cincinnati, formed "helping pairs" among new teachers. Here the partners are in the same boat—both learning, presumably helping and being helped by each other—a symmetrical arrangement that reduced the threat.

The usefulness of peer observation depends partly on what you want to find out. If there is a particular aspect of your teaching that you are concerned about, be sure that the observer knows what to look for. Knowing what to look for is in fact a general principle applying to observations. Meeting with the observer to tell him or her before the observation what your goals are and what you are planning to do will increase the helpfulness of the observation. Centra (1993) gives some sample forms used for colleague observations, and you may work out your own observation form using items from these forms.

But the major usefulness of colleague observation comes from your discussion after the observation. Here you have a chance to question, probe for examples, and ask for suggestions.

Feedback from Faculty Development Specialists

Most colleges and universities now have faculty or staff members who are assigned the task of improving instruction. Often they are available to videotape or observe classes. Videotaping would seem on the face of it to be especially helpful. "To see oursels as others see us . . . would frae monie a blunder free us." There is certainly some truth in Robert Burns's familiar saying. Nonetheless, videotaping may not be the best feedback. Research on feedback from films half a century ago demonstrated that when we see our teaching on film (or videotape), we are so captured by our minor mannerisms and appearance that we are likely to miss the critical items of feedback. Only when the videotape is viewed with a consultant who calls our attention to the more important items is seeing the videotape likely to result in improvement.

One method used by many faculty developers is small-group instructional diagnosis (SGID), originated by D. Joseph Clark at the University of Washington. This combines observation with feedback from students.

Typically a consultant using SGID meets before the class with the instructor who desires feedback, to learn about the class and the instructor's goals and needs, as well as to establish the procedures. The instructor explains the procedure to the class, assuring the class that comments will be confidential and used only to help him or her learn how the course is going. After teaching for about half the class period, the instructor turns the class over to the observer and leaves the room. The observer then asks the students to form small groups to discuss their learning experiences in the group. Often the observer asks the groups to answer such questions as "What aspects of the class have helped you learn? What aspects have been unhelpful? What suggestions do you have?"

After about 10 minutes, a member previously designated as reporter gives each group's answers to the questions. The consultant summarizes the reports and asks for student comments. After the class, the consultant discusses the reports with the teacher and offers encouragement, suggestions if the instructor is unsure about what alternatives might help, and clarification if the instructor finds some comments confusing or contradictory. At the next class meeting, the instructor discusses the feedback, indicating what changes will be made or why certain things cannot be changed.

Feedback from Students

Probably the most familiar form of feedback from students is student ratings of teaching. Student ratings are now administered in almost all colleges and universities in the United States and are becoming common in other countries. However, their primary purpose is often to collect data for personnel evaluation, and this complicates and sometimes conflicts with their usefulness for improving teaching. One problem is that those who use student ratings for personnel purposes often feel (unjustifiably) that they need to use a standard form that can be used to compare teachers, across disciplines, in a variety of types of classes, in required as well as elective courses, in large and small classes, and in a variety of contexts. The result is that the questions on the form are so general that they may be irrelevant to a particular class and, even if relevant, are worded so generally that they offer little guidance for improvement. Moreover, they are typically given at the end of the semester, when it is too late to make much improvement for the class from which the feedback comes.

An additional barrier to the use of these forms for improvement is that faculty members are likely to be defensive about low ratings, rejecting the validity of the student responses. Among the common defenses are such responses as

- "Students aren't competent observers or respondents."
- "Students want easy courses. I set high standards."
- "Student ratings are determined primarily by the instructor's personality rather than by competence."
- "Students may give low ratings now but will appreciate my teaching after they've been out of college a few years."

As you may suspect, each of these excuses is invalid. There has been more research on student ratings than on any other topic—something over 2,000 studies. Here's what the research says about each of the aforementioned rationalizations.*

1. *The validity of student ratings.* Because we've said that you can't be a good teacher unless students have learned, the question becomes: Can students judge whether or not they are learning? The answer is clearly "yes." In multisection courses, average ratings of the value of the course or of the teacher's effectiveness correlate significantly with average scores on achievement tests, both final examinations and standardized tests. Moreover, they correlate with other course outcomes, such as motivation for further learning or measures of attitude change. In addition, when an instructor is teaching more than one section or more than one course, student ratings correlate well with the instructor's own judgments of which classes were taught most successfully.

2. *Hard versus easy courses.* Large national studies reveal that, on the average, more difficult courses are given higher student ratings than easy courses. Very likely this is a curvilinear relationship. Although students prefer challenging courses, courses that are so difficult that students cannot meet the challenge will receive lower ratings (Marsh, 2001).

3. *Teacher personality.* There is little doubt that some personality characteristics affect ratings. Enthusiastic, expressive, warm,

---

*Probably the best reviews of this research may be found in Perry and Smart (1997).

friendly teachers will in general receive higher ratings than teachers who are more reserved and distant from their students. However, these personality characteristics are also related to student learning. This doesn't mean that you need to change your personality to become effective, but if you don't have an outgoing, warm personality, you can still be effective and could become even more effective by, for example, using more gestures and learning student names.

4. *I'll be appreciated later.* I often wish this were true when I get a negative comment (and there are always a few). But both the classic studies by Drucker and Remmers (1951) half a century ago and my more recent ones found that alumni ratings of faculty members correlate highly with those given 10 years or more before. There are very likely some cases when there is delayed appreciation of what a teacher did, but it's the exception rather than the rule.

So, how can we use student ratings for continued growth in teaching effectiveness?

Keys to Improvement with Feedback from Students

1. *Get the feedback early enough to make a difference for the students who give it.* I typically collect feedback from students after the third or fourth week of the term. Others collect ratings about the middle of the term. In either case, the important thing is that you have a chance to adjust to this particular class. (Remember that each class is different. What works well in one class may not in the next.) As I mentioned with respect to SGID, I review the feedback with the class, indicating which suggestions I intend to implement, and I discuss differences of opinion among students. (Usually some students want more discussion, some want less, and all assume that everyone else feels as they do.) I also explain why I am not adopting some suggestions and give the reasons why I believe that what I have done, and will do, is important for their learning.

2. *Don't feel that you need to use the standard form.* If you want ratings, choose items that will be useful to you. The advantage of ratings

is that you can cover a number of aspects of teaching relatively quickly. But open-ended questions are often equally or more useful. Usually I simply ask students to write on two questions:

- "What have you liked about the course so far?" or "What aspects of the course have been valuable for your learning so far?"
- "What suggestions do you have for improvement?"

Sometimes I use questions such as

- "What have you done that has helped you learn effectively in this course?"
- "What do you need to do to improve your learning in this course?"
- "What have you done to help other students in the course to learn?" (Helping other learners not only provides altruistic satisfaction but also aids one's own learning. And this is true for teachers as well.)
- "What has the teacher done that has helped you learn?"
- "What would you like the teacher to do that would facilitate your learning?"

If I am teaching a large multisection course, I sometimes ask each section to choose two representatives to meet with me to provide feedback. The representatives are given a few minutes at the end of their discussion section to talk with their classmates about suggestions, and then meet with me. Because they can say, "Some students say . . . ," they feel free to relay negative as well as positive reactions, and the face-to-face meeting gives me a chance to question more deeply as well as to get their suggestions about what to do.

Feedback need not be limited to midterm or end-of-term assessment. You can ask students for comments on a particular class session in the last five minutes of class.

3. *Supplement end-of-course ratings.* All faculty members in our college are required to collect student ratings at the end of the term. Five items are mandatory, and the rest of the items may be chosen by the department and instructor from a large list of

possible items, including some open-ended items. I choose two types of items—those having to do with goals of education and those dealing with specific behaviors.

The items with respect to goals that I choose are usually something like

- "I became more interested in the subject matter of this course."
- "My intellectual curiosity has been stimulated by this course."
- "I am learning to think more clearly about the area of this course."

Behavioral items include

- "The instructor knew students' names."
- "The instructor gestures with hands and arms."
- "The instructor gives multiple examples."
- "The instructor points out practical applications."
- "The instructor encourages student questions and student comments."
- "The instructor signals transitions to a new topic."

Although faculty members often make some improvements as a result of feedback from student ratings, Murray (1983, 1997) has shown that improvement is much more likely to occur when behavioral items are used rather than more generic abstract items.

Whether or not there is a choice of items, I find it helpful to ask students to rate or comment on specific aspects of the course. Some of these change from term to term whereas some carry over if they have worked well. These include such aspects as the syllabus, the team research project, the textbook they used, videotapes, field trips, and journals.

Consultation

Whatever form of feedback you use, research clearly shows that you are more likely to improve if you discuss the feedback with someone. Your consultant can help you put ratings in perspective, pointing out the positives and reducing the sting of the negatives. (I and, I think, most of us tend to note and remember the negative comments more than the positives.) The consultant can also suggest strategies to try that may help deal with areas that seem to need improvement. A consultant can offer support and encouragement. All too often, poor student ratings lead to defensiveness, dislike for students, and poorer teaching rather than to improvement. In such cases, hope is important, and a consultant can help promote hope.

Classroom Assessment and Research

A little over a decade ago, Pat Cross and Tom Angelo compiled a set of 30 techniques to help faculty members monitor student learning. Five years later, they published a second edition of classroom assessment techniques, including 50 techniques (Angelo & Cross, 1993). Some of these, such as the minute paper and one-sentence summary, have been described earlier in this textbook. But you cannot fail to find among the 50 several that will help you get feedback on your students' learning, including directed paraphrasing, misconception check, pro and con grid, concept maps, course-related self-confidence surveys, and "what's the principle?"

Classroom Research (Cross & Steadman, 1996) is an example of the *scholarship of teaching*—systematically evaluating methods, approaches, or techniques that you are using in your teaching. In classroom research you may use some of the classroom assessment techniques to get evidence about the effectiveness of an innovation you are trying (or of something you have been doing for a long time). In addition, you may use regular classroom tests or other measures of achievement. You may even carry out an experiment comparing two alternative methods or the method you formerly used with one you would like to try.

Both classroom assessment techniques and classroom research not only provide useful data but also are motivating. They stimulate you to think about your teaching and what you expect students to gain from it. They enrich both your conceptual thinking about education and your repertoire of skills.

Self-Evaluation

Our emphasis on gathering data and getting consultation may have implied that improvement depends on external sources of feedback and help. But self-evaluation is also a potential resource for continued growth—perhaps the most important of all. In recent years, portfolio assessment has become a major element in evaluating teaching. Although portfolios have been used primarily in evaluation for personnel decisions, preparing and maintaining a portfolio can be an important aid to improvement even if it won't be used for promotion or salary purposes. The portfolio provides a stimulus to thinking about your teaching, about your goals and the evidence that will tell you how well you've achieved your goals—all this will contribute to your continued development.* Preparing a portfolio takes time, but all useful activities take time. If you feel that you don't have time for a portfolio, at least keep a journal in which you write regularly about your teaching, your students, and your classes.

IN CONCLUSION

The great thing about teaching is that there is always more to learn. The various sources of ideas and feedback that I have described help us to improve. As we improve, our students respond more positively, and their increased interest and enthusiasm sparks us to even more effort and enjoyment. Obviously, the course is not always onward and upward. There are moments of frustration and despair, but there are enough good times to help us through those that are not so good. And as we gain additional skill and assurance, our relations with students become more satisfying.

Most of this book has dealt with interactions in the classroom, but research has shown that those faculty members who have the most impact on students spend time with students outside the classroom.

---

*As compared with some earlier editions of *Teaching Tips*, this chapter has paid much less attention to evaluation for tenure or for post-tenure review. I have deliberately focused on improvement because I believe that a teacher who uses the methods discussed here for continual development will be well equipped for personnel evaluations.

This is not only important for the students' development, it also contributes to one's continuing vitality as a teacher. Our interactions with students and faculty are critical to the development of a community of learners—teachers and students, learners all.

Over the years, I have visited hundreds of colleges and universities, both in this country and in others. What most impresses me is that, no matter how difficult the circumstances, there are always some vital, effective teachers. They come in no one personality, no one discipline, no one institution. Somehow teachers find a way to cope with adverse environments and are able to stimulate effective learning. They enjoy teaching despite unfavorable circumstances.

This chapter has discussed at length ways to grow. However much you are intrigued by new possibilities, it is important not to forget what you enjoy doing. My final advice is "HAVE FUN!"

As I look back at my discussion of basic human motives at the beginning of this chapter, I think once again, "What a marvelous career teaching provides for satisfying our fundamental human needs!"

In Robert Bolt's *A Man for All Seasons,* Sir Thomas More assures his protégé that, if he becomes a teacher, he will be an outstanding teacher. "But if I were," demurs the ambitious young man, "who would know it?" More replies, "You, your friends, your students, God. Not a bad audience that."*

Not a bad audience indeed!

Supplementary Reading

The many books recommended as supplementary reading in previous chapters are relevant to your lifelong learning, but to save you the trouble of looking back, I will mention here once again several books that nicely cover the major areas of teaching:

▮▮ J. Biggs, *Teaching for Quality Learning at University* (Buckingham, UK: SRHE, and Philadelphia: Open University Press, 1999).

---

*For the reference to Sir Thomas More I am indebted to Nick Skinner, who used these words in concluding his address as recipient of the Canadian Psychological Association Award for Distinguished Contribution to Psychology in Education and Training (Skinner, 2001).

- B. G. Davis, *Tools for Teaching*, 2nd ed. (San Francisco: Jossey-Bass, 1993).
- J. Lowman, *Mastering the Techniques of Teaching*, 2nd ed. (San Francisco: Jossey-Bass, 1995).
- P. Ramsden, *Learning to Teach in Higher Education* (London and New York: Routledge, 1992).
- W. A. Wright and associates, *Teaching Improvement Practices: Successful Strategies for Higher Education* (Bolton, MA: Anker, 1995).

Stephen Brookfield's *Becoming a Critically Reflective Teacher* (San Francisco: Jossey-Bass, 1995) will help you with one of the most important aspects of your development—reflecting on your experience—and fits nicely with your use of classroom assessment techniques.

I am probably biased, but I do think that *Student Motivation, Cognition, and Learning: Essays in Honor of Wilbert J. McKeachie,* edited by Paul Pintrich, Donald Brown, and Claire Ellen Weinstein (Hillsdale, NJ: Erlbaum, 1994), gives you an excellent introduction to a variety of research areas relevant to teaching.

A briefer useful resource is Janet G. Donald and Arthur M. Sullivan (eds.), "Using Research to Improve Teaching," *New Directions for Teaching and Learning,* no. 23, 1985.

Three volumes are particularly helpful in the area of evaluation and assessment of teaching:

- J. Centra, *Reflective Faculty Evaluation: Enhancing Teaching and Determining Faculty Effectiveness* (San Francisco: Jossey-Bass, 1993).
- R. P. Perry and J. C. Smart (eds.), *Effective Teaching in Higher Education: Research and Practice* (New York: Agathon, 1997).
- P. Seldin and associates, *Changing Practices in Evaluating Teaching* (Bolton, MA: Anker, 1999).

Finally, for a thoughtful, stimulating perspective differing from American cognitivist/constructivist approaches, read Ference Marton and Shirley Booth's *Learning and Awareness* (Mahwah, NJ: Erlbaum, 1997). Marton's phenomenographic research at Gothenburg, Sweden, has been enormously influential in thinking about learning and teaching in higher education.

References

ABCNEWS.com. (2004, April 29). *Full-service fakery: Inside the life of a professional essay writer and test taker* [Online]. Available: http://abcnews.go.com/sections/Primetime/US/cheating_andy_040429.html

Achacoso, M., & Svinicki, M. (Eds.). (2005, Spring). New testing alternatives. In *New directions for teaching and learning* (no. 100). San Francisco: Jossey-Bass.

Adams, M. (1992). Cultural inclusion in the American college classroom. In *New directions for teaching and learning* (no. 49, pp. 5–17). San Francisco: Jossey-Bass.

Adelman, C. (1999). *The new college course map and transcript files: Changes in course-taking and achievement, 1972–1993* (2nd ed., pp. 198–204). Washington, DC: U.S. Department of Education.

Albanese, M. A., & Mitchell, S. (1993). Problem-based learning: A review of literature on its outcomes and implementation issues. *Academic Medicine, 68,* 52–81.

Alexander, P. A. (1995). Superimposing a situation-specific and domain-specific perspective on an account of self-regulated learning. *Educational Psychologist, 30,* 189–193.

Alexander, P. A., & Judy, J. E. (1988). The interaction of domain-specific and strategic knowledge in academic performance. *Review of Educational Research, 58*(4), 375–404.

Alger, J., Chapa, J., Gudeman, R., Marin, P., Maruyama, G., Milem, J., Moreno, H., & Wilds, D. (2000). *Does diversity make a difference?* Washington, DC: American Council on Education and American Association of University Professors.

Allen, B. P., & Niss, J. F. (1990). A chill in the college classroom? *Phi Delta Kappan, 71,* 607–609.

Altmiller, H. (1973). Another approach to freshman chemistry. *Journal of Chemical Education, 50,* 249.

Alverno College Faculty. (1994). *Student Assessment Learning at Alverno College.* Milwaukee, WI: Alverno Productions.

American Association of University Professors (AAUP). (1987). Statement on professional ethics. *Academe, 73*(4), 49.

American Council on Education and University of California at Los Angeles Higher Education Research Council. (1996). *The American freshman: National norms for fall 1996.* Washington, DC: American Council on Education.

Ames, C. (1992). Classrooms: Goals, structures, and student motivation. *Journal of Educational Psychology, 84*, 261–271.

Anderson, J. A., & Adams, M. (1992). Acknowledging the learning styles of diverse populations: Implications for instructional design. In *New directions for teaching and learning* (no. 49, pp. 19–33). San Francisco: Jossey-Bass.

Anderson, L. W., & Krathwohl, D. R. (Eds.). (2001). *A taxonomy for learning, teaching, and assessing: A revision of Bloom's taxonomy of educational objectives.* New York: Longman.

Andre, T. (1987). Questions and learning from reading. *Questioning Exchange, 1*(1), 47–86.

◆ Angelo, T. A., & Cross, K. P. (1993). *Classroom assessment techniques: A handbook for college faculty* (2nd ed.). San Francisco: Jossey-Bass.

Annis, L. F. (1981). Effect of preference for assigned lecture notes on student achievement. *Journal of Educational Research, 74*, 179–181.

———. (1983a). The processes and effects of peer tutoring. *Human Learning, 2*, 39–47.

———. (1983b). *Study techniques.* Dubuque: Wm. C. Brown.

Apple, T., & Cutler, A. (1999). The Rensselaer studio General Chemistry course. *Journal of Chemical Education, 76*, 462–463.

Arce, J., & Betancourt, R. (1997). Student-designed experiments in scientific lab instruction. *Journal of College Science Teaching, 27*, 114–118.

Arredondo, P. (1991). Counseling Latinas. In C. Lee & B. Richardson (Eds.), *Multicultural issues in counseling: New approaches to diversity* (pp. 143–156). Alexandria, VA: American Counseling Association.

Asante, M. K. (1987). *The Afrocentric idea.* Philadelphia: Temple University Press.

———. (1988). *Afrocentricity.* Trenton, NJ: Africa World Press.

Association of American Colleges and Universities. (2000). *Americans see many benefits to diversity in higher education, finds first-ever national poll on topic* [Online]. Available: http://www.aacu-edu.org/Initiatives/legacies.html

◆ Astin, A. (1975). *Preventing students from dropping out.* San Francisco: Jossey-Bass.

Astin, A. W., & Astin, H. S. (1999). *Meaning and spirituality in the lives of college faculty: A study of values, authenticity, and stress.* Los Angeles: UCLA Higher Education Research Institute.

Note: References marked with a diamond ◆ are classic, seminal works that still offer the most reliable scholarship on their topics.

Attneave, C. (1982). American Indian and Alaskan native families: Emigrants in their own homeland. In M. McGoldrick, J. Pearce, & J. Giordano (Eds.), *Ethnicity and family therapy* (pp. 55–83). New York: Guilford Press.

Avila, D., & Avila, A. (1995). Mexican Americans. In N. Vacc, S. Devaney, & J. Wittmer (Eds.), *Experiencing and counseling multicultural and diverse populations* (3rd ed., pp. 119–146). Bristol, PA: Accelerated Development.

Bailey, C. A., Kingsbury, K., Kulinowski, K., Paradis, J., & Schoonover, R. (2000). An integrated lecture-laboratory environment of General Chemistry. *Journal of Chemical Education, 77*, 195–199.

◆ Bargh, J. A., & Schul, Y. (1980). On the cognitive benefits of teaching. *Journal of Educational Psychology, 72*(5), 593–604.

Barr, R. B., & Tagg, J. (1995). From teaching to learning—A new paradigm for undergraduate education. *Change, 27*, 12–25.

Baruth, L., & Manning, M. (1991). *Multicultural counseling and psychotherapy*. New York: Merrill.

◆ Baxter Magolda, M. B. (1992). *Knowing and reasoning in college: Gender-related patterns in students' intellectual development*. San Francisco: Jossey-Bass.

Beach, R., & Bridwell, L. (1984). Learning through writing: A rationale for writing across the curriculum. In A. Pellegrini & T. Yawkey (Eds.), *The development of oral and written language in social contexts*. Norwood, NJ: Ablex.

◆ Belenky, M. F., Clinchy, B. M., Goldberger, N. R., & Tarule, J. M. (1986). *Women's ways of knowing: The development of self, voice, and mind*. New York: Basic Books.

Benjamin, L. (1991). Personalization and active learning in the large introductory psychology class. *Teaching of Psychology, 18*(2), 68–74.

Berge, Z. (2000). *Concerns of online teachers in higher education* [Online]. Available: http://www.emoderators.com/zberge/iste98.html

Berlyne, D. E. (1954a). An experimental study of human curiosity. *British Journal of Psychology, 45*, 256–265.

———. (1954b). A theory of human curiosity. *British Journal of Psychology, 45*, 180–181.

◆ ———. (1960). *Conflict, arousal, and curiosity*. New York: McGraw-Hill.

Bieron, J. F., & Dinan, F. J. (2000). Not your ordinary lab day. *Journal of College Science Teaching, 30*(1), 44–47.

Biggs, J. (1999). *Teaching for quality learning at university*. Buckingham, UK: SRHE, and Philadelphia: Open University Press.

Blackwell, J. E. (1990). Operationalizing faculty diversity. *AAHE Bulletin, 42*(10), 8–9.

Bligh, D. (2000). *What's the use of lectures?* San Francisco: Jossey-Bass.

Block, C. (1981). Black Americans and the cross-cultural counseling and psychotherapy experience. In A. Marsella & P. Pedersen (Eds.), *Cross-cultural counseling and psychotherapy* (pp. 177–194). New York: Pergamon Press.

Bloom, B. S. (Ed.). (1956). *Taxonomy of educational objectives: The classification of educational goals.* New York: Longman.

Bloom, B. S. (Ed.). (1956). *Taxonomy of educational objectives, handbook I: Cognitive domain.* New York: Longmans, Green.

Bloom, B. S., Englehart, M. D., Furst, E. J., & Krathwohl, D. R. (1956). *Taxonomy of educational objectives: Cognitive domain.* New York: McKay.

Boekaerts, M. (1995). Self-regulated learning: Bridging the gap between metacognitive and metamotivational theories. *Educational Psychologist, 30,* 195–200.

Boekaerts, M., & Niemivirta, M. (2000). Self-regulation in learning: Finding a balance between learning- and ego-protective goals. In M. Boekaerts, P. R. Pintrich, & M. Zeidner (Eds.), *Handbook of self-regulation* (pp. 417–450). San Diego: Academic Press.

Boekaerts, M., Pintrich, P. R., & Zeidner, M. (Eds.). (2000). *Handbook of self-regulation.* San Diego: Academic Press.

Bonk, C. J., & Cunningham, D. J. (1998). Searching for learner-centered, constructivist, and sociocultural components of collaborative educational learning tools. In C. J. Bonk & S. K. King (Eds.), *Electronic collaborators: Learner-centered technologies for literacy, apprenticeship, and discourse* (pp. 25–50). Mahwah, NJ: Erlbaum.

Border, L. B., & Chism, N. V. N. (Eds.). (1992). Teaching for diversity. In *New directions for teaching and learning* (no. 49). San Francisco: Jossey-Bass.

Boss, J. (1994). The effect of community service on the moral development of college ethics students. *Journal of Moral Education, 23,* 183–198.

Bowser, B. P., Jones, T., & Young, G. A. (Eds.). (1995). *Toward the multicultural university.* Westport, CT: Praeger.

◆ Boyer, E. (1990). *Scholarship reconsidered: Priorities of the professoriate.* Princeton, NJ: Carnegie Foundation for the Advancement of Teaching.

Brandell, M., & Hinck, S. (1997). Service learning: Connecting citizenship with the classroom. *NASSP Bulletin, 81,* 49–56.

Braxton, J. M., & Bayer, A. (1999). *Faculty misconduct in collegiate teaching.* Baltimore: Johns Hopkins Press.

Bridges, E. M., & Hallinger, P. (1996, Winter). Problem-based learning in leadership education. In L. Wilkerson & W. H. Gijselaers (Eds.), Bringing problem-based learning to higher education: Theory and practice. *New directions for teaching and learning* (no. 68, pp. 53–61). San Francisco: Jossey-Bass.

Brown, J. S. (2000). Growing up digital: How the web changes work, education, and the ways people learn. *Change, 32*(2), 11–20.

Brown, G., & Atkins, M. (1988). *Effective teaching in higher education.* London: Methuen.

Brown, R. D., & Krager, L. (1985). Ethical issues in graduate education: Faculty and student responsibilities. *Journal of Higher Education, 56,* 403–418.

Brown, S., & Glassner, A. (Eds.). (1999). *Assessment matters in higher education: Choosing and using diverse approaches.* Buckingham, UK: Open University Press.

Cahn, S. (1994). *Saints and scamps: Ethics in academia.* Lanham, MD: Rowan and Littlefield Publishers, Inc.

Cambridge, B. (1996). Looking ahead. *AAHE Bulletin,* 10–11.

Campbell, R. (1999). Mouths, machines, and minds. *The Psychologist, 12,* 446–449.

Caron, M. D., Whitbourne, S. K., & Halgin, R. P. (1992). Fraudulent excuse making among college students. *Teaching of Psychology, 19*(2), 90–93.

Carr, D. (2000). *Professionalism and ethics in teaching.* New York: Routledge.

Center for Teaching and Learning. (1998). *Teaching for inclusion.* Chapel Hill, NC: University of North Carolina at Chapel Hill.

Centra, J. A. (1975). Colleagues as raters of classroom instruction. *Journal of Higher Education, 46,* 327–337.

◆ ———. (1993). *Reflective faculty evaluation: Enhancing teaching and determining faculty effectiveness.* San Francisco: Jossey-Bass.

Champagne, A. B., Klofper, L. E., & Anderson, J. H. (1980). Factors influencing the learning of classical mechanics. *American Journal of Physics, 48,* 1074–1079.

Chang, T. M., Crombag, H. F., van der Drift, K. D. J. M., & Moonen, J. M. (1983). *Distance learning: On the design of an open university.* Boston: Kluwer-Nijhoff.

Chesler, M. A. (1994). *Perceptions of faculty behavior by students of color.* Ann Arbor, MI: Center for Research on Learning and Teaching, University of Michigan [Online]. Available: http://www.crlt.umich.edu/occ7.html

Chi, M. T. H., Glaser, R., & Farr, M. J. (Eds.). (1988). *The nature of expertise.* Hillsdale, NJ: Erlbaum.

Chronicle of Higher Education. (September 1, 2000a). *The Chronicle of Higher Education 2000–01 almanac issue, 47*(1).

Chronicle of Higher Education. (June 2, 2000b). *College campuses will grow more diverse, report says, 46*(27), A51.

Churchill, L. R. (1982). The teaching of ethics and moral values in teaching. *Journal of Higher Education, 53*(3), 296–306.

Clark, R. E. (1994a). Media and method. *Educational Technology Research and Development, 42*(3), 7–10.

———. (1994b). Media will never influence learning. *Educational Technology, Research and Development, 42*(2), 21–29.

Cohen, P., Kulik, J., & Kulik, C.-L. (1982). Educational outcomes of tutoring: A meta-analysis of findings. *American Educational Research Journal, 19*(2), 237–248.

Collett, J., & Serrano, B. (1992). Stirring it up: The inclusive classroom. In *New directions for teaching and learning* (no. 49, pp. 35–48). San Francisco: Jossey-Bass.

Collins, A. (1977). Processes in acquiring knowledge. In R. C. Anderson, R. J. Spiro, & W. E. Montague (Eds.), *Schooling and the acquisition of knowledge* (pp. 339–363). Hillsdale, NJ: Erlbaum.

Collins, A., & Stevens, A. L. (1982). Goals and strategies of inquiry teaching. In R. Glaser (Ed.), *Advances in instructional psychology* (pp. 65–119). Hillsdale, NJ: Erlbaum.

Connor-Greene, P. (2000). Making connections: Evaluating the effectiveness of journal writing in enhancing student learning. *Teaching of Psychology, 27*(1), 44–46.

Cooper, J. L., Robinson, P., & Ball, D. (Eds.). (2003). *Small group instruction in higher education: Lessons from the past, visions of the future.* Stillwater, OK: New Forums Press.

Coppola, B. P. (1995, Summer). Progress in practice: Using concepts from motivation and self-regulated learning research to improve chemistry instruction. In P. R. Pintrich (Ed.), Understanding self-regulated learning. *New directions for teaching and learning* (no. 63, pp. 87–96). San Francisco: Jossey-Bass.

———. (2000). Targeting entry points for ethics in chemistry teaching and learning. *Journal of Chemical Education, 77,* 1506–1511.

Coppola, B. P., Ege, S. N., & Lawton, R. G. (1997). The University of Michigan undergraduate chemistry curriculum: 2. Instructional strategies and assessment. *Journal of Chemical Education, 74,* 84–94.

Coppola, B. P., & Lawton, R. G. (1995). "Who has the same substance that I have?" A blueprint for collaborative learning activities. *Journal of Chemical Education, 72,* 1120–1122.

Costin, F. (1972). Three-choice versus four-choice items: Implications for reliability and validity of objective achievement tests. *Educational and Psychological Measurement, 32,* 1035–1038.

Covington, M. V. (1999). Caring about learning: The nature and nurture of subject-matter appreciation. *Educational Psychologist, 34,* 127–136.

Creed, T. (1997). PowerPoint, No! Cyberspace, Yes. *National Teaching and Learning Forum, 6*(4), 5–7.

◆ Cronbach, L. J., & Snow, R. E. (1977). *Aptitudes and instructional methods: A handbook for research on interaction.* New York: Irvington.

◆ Cross, K. P., & Steadman, M. H. (1996). *Classroom research: Implementing the scholarship of teaching.* San Francisco: Jossey-Bass.

Darder, A. (1996). Creating the conditions for cultural democracy in the classroom. In C. Turner, M. Garcia, A. Nora, & L. Rendon (Eds.), *Racial and ethnic diversity in higher education* (pp. 134–149). New York: Simon & Schuster.

Davies, P. (2000, November). Computerized peer assessment. *Innovation in Education and Training International, 37*(4), 346–355.

Day, R. S. (1980). Teaching from notes: Some cognitive consequences. In *New directions for teaching and learning* (no. 2, pp. 95–112). San Francisco: Jossey-Bass.

Deci, E., & Ryan, R. M. (1985). *Intrinsic motivation and self-determination in human behavior.* New York: Plenum.

Deci, E., & Ryan, R. (2000). The "what" and "why" of goal pursuits: Human needs and the self-determination of behavior. *Psychological Inquiry, 11,* 227–268.

Deutsch, M. (1949). An experimental study of the effects of cooperation and competition upon group processes. *Human Relations, 2,* 199–232.

Dewey, R. (1995, March). Finding the right introductory psychology textbook. *APS Observer,* 32–35.

DiBiase, W. J., & Wagner, E. P. (2002). Aligning General Chemistry laboratory with lecture at a large university. *School of Science and Mathematics, 102,* 158–171.

Diederich, P. (1974). *Measuring growth in English.* Urbana: NCTE.

Dillon, J. T. (1982). The effect of questions in education and other enterprises. *Journal of Curriculum Studies, 14,* 127–152.

Domin, D. S. (1999). A review of laboratory instruction styles. *Journal of Chemical Education, 76,* 543–547.

Donald, J. G. (1995, Summer). Disciplinary differences in knowledge validation. In P. R. Pintrich (Ed.), Understanding self-regulated learning. *New directions for teaching and learning* (no. 63, pp. 7–17). San Francisco: Jossey-Bass.

◆ Drucker, A. J., & Remmers, H. H. (1951). Do alumni and students differ in their attitudes toward instructors? *Journal of Educational Psychology, 42,* 129–143.

Duchastel, P. C., & Merrill, P. F. (1973). The effects of behavioral objectives on learning: A review of empirical studies. *Review of Educational Research, 43,* 53–69.

Dweck, C. S. (1986). Motivational processes affecting learning. *American Psychologist, 41,* 1040–1048.

D'Ydewalle, G., Swerts, A., & de Corte, E. (1983). Study time and test performance as a function of test expectations. *Contemporary Educational Psychology, 8*(1), 55–67.

Eccles, J. (1994). Understanding women's educational and occupational choices. *Psychology of Women Quarterly, 18,* 585–609.

Eccles, J. S., Midgley, C., Wigfield, A., Buchanan, C. M., Reuman, D., Flanagan, C., & MacIver, D. (1993). Development during adolescence: The impact of stage-environment fit on young adolescents' experiences in schools and in families. *American Psychologist, 48,* 90–101.

Ehrmann, S. C. (1995, March/April). Asking the right questions: What does research tell us about technology and higher learning? *Change, 27*(2), 20–27.

Elbow, P. (2000a). Using the collage for collaborative writing. In *Everyone can write: Essays toward a hopeful theory of writing and teaching writing* (pp. 372–378). New York: Oxford University Press.

———. (2000b). Your cheatin' art: A collage. In *Everyone can write: Essays toward a hopeful theory of writing and teaching writing* (pp. 300–313). New York: Oxford University Press.

Elbow, P., & Belanoff, P. (2003). *Sharing and responding.* New York: McGraw-Hill.

El-Ghoroury, N., Salvador, D., Manning, R., & Williamson, T. (1999). *A survival guide for ethnic minority graduate students* [Online]. Available: http://www.apa.org/apags/diversity/emsg.html

Elshout, J. J. (1987). Problem solving and education. In E. DeCorte, H. Lodewijks, R. Permentier, & P. Span (Eds.), *Learning and instruction: European research in an international context* (Vol. 1). Oxford: Leuven University Press/Pergamon Press.

Entwistle, N. J. (1992). Student learning and study strategies. In B. R. Clark & G. Neave (Eds.), *Encyclopedia of higher education.* Oxford: Pergamon.

Eriksen, S. C. (1983). Private measures of good teaching. *Teaching of Psychology, 10,* 133–136.

Eyler, J., & Giles, Jr., D. E. (1999). *Where's the learning in service-learning?* San Francisco: Jossey-Bass.

Falk, D. (1995, Winter). Preflection. A strategy for enhancing reflection. *NSEE Quarterly, 13.*

Fallon, M. (1997). The school counselor's role in first generation students' college plans. *School Counselor, 44*(5), 384–393.

◆ Feldman, K. A., & Newcomb, T. M. (1969). *The impact of college on students* (Vol. 2). San Francisco: Jossey-Bass.

Feldman, S., & Rosenthal, D. (1990). The acculturation of autonomy expectations in Chinese high schoolers residing in two western nations. *International Journal of Psychology, 25,* 259–281.

Ferguson, M. (1990). The role of faculty in increasing student retention. *College and University, 65,* 127–134.

Fisch, L. (2001). The devil's advocate strikes again. *Journal of Staff, Program, and Organizational Development, 18*(1), 49–51.

Fisch, L. (Ed.). (1996). Ethical dimensions of college and university teaching: Understanding and honoring the special relationship between teachers and students. In *New directions for teaching and learning* (no. 66). San Francisco: Jossey-Bass.

Flavell, J. H. (1979). Metacognition and cognitive mentoring: A new area of cognitive-developmental inquiry. *American Psychologist, 34,* 906–911.

Foos, P. W., & Fisher, R. P. (1988). Using tests as learning opportunities. *Journal of Educational Psychology, 88*(2), 179–183.

Frew, E. A., & Weber, K. (1995). Towards a higher retention rate among distance learners. *Open Learning, 10*(2), 58–61.

Friedman, E. G., Kolmar, W. K., Flint, C. B., & Rothenberg, P. (1996). *Creating an inclusive curriculum.* New York: Teachers College Press.

Fry, R. (2003). *Hispanic youth dropping out of U.S. schools: Measuring the challenge.* Washington, DC: Pew Hispanic Center.

Fuentes, M., Kiyana, A., & Rosario, E. (2003). *Keeping Latinos in high school: The role of context.* Paper presented at the annual meeting of the American Psychological Association, Toronto, Canada.

Fuligni, A., Burton, L., Marshall, S., Perez-Febles, A., Yarrington, J., Kirsch, L., & Merriwether-DeVries, C. (1999). Attitudes toward family obligations among American adolescents with Asian, Latin American, and European backgrounds. *Child Development, 70,* 1030–1044.

Gamson, W. A. (1966). *SIMSOC: A manual for participants.* Ann Arbor, MI: Campus Publishers.

Garrett, J., & Garrett, M. (1994). The path of good medicine: Understanding and counseling Native American Indians. *Journal of Multicultural Counseling and Development, 22,* 134–144.

Garwick, A., & Auger, S. (2000). What do providers need to know about American Indian culture? Recommendations from urban Indian family caregivers. *Families, Systems & Health, 18,* 177–190.

Gay, G. (1995). Curriculum theory and multicultural education. In J. A. Banks & C. A. Banks (Eds.), *Handbook of research on multicultural education* (pp. 25–43). New York: Simon & Schuster Macmillan.

Gerdeman, R. (2000). Academic dishonesty and the community college. *ERIC Digest.* ERIC Clearinghouse for Community Colleges. (ED447840).

Gibbs, G. (1999). Using assessment strategically to change the way students learn. In S. Brown & A. Glassner (Eds.), *Assessment matters in higher education: Choosing and using diverse approaches* (pp. 41–54). Buckingham, UK: Society for Research in Higher Education/Open University Press.

Goldschmid, M. L. (1971). The learning cell: An instructional innovation. *Learning and Development, 2*(5), 1–6.

———. (1975, May). *When students teach students.* Paper presented at the International Conference on Improving University Teaching, Heidelberg, Germany.

◆ Goldschmid, M. L., & Shore, B. M. (1974). The learning cell: A field test of an educational innovation. In W. A. Verreck (Ed.), *Methodological problems in research and development in higher education* (pp. 218–236). Amsterdam: Swets and Zeitlinger.

Gonzalez, B. L., Wegner, P. A., Foley, B., & Thadani, V. (1999). Studio classroom and conceptual learning in chemistry. *Abstracts of Papers of the American Chemical Society,* 217th ACS National Meeting, Anaheim, CA, March 21–25, 1999; American Chemical Society: Washington, DC, 1999; CHED 071.

Gottfried, A. C., Hessler, J. A., Sweeder, R. D., Bartolin, J. M., Coppola, B. P., Banaszak Holl, M. M., Reynolds, B. P., & Stewart, I. C. (2003). Studio 130: Design, testing, and implementation. *Abstracts of Papers of the American Chemical Society, 225,* 647.

Grasha, A., & Yangarber-Kicks, N. (2000). Integrating teaching styles and learning styles with instructional technology. *College Teaching, 48*(1), 2–10.

Grauerholz, E., & Copenhaver, S. (1994). When the personal becomes problematic: The ethics of using experiential teaching methods. *Teaching Sociology, 22*(4), 319–327.

Green, M. C. (2004). Storytelling in teaching. *APS Observer, 17*(4), 37–39.

Greeno, J. G. (1991). Number sense as situated knowing in a conceptual domain. *Research in Mathematical Education, 22,* 170–218.

Greeno, J. G., & the Middle-School Mathematics Through Applications Project Group. (1997, November). Theories and practices of thinking and learning to think. *American Journal of Education, 106*(1), 85–126.

Grigorenko, E., Jarvin, L., & Sternberg, R. (2002). School-based tests of the triarchic theory of intelligence: Three settings, three samples, three syllabi. *Contemporary Educational Psychology, 27*(2), 167–208.

Gruber, H. E., & Weitman, M. (1960, April). *Cognitive processes in higher education: Curiosity and critical thinking.* Paper read at Western Psychological Association, San Jose, CA.

———. (1962, April). *Self-directed study: Experiments in higher education* (Report No. 19). Boulder: University of Colorado, Behavior Research Laboratory.

Gudykunst, W. (1998). *Bridging differences: Effective intergroup communication* (3rd ed.). Thousand Oaks, CA: Sage.

Gudykunst, W., & Matsumoto, Y. (1996). Cross-cultural variability of communication in personal relationships. In W. Gudykunst, S. Ting-Toomey, & T. Nishida (Eds.), *Communication in personal relationships across cultures* (pp. 19–56). Thousand Oaks, CA: Sage.

Gudykunst, W., Ting-Toomey, S., & Nishida, T. (Eds.). (1996). *Communication in personal relationships across cultures*. Thousand Oaks, CA: Sage.

Gurin, P. (1999). Expert report of Patricia Gurin. In *The compelling need for diversity in higher education, Gratz et al. v. Bollinger et al.* Ann Arbor, MI: University of Michigan [Online]. Available: http://www.umich.edu/~urel/admissions/legal/expert/gurintoc/html

Haines, D. B., & McKeachie, W. J. (1967). Cooperative vs. competitive discussion methods in teaching introductory psychology. *Journal of Educational Psychology, 58*, 386–390.

Hall, R. M., & Sandler, B. R. (1982). *The classroom climate: A chilly one for women?* Project on the Status and Education of Women. Washington, DC: Association of American Colleges.

Halpern, D. F. (1996). *Thought and knowledge: An introduction to critical thinking.* Mahwah, NJ: Erlbaum.

Halpern, D. F., & Hakel, M. D. (2003). Applying the science of learning to the university and beyond. *Change, 35*(4), 36–41.

Hannafin, M., Land, S., & Oliver, K. (1999). Open learning environments: Foundations, methods, and models. In C. M. Reigeluth (Ed.), *Instructional-design theories and models* (Vol. 2, pp. 115–140). Mahwah, NJ: Erlbaum.

Hanson, K. (1996). Between apathy and advocacy: Teaching and modeling ethical reflection. In *New directions for teaching and learning* (no. 66, pp. 33–36). San Francisco: Jossey-Bass.

Harackiewicz, J., Barron, K. E., & Elliott, A. J. (1998). Rethinking achievement goals: When are they adaptive for college students and why? *Educational Psychologist, 33*, 1–21.

Harasim, L. (1990). Online education: An environment for collaboration and intellectual amplification. In L. Harasim (Ed.), *Online education: Perspectives on a new environment* (pp. 39–64). New York: Praeger.

———. (1993). Networlds: Networks as a social space. In L. M. Harasim (Ed.), *Global networks* (pp. 15–34). Cambridge: MIT Press.

Harter, S. (1978). Effective motivation reconsidered: Toward a developmental model. *Human Development, 21*, 34–64.

Hartley, J., & Cameron, A. (1967). Some observations on the efficiency of lecturing. *Educational Review, 20*(1), 30–37.

◆ Hartley, J., & Davies, I. K. (1978). Note-taking: A critical review. *Programmed Learning and Educational Technology, 15,* 207–224.

Hartman, F. R. (1961). Recognition learning under multiple channel presentation and testing conditions. *Audio-Visual Communication Review, 9,* 24–43.

Hartman, H. J. (1990). Factors affecting the tutoring process. *Journal of Developmental Education, 14*(2), 2–6.

Helton, P. (2000, Fall). Diversifying the curriculum: A study of faculty involvement. *Diversity Digest* [Online]. Available: http://www.inform.umd.edu/diversityweb/Digest/F00/research.html

Henderson, L., & Buising, C. (2000). A research-based molecular biology laboratory. *Journal of College Science Teaching, 30*(5), 322–327.

Herring, R. (1997). Counseling indigenous American youth. In C. Lee (Ed.), *Multicultural issues in counseling: New approaches to diversity* (2nd ed., pp. 53–70). Alexandria, VA: American Counseling Association.

Hettich, P. (1990). Journal writing: Old fare or nouvelle cuisine? *Teaching of Psychology, 17,* 36–39.

Higginbotham, C., Pike, C. F., & Rice, J. K. (1998). Spectroscopy in sol-gel matrices: An open-ended laboratory experience for upper-level undergraduates. *Journal of Chemical Education, 75,* 461.

Hillocks, G. (1982). The interaction of instruction, teacher comment, and revision in teaching the composing process. *Research in Teaching of English, 16,* 261–278.

Hodges, E. (1994, Summer). Some realities of revision: What students don't or won't understand. *English in Texas, 25*(4), 13–16.

Hodgkinson, H. L. (1995). Demographic imperatives for the future. In B. P. Bowser, T. Jones, & G. A. Young (Eds.), *Toward the multicultural university* (pp. 3–19). Westport, CT: Praeger.

Hofer, B. (1997). *The development of personal epistemology: Dimensions, disciplinary differences, and instructional practices.* Unpublished doctoral thesis, University of Michigan.

◆ Hofer, B. K., Yu, S. L., & Pintrich, P. R. (1998). Teaching college students to be self-regulated learners. In D. H. Schunk & B. J. Zimmerman (Eds.), *Self-regulated learning: From teaching to self-reflective practice* (pp. 57–85). New York: Guilford.

Hofstede, G. (1986). Cultural differences in teaching and learning. *International Journal of Intercultural Relations, 10,* 301–320.

Hofstein, A., & Lunetta, V. N. (1982). The role of the laboratory in science teaching: Neglected aspects of research. *Review of Educational Research, 52*(2), 201–217.

Hogan, P., & Kimmel, A. (1992). Ethical teaching of psychology: One department's attempts at self-regulation. *Teaching of Psychology, 19*(4), 205–210.

Horowitz, G. (2003). A discovery approach to three organic laboratory techniques: Extraction, recrystallization, and distillation. *Journal of Chemical Education, 80,* 1039–1043.

Houston, J. P. (1983). Alternate test forms as a means of reducing multiple-choice answer copying in the classroom. *Journal of Educational Psychology, 75*(4), 572–575.

◆ Hovland, C. I. (Ed.). (1957). *The order of presentation in persuasion.* New Haven, CT: Yale University Press.

Huang, L. (1994). An integrative approach to clinical assessment and intervention with Asian-American adolescents. *Journal of Clinical Child Psychology, 23,* 21–31.

Hurtado, S. (1997). How diversity affects teaching and learning. *Educational Record, 77*(4), 27–29.

Husman, J., Derryberry, P. W., & Crowson, H. M. (2000, August). *Instrumentality: An important motivational construct for education?* Poster presented at the annual meeting of the American Psychological Association, Washington, DC.

Irvine, J. J., & York, D. E. (1995). Learning styles and culturally diverse learners: A literature review. In J. A. Banks & C. A. Banks (Eds.), *Handbook of research on multicultural education* (pp. 484–497). New York: Simon & Schuster Macmillan.

Jensen, J. (1985). Perspective on nonverbal intercultural communication. In L. Samovar & R. Porter (Eds.), *Intercultural communication: A reader* (pp. 256–272). Belmont, CA: Wadsworth.

Johnson, D. M. (1975). Increasing originality on essay examinations in psychology. *Teaching of Psychology, 2,* 99–102.

◆ Johnson, D. W., Maruyama, G., Johnson, R., Nelson, D., & Skon, L. (1981). The effects of cooperative, competitive, and individualistic goal structures on achievement: A meta-analysis. *Psychological Bulletin, 89,* 47–62.

Johnstone, D. B. (1992). *Learning productivity: A new imperative for American higher education* [Monograph]. State University of New York, Studies in Public Higher Education [Edited Version Online]. Available: http://192.52.179.128/program/nlii/articles/johnstone .html

Jonassen, D. H. (2000). *Computers as mindtools for schools: Engaging critical thinking.* Upper Saddle River, NJ: Merrill.

Jonassen, D. H., & Brabowski, B. L. (1993). *Individual differences, learning, and instruction.* Hillsdale, NJ: Erlbaum.

Jones, T., & Young, G. S. (1997). Classroom dynamics: Disclosing the hidden curriculum. In A. I. Morey & M. K. Kitano (Eds.), *Multicultural course transformation in higher education: A broader truth* (pp. 89–103). Needham Heights, MA: Allyn & Bacon.

Jordan, A. E. (2001). College student cheating: The role of motivation, perceived norms, attitudes, and knowledge of institutional policy. *Ethics and Behavior, 11*, 233–247.

Karenga, M. (1995). Afrocentricity and multicultural education: Concept, challenge, and contribution. In B. P. Bowser, T. Jones, & G. A. Young (Eds.), *Toward the multicultural university* (pp. 41–64). Westport, CT: Praeger.

Katz, D. (1950). *Gestalt psychology.* New York: Ronald Press.

Keith-Spiegel, P., Wittig, A., Perkins, D., Balogh, D. W., & Whitley, B. (1996). Intervening with colleagues. In *New directions for teaching and learning* (no. 66, pp. 75–78). San Francisco: Jossey-Bass.

Keller, F. S. (1968). Goodbye teacher, . . . *Journal of Applied Behavior Analysis, 10*, 165–167.

Kendrick, J. R. (1996). Outcomes of service learning in an introduction to sociology course. *Michigan Journal of Community Service Learning, 3*, 72–81.

Kerr, C. (1994). Knowledge ethics and the new academic culture. *Change, 26*(1), 8–16.

Khan, F. A., Leavitt, A. J., Garmon, L. B., & Harper, W. D. (2003). An integrated chemistry environment using studio, workshop, and labworks: Systematically changing the teaching of General Chemistry. *Abstracts of Papers of the American Chemical Society*, 226th ACS National Meeting, New York, September 7–11, 2003; American Chemical Society: Washington, DC, 2003; CHED 262.

Kiewra, K. A. (1989). A review of notetaking: The encoding storage paradigm and beyond. *Educational Psychology Review, 1*(2), 147–172.

King, A. (1990). Enhancing peer interaction and learning in the classroom. *American Educational Research Journal, 27*, 664–687.

———. (1997). Ask to think—Tell why: A model of transactive peer tutoring for scaffolding higher-level complex learning. *Educational Psychologist, 32*, 221–235.

Kirschenbaum, H., Simon, S., & Napier, R. (1971). *Wad-ja-get? The grading game in American education.* New York: Hart Publishing.

Kitano, M. K. (1997). What a course will look like after multicultural change. In A. I. Morey & M. K. Kitano (Eds.), *Multicultural course transformation in higher education: A broader truth* (pp. 18–34). Needham Heights, MA: Allyn & Bacon.

Kluger, A. N., & DeNisi, A. (1996). The effects of feedback intervention on performance: A historical review, a meta-analysis, and a preliminary feedback intervention theory. *Psychological Bulletin, 119*, 254–284.

Knoedler, A. S., & Shea, M. A. (1992). Conducting discussion in the diverse classroom. In D. H. Wulff & J. D. Nyquist (Eds.), *To improve the academy* (Vol. 11, pp. 123–135). Stillwater, OK: New Forums Press.

Komada, N. M. (2002). First generation college students and resiliency. *Dissertation Abstracts International, 63*(6-A), 2158.

Koocher, G., & Keith-Spiegel, P. (1998). *Ethics in psychology: Professional standards and cases.* Mahwah, NJ: Erlbaum.

Kovac, J. (1999). Professional ethics in the college and university science curriculum. *Science & Education, 8,* 309–319.

Kozma, R. (1994). Will media influence learning? Reframing the debate. *Educational Technology, Research and Development, 42*(2), 7–19.

Krathwohl, D., Bloom, B. S., & Masia, B. (Eds.). (1964). *Taxonomy of educational objectives, handbook II: Affective domain.* New York: David McKay.

Kulik, J. (2003). *Effects of using instructional technology in colleges and universities: What controlled evaluation studies say* [Online]. Available: http://sri.com/policy/csted/reports/sandt/it/

Kulik, J. A., Kulik, C.-L., & Bangert-Drowns, R. L. (1988). *Effectiveness of mastery learning programs: A meta-analysis.* Ann Arbor: University of Michigan, Center for Research on Learning and Teaching.

LaFromboise, T., Berman, J., & Sohi, B. (1994). American Indian women. In L. Comas-Diaz & B. Greene (Eds.), *Women of color: Integrating ethnic and gender identities in psychotherapy* (pp. 30–71). New York: Guilford Press.

LaFromboise, T., Coleman, H., & Gerton, J. (1998). Psychological impact of biculturalism. In P. Organista, K. Chun, & G. Marin (Eds.), *Readings in ethnic psychology* (pp. 123–155). New York: Routledge.

LaPree, G. (1977). Establishing criteria for grading student papers: Moving beyond mysticism. *Teaching and Learning, 3*(1).

Larson, C. O., et al. (1984). Verbal ability and cooperative learning: Transfer of effects. *Journal of Reading Behavior, 16,* 289–295.

Lawrence, S. (1998). Unveiling positions of privilege: A hands-on approach to understanding racism. *Teaching of Psychology, 25*(3), 198–200.

Leamnson, R. (2000). Learning as biological brain change. *Change, 32,* 34–40.

Lee, W. (1999). *An introduction to multicultural counseling.* Bristol, PA: Accelerated Development.

Lehrer, R. (1993). Authors of knowledge: Patterns of hypermedia design. In S. P. Lajoie & S. J. Derry (Eds.), *Computers as cognitive tools* (pp. 197–227). Hillsdale, NJ: Erlbaum.

Leith, G. O. M. (1977). Implications of cognitive psychology for the improvement of teaching and learning in universities. In B. Massey (Ed.), *Proceedings of the Third International Conference, Improving University Teaching* (pp. 111–138). College Park: University of Maryland.

Lenhart, A., Horrigan, J., Rainie, L., Allen, K., Boyce, A., Madden, M., & O'Grady, E. (2003, April 16). *The ever-shifting Internet population: A new look at Internet access and the digital divide. The Pew Internet & American Life Project* [Online]. Retrieved June 21, 2004, from http://www.pewinternet.org

Lepper, M. R., & Hodell, M. (1989). Intrinsic motivation in the classroom. In C. Ames & R. Ames (Eds.), *Research on motivation in education* (Vol. 3, pp. 73–105). San Diego: Academic Press.

Lepper, M. R., & Malone, T. W. (1985). Intrinsic motivation and instructional effectiveness in computer-based education. In R. E. Snow & M. J. Farr (Eds.), *Aptitude, learning and instruction: III. Conative and affective process analyses.* Hillsdale, NJ: Erlbaum.

Lewis, M. (1997). *Poisoning the ivy: The seven deadly sins and other vices of higher education in America.* Armonk, NY: Sharpe.

Lidren, D. M., Meier, S. E., & Brigham, T. A. (1991). The effects of minimal and maximal peer tutoring systems on the academic performance of college students. *Psychological Record, 41,* 69–77.

Lin, Y-G., McKeachie, W. J., & Kim, Y. C. (2003). College students intrinsic and/or extrinsic motivation and learning. *Learning and Individual Differences, 13,* 251–258.

Lone-Knapp, F. (2000). Rez talk: How reservation residents describe themselves. *American Indian Quarterly, 24,* 635–640.

Lopez, G., & Chism, N. (1993). Classroom concerns of gay and lesbian students. *College Teaching, 41*(3), 97–103.

Lynch, E. W. (1997). Instructional strategies. In A. I. Morey & M. K. Kitano (Eds.), *Multicultural course transformation in higher education: A broader truth* (pp. 56–70). Needham Heights, MA: Allyn & Bacon.

MacGregor, J. (Ed.). (1993, Spring). Student self-evaluation: Fostering reflective learning. In *New directions for teaching and learning* (no. 56). San Francisco: Jossey-Bass.

Maehr, M., & Midgley, C. (1991, Summer–Fall). Enhancing student motivation—A schoolwide approach. *Educational Psychologist, 26*(3–4), 399–427.

Maier, N. R. F. (1952). *Principles of human relations.* New York: Wiley.

———. (1963). *Problem-solving discussions and conferences.* New York: McGraw-Hill.

◆ Maier, N. R. F., & Maier, L. A. (1957). An experimental test of the effects of "developmental" vs. "free" discussion on the quality of group decisions. *Journal of Applied Psychology, 41,* 320–323.

Maki, M., & Kitano, H. (1989). Counseling Asian Americans. In P. Pedersen, J. Draguns, W. Lonner, & J. Trimble (Eds.), *Counseling across cultures* (5th ed., pp. 109–132). Thousand Oaks, CA: Sage.

◆ Mann, R. D., et al. (1970). *The college classroom: Conflict, change, and learning.* New York: Wiley.

Marbach-Ad, G., & Sokolove, P. G. (2000). Can undergraduate biology students learn to ask higher-level questions? *Journal of Research in College Teaching, 37*, 854–870.

Marcinkiewicz, H. R., & Clariana, R. B. (1997). The performance effects of headings within multiple-choice tests. *British Journal of Educational Psychology, 67*, 111–117.

Markie, P. (1994). *A professor's duties: Ethical issues in college teaching.* Totowa, NJ: Rowman & Littlefield.

Markies, G. B., Howard, J., & King, D. C. (1993). Integrating community service and classroom instruction enhanced learning: Results from an experiment. *Educational Evaluation and Policy Analysis, 15*, 410–419.

Marsh, H. W. (2001). Distinguishing between good (useful) and bad workloads on students' evaluations of teaching. *American Educational Research Journal, 38*, 183–212.

◆ Marton, F., & Säljö, R. (1976a). On qualitative differences in learning: I—Outcome and process. *British Journal of Educational Psychology, 46*, 4–11.

———. (1976b). On qualitative differences in learning: II—Outcome as a function of the learner's conception of the task. *British Journal of Educational Psychology, 46*, 115–127.

Maruyama, M. (1982). Yellow youth's psychological struggle. *AAPA Journal, 7*(1), 21–29.

Matthews, J. (1991). The teaching of ethics and the ethics of teaching. *Teaching of Psychology, 18*(2), 80–85.

Matthews, R. S., Cooper, J. L., Davidson, N., & Hawkes, P. (1995). Building bridges between cooperative and collaborative learning. *Change, 27*(4), 35–40.

Mayer, R. (1997). Multimedia learning: Are we asking the right questions? *Educational Psychologist, 31*, 1–19.

———. (2001). *Multimedia learning.* New York: Cambridge University Press.

———. (2003). The promise of multimedia learning: Using the same instructional design methods across different media. *Learning and Instruction, 13*, 125–139.

Mazur, E. (1997). *Peer instruction: A user's manual.* Upper Saddle River, NJ: Prentice Hall.

McAdoo, H. (Ed.). (1999). *Family ethnicity: Strength in diversity* (2nd ed.). Thousand Oaks, CA: Sage.

McCabe, D. (2002, May 21). *All things considered* [Radio broadcast]. New York: National Public Radio.

McCabe, D. L., & Trevino, L. K. (1996). What we know about cheating in college: Longitudinal trends and recent developments. *Change, 28*(1), 29–33.

McCabe, D., & Trevino, L. (1996, January/February). What we know about cheating in college. *Change, 28*(1), 28–33.

McCabe, D., Trevino, L., & Butterfield, K. (2001, January–February). Dishonesty in academic environments: The influence of peer reporting requirements. *Journal of Higher Education, 72*(1), 29–45.

◆ McClelland, D., Atkinson, J. W., Clark, R. A., & Lowell, E. L. (1953). *The achievement motive.* New York: Appleton-Century-Crofts.

McCluskey, H. Y. (1934). An experimental comparison of two methods of correcting the outcomes of examination. *School and Society, 40,* 566–568.

McDavis, R., Parker, W., & Parker, W. (1995). Counseling African Americans. In N. Vacc, S. DeVaney, & J. Wittmer (Eds.), *Experiencing and counseling multicultural and diverse populations* (pp. 217–250). Bristol, PA: Accelerated Development.

McKeachie, W. J. (1990). Learning, thinking, and Thorndike. *Educational Psychologist, 25*(2), 127–141.

McKeachie, W. J., Lin, Y-G., Forrin, B., & Teevan, R. (1960). Individualized teaching in elementary psychology. *Journal of Educational Psychology, 51,* 285–291.

◆ McKeachie, W. J., Pintrich, P. R., & Lin, Y-G. (1985). Teaching learning strategies. *Educational Psychologist, 20*(3), 153–160.

McKeachie, W. J., Pintrich, P. R., Lin, Y-G., Smith, D. A. F., & Sharma, R. (1990). *Teaching and learning in the college classroom: A review of the research literature* (2nd ed.). Ann Arbor: NCRIPTAL, University of Michigan.

McKeachie, W. J., Pollie, D., & Speisman, J. (1955). Relieving anxiety in classroom examinations. *Journal of Abnormal and Social Psychology, 50,* 93–98.

McKinnon, M. (1999). PBL in Hong Kong. *PBL Insight, 2*(1), 1–6.

McLeod, S. H. (1992). Responding to plagiarism: The role of the WPA. *WPA: Writing Program Administration, 15*(3), 7–16.

McMurtry, K. (2001, November). E-cheating: Combating a 21st century challenge. *T.H.E. Journal Online* [Online]. Available: http://www.thejournal.com/magazine/vault/A3724.cfm

McNett, J. M., Harvey, C., Athanassiou, N., & Allard, J. (2000). Cognitive development in the management classroom: Bloom's taxonomy as a teaching tool. In T. B. Massey (Ed.), *Contributed papers: 25th International Conference on Improving Learning and Teaching.* Johann Wolfgang Goethe University, Frankfurt, Germany. College Park, MD: Improving Learning and Teaching.

Mentkowski, M., & Associates. (2000). *Learning that lasts.* San Francisco: Jossey-Bass.

Mentkowski, M., & Loacker, G. (1985, September). Assessing and validating the outcomes of college. *New Directions for Institutional Research, 47*–64.

Metzger, R. L., Boschee, P. F., Haugen, T., & Schnobrich, B. L. (1979). The classroom as learning context: Changing rooms affects performance. *Journal of Educational Psychology, 71*(4), 440–442.

Michaelsen, L. K., Knight, A. B., & Fink, L. D. (Eds.). (2004). *Team-based learning: A transformative use of small groups.* Sterling, VA: Stylus Publications.

Milem, J. F. (2001). The educational benefits of diversity: Evidence from multiple sectors. In M. J. Chang, D. Witt-Sandis, J. Jones, & K. Hakuta (Eds.), *Compelling interest: Examining the evidence on racial dynamics in higher education.* Palo Alto: Stanford University Press.

Milem, J. F., & Hakuta, K. (2000). The benefits of racial and ethnic diversity in higher education. In D. W. Wilds (Ed.), *Minorities in higher education, 1999–2000* (pp. 39–67). Washington, DC: American Council on Education.

Miller, H. (1998). Assessment with a purpose. *Innovation Journal 1998,* 35–37.

Miller, J. (1993). Psychology in the community. In J. Howard (Ed.), *A faculty casebook on community service learning* (pp. 123–134). Ann Arbor: DCSL Press, University of Michigan.

Miller, J. E., & Groccia, J. E. (1997). Are four heads better than one? A comparison of cooperative and traditional teaching formats in an introductory biology course. *Innovative Higher Education, 21,* 253–273.

Mills, P., Sweeney, W. V., Marino, R., & Clarkson, S. A. (2000). New approach to teaching introductory science: The gas module. *Journal of Chemical Education, 77,* 1161–1165.

Mindess, A. (1999). *Reading between the signs.* Yarmouth, ME: Intercultural Press.

Monaco, G. E. (1977). *Inferences as a function of test-expectancy in the classroom.* Kansas State University Psychology Series, KSU-HIPI Report 73–3.

Mousavi, S., Lowe, R., & Sweller, J. (1995). Reducing cognitive load by mixing auditory and visual presentation modes. *Journal of Psychology, 87,* 319–334.

Mueller, D. J., & Wasser, V. (1977). Implications of changing answers on objective test items. *Journal of Educational Measurement, 14*(1), 9–13.

Murphy, K. L., Drabier, R., & Epps, M. L. (1997). *Incorporating computer conferencing into university courses.* Fourth annual Distance Education Conference [Online]. Available: http://disted.tamu.edu/~kmurphy/dec97pap.htm

Murphy, P. K., & Alexander, P. A. (2000). A motivated exploration of motivation terminology. *Contemporary Educational Psychology, 25*, 3–53.

Murray, H. G. (1983). Low-inference classroom teaching behaviors and student ratings of college teaching effectiveness. *Journal of Educational Psychology, 75*, 138–149.

◆ ———. (1997). Effective teaching behaviors in the college classroom. In R. P. Perry & J. C. Smart (Eds.), *Effective teaching in higher education: Research and practice* (pp. 171–204). New York: Agathon.

Murray, H., Gillese, W., Lennon, M., Mercer, P., & Robinson, M. (1996). Ethical principles for college and university teaching. In *New directions for teaching and learning* (no. 66, pp. 57–64). San Francisco: Jossey-Bass.

Musil, C., Garcia, M., Hudgins, C., Nettles, M., Sedlacek, W., & Smith, D. (1999). *To form a more perfect union: Campus diversity initiatives.* Washington, DC: Association of American Colleges and Universities.

Myers-Lipton, S. (1994). *The effects of service-learning on students' attitudes toward civic responsibility, international understanding, and racial prejudice.* (Doctoral dissertation, University of Colorado).

———. (1996). Effect of a comprehensive service-learning program on college students' level of modern racism. *Michigan Journal of Community Service Learning, 3*, 44–54.

Naveh-Benjamin, M., & Lin, Y-G. (1991). *Assessing students' organization of concepts: A manual of measuring course-specific knowledge structures.* Ann Arbor: NCRIPTAL, University of Michigan.

◆ Naveh-Benjamin, M., Lin, Y-G., & McKeachie, W. J. (1989). Development of cognitive structures in three academic disciplines and their relations to students' study skills, anxiety and motivation: Further use of the ordered-tree technique. *Journal of Higher Education Studies, 4*, 10–15.

Naveh-Benjamin, M., McKeachie, W. J., Lin, Y-G., & Tucker, D. G. (1986). Inferring students' cognitive structures and their development using the "ordered tree" technique. *Journal of Educational Psychology, 78*, 130–140.

National Research Council. (2000). *Inquiry and the national science education standards: A guide for teaching and learning.* Washington, DC: National Academy Press.

Nessler, M. S. (1999, November). *Factors associated with retention in a distance-based liberal arts program. Higher Education.* Paper presented at the North East Association for Institutional Research Conference, Newport, RI.

Nishida, T. (1996). Communication in personal relationships in Japan. In W. Gudykunst, S. Ting-Toomey, & T. Nishida (Eds.), *Communication in personal relationships across cultures* (pp. 102–121). Thousand Oaks, CA: Sage.

Okun, B., Fried, J., & Okun, M. (1999). *Understanding diversity: A learning-as-practice primer.* Pacific Grove, CA: Brooks/Cole.

Oliver-Hoyo, M. T., Allen, D. A., Hunt, W. F., Hutson, J., & Pitts, A. (2004). Effects of an active learning environment: Teaching innovations at a Research I institution. *Journal of Chemical Education, 81,* 441–448.

Oppenheimer, T. (1997). The computer delusion. *The Atlantic Monthly, 280*(1), 45–62.

Palomba, C., & Banta, T. (1999). *Assessment essentials: Planning, implementing, and improving assessment in higher education.* San Francisco: Jossey-Bass.

Paris, S. G., Lipson, M. Y., & Wixson, K. K. (1983). Becoming a strategic reader. *Contemporary Educational Psychology, 8,* 293–316.

Paris, S. G., & Paris, A. H. (2001). Classroom applications of research on self-regulated learning. *Educational Psychologist, 36,* 89–101.

Parsons, T. S. (1957). A comparison of instruction by kinescope, correspondence study, and customary classroom procedures. *Journal of Educational Psychology, 48,* 27–40.

Parsons, T. S., Ketcham, W. A., & Beach, L. R. (1958, August). *Effects of varying degrees of student interaction and student-teacher contact in college courses.* Paper presented at American Sociological Society, Seattle, WA.

Pascarella, E. T., & Terenzini, F. (1991). *How college affects students.* San Francisco: Jossey-Bass.

Patrick, H., Hicks, L., & Ryan, A. M. (1997). Relations of perceived social efficacy and social goal pursuit to self-efficacy for academic work. *Journal of Early Adolescence, 17*(2), 109–128.

Paul, J. B. (1932). The length of class periods. *Educational Research, 13,* 58–75.

Peckham, G., & Sutherland, L. (2000). The role of self-assessment in moderating students' expectations. *South African Journal of Higher Education, 14,* 75–78.

Peper, R. J., & Mayer, R. E. (1978). Note taking as a generative activity. *Journal of Educational Psychology, 70*(4), 514–522.

Perry, R. P., & Smart, J. C. (Eds.). (1997). *Effective teaching in higher education: Research and practice.* New York: Agathon.

◆ Perry, W. G., Jr. (1970). *Forms of intellectual and ethical development in the college years: A scheme.* New York: Holt, Rinehart, and Winston.

———. (1981). Cognitive and ethical growth: The making of meaning. In A. W. Chickering (Ed.), *The modern American college* (pp. 76–116). San Francisco: Jossey-Bass.

Pintrich, P. R. (Ed.). (1995, Summer). Understanding self-regulated learning. In *New directions for teaching and learning* (no. 63). San Francisco: Jossey-Bass.

Pintrich, P. R. (2002). The role of metacognitive knowledge in learning, teaching and assessing. *Theory into Practice, 41*(4), 219–225.

———. (2003). Motivation and classroom learning. In W. M. Reynolds & G. E. Miller (Eds.), *Handbook of psychology: Educational psychology* (Vol. 7, pp. 103–122). New York: Wiley.

Pintrich, P. R., & De Groot, E. V. (1990). Motivational and self-regulated learning components of classroom academic performance. *Journal of Educational Psychology, 82,* 33–40.

Pintrich, P. R., & Garcia, T. (1991). Student goal orientation and self-regulation in the college classroom. In M. Maehr & P. R. Pintrich (Eds.), *Advances in motivation and achievement: Goals and self-regulatory processes* (Vol. 7, pp. 371–402). Greenwich, CT: JAI Press.

———. (1994). Self-regulated learning in college students: Knowledge, strategies, and motivation. In P. R. Pintrich, D. R. Brown, & C. E. Weinstein (Eds.), *Student motivation, cognition, and learning: Essays in honor of Wilbert J. McKeachie* (pp. 113–133). Hillsdale, NJ: Erlbaum.

◆ Pintrich, P. R., & Schunk, D. H. (1996). *Motivation in education.* Englewood Cliffs, NJ: Prentice Hall.

———. (2002). *Motivation in education: Theory, research and applications* (2nd ed.). Upper Saddle River, NJ: Merrill/Prentice Hall.

Pintrich, P. R., Smith, D. A. F., Garcia, T., & McKeachie, W. J. (1991). *A manual for the use of the Motivated Strategies for Learning Questionnaire (MSLQ).* Ann Arbor: National Center for Research to Improve Postsecondary Teaching and Learning, University of Michigan.

Pintrich, P. R., Wolters, C., & Baxter, G. (2000). Assessing metacognition and self-regulated learning. In G. Schraw & J. Impara (Eds.), *Issues in the measurement of metacognition* (pp. 43–97). Lincoln, NE: Buros Institute of Mental Measurements.

Prenger, S. M. (Ed.). (1999). *Teaching for inclusion: A resource book for UN faculty.* Lincoln, NE: Teaching and Learning Center, University of Nebraska.

Pressley, M., & McCormick, C. B. (1995). *Cognition, teaching and assessment.* New York: HarperCollins.

◆ Pressley, M., et al. (1992). Encouraging mindful use of prior knowledge: Attempting to construct explanatory answers facilitates learning. *Educational Psychologist, 27*(1), 91–109.

Pulvers, K., & Diekhoff, G. (1999). The relationship between academic dishonesty and college classroom environment. *Research in Higher Education, 40*(4), 487–498.

Reyes, P., Scribner, J., & Scribner, A. (Eds.). (1999). *Lessons from high performing Hispanic schools*. New York: Teachers College Press.

Rhoads, R., & Howard, J. (1998, Winter). Academic service learning: A pedagogy of action and reflection. In *New directions for teaching and learning* (no. 73). San Francisco: Jossey-Bass.

Roberts, M. S., & Semb, G. B. (1990). Analysis of the number of student-set deadlines in a personalized psychology course. *Teaching of Psychology, 17,* 170–173.

Robinson, R. (2001, September). An application to increase student reading and writing skills. *American Biology Teacher, 63*(7), 478–480.

Rodabaugh, R. (1996). Institutional commitment to fairness in teaching. In *New directions for teaching and learning* (no. 66, pp. 37–46). San Francisco: Jossey-Bass.

Rojewski, J. W., & Schell, J. W. (1994). Instructional considerations for college students with disabilities. In K. W. Prichard & R. M. Sawyer (Eds.), *Handbook of college teaching* (pp. 387–400). Westport, CT: Greenwood Press.

Ross, I. C. (1957). Role specialization in supervision. (Doctoral dissertation, Columbia University). *Dissertation Abstracts, 17,* 2701–2702.

Royer, P. N. (1977). Effects of specificity and position of written instructional objectives on learning from a lecture. *Journal of Educational Psychology, 69,* 40–45.

Ruhl, K. L., Hughes, C. A., & Schloss, P. J. (1987). Using the pause procedure to enhance lecture recall. *Teacher Education and Special Education, 10,* 14–18.

Ruiz, P. (1995). Assessing, diagnosing and treating culturally diverse individuals: A Hispanic perspective. *Psychiatric Quarterly, 66,* 329–341.

Ruiz, R., & Padilla, A. (1977). Counseling Latinos. *Personnel and Guidance Journal, 55,* 401–408.

Russell, T. L. (1999). *No significant difference phenomenon*. North Carolina State University, Raleigh, NC.

Ryan, R., & Deci, E. (2000). When rewards compete with nature: The undermining of intrinsic motivation and self-regulation. In C. Sansone & J. Harackiewicz (Eds.), *Intrinsic and extrinsic motivation: The search for optimal motivation and performance*. San Diego: Academic Press.

Sadker, M., & Sadker, D. (1992). Ensuring equitable participation in college classes. In *New directions for teaching and learning* (no. 49, pp. 49–56). San Francisco: Jossey-Bass.

Sadler, D. R. (1987). Specifying and promulgating achievement standards. *Oxford Review of Education, 13*(2), 191–209.

Sage, G. (1991). Counseling American Indian adults. In C. Lee & B. Richardson (Eds.), *Multicultural issues in counseling: New approaches to diversity* (pp. 23–35). Alexandria, VA: American Counseling Association.

Sanchez, A., & Atkinson, D. (1983). Mexican American cultural commitment, preference for counselor ethnicity, and willingness to use counseling. *Journal of Counseling Psychology, 30,* 215–220.

Saunders, S., & Kardia, D. (1997). *Creating inclusive college classrooms.* Ann Arbor, MI: Center for Research on Learning and Teaching, University of Michigan [Online]. Available: http://www.crlt.umich.edu/F6.html

Sax, L. J., Astin, A. W., Korn, W. S., & Gilmartin, S. K. (1999). *The American college teacher: National norms for the 1998–1999 HERI Faculty Survey.* Los Angeles: Higher Education Research Institute, UCLA.

Schank, R., Berman, T. R., & Macpherson, K. A. (1999). Learning by doing. In C. M. Reigeluth (Ed.), *Instructional-design theories and models* (Vol. 2, pp. 141–160). Mahwah, NJ: Erlbaum.

Schoem, D., Frankel, L., Zúñiga, X., & Lewis, E. A. (Eds.) (1993). *Multicultural teaching in the university.* Westport, CT: Praeger.

Schomberg, S. F. (1986, April). *Involving high ability students in learning groups.* Paper presented at AERA in San Francisco.

Schön, D. (1983). *The reflective practitioner.* San Francisco: Jossey-Bass.

Schultz, P. A., & Weinstein, C. E. (1990). Using test feedback to facilitate the learning process. *Innovation Abstracts, 12*(22).

Schunk, D. H., & Ertmer, P. A. (1999). Self-regulatory processes during computer skill acquisition: Goal and self-evaluative influences. *Journal of Educational Psychology, 91,* 251–260.

◆ Schunk, D. H., & Zimmerman, B. J. (Eds.). (1998). *Self-regulated learning: From teaching to self-reflective practice.* New York: Guilford.

———. (2003). Self-regulation and learning. In W. M. Reynolds & G. E. Miller (Eds.). *Handbook of psychology: Educational psychology* (Vol. 7, pp. 59–78). New York: John Wiley.

Schutz, P. A., & Davis, H. A. (2000). Emotions and self-regulation during test taking. *Educational Psychologist, 35,* 243–356.

Seymour, E., & Hewitt, N. (1997). *Talking about leaving: Why undergraduates leave the sciences.* Boulder, CO: Westview Press.

Shapiro, R. J., & Rohde, G. L. (2000, October). *Falling through the net: Toward digital inclusion.* Washington, DC: U.S. Department of Commerce [Online]. Available: http://www.esa.doc.gov/fttn00.htm

Shields, N. (2002). Anticipatory socialization, adjustment to university life, and perceived stress: Generational and sibling effects. *Social Psychology of Education, 5*(4), 365–392.

Siebert, A., Gilpin, B., Karr, M., & Ritter, B. (2000). *The adult student's guide to survival and success* (4th ed.). Portland, OR: Practical Psychology Press.

Silverman, R., Welty, W. M., & Lyon, S. (1994). *Educational psychology cases for teacher problem solving.* New York: McGraw-Hill.

Skinner, N. F. (2001). A course, a course, my kingdom for a course: Reflections of an unrepentant teacher. *Canadian Psychology, 42,* 49–60.

Sleeter, C. E. (1991). *Empowerment through multicultural education.* Albany, NY: State University of New York Press.

Smith, D. (1996). The ethics of teaching. In *New directions for teaching and learning* (no. 66, pp. 5–14). San Francisco: Jossey-Bass.

Smith, D. G., Gerbick, G. L., Figueroa, M. A., Watkins, G. H., Levitan, T., Moore, L. C., Merchant, P. A., Beliak, H. D., & Figueroa, B. (1997). *Diversity works: The emerging picture of how students benefit.* Washington, DC: Association of American Colleges and Universities.

Smith, W. F., & Rockett, F. C. (1958). Test performance as a function of anxiety, instructor, and instructions. *Journal of Educational Research, 52,* 138–141.

Snow, R. E., & Peterson, P. L. (1980). Recognizing differences in student attitudes. In *New directions for teaching and learning* (no. 2). San Francisco: Jossey-Bass.

◆ Solomon, D., Rosenberg, L., & Bezdek, W. E. (1964). Teacher behavior and student learning. *Journal of Educational Psychology, 55,* 23–30.

Springer, L., Palmer, B., Terenzini, P., Pascarella, E., & Nora, A. (1996). Attitudes towards campus diversity. *Review of Higher Education, 20*(1), 53–68.

Stanton, H. (1992). *The University Teacher, 13*(1).

Stark, J. S., & Lattuca, L. R. (1997). *Shaping the college curriculum: Academic plans in action.* Boston: Allyn & Bacon.

◆ Stern, G. G. (1962). Environments for learning. In N. Sanford (Ed.), *The American college.* New York: Wiley.

Stern, G. G., & Cope, A. H. (1956, September). *Differences in educability between steropaths, non-steropaths and rationals.* Paper presented at the American Psychological Association meeting, Chicago.

Sternberg, R. (2003). *The Rainbow Project: What's wrong with college admissions and how psychology can fix it.* Invited address at the annual convention of the American Psychological Association, Toronto, Canada.

Sterngold, A. (2004, May/June). Confronting plagiarism: How conventional teaching invites cyber-cheating. *Change, 36*(3), 16–21.

Strage, A. A. (2000). Service learning: Enhancing student learning outcomes in a college-level lecture course. *Michigan Journal of Community Service Learning, 7,* 5–13.

Strike, K. (1988). The ethics of teaching. *Phi Delta Kappan, 70(2),* 156–158.

Stuart, R. (2004). Twelve practical suggestions for achieving multicultural competence. *Professional Psychology, 35,* 3–9.

Sue, D. W. (2003). *Overcoming our racism: The journey to liberation.* San Francisco: Jossey-Bass.

———. (2004). *Whiteness and ethnocentric monoculturism: Making the "invisible" visible.* Invited address at the annual convention of the American Psychological Association, Honolulu, Hawaii.

Sue, D. W., & Sue, D. (2003). *Counseling the culturally diverse: Theory and practice* (4th ed.). New York: Wiley.

Sutman, F. X., Schmuckler, J. S., Hilosky, A., Priestley, W. J., Priestley, H., & White, M. (1998, April). *Evaluating the use of the inquiry matrix.* Paper presented at the annual conference of the National Association for Research in Science Teaching, San Diego [Online]. Available: http://www.narst.org/conference/98conference/sutman.pdf

Sutton, C., & Broken Nose, M. (1996). American Indian families: An overview. In M. McGoldrick, J. Giordano, & J. Pearce (Eds.), *Ethnicity and family therapy* (2nd ed., pp. 31–44). New York: Guilford Press.

Sutton, S. E. (1993). Seeing the whole of the moon. In D. Schoem, L. Frankel, X. Zúñiga, & E. A. Lewis (Eds.), *Multicultural teaching in the university* (pp. 161–171). Westport, CT: Praeger.

◆ Svinicki, M. D., Hagen, A. S., & Meyer, D. K. (1995). Research on learning: A means to enhance instructional methods. In R. Menges & M. Weimer (Eds.), *Better teaching and learning in college: Toward more scholarly practice* (pp. 257–296). San Francisco: Jossey-Bass.

Swearingen, C. J. (1999). Originality, authenticity, imitation, and plagiarism: Augustine's Chinese cousins. In L. Buranen & A. M. Roy (Eds.), *Perspectives on plagiarism and intellectual property in a postmodern world* (pp. 5–18). Albany: State University of New York Press.

Sweeting, L. (1999). Ethics in science for undergraduate students. *Journal of Chemical Education, 76,* 369–372.

Swinomish Tribal Mental Health Project. (1991). *A gathering of wisdoms.* LaConner, WA: Swinomish Tribal Community.

Tabachnick, B., Keith-Spiegel, P., & Pope, K. (1991). Ethics of teaching: Beliefs and behaviors of psychologists as educators. *American Psychologist, 46(5),* 506–515.

Tatum, B. (1993). *Coming of age: Black youth in white communities. Focus, 7(2),* 15–16.

Tchudi, S. (Ed.). (1997). *Alternatives to grading student writing.* Urbana: NCTE.

◆ Thistlethwaite, D. L. (1960). *College press and changes in study plans of talented students.* Evanston, IL: National Merit Scholarship Corporation.

Thompson, V., Bazile, A., & Akbar, M. (2004). African Americans' perceptions of psychotherapy and psychotherapists. *Professional Psychology: Research and Practice, 35,* 19–26.

Tien, L. T., Rickey, D., & Stacy, A. M. (1999). The MORE thinking frame: Guiding students' thinking in the laboratory. *Journal of College Science Teaching, 28*(5), 318–324.

Toombs, W., & Tierney, W. (1992). *Meeting the mandate: Renewing the college and department curriculum.* Washington, DC: Association for the Study of Higher Education. (ASHE-ERIC Higher Education Report No. 91–6).

Topping, K. (1998, Fall). Peer assessment between students in colleges and universities. *Review of Educational Research, 68*(3), 249–276.

Toppino, T. C., & Brochin, H. A. (1989). Learning from tests: The case of true-false examinations. *Journal of Educational Research, 83,* 119–124.

Travers, R. M. W. (1950a). Appraisal of the teaching of the college faculty. *Journal of Higher Education, 21,* 41–42.

———. (1950b). *How to make achievement tests.* New York: Odyssey Press.

Trawick, L., & Corno, L. (1995, June). Expanding the volitional resources of urban community college students (pp. 57–70). In P. Pintrich (Ed.), Understanding self-regulated learning. *New directions for teaching and learning* (no. 63, pp. 57–70). San Francisco: Jossey-Bass.

Trujillo, C. M. (1986). A comparative examination of classroom interactions between professors and minority and non-minority college students. *American Educational Research Journal, 23,* 629–642.

Trusty, J., & Harris, M. (1999). Lost talent: Predictors of the stability of educational expectations across adolescence. *Journal of Adolescent Research, 14,* 359–382.

Twigg, C. A. (1992). Improving productivity in higher education: The need for a paradigm shift. *Cause/Effect, 15*(2), 39–45.

Upcraft, M. L. (1996). Teaching and today's college students. In R. Menges, M. Weimer, & Associates (Eds.), *Teaching on solid ground: Using scholarship to improve practice* (pp. 21–41). San Francisco: Jossey-Bass.

Van Overwalle, F., Segebarth, K., & Goldchstein, M. (1989). Improving performance of freshmen through attributional testimonies from fellow students. *British Journal of Educational Psychology, 59,* 75–85.

Vasquez, M. (1982). Confronting barriers to participation of Mexican American women in higher education. *Hispanic Journal of Behavioral Sciences, 4,* 147–165.

Veenstra, M. V. J., & Elshout, J. J. (1995). Differential effects of instructional support on learning in simulation environments. *Instructional Science, 22,* 363–383.

Von Secker, C. (2002). Effects of inquiry-based teacher practices on science excellence and equity. *Journal of Educational Research, 95,* 151–160.

Von Secker, C., & Lissitz, R. W. (1999). Estimating the impact of instructional practices on student achievement in science. *Journal of Research in Science Teaching, 36,* 110–112.

Vontress, C., & Epp, L. (1997). Historical hostility in the African American client: Implications for counseling. *Journal of Multicultural Counseling and Development, 25,* 170–184.

Wager, E. D., & McCombs, B. L. (1995). Learner-centered psychological principles in practice: Designs for distance education. *Educational Technology, 35*(2), 32–35.

Wakely, J. H., Marr, J. N., Plath, D. W., & Wilkins, D. M. (1960, March). *Lecturing and test performance in introductory psychology.* Paper presented at Michigan Academy, Ann Arbor.

Wales, C. E., & Nardi, A. (1982, November). *Teaching decisionmaking with guided design* (Idea paper no. 9). Kansas State University, Center for Faculty Evaluation and Development.

Walvoord, B., & Anderson, V. (1998). *Effective grading: A tool for learning and assessment.* San Francisco: Jossey-Bass.

Weaver, R. L., II, & Cotrell, H. W. (1985). Mental aerobics: The half-sheet response. *Innovative Higher Education, 10,* 23–31.

Weiner, B. (1986). *An attributional theory of motivation and emotion.* New York: Springer-Verlag.

Weiner, B. (2001). Intrapersonal and interpersonal theories of motivation from an attribution perspective. In F. Salili, C. Chiu, & Y. Hong (Eds.), *Student motivation: The culture and context of learning* (pp. 17–30). New York: Kluwer.

Weinstein, C. E. (1988). Executive control processes in learning: Why knowing about how to learn is not enough. *Journal of College Reading and Learning, 21,* 48–56.

———. (1994). Strategic learning/strategic teaching: Flip sides of a coin. In P. R. Pintrich, D. R. Brown, & C. E. Weinstein (Eds.), *Student motivation, cognition, and learning: Essays in honor of Wilbert J. McKeachie.* Hillsdale, NJ: Erlbaum.

Weinstein, C. E., Beth, A. D., Corliss, S. B., Cho, Y. (in press). Learning how to learn for e-learning: The importance of strategic learning in technology-rich environments. In R. Nyberg (Ed.), Invited Book Chapter.

Weinstein, C. E., Husman, J., & Dierking, D. R. (2000). Self-regulation interventions with a focus on learning strategies. In M. Boekaerts, P. Pintrich, & M. Zeidner (Eds.), *Handbook of self-regulation.* San Diego: Academic Press.

◆ Weinstein, C. E., & Mayer, R. E. (1986). The teaching of learning strategies. In M. Wittrock (Ed.), *Handbook of research on teaching* (3rd ed., pp. 315–327). New York: Macmillan.

Weinstein, G., & Obear, K. (1992). Bias issues in the classroom: Encounters with the teaching self. In *New directions for teaching and learning* (no. 52, pp. 39–50). San Francisco: Jossey-Bass.

Wentzel, K., & Wigfield, A. (1998). Academic and social motivational influences on students' academic performance. *Educational Psychology Review, 10*, 155–175.

Wenzel, T. J. (1995). A new approach to undergraduate analytical chemistry. *Analytical Chemistry, 67*, 470A–475A.

———. (1998). Cooperative group learning in undergraduate analytical chemistry. *Analytical Chemistry, 70*(23), 790A–795A.

White, J., & Parham, T. (1990). *The psychology of blacks: An African-American perspective* (2nd ed.). Englewood Cliffs, NJ: Prentice Hall.

Whitley, B. (1998). Factors associated with cheating among college students: A review. *Research in Higher Education, 39*(3), 235–274.

Wigfield, A., & Eccles, J. S. (2000). Expectancy-value theory of achievement motivation. *Contemporary Educational Psychology, 25*, 68–81.

Wilhite, S. C. (1983). Prepassage questions: The influence of structural importance. *Journal of Educational Psychology, 75*(2), 234–244.

Williams, K. (2000, February). Internet access in U.S. public schools and classrooms: 1994–99 (NCES 2000-086). *Education Statistics Quarterly: Elementary and Secondary Education.* Washington, DC: U.S. Department of Education, Office of Educational Research and Improvement, National Center for Education Statistics [Online]. Available: http://nces.ed.gov/pubs2000/qrtlyspring/4elem/q4-8.html

Willie, C. V. (1975). *Oreo: Race and marginal men and women.* Wakefield, MA: Parameter Press.

Wilson, J. M. (1994). The CUPLE physics studio. *Physics Teacher, 32*, 518–523.

◆ Wilson, R. C. (1986). Improving faculty teaching: Effective use of student evaluations and consultation. *Journal of Higher Education, 57*, 196–211.

Wilson, T. D., & Linville, P. W. (1982). Improving the academic performance of college freshmen: Attribution therapy revisited. *Journal of Personality and Social Psychology, 42*, 367–376.

Winne, P. (1996). A metacognitive view of individual differences in self-regulated learning. *Learning and Individual Differences, 8*, 327–353.

Witkin, H. A., & Moore, C. A. (1975). *Field-dependent and field-independent cognitive styles and their educational implications.* Princeton, NJ: Educational Testing Service.

Wlodkowski, R., & Ginsberg, M. (1995). *Diversity and motivation: Culturally responsive teaching*. San Francisco: Jossey-Bass.

Yan, L., & Kember, D. (2004). Avoider and engager approaches by out-of-class groups: The group equivalent to individual learning approaches. *Learning and Instruction, 14*, 27–49.

Young, A. (1997, Winter). Mentoring, modeling, monitoring, motivating: Response to students' ungraded writing as academic conversation. In M. D. Sorcinelli & P. Elbow (Eds.), Writing to learn: Strategies for assigning and responding to writing across the disciplines. *New directions for teaching and learning* (no. 69). San Francisco: Jossey-Bass.

Zimbardo, P. G., & Newton, J. W. (1975). *Instructor's resource book to accompany psychology and life*. Glenview, IL: Scott, Foresman.

Zimmerman, B. J. (1989). Models of self-regulated learning and academic achievement. In B. J. Zimmerman & D. H. Schunk (Eds.), *Self-regulated learning and academic achievement: Theory, research, and practice* (pp. 1–25). New York: Springer-Verlag.

———. (1990). Self-regulated learning and academic achievement [Special issue]. *Educational Psychologist, 25*(1).

———. (1994). Dimensions of academic self-regulation: A conceptual framework for education. In D. H. Schunk & B. J. Zimmerman (Eds.), *Self-regulation of learning and performance: Issues and educational applications* (pp. 3–19). Hillsdale, NJ: Erlbaum.

———. (1995). Self-regulation involves more than metacognition: A social cognitive perspective. *Educational Psychologist, 30*(4), 217–222.

◆ ———. (1998). Developing self-fulfilling cycles of academic regulation: An analysis of exemplary instructional models. In D. H. Schunk & B. J. Zimmerman (Eds.), *Self-regulated learning: From teaching to self-reflective practice* (pp. 1–19). New York: Guilford.

———. (2001). Theories of self-regulated learning and academic achievement: An overview and analysis. In B. J. Zimmerman & D. H. Schunk (Eds.), *Self-regulated learning and academic achievement: Theoretical perspectives* (2nd ed., pp. 1–37). Mahwah, NJ: Erlbaum.

Zimmerman, B. J., & Paulson, A. S. (1995, Summer). Self-monitoring during collegiate studying: An invaluable tool for academic self-regulation. In P. R. Pintrich, (Ed.), Understanding self-regulated learning. *New directions for teaching and learning* (no. 63, pp. 13–18). San Francisco: Jossey-Bass.

Zimmerman, B. J., & Schunk, D. H. (2001). Reflections on theories of self-regulated learning and academic achievement. In B. J. Zimmerman & D. H. Schunk (Eds.), *Self-regulated learning and academic achievement: Theoretical perspectives* (2nd ed., pp. 289–307). Mahwah, NJ: Erlbaum.

Index